MODERN PUBLIC ADMINISTRATION

MODERN PUBLIC ADMINISTRATION

Felix A. Nigro
San Diego State College

HARPER & ROW, PUBLISHERS
NEW YORK, EVANSTON, AND LONDON

MODERN PUBLIC ADMINISTRATION
 For information address Harper & Row, Publishers, Incorporated, 49 East 33rd Street, New York 16, N.Y.

A-P

Library of Congress Catalog Card Number: 65-11140

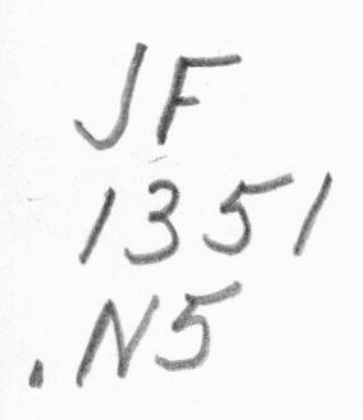

To LLOYD

Contents

PART IV/PERSONNEL ADMINISTRATION

PART V/FINANCIAL ADMINISTRATION

PART VI/ADMINISTRATIVE RESPONSIBILITY

PART VII/INTERNATIONAL ADMINISTRATION

Preface

This book is written for persons who seek an introduction to the essential principles, qualities, and problems of public administration, and to meet the challenges to administration that arise in an increasingly complex society. As areas of public interest grow ever greater in sheer number and importance, the need for effective administration also grows. The author strives to present an up-to-date picture of the field of administration, both from the standpoint of the newer theoretical emphases and from that of the practical problems which confront every administrator in his daily operations.

Administration at every level of government is discussed. International administration is given as full a treatment as is possible within a text of this scope, and topics such as "Leadership," "Informal Organization," and "Administration and Culture" are developed in detail because of the growing awareness of their importance in recent years. The standard subjects, such as personnel and financial administration, are not neglected; indeed, the author gives some aspects of them greater attention than is customary. The treatment of certain administrative agencies—for example, the Federal Aviation Agency and the National Aeronautics and Space Administration, which are discussed in Chapter 6—relates administration as directly as possible to the events and developments of the modern era in which the reader lives. In fact, in the writing of this book, one aim is to make the reader more aware of the world of administration which surrounds him as he goes about his daily affairs.

The bibliographies at the end of each chapter should prove useful to readers who are interested in exploring the topics more intensively. It is hoped that every reader will succumb to this temptation.

In writing any book of this sort, it is difficult not to let one's own particular views slip in and color the text; yet every effort has been made to present the field without bias or distortion. A possible exception may lie in the treatment of the modern, humanistic approach to administration as opposed to the traditional approach, for the present author admits an inclination toward the former.

The writer is indebted to his wife for her assistance in typing and proofreading, and, most of all, for her devoted encouragement.

F. A. N.

San Diego, California
February, 1965

PART I

NATURE AND SCOPE OF THE FIELD

CHAPTER 1

What is Public Administration?

One-sentence definitions are desirable, particularly in textbooks, but, in the case of public administration, so brief a description of the field would tell us very little. Indeed, a review of the literature of public administration shows that where a one-sentence definition is attempted, the writer usually hastens to add to it in subsequent paragraphs. This is understandable—first, because the boundaries of the field have never been precisely delimited, and, second, because in recent years both the scholar's and practitioner's concept of what it includes has broadened considerably. "The scope of public administration has so grown," writes Frederick C. Mosher, "that it almost defies classification. In fact, it would appear that any definition of this field would be either so encompassing as to call forth the wrath or ridicule of others, or so limiting as to stultify its own disciples. Perhaps it is best that it not be defined."[1] Mosher accurately states the difficulties, but, still, a reasonably satisfactory answer can be given to the question, "What is public administration?" provided the writer does not attempt to give the answer in only a sentence or two.

Let us, therefore, take our time in reaching a final definition. First, we shall explore a number of different considerations which bear upon the determination of the proper scope of public administration. The advantage of this procedure is that it will show clearly why we

[1] Frederick C. Mosher, "Research in Public Administration: Some Notes and Suggestions," *Public Administration Review*, XVI, No. 3 (Summer, 1956), 170, 177.

include some things in the definition and exclude others. One approach is to identify public administration as it relates to the three traditional branches of government: executive, legislative, and judicial. Does it cover all three of these branches? To what extent, if any, does each of them have administrative responsibilities?

THE ROLE OF THE EXECUTIVE

According to the Oxford English dictionary, the *executive* is "that branch of government which is charged with the execution of the laws." The executive branch consists of *administrative* agencies which put the laws into effect. Clearly, public administration includes the executive branch. This part of the definition is not in dispute, since the everyday activity of postmen, policemen, firemen, public-health nurses, diplomats, tax collectors, and a host of others employed in the administrative agencies of federal, state, and local governments illustrates it well enough. The executive branch of government is public administration in a truly visible form.

THE ROLE OF THE LEGISLATURE

The legislative branch does not execute the laws; it passes them. However, to a limited extent, legislative bodies are also directly engaged in administrative activities. As one example, if you consult the *United States Organization Manual,*[2] you will find that the nation's highest lawmaking body, Congress, has several administrative agencies immediately under it. Congress, not the President, is responsible for directly supervising them. These agencies are the Government Printing Office (GPO), the Library of Congress, the Office of the Architect of the Capitol, the United States Botanic Garden, and the General Accounting Office (GAO). True, since the number of agencies supervised is small, these direct administrative responsibilities are not as extensive as are those of the executive branch. The point is, however, that they do exist.

Much more important is the legislative body's role in generally overseeing the activities of the executive branch. It is long-established

D.C.: Government Printing Office, pp. 29–42.

[2] *United States Government Organization Manual 1963–64,* Washington,

American doctrine that, at all levels of government, the lawmakers should maintain a close watch on what is going on in the administrative agencies. Although the legislature is not normally expected to assume direct responsibility for administering the laws it passes, we assume that it will accept positive responsibility for checking up on how those laws are carried out by the administrative establishment. Legislative investigations of administrative agencies, as one example of this role of the lawmaking body, are a commonplace.

Just how effective legislatures have been in controlling the executive branch in the public interest is taken up in Part VI of this book. Our concern here has been to make clear at the outset that, in the American scheme of things, the legislature is supposed to have a vital role in public administration. It was never intended that it should keep out of this area, as a quick perusal of *The Federalist* will confirm.[3]

The Concept of Codirectorship

There has been, however, an increasing tendency in recent years for the national Congress to want to participate in the decisions which must be made daily by administrative officials in carrying out the various government programs. This is not to say that Congress has only recently injected itself into detailed questions of administration, because it has done so for many years. What we are now witnessing, however, is a definite trend for it to assume in some areas of public policy the role of codirectors, together with the heads of the administrative agencies operating in the particular fields.

Morton Grodzins cites numerous cases of such "legislative involvement with executive business," based on recent statutes which "require administrators to report either past actions or future plans to committees of Congress or to Congress as a whole."[4] Sometimes the statutes instruct the administrative agencies merely to "consult" with certain Congressional committees. In other cases, the law may provide for a suspensive veto, by Congress or by one of its committees,

[3] Alexander Hamilton, James Madison, and John Jay, *The Federalist*, Cambridge, Mass.: Harvard Univ. Press, 1961.

[4] Morton Grodzins, "American Political Parties and The American System," *Western Political Quarterly*, XIII, No. 4 (December, 1960), 980–982.

over a proposed administrative action. The President and the heads of the agencies in question resist this legislative concept of codirectorship when, in their opinion, Congress has encroached on the domain of the executive branch and has violated the constitutional doctrine of the separation of powers. Such poaching, however, takes place largely as the result of informal agreements between Congressional committees and administrative officials, in which the latter, dependent upon Congress for appropriations, find it necessary to acquiesce. Since this encroachment is not based on a provision of law, it is much more difficult for the offended parties in the executive branch to charge Congress with violation of separation of powers. Grodzins cites examples in recent years of such informal agreements. A House subcommittee prevents the Defense Department from closing military hospitals which the Department itself has decided are no longer needed. The Committee on Interstate and Foreign Commerce tells the Department of Commerce and federal regulatory agencies what licensing fees to impose. The House Armed Services Committee—perturbed by possible competition between the military post exchanges and local retailers—negotiates detailed agreements with the military, specifying what may and may not be sold at the PXs.

Thus, department heads increasingly find that they cannot act without first consulting Congressional committees or without having to obtain the approval of the entire Congress. The latter has always tended to consider itself a kind of Board of Directors for the executive branch, but now the members of this Board step down frequently into the realm of current agency management. We are not concerned, at this point, with the question of whether or not this is a desirable trend. The object is merely to describe the reality.

Case Work

A more frequent kind of legislative participation in administration is *case work*. This refers to the individual legislator's numerous contacts with administrative officials on behalf of his constituents. If anyone wants to accomplish something which requires action by some federal agency or official, "get in touch with your Congressman" is considered good advice. So it must be because, typically, much of the Congressman's time and that of his staff is taken up attending to requests of this kind. The Office of Price Administration, during the calendar year 1944, averaged 1397 congressional contacts a week, including phone calls, letters, and visits from Congressmen and their staffs. In the ten working days between May 21 and June 4, 1958, the Department of Interior, by actual count, received 553 pieces of congressional mail, plus an estimated 200 phone calls.[5]

Administrative officials are anxious to build support for their agencies' programs both in Congress and among the general public. Just as the Congressman is glad to act upon a constituent's reasonable request, so are the agencies happy to accomodate the Congressman, if at all possible, when he refers that request to them. The result is that every day's work in an administrative agency is characterized by very close relationships between the executive and legislative branches. The same pattern of executive-legislative relationships is found in state and local governments, as well.

Internal Administration of Legislatures

Lawmaking bodies also face a formidable problem of *internal administration*. At this point, we will direct our attention to administration *as a process*; that is, as a body of knowledge and techniques for the effective management of any enterprise.

Legislatures should, of course, be efficient. For one thing, they should be properly organized; for example, the number of committees should not be excessive and their respective jurisdictions should be clearly defined so as to prevent overlapping. The time of the individual legislator should be effectively utilized; he should have neither too many nor too few committee assignments. The committee and the individual legislators should have the staff they need in order to do the best possible job; office space, equipment, and other housekeeping services must be provided. In short, if it is to do its job well, the legislature must be concerned with constantly improving its own internal organization and procedures.

Congress has been aware of the need to improve its internal management, and, for that reason, it passed the Legislative Reorganization Act of 1946. It is not necessary here to give the detailed

[5] *Ibid.*, pp. 984–985.

provisions of this Act, for we are merely citing it as an example of a major effort to improve the administrative process within a legislative body. State legislatures and local governing bodies, similarly, have been sensitive to the need to eliminate excessive delays and otherwise to get their jobs done more expeditiously.

THE ROLE OF THE JUDICIARY

Just as in the case of the legislature, the courts participate directly in administration to some extent. For example, the Constitution states in Article 1, Section 8, that Congress shall provide "uniform laws on the subject of bankruptcies throughout the United States." This gives the federal courts jurisdiction over bankruptcy proceedings, and control of the disposition of the property of the bankrupt firm is, therefore, the responsibility of the court. If the property is placed in the hands of a receiver, the court appoints him. If a decision is made to sell the property to pay off the creditors, the receiver conducts the sale in accordance with the court's instructions. The judge and the receiver whom he appoints are, in effect, the managers of the properties, with the same responsibilities as any business entrepreneur. Similarly, in the field of local government, county probate courts are responsible for administering and settling the estates of persons who die without leaving wills. The court names an administrator who is in charge of the details under the supervision of the court. Both these examples show how, in addition to their primary function of deciding cases, courts do sometimes actually discharge administrative functions.

Judicial Review and Public Administration

Of much greater importance is the role of the courts—both federal and state—in passing upon the constitutionality of legislative enactments and administrative acts. This, of course, is what is known as "judicial review," and it has far-reaching implications for both the scope of government activities and the range of permissive action of public officials.

One of the most essential government services is public education.

It is largely due to the decisions of the federal judges that schools are still open in those states which resorted to the last-ditch method of warding off desegregation by passing laws that provide for closing the schools.[6] The purpose of these laws was to divert the white pupils to "private" schools which would be subsidized by the state governments through tuition grants, tax benefits, and the like. By striking down these statutes, the federal courts preserved the public-school system in the states concerned. At the moment of writing, some schools closed still remain so, but in the main, the federal courts have thwarted this last stratagem to avoid desegregation.

Judicial review also affects the more routine aspects of public administration. One day, a property owner in Baltimore, Md. refused to allow a city housing inspector to enter his residence in order to check on compliance with municipal rat-control regulations. He requested the inspector to produce a search warrant in accordance with the constitutional prohibition of "illegal searches and seizures." The case was finally heard in the United States Supreme Court[7] which held that the municipal regulations were constitutional. Its reasoning was that the overriding responsibility of the municipal government to protect the health of its citizens rendered invalid any claim of invasion of privacy. The administration of the municipal sanitary ordinances would have been seriously impeded by the delay and extra work involved if the inspectors were forced to obtain search warrants for the inspection of each and every house.

Naturally, there is disagreement as to whether the courts decide some of the cases of this kind correctly; however, whether the individual rulings are correct or not, they do lay down for the public officials concerned what they can and cannot legally do. Sometimes, the issue that arises is not concerned with the constitutionality of a law or of an administrative act, but rather with the claim that the official exceeded his powers; in other cases, the court decides whether the rule or other action of a regulatory commission should be sustained. Suffice it to say that the administrator in charge of a particular program must constantly weigh his acts in terms of possible later invalidation by the courts.

[6] See Daniel H. Pollitt, "Equal Protection in Public Education: 1954–61," *AAUP Bulletin*, XLVII, No. 3 (September, 1961), 203–204.

[7] *Frank v. Maryland*, 359 U.S. 360 (1959).

Internal Administration

Just as in the case of legislatures, courts are faced with the problem of organizing their work in such a way as to render maximum service to the public. Since court systems—national, state, and local—consist of several different kinds of courts, and their work load is heavy in our ever more complex society, judicial administration has emerged as a leading problem area in modern public administration. This is regarded as such an important problem by the National Conference of Commissioners on Uniform State Laws that it has prepared a *Model Act to Provide for An Administrator For the State Courts.* The Act puts the arguments for establishing such a position very succinctly:

> There should be a responsible head to aid in directing the business affairs of the courts but without any power of supervision over the judicial function vested in the courts. The judiciary should be more closely integrated in order that the business end of the judiciary may be operated in a more efficient manner. In most states there are probably a sufficient number of judges to handle all of the judicial business promptly; but there may be congested dockets in some districts while in others the judges are idle. How many judges are needed in a county or district; is the judicial manpower so used that the services of all the judges is being fully utilized; are some areas overstaffed and others understaffed; are some judges overloaded and unable to keep their dockets current? An administrator could ascertain the facts and suggest the appropriate remedy. Efficient modes of procedure may be in operation in some districts while outmoded methods prevail in others. To minimize delay the courts must be so manned, equipped, and organized that they may handle the maximum load promptly and efficiently.[8]

The American Judicature Society reports that 26 states now have court systems with administrative officers. These court administrators usually function under the direction of judicial councils which now exist in the great majority of states. A good example is the California Judicial Council which is composed of 11 members, with the Chief Justice as chairman and 10 other justices whom he appoints from among the judges of the different state courts. Its principal function, like that of other judicial councils, is to improve the internal admini-

[8] National Conference of Commissioners on Uniform State Laws, *Model Act to Provide for An Administrator For the State Courts*, 1948, p. 3.

stration of the state's court system.[9] At the national level, the Judicial Conference of the United States has the same role. In 1939, Congress established the Administrative Office of the United States Courts. The director of this Office has, in general, the same responsibilities as those proposed in the Model Act for state court administrators.[10] So far has the movement for such administrative officers progressed, that Los Angeles County recently established such a position, with the title of Executive Officer, for its Superior Court.

Thus, public administration, both as a field of study and in practice, cannot be said to be limited to the executive agencies; it covers all three branches. In one of *The Federalist* papers, Alexander Hamilton wrote:

> . . . The administration of government, in its largest sense, comprehends all the operations of the body politic, whether legislative, executive, or judiciary; but in its most usual and perhaps in its most precise signification, it is limited to executive details, and falls peculiarly within the province of the executive department. The actual conduct of foreign negotiations, the preparatory plans of finance, the application and disbursement of the public moneys in conformity to the general appropriations of the legislature, the arrangement of the army and navy, the direction of the operations of war,—these, and other matters of a like nature, constitute what seems to be most properly understood by the administration of government.[11]

Hamilton, we can be sure, knew that, in its daily activities, the executive branch would have numerous contacts and interrelationships with the legislature and the judiciary. His statement, however, emphasizes that the executive branch does most of the direct implementation of the laws. It has by far the largest number of employees and also the most complex problems of internal management.

ADMINISTRATION AND POLICY

Although, in the quotation above, Hamilton speaks of "executive details," the executive branch does play a very important role in the

[9] See Winston W. Crouch, *et al., California Government and Politics*, Englewood Cliffs, N.J.: Prentice-Hall, 1960, p. 187.

[10] See Henry P. Chandler, "The Problem of Congestion and Delay in the Federal Courts," *Annals of the American Academy of Political and Social Sciences*, CCCXXVIII (March, 1960), 147.

[11] Alexander Hamilton, James Madison, and John Jay, *op. cit.*, 462–463.

formulation of public policy. At one time, the simplified explanation held sway that the legislature determined public policies when it passed the laws, and that the task of the executive agencies was merely to put these policies into effect. This is the famous dichotomy between policy and administration which is now, for good reasons, rejected by most writers. In fact, the administrative branch has always exercised discretion in carrying out the laws. Leonard D. White shows how attempts were made to keep administrative discretion to a minimum during the administrations of George Washington and John Adams, and how this could not be accomplished even in the relatively simple society of the first years of the new Republic. For example, when Congress decided to raise money by taxing carriages, it wrestled with the problem of establishing a uniform classification of the carriages for tax purposes, but, in the end, it had to "recognize a substantial degree of administrative leeway."[12] The problem was how to differentiate between chariots, coaches, four-wheeled carriages, and similar vehicles with the unstandardized structural features characteristic of the times. Congress did the best it could in trying to describe each class of carriage in the law, "but added that in cases of doubt any carriage should be deemed to belong to that class to which it bore the greatest resemblance." Exercising this discretion, the New Jersey collector applied the tax to wagons of farmers going to market.

An even better example of the need for administrative discretion is an early law of Congress authorizing the superintendents of the Indian Department to grant licenses to trade with Indians to "any proper person." Obviously, Congress could not specify in the legislation the kinds of individuals to whom such licenses could safely be entrusted, nor could it itself assume the responsibility for passing upon applications for such licenses.[13]

Today, American society is much more complex. Legislatures pass laws in highly complicated fields where great reliance must be placed on trained officials in the administrative branch to make the right decisions in applying the laws to particular cases. This is true at all levels of government, but naturally the extent of administrative discretion and the importance of its exercise vary. As William W. Boyer has written:

[12] Leonard D. White, *The Federalists*, New York: Macmillan, 1948, p. 452.
[13] *Ibid.*, p. 380.

Numerous statutes confer policymaking authority upon administrative agencies, but the number of such grants does not necessarily indicate the scope of an agency's authority to make policies. Some grants are very broad, for example, the delegation of authority to agencies to make reasonable rules for the protection of public health, or for the elimination of unfair trade practices or unfair labor practices. Other grants of authority may be relatively narrow as, for example, a statutory directive that an agency make rules to prevent, eradicate, and control communicable diseases of honey bees, or an even narrower grant—that an agency prescribe a definition of "epilepsy."[14]

Whether the discretion is ample or limited, the common factor in Boyer's examples is that the legislature finds it cannot go beyond stating the objectives of the law and the broad policies to govern its execution. "Protect the public health," "eliminate unfair trade or labor practices," "control communicable diseases"—these indicate the legislative purpose, but the rest is necessarily left to the experts in the administrative branch to define.

Much discretion is normally exercised by administrative officials, whether in national, state, or local governments. In the space of several days' reading of the newspapers, numerous examples of their policy decisions can be noted. Try this for a week or so and you will accumulate a bundle of clippings that range from the President's momentous decisions about nuclear testing to the city health department's routine order to close a restaurant as a menace to the public health.

Not only does the executive branch have a policy role in executing the laws, but it also participates actively in the original formulation of the laws themselves. The writers of the Constitution did not intend that the President should not lead, but it is doubtful that they expected most major legislation to originate with the recommendations of the Administration in power. Yet this has been the pattern in recent American history: the President proposes and Congress decides. Specifically, bills are frequently drafted within the executive branch and then introduced by administration supporters in the House and the Senate, frequently simultaneously. True, in some cases a Presi-

[14] William W. Boyer, "Policy Making by Government Agencies," *Midwest Journal of Political Science*, IV, No. 3 (August, 1960), 269. See also Herman Goldstein, "Police Discretion: The Ideal Versus the Real," *Public Administration Review*, XXIII, No. 3 (September, 1963), 140–148.

dential request for legislation is the result of pressure from leading members of his party in Congress, and certainly it cannot be said that Congressmen never propose but would always rather sit in review on the bills suggested by the executive branch. It is correct, however, to state that, in the main, Congress now concentrates on critical examination of the President's legislative proposals. This is particularly true, of course, when the Chief Executive believes that his function is to exert leadership. Eisenhower at first differed from most recent Chief Executives with the view that Congress should decide, and hence lead. However, he later changed his mind, as his extremely frequent use of the veto power demonstrated. While Eisenhower did not always want to lead, he did not, on the other hand, want to be led. The same attitude is often true of chief executives in state and local governments. They sponsor legislative programs and are directly responsible for many of the laws passed.

ADMINISTRATION AND POLITICS

In pursuing our definition of public administration, we may seem to have delayed unduly in coming to the cardinal question of the relationship between administration and politics. Our purpose was first to explore the nature and extent of administrative discretion, because these are among the clues to the relationship.

Let us examine what we mean by the word, *politics.* Dictionary definitions are of limited use here, because they do not adequately reflect all the different meanings that social scientists now give to the word. One interpretation is that any participation in the formulation of public policies means, *ipso facto,* involvement in politics. In other words, it is a political act when an administrator recommends legislation and when he makes policy decisions in carrying out a law. If we accept this, and there are strong reasons for doing so, the preceding discussion of administration and policy clearly puts administration into the arena of politics. Another view of politics is that it is "the process by which power and influence are acquired and exercised."[15] Harold Lasswell's book, *Politics—Who Gets What, When, How,*[16] conveys the meaning of this definition very well. Public officials seek

[15] John M. Pfiffner and Frank P. Sherwood, *Administrative Organization,* Englewood Cliffs, N.J.: Prentice-Hall, 1960, p. 311.

[16] Harold Lasswell, *Politics—Who Gets What, When, How,* New York: Whittlesey House, 1936.

power and influence with legislators and interest groups in order to build support for the programs they administer. We need go no farther: in this sense, administration certainly is politics.

Social scientists do not limit the use of the term *politics* to political-party activity or even to governmental affairs. Policymaking and power struggles take place in many areas of human activity. A *political* approach—which, in everyday usage, means being shrewd and engaging in "horsetrading"—can take place in any kind of organization. *Politics* does have a bad connotation, and this brings us to the unfortunate dichotomy between *administration* and *politics* which characterized early writings in the field of political science. These writers were anxious to keep partisan influence out of the daily work of public administration. What they feared was the spoilsman and the evil consequences of handing out government jobs as rewards for supporting the political party in power. Such *politics* they despised because it stood in the way of administrative reform. They wanted administration separated from politics in this sense, but to drive their point home, they went too far in arguing the separability of administration.[17] Today, the same determination exists to keep out the spoilsman, but the broader definition of *politics* now holds sway. This broader view equates policymaking with politics, and thus regards administration as part of the political process. Wallace S. Sayre states this point of view very well: "The exercise of discretionary power, the making of value choices, is a characteristic and increasing function of administrators and bureaucrats; they are thus importantly engaged in politics."[18]

PRIVATE AND PUBLIC ADMINISTRATION

The Cooperative Element

Administration as a process is by no means limited to the public sector; it is also found in private organizations. Factories, hospitals, labor unions, charitable agencies, churches—in all these and every other kind of human organization, the key to successful operations is

[17] See Albert Lepawsky, *Administration, The Art and Science of Organization and Management*, New York: Knopf, 1955, pp. 41–51.

[18] Wallace S. Sayre, "Premises of Public Administration: Past and Emerging," *Public Administration Review*, XVIII, No. 2 (Spring, 1958), 104.

the effective utilization of human and physical resources. This is the work of administration, or, as it is also frequently called, management. Another way of expressing this is that administration is cooperative group effort, in a public or private setting. The common factor is the element of cooperation, but the purposes or goals of human organizations, as is evident from the examples above, naturally vary. Furthermore, the problems of all public organizations are not the same, just as the problems of private ones vary from company to company. Each organization, public or private, must meet the challenges of its particular environment. The risk element, for example, in a private, atomic-energy plant is at present much greater than that in a telephone company. The military regiments the individual soldier in ways which would be considered intolerable in civilian public agencies. The exact form administration takes varies, depending upon the kind of undertaking.

The Bureaucratic Element

Besides the common element of cooperation, there is, in modern industrial societies, another similarity: the element of large size. In fact, so large have modern organizations grown that some people feel that they stifle human initiative and curb individual freedom. Frequently, this criticism takes expression in a condemnation of "bureaucracy." As Robert Dubin paints the popular picture of the bureaucrat, he is an "expert in wasting, time, money, and energy." Far from being efficient, he "institutionalizes his inefficiency and raises it to the level of a fine art."[19]

However, bureaucracy can produce good results as well as undesirable ones. To the social scientists, a bureaucratic organization is one characterized by certain features, the end purpose of which is to produce efficient results. "Every organization," writes Dubin, "that is big enough will develop a bureaucracy."[20] The bureaucratic element enters when the number of employees becomes so great that the head man cannot have personal contact with all of them. He must designate some of them to serve as intermediate supervisors, and, as the organization grows in complexity, they in turn find it necessary to channel their instructions through subordinate levels of supervisors.

[19] Robert Dubin (ed.), *Human Relations in Administration*, Englewood Cliffs, N.J.: Prentice-Hall, 1961, p. 139.

[20] *Ibid.*, p. 140.

This is the principle of hierarchy, with the directive positions arranged in descending order of importance. Bureaucracy consists, then, of these layers of officials interposed between the head man and the lowest level of employees. Objectivity and impersonal relations come to characterize such an organization, whether in government or business. Individuals are selected to fill each directive post on the basis of professional qualifications for the assignment. Some of these professionals are managers; their responsibilities are predominantly of an administrative character. Others are technicians in the different occupational lines represented in the organization.

Nothing is wrong with all of this—except that the size of the operations forces the bureaucrat to develop rules and regulations for dealing with specific cases, and though this promotes orderliness, it angers the citizen who finds that some officials seem to regard the rules as ends in themselves. The human personality rails against being catalogued as a *case,* to be treated in the same way as thousands of others whatever the circumstances. That some officials adopt this attitude cannot be disputed, but, again, this happens not only in public, but also in private agencies.

This is an abbreviated discussion of bureaucracy, but it gives its essential distinguishing characteristics, as stated by contemporary social scientists, who have been greatly influenced by the German sociologist, Max Weber, one of the first scholars to identify the special features of bureaucratic organization.[21] Human efforts to cooperate may go astray, as happens when bureaucrats become wedded to red tape, but one would be naive to suppose that the solution is to escape to the private sector of the economy. Accordingly, our second point is that bureaucracy, for good or bad, is another major element of similarity between public and private administration.

Scientific Management

A third observation is that the concepts and techniques of scientific management are applicable to both industry and government. The scientific-management movement was pioneered by Frederick W. Taylor who became prominent in American industrial circles towards the close of the nineteenth century. Taylor believed that sound scien-

[21] See Dwight Waldo (ed.), *Ideas and Issues in Public Administration,* New York: McGraw-Hill, 1953, pp. 41–49, for selections from Weber's writings.

tific analysis of any operation would lead to discovery of the "one best way" of carrying it out. Scientific analysis involves breaking down each task into its component parts, studying the movements of the workers, the use made of materials and equipment, experimenting with different work methods and procedures, and finally adopting those which proved most efficient. Taylor concentrated on studies at the level of the individual worker and his workbench. He was very successful in this kind of analysis, and when his recommendations were followed, they did, in many cases, make for appreciably more efficient operations.[22]

Why not move the focus from the individual worker and apply this same "scientific" approach to larger questions, such as basic organization structure? This question intrigued some of Taylor's followers, and they proceeded to develop what came to be known as "principles of organization." Orderliness, they felt, should be the keynote in developing the organization plan—again, to promote efficiency. By around 1910, scientific management was already being used in government shops and arsenals. As the movement expanded to include problems of management in general, it led to the creation of administrative-planning offices in government agencies, paralleling a similar development in industry. The titles of such offices vary, but their mission is to improve organization and their methods are now generally accepted.[23] This is why it is frequently said that administration in government is part of the larger field of management, meaning a particular application of *Taylorism*. But some writers have gone too far in emphasizing the similarity of private and public administration. Scientific-management principles can and are profitably used in both sectors, but essential differences from the standpoint of the *purposes* sought still remain. For reasons which will be explained shortly, no private organization can ever be exactly the same as a public one.

The Human Relations Approach

Taylorism is associated with what is called the "traditional approach" to administration. As Dwight Waldo so ably points out, scientific management, "taking efficiency as the objective, views ad-

[22] Frederick W. Taylor, *Scientific Management*, New York: Harper & Row, 1947.

[23] See Dwight Waldo, *The Administrative State*, New York: Ronald, 1948, pp. 47–61.

ministration as a technical problem concerned basically with the division of labor and the specialization of function."[24] Thus, task analysis and the development of logical organization structure are central considerations in this approach, the symbol of which is the organization chart. Taylor concentrated on work methods, machines, and materials; he was primarily concerned with questions of mechanical efficiency. It is a striking fact that one of his disciples should write:

> It is being realized with increasing clarity that, in addition to the problems of the task, adjusting the individual to the task, and arranging and correlating tasks, there is a fourth issue, *motivating and energizing the group as a group. And that this fourth aspect of management is probably the most important and complex of the four.*[25]

Of course, what Taylor sought to accomplish was exceedingly important, as it still is today, namely, to develop efficient work procedures and to eliminate waste. In neglecting the human element, however, he missed the clue which would have permitted him to make an even greater contribution to the effectiveness of human organizations.

Writing about those who still cling to the traditional approach, Robert Tannenbaum states:

> Many who take this view see business units as essentially economic and technological entities (which certainly they are) but not importantly as social organizations (which certainly they also are). To them, people are not unique human beings in unique social groupings, but rather names on organization charts whose on-the-job behavior is primarily determined (or ought to be) by job descriptions and the desires of their bosses.
>
> An increasing number of scholars, however, are becoming aware of and are able to accept the fact that people (with all their really human qualities) are a fundamental part of any business organization. They are there as individuals with their peculiar personalities; they are there as members of many types of groups; they are units in the total organization; and they are affected by the culture that surrounds them.
>
> While the effective manager must, without question, be able to understand and deal with economic and technological phenomena, he must *also* be able to deal with interpersonal phenomena. Managerial problems

[24] Dwight Waldo, "Organization Theory: An Elephantine Problem," *Public Administration Review*, XXI, No. 4 (Autumn, 1961), 219–220.

[25] Lyndall F. Urwick, *The Pattern of Management*, Minneapolis: Univ. of Minnesota Press, 1956, pp. 50–51. (Italics ours.)

involving motivation, morale, teamwork, creativity, introduction of change, demand creation, public relations, etc., can adequately be solved only through a keen understanding of human-relations variables and an ability to behave appropriately in light of such understanding.[26]

In later chapters of this book, these "interpersonal phenomena" will be the center of interest as such topics as leadership, informal organization, and supervision are explored in detail. It should be made clear here, however, that the traditional approach is not being abandoned, either in government or in industry. Waldo expects it "to be around a long, long, time," because it does have "much truth in it, both descriptively and prescriptively, that is to say both as a description of organizations as we find them in our society and as a prescription for achieving the goals of these organizations 'efficiently'."[27]

In both sectors, a synthesis of the traditional and the human relations approaches is emerging. As we shall see later, the traditional approach did lead to certain misconceptions about the nature of authority and worker motivations. In the main, however, combining both the traditional and the newer viewpoints produces a fuller picture of organization life than when the focus is limited to only one of them.

Differences Between Public and Private Agencies

We must now explain the statement made previously that "no private organization can ever be exactly the same as a public one." The peculiar element in public administration is that everything a government agency does is the public's business. Tax money is being used, so every citizen has the right to know how it is spent and to criticize public officials with whose decisions they do not agree. As has often been said, the public official operates in a "goldfish bowl"; he is subject to searching and constant outside scrutiny. In fact, it is a cardinal principle of democratic government that civil servants be guided by public opinion. While the officials of a private company also have important public contacts, they are not operating in a "goldfish bowl." Companies want satisfied clients, and they are also increasingly subject to government regulation, all of which makes *public relations* an

[26] Robert Tannenbaum, "Some Current Issues in Human Relations," *California Management Review*, II, No. 1 (Fall, 1959), 53.

[27] Waldo, "Organization Theory: An Elephantine Problem," in *op. cit.*, 220.

important element in business success. Nevertheless, companies still remain private in character, and their internal operations are pretty much their own business and not that of the general public.

James Forrestal once said that "the difficulty of government work is that it not only has to be well done, but the public has to be convinced that it is being well done. In other words, there is a necessity both for competence and exposition, and I hold it is extremely difficult to combine the two in the same person."[28] This is why some businessmen fail in government positions. Impatient over the need to justify their decisions to the public and accustomed in their companies to giving orders which quickly produce action, they complain that in the government they are thwarted by red tape. Yet it is the public that insists on this paperwork, because, to repeat, it is their money that is being spent. Civil service, conflict of interest, and numerous other laws and regulations must be observed. This is what creates the red tape so exasperating to the typical businessman, but, while some of it may safely be eliminated, a sizeable residue will always be necessary to protect the public interest.

It is sometimes bluntly stated that a public official needs a thick skin. Criticism of government workers has, from time to time, been so intense that Senator Javits of New York has suggested creation of a new congressional committee to function as a kind of public defender for maligned federal employees.[29] Along with other members of the Senate Subcommittee on National Policy Machinery, he had listened to numerous witnesses testify that the government was handicapped in its efforts to recruit scientific and other valuable personnel because of the savage attacks on public employees. Such concern by a legislator for the feelings of administrative officials is rare, so it is not surprising that such a "public-defender" committee has not been established.

Government is also different because no private company can equal it in size and diversity of activities. In recent years, federal employment has stabilized at around 2,500,000; no one firm, including even the giants such as General Motors and the American Telephone and Telegraph Company, employs anywhere near this figure. Even

[28] Quoted in John J. Corson, "Distinguishing Characteristics of Public Administration," *Public Administration Review*, XII, No. 2 (Spring, 1952), 124.

[29] *Mobilizing Talent for Government Service*, Senate Subcommittee on National Policy Machinery, 86th Congress, 2nd Session, Washington, D.C.: Government Printing Office, 1960, pp. 422–423.

more important is the great scope of government activities. These range from "rehabilitating mentally shattered veterans, teaching Indian children to draw, incarcerating hardened criminals, rescuing ships in distress at sea, manufacturing A-bombs, building airstrips in North Africa and weather stations in Greenland, blockading the coast of Korea, and fixing a ceiling price on hamburger, to mention a random selection."[30]

Furthermore, the comparison need not be made with the federal government. State and municipal governments have also greatly expanded their activities. These range from much bigger educational systems and multimillion dollar superhighways to air- and water-pollution programs, civil defense, urban redevelopment, educational television, airports, heliports, picnic areas, public housing, and many other programs. The billion-dollar mark in some state and municipal budgets was passed some time ago. At the same time, for reasons discussed in the next chapter, the outlook for the future is for a continued increase in the load on government at all levels. The variety of skills required in public employment in state and local governments is usually much wider than that found in private business, except for a few multi-purpose corporations like General Electric.

THE PUBLIC–PRIVATE PARTNERSHIP

Whenever comparisons are made between public and private administration, the impression may be given that each is opposed to the other and occupies a separate, distinct field. Actually, much of what takes place in public administration is accomplished with the collaboration of numerous private groups and individuals. A strict separation between public and private administration does not exist.

Examples in Community Organizations

This can be easily demonstrated with just one or two examples. The South East Chicago Commission (SECC) is a private organization representing certain communities in that part of the city. Its mis-

[30] *Improvement of Management in the Federal Government*, President's Advisory Committee on Management, Washington, D.C.: Government Printing Office, 1952. Quoted in *Public Administration Review*, XIII, No. 1 (Winter, 1953), 40.

sion is to fight physical blight and generally to rehabilitate these communities. It was originally created in 1952 as the result of pressure by private civic and other groups. Recently a resident in the area called the SECC to complain about deplorable conditions in certain dwellings. There was no light or heat in these buildings, and they were rat-infested. An SECC building inspector arrived, called in a city inspector, and they both found no fewer than 278 violations of the building code. They asked the Community Conservation Board (CCB), an agency of the city of Chicago, to take emergency action. The CCB ordered coal, had the lights turned on, and took steps to speed up acquisition of the property which happened to be one of the parcels still to be acquired under the urban renewal program. Charges were brought against the owners and sustained in the courts, and the buildings were ordered closed. The CCB then, at the urgent request of the SECC, made arrangements to relocate the tenants.[31] The entire incident illustrates how citizen groups in local communities spur public action and cooperate with government officials in assuring the success of different programs.

Examples from the Field of Recreation

In a staff paper prepared for the Outdoor Recreation Resources Commission, Morton Grodzins cites numerous evidences of private—public collaboration.[32] Most private recreational camps are adjacent to public parks or water and many operate on public land, as at Tennessee Valley Authority Reservoirs, and in the national parks. Without the public bridle paths, the market would be greatly reduced for the sale of riding boots and clothes and for the rental of horses. The sale of fishing gear, which amounted to almost $160 million in 1959, is largely dependent upon public waters and reservoirs built by government agencies. The reverse is also true, for most of the nation's large timber growers allow their lands to be used by the general public for recreational purposes. Among the activities invited are hunting, fishing, hiking, and picnicking.

[31] *St. Louis Post-Dispatch*, April 4, 1961, editorial page.

[32] Morton Grodzins, *Trends in American Living and Outdoor Recreation*, The Outdoor Recreation Resources Review Commission, Study Report 22, Washington, D.C.: Government Printing Office, 1962, pp. 4–7.

Private groups, too, work closely with public agencies in the passage of important legislation in the field of recreation. The boating industry, for example, helped in drawing up the Federal Boat Registration Act of 1958 and a complementary draft statute recommended for passage by the states. Private agencies sometimes even purchase land with their own funds and then donate it to the government as public recreational areas. The Massachussetts Trustees of Public Reservations makes statewide surveys of scenic sites, purchases desirable tracts with privately raised funds, and then either maintains them for public use or turns them over to the state or to a local government. In California, the Save-the-Redwoods League "has had an important role in establishing the state park system, not least of all through its purchase by private subscription of prime park land." In all, Grodzins concludes that the recreational field provides an excellent example of the "overlap of the private and public in the American culture."

Government by Contract

It was stated above that federal employment alone totals about 2,500,000. Victor K. Heyman reveals, however, that "the time appears to be rapidly approaching when the employees of the federal government, like the classic iceberg, are nine-tenths 'invisible'."[33] He estimates that the real total is around 11 million, 5 million of them in the civilian and military branches and the remaining 6 million recruited through *contracts* and similar arrangements. Of course, the bottom part of this "iceberg" is visible, but most people do not recognize it for what it is. These are the plants, scientific laboratories, and other installations of defense and other contractors. They employ some 6 million workers, principally on research and development, weapons-system management, and technical supervision of weapons programs. No discussion of the intermingling of private and public activities would be complete without mentioning this extensive use by the government of private contractors.

Heyman states that more than 30 federal agencies contract for re-

[33] Victor K. Heyman, "Government by Contract: Boon or Boner?" *Public Administration Review*, XXI, No. 2 (Spring, 1961), 59.

search and development. This money is expended in general on three types of activities:

1. research projects selected by the contractor himself, consisting generally of basic research conducted at universities;
2. specific research undertaken by a contractor at the request of a federal agency which needs help in solving certain problems;
3. research and development contracts under which the contractor manages and operates a government-owned facility.

In addition, the federal government contracts for a great variety of consultant services, including those of the "think groups," such as the Rand Corporation. Many of the services made available to foreign governments under technical-assistance programs are provided through contracts made by the Agency for International Development (AID) with private American companies, educational institutions, and different private individuals. Other examples of the growing use of the contract device could be given, but those already mentioned indicate how extensively it is used.

DEFINITION OF PUBLIC ADMINISTRATION

We have travelled a long way in the search for a satisfactory definition of public administration, but why we had to do so can now readily be appreciated. No condensed definition can encompass all of the above points. They can, however, be presented in the form of a brief summary which will constitute the definition. Public administration:

1. is cooperative group effort in a public setting.
2. covers all three branches—executive, legislative, and judicial—and their interrelationships.
3. has an important role in the formulation of public policy and is thus a part of the political process.
4. is more important than, and also different in significant ways from, private administration.
5. as a field of study and practice, has been much influenced in recent years by the human-relations approach.
6. is closely associated with numerous private groups and individuals in providing services to the community.

BIBLIOGRAPHY

A Handbook of Public Administration, Current Concepts and Practice With Special Reference to Developing Countries, New York: United Nations, 1961.

Dahl, Robert A., and Lindblom, Charles E., *Politics, Economics and Welfare*, New York: Harper & Row, 1953.

Dubin, Robert (ed.), *Human Relations in Administration*, Englewood Cliffs, N.J.: Prentice-Hall, 1961.

Gaus, John M., *Reflections on Public Administration*, University, Univ. of Alabama Press, 1947.

Gaus, John M., White, Leonard D., and Dimock, Marshall E., *The Frontiers of Public Administration*, Chicago: Univ. of Chicago Press, 1936.

Grodzins, Morton, "Public Administration and the Science of Human Relations," *Public Administration Review*, **XI**, No. 2 (Spring, 1951).

Homans, George C., *The Human Group*, New York: Harcourt, Brace, 1950.

Hyneman, Charles S., *Bureaucracy in a Democracy*, New York: Harper & Row, 1950.

Lepawsky, Albert (ed.), *Administration: The Art and Science of Organization and Management*, New York: Knopf, 1949.

Likert, Rensis, "An Emerging Theory of Organization, Leadership, and Management," in L. Petrullo and B. M. Bass (eds.), *Leadership and Interpersonal Behavior*, New York: Holt, Rinehart and Winston, 1961.

Redford, Emmette S., *Ideal and Practice in Public Administration*, University: Univ. of Alabama Press, 1958.

Sayre, Wallace S., "Trends of a Decade in Administrative Values," *Public Administration Review*, **XI**, No. 1 (Winter, 1951).

Sayre, Wallace S., "Premises of Public Administration: Past and Emerging," *Public Administration Review*, **XVIII**, No. 2 (Spring, 1958).

Simon, Herbert A., *Administrative Behavior*, New York: Macmillan, 1957.

Simon, Herbert A., and March, James G., *Organizations*, New York: Wiley, 1958.

Standards and Techniques of Public Administration, New York: United Nations, 1951.

Tannenbaum, Robert, "Some Current Issues in Human Relations," *California Management Review*, **II**, No. 1 (Fall, 1959).

Tead, Ordway, *The Art of Administration*, New York: McGraw-Hill, 1951.

Tead, Ordway, *Democratic Administration*, New York: Association Press, 1945.

Waldo, Dwight, "Organizational Analysis: Some Notes on Methods and Criteria," *Public Administration Review*, **VII,** No. 4 (Autumn, 1947).

Waldo, Dwight, *The Administrative State*, New York: Ronald, 1948.

Waldo, Dwight, *The Study of Public Administration*, (Doubleday Short Studies in Political Science) New York: Doubleday, 1955.

Waldo, Dwight, *Perspectives on Administration*, University: Univ. of Alabama Press, 1956.

CHAPTER 2

The Environment of Public Administration in the United States

In the preceding chapter it was shown how the role of public administration has grown in importance as society has become more complicated. The more complex the society, the greater the scope and diversity of the public services it must provide. Moreover, as changes take place in the physical and human settings, efforts must be made to reorient government programs accordingly. Specifically, what are some of the outstanding characteristics of American society and how do they affect public administration? No exhaustive treatment will be attempted, but several of the most important such factors will be discussed in some detail.

POPULATION CHANGES

Increase in Population

Almost everyone has heard of the "population explosion," but too few people appreciate its consequences for government. First, let us present the facts, and then we will show their numerous effects upon public administration. At the latest count, the total population of the United States was 192 million, and it was increasing at the rate of 3 million a year. It was expected to reach, by 1966, the 200-million mark, and, by 1980, to be about 256 million. One expert estimates that, in the next 50 years, the country's population will more than double, and that, eventually, it should total 910 millions—not including Alaska, which could probably support an additional 30 million![1] The staggering nature of this increase is seen most clearly when we make comparisons with population figures for the recent past. In 1950, the country had 151,325,798 inhabitants; in 1960, it had 179,323,175—an increase of 27,997,377, or 18.5 percent. In 1930, when the author of this textbook enrolled in college, the figure was about 130 million. Despite the decelerated birth rate of the depression years, in three decades the country's population increased almost 40 percent.

Changes in Composition

Not only has the population grown greatly, but significant changes have also taken place in its composition. First, the proportion of aged persons is much larger that it used to be: In 1950, the number of individuals 65 years of age or older was 12,295,000, or approximately 8 percent of the total population; the 1960 census showed that it had jumped to 16,559,580, or more than 9 percent. Furthermore, it is estimated that, by 1975, it will be close to 22 million, or almost 10 percent of the American population. Second, there has been, at the same time, a sizeable increase in the number of youngsters of school age: In 1950, there were 46,967,000 persons under 18; by 1960, this had risen to 64,202,000, an increase of 36.7 percent. This exceeded even the rate of increase during the same period for people of 65 and over, which was 34.7 percent. The middle group, 18 to 65, moved from 92,064,000 to 98,561,000, or an increase of only 7.1 percent.

Changes in Geographic Distribution

How about the location of the population? For some time now, people have been moving from the farms and the rural countryside to the cities and the metropolitan areas. We knew before the 1960 census that the majority of Americans lived in urban settlements. That census revealed, however, that, collectively, the nation's cities grew

[1] Harrison Brown, "The Prospective Environment For Policymaking and Administration," reproduced in *The Formulation and Administration of United States Foreign Policy*, Senate Foreign Relations Committee, 86th Congress, 2nd Session, Washington, D.C.: Government Printing Office, 1960, p. 141.

only moderately between 1950 and 1960, despite the fact that Americans left the farms at the rate of nearly half a million a year during the decade. The explanation is very simple and is known to all of us in a general way, but again, it is not fully appreciated: By far the greatest population increase took place in the suburbs.

The Bureau of the Census defines a standard metropolitan statistical area (SMSA) as a county or group of contiguous counties which contains at least one city of 50,000 inhabitants or more, or "twin cities" with a combined population of at least 50,000. In addition to the county or counties containing such a city or cities, contiguous counties are included in the SMSA if they are essentially metropolitan in character and are socially and economically integrated with the central city. These contiguous areas—or satellite communities, as they are sometimes called—constitute the suburbs. Their residents work and shop in the core city and otherwise participate in its life. Whereas between 1950 and 1960 the population increase was only 10.7 percent in the core cities, it was 48.6 percent in the suburbs. In fact, with the sole exception of Los Angeles, the nation's largest cities lost, rather than gained, population. Almost two-thirds of the nation's population now lives in metropolitan areas. The total urban population is even larger, because some of it is found in cities with a population of 2500 or more outside metropolitan areas. Since the Census Bureau includes all cities of this size in the total urban count, this means that seven of every ten Americans is an urbanite. The rest of the population resides in the small towns and the rural areas; by 1960, only 8.7 percent of the total United States population actually lived on the farms.

Another kind of population movement of great dimensions has been taking place: the westward migration. The states growing the fastest are principally in the "sunny" part of the country—in other words, the western states and Florida. This westward movement increased greatly during the past decade and shows no signs of abating. As Richard M. Scammon, the Director of the Census Bureau, explains: "What we are seeing, really, is a picture of mobility and of people being able to go where they want to go, rather than going where the mines are or where the farming is good."[2]

[2] "The America the '60 Census Shows," *U.S. News & World Report*, July 3, 1961, p. 48.

Impact on Public Administration

The great increase in population makes it necessary for governments at all levels to expand their budgets. At the local level, more money must be spent on streets, sewers, refuse and garbage collection, water supply, police and fire protection, parks and recreation, and similar services. The states must increase the amounts of their grants-in-aid to local school districts because of the large numbers of new pupils. Similarly, state expenditures for public assistance and other welfare programs must be boosted. State governments also must spend more on highways, parks, dams, aqueducts, prisons, mental hospitals, and other institutions. At the national level, the federal government must increase the size, not only of the programs it directly administers—such as the national parks and forests—but also of its grants to the state and local governments for highways, airports, urban renewal, social security, and other purposes. Furthermore, as the great increase in population creates complex conditions which state and local governments find they can no longer solve, new federal programs become necessary. Public administration has to carry a much heavier load, and, what is more, to make arrangements to do so in a very short period of time. When whole cities seem to spring up overnight, and when population increases quickly lead to pressing problems on which the community knows it must take action, the challenge facing public officials all over the nation becomes clear. They must function efficiently and with dispatch as the people's agents for adjusting to the accelerated social change which so characterizes our complicated society.

REQUIREMENTS OF PARTICULAR POPULATION GROUPS

Needs of the Aged and Aging

Let us now turn to the special needs of certain groups in the population, and see first how the sizeable increase in the number of aged and aging persons affects public administration. Naturally, there are strong differences of opinion about what the government should do for this segment of the population. We see this in the controversy raging over the proposal to increase social security taxes in order to finance medical insurance for persons retired under that program. Nonetheless, it is evident that the government must give more attention to this group than it has in the past, simply because it is now so much larger.

A large proportion of the aged have very low incomes, but their needs are not economic alone. Because they seem forgotten, many of them have withdrawn from active participation in community life. Four-fifths of those 65 and over are fully retired from regular employment. They want to live decently, from the standpoint of food, clothing, shelter, and other material resources but, as one official puts it, they also do not want to "go to seed." This official gave a speech in December 1961 in which he described new federal programs for the aged in the field of housing. These programs cover both federally aided, low-rent public housing and privately financed housing, such as that built with loans guaranteed by the Federal Housing Administration. One example from his speech[3] will show how these programs are being adapted to meet the needs of the senior citizens. In Victoria Plaza, a 185–unit, public-housing development in San Antonio, Texas, the entire first floor is taken up by a large Senior Center. Besides recreational facilities, this Center contains a beauty salon—operated by the project residents themselves—a branch of the San Antonio Public Library, and two counselling offices staffed by local social agencies. It also houses an eight-room, public-health clinic maintained by the City Department of Public Health for children in the neighborhood, and a community kitchen for the preparation of food or refreshments for parties held in adjoining recreation rooms. In the future, these kitchen facilities may also be used to provide a "meals-on-wheels" service for those residents who are confined to their rooms.

This is only one example, taken from just a single kind of government program. Many other illustrations could be given, such as the activities of municipalities in providing special facilities in the public parks for bridge playing and other activities by senior citizens. How-

[3] E. Everett Ashley, 3rd, "Better Living Through Better Housing for Senior Citizens," a talk delivered at round table conference of American Public Welfare Association, Chicago, December 1, 1961.

ever, the Victoria Plaza example suffices to show clearly how population change has a definite impact on public administration.

Problems of Younger Americans

Turning to the under-18 age group, mention has already been made of the soaring education budgets. The United States Office of Education estimated that the 1964 fall enrollment in the public elementary schools would be 26.1 million. The estimate for the public secondary schools was 14.9 million. For higher-education, degree-credit enrollment, it was 4.7 million.

Apart from this pressure on educational facilities, local communities also face the serious problem of a relatively high rate of unemployment among those seeking employment for the first time. In recent months, teen agers have accounted for as much as 40 percent of the total unemployed.

Plight of the Suburban Communities

When people move in large numbers to the suburbs, the problem of providing basic public services becomes acute. Note the following statement from a recent report on metropolitan problems:

> With increased numbers and concentration of people and improved standards of service, discrepancies arise in suburbs between what can be provided and what the people expect. More schools, parks, and playgrounds are needed in suburban communities. Such facilities are expensive, and many neighborhoods must do without them or get along with fewer facilities than are needed. Other communities must strain their taxing ability to provide them. There is no indication that the demands will decrease; instead, they will become more urgent and the levels of service demanded will continue to rise as the levels of education, occupation and income of the citizens increase.
>
> Suburbanites who are home owners and expect to be suburban residents for a long time care greatly about services which affect the character of their neighborhood. Thus we find, from the extensive sample survey of citizen opinion, much concern over improvement of local streets and street cleaning, maintenance of sidewalks and provision of street lighting. The quality of these services enhances or detracts from the neighborhood

as a pleasant place in which to live. Yet the rapid expansion of new subdivisions, frequently with little regard for basic planning needs, is already leading to public service deficiencies in many suburban areas.[4]

The "public service deficiencies" referred to have, in some cases, already produced what are known as suburban slums. *Suburb,* today, does not mean, as it usually did in previous decades, an exclusive section, very well maintained and catering to high-income families. All too often it refers to untidy, hastily laid-out settlements, that are occupied by many families of relatively modest means. As a result, government needs to be as much concerned with developing a better life for the inhabitants of some suburbs as it is with improving the lot of those living in the core cities.

The Pressure on the Western States

The movement of the population to the "sunny" part of the country has been in such large numbers as to place these states under a great strain to provide the necessary public services. California is a case in point. Between 1950 and 1960, its population increased 48.5 percent, from 10,586,223 to 15,717,204. As a result, its budget for the 1962–1963 fiscal year was $2.887 billion. Of this amount, more than 40 percent was spent for education alone. Its budget for the 1964–1965 fiscal year was $3,600,000,000.

The concentration of defense industry in California and other western states greatly influences decisions which are made, not only at the state capitals, but also in Washington. One illustration of this is California's concern that the federal government may siphon important defense contracts from the West Coast to areas of unemployment in other parts of the country. California rests its case on the principle of efficiency: It has the skilled workers and the demonstrated capacity to do a good job on defense business. On the other hand, the states with long-term, "hard-core" unemployment want the chance to prove that they can handle defense business just as efficiently as California. Of course, any decision in this sort of situation

[4] *Path of Progress For Metropolitan St. Louis,* Metropolitan St. Louis Survey, University City, Mo.: August, 1957, p. 18.

has important political implications, but this is merely to restate that public officials have an important political role. The governors naturally put pressure on Washington to obtain defense contracts for their states. Washington is caught in the middle, and does its best to satisfy the needs of all states whenever it is possible to do so.

Increased Needs for Water and Electric Power

As the population growth in the West makes old problems even more acute, these problems inevitably come to loom larger in policy-making at the national level. An excellent example is the question of water supply. Precipitation is very low in extensive parts of the region, such as Southern California. At the same time, both domestic and industrial needs for water have increased tremendously. This, of course, is a national problem, because all over the country we are rapidly running out of good water. Accordingly, plans must now be made to assure that, through construction of new reservoirs, reclaiming water from sewage for industrial reuse, and other methods, these vastly expanded needs will be met.

Further, as new industry and thousands of new families have poured into the West, the need for electric power has greatly increased. Thus, in a region where a battle has raged for some time over public- or private-power developments, the issue has now become an even more sensitive one. Again, policy decisions of federal officials are of great significance. The Federal Power Commission (FPC) is authorized under the law to decide which proposed dam projects would provide the most "comprehensive" development of the resources of a particular area. The FPC passes upon rival applications by public utility districts and private companies to develop the hydroelectric potential of the country's rivers. Sometimes the FPC decides in favor of the private interests, as it did in 1955 in the controversy over Hell's Canyon in the Pacific Northwest. Sometimes, however, the FPC decides that the better development plan is the one offered by public bodies. Every decision of this kind by the FPC is the subject of intensive debate not only in the particular region involved, but also in the national Congress where the West now wields more power because of its increased population.

ADVANCES IN PHYSICAL TECHNOLOGY

Inventions, scientific discoveries, and other advances in physical technology constitute a whole complex of factors which have greatly influenced American society.

The Automobile Age

The automobile is a case in point. As one writer notes, "In 1920 automobiles were a luxury—few persons could afford them. By 1930, however, the automobile had become a necessity for millions of persons. The new mode of transportation made possible new ways of life. And new patterns of life quickly evolved around the automobile."[5] He comments that the point seems already to have been reached where every person qualified by age to drive wants to have a car at his disposal. Eventually, he believes, there will be one self-propelled vehicle in existence for every person of driving age. In another 50 years, there may be more than 200 million private cars in the country.

The automobile has made possible the movement to the suburbs. Some commuters travel by train, but most commuting is by private car. As a result, railroad commuter lines have in recent years been in serious financial straits, and many have gone out of business. Furthermore, the great majority of those who live in or close to the big cities prefer to drive their own vehicles to work, instead of using the buses and street cars. This situation explains the recent proposals for the federal government to extend aid to local governments for improvement of mass-transit facilities. Senator Williams of New Jersey has said:

> . . . The problems of skyrocketing metropolitan-area growth, the paralysis of traffic congestion, and the obstacles to the free flow of interstate commerce are of such magnitude and consequence that it just does not make sense to call the problems of mass transportation "a merely local concern" or even "primarily a local problem."[6]

[5] Brown, *op. cit.*, p. 145.
[6] *St. Louis Post-Dispatch*, May 12, 1960, editorial page.

Limited recognition of national responsibility in this area came in 1961 when Congress appropriated $50 million for exploratory studies on urban transportation problems. In 1964, legislation was passed providing for an expenditure, over a three-year period, of $375 million in grants to the cities for large-scale improvement of commuter facilities.

Millions of Americans also prefer to use their own cars for both short and long vacation trips. As the leisure time of the individual increases, he naturally uses his automobile more, all of which leads to a "demand not only for private resorts, service stations, and motor inns that line the main highways, but for governmentally financed facilities such as roads, bridges, parks, golf courses, camping sites, swimming pools, and the like."[7]

This is the brighter side of the picture, because the automobile does contribute greatly to a more enjoyable existence for Americans, young and old. Unfortunately, it is also a menace in various ways. The greater the number of vehicles on the highways, the greater, naturally, are the possibilities of accidents. A public health hazard also exists in those cities where exhaust fumes from automotive vehicles are a major cause of air pollution. As these problems have become more serious in recent years, the pressures on government to deal with them have mounted.

The Airplane

We have also moved into the "Air Age," and this has also meant new challenges and problems for government. In Chapter 6, the Federal Aviation Agency (FAA) is discussed in some detail as part of an analysis of the pressures leading to the creation of new administrative agencies. Here we will simply note some of the outstanding consequences of the Air Age for public administration.

The airlines now carry far more passengers than the railroads. In 1950, the latter carried three times as many first-class passengers as the scheduled domestic airlines; by 1960, the ratio was reversed. Furthermore, although the quantity of freight carried by air is very

[7] George Soule, "The Economics of Leisure," *Annals of the American Academy of Political and Social Sciences*, CCCXIII (September, 1957), 21.

small by comparison with that moved by rail, pipeline, and truck, it is expected to increase tenfold during the next 50 years. Government regulation of the commercial-aviation industry is thus far more important than it used to be. At the national level, the Civil Aeronautics Board (CAB) passes upon applications for certificates to provide air service between different points. It approves or disapproves requests for rate increases, changes in service, and mergers, just as the Interstate Commerce Commission does in the case of the railroads and motor carriers. The importance of these determinations of the CAB is clearly seen in the present concern over the financial positions of the major airlines. With the introduction of jet aircraft, competition between companies serving the same routes has intensified. The jets carry many more passengers than the piston-powered planes which they have now largely replaced. Too many vacant seats make it difficult for the airlines to operate profitably. This largely explains the growing number of requests for mergers and the consequent debate over whether or not they are in the public interest. The CAB is concerned, because its job is as much to regulate the airlines as to encourage—rather than to discourage—their profitable operation by the owners. It must also protect the interests of the millions of passengers.

The FAA has complete control over the use of the navigable airspace of the United States, by both civilian and military aircraft. It regulates the country's airways and employs the air-traffic controllers who direct takeoffs and landings. It also makes the air-safety regulations, although investigation of accidents remains the responsibility of the CAB. State Aeronautics Commissions regulate small airlines and private aircraft operating within the particular state. Cities and counties operate airports, many so big as to represent a management activity far exceeding in importance that of some other local government functions.

The Communications Revolution

With the successful launching of the first Telstar, communications satellites have demonstrated their practicability, and television programs will be relayed from one continent to another. Already, the policymakers of the various nations of the world have had to give their attention to certain basic questions, such as the respective roles of government and of private enterprise in this new development. Congress passed legislation recommended by President Kennedy providing that the American part of the world network would be privately owned, but with some stock available for sale to the general public. Additional responsibilities of an extremely important character have thus been placed on the Federal Communications Commission (FCC). Besides regulating the activities of domestic radio and television stations, it must now oversee the United States part of the international communications satellite system.

Because of the jet airplane and the cheaper fares, far more Americans now visit foreign countries, both on business trips and on vacation. This makes for greater personal communication with the peoples of these countries, and there is evidence that such direct contacts have made many Americans more internationally minded. Improved communications have also served to raise the aspirations of the peoples of the underdeveloped nations and to make them much more aware of the better life they could attain. This has led to the "revolution of rising expectations," about which we will have more to say later. Whether communication takes place by radio, television, in writing, or by personal contact, the net impact is to increase greatly the spread of ideas and values, and eventually, it is hoped, of international understanding.

The Agricultural Revolution

Yet another revolution has taken place—in agriculture. The number of persons working on farms has declined so sharply that one might think it should by now decrease no further. This is not so, because, as Walter Lippmann put it, "Underneath the crop surpluses there is a surplus of farmers."[8] Yields per acre have risen so greatly that President Kennedy told Congress early in 1962 that, in the next 20 years, the country probably could retire 50 million acres from production and still meet all its needs. This increase has been due to the new farm technologies which continue to expand. Tractors and electric energy have replaced horse and mule power; greatly improved fertilizers, hybrid seeds, and more scientific methods of cul-

[8] *St. Louis Post-Dispatch*, Feb. 23, 1962, editorial section.

tivation have combined to raise yields to unprecedented levels. The nation still has three and one half million farmers, but this is twice as many as it really needs. One and a half million of them are now responsible for 87 percent of the total production, and they could easily produce the remaining 13 percent.

The approach of the Kennedy administration was to continue and to strengthen the government's role in agricultural planning, instead of curtailing it. Through tighter production controls, larger withdrawals of land from cultivation, and training of surplus farm workers in industrial skills, it hoped to avoid the huge surpluses of the past. Here again there is room for differences of opinion, as was evidenced by the sharp opposition of some groups to the Kennedy program. No one, however, can deny the existence of the agricultural revolution, nor can it be disputed that, so far, the efforts to deal with it have proved largely unsuccessful.

Besides the drain on the domestic taxpayer, the huge government-owned farm surpluses create difficult problems in international relations. Should some be sold at reduced prices in foreign markets? Such a move would antagonize nations like Canada, which depend heavily on these markets. Should it be donated to underdeveloped countries? In that case, how can we assure that the commodities actually reach the needy people of such lands and are not diverted into other channels by dishonest individuals?

Automation

Automation, both in agriculture and industry, is one of the principal forces for change in American life today, and its many manifestations have an important influence on public administration. In 1961, a Congressional committee found that, in the previous ten years, automation had progressed greatly. In the electrical industry alone, it had meant an increase of 21 percent in output, but also the elimination of 89,000 jobs, or 10 percent of the total. In 1960, as much steel was produced as in 1950, but with 80,000 fewer mill hands. In the soft-coal industry, productivity rose 96 percent, but 262,000 miners lost their jobs in the process. In the railroad industry, labor productivity went up 65 percent, but employment dropped by 540,000. In New York City, 25,000 elevator operators were replaced by automatic lifts within a ten-year period. Despite the fact that the United States work force had increased greatly, there had been a sharp decrease in the number of production-line jobs. On the other hand, the number of clerks—and particularly of professional employees—had shown a large increase. This is because the newer industries like electronics need large numbers of technicians, and because automation itself requires the employment of machine experts.

President Kennedy labeled automation the major domestic challenge of the sixties; the question is, what can the government do to soften the impact of this "machine revolution?" The exact number of those out of work as the result of automation is not known, but it is believed to constitute a large part of what is known as "hard-core unemployment." In this category are an estimated one million workers who remain unemployed even when business generally improves all over the country. They, like many young people entering the labor market for the first time, do not have the skills to qualify for the jobs which are open. In 1961 Congress passed the Federal Area Redevelopment Act which provided for the training of a limited number of persons lacking marketable skills. Then, in March of 1962, it passed a new law providing for a much bigger retraining program. Specifically, this law called for federal expenditures of $435 million over a three-year period to help not only those who lose their jobs because of automation, but also those whose skills limit them to low-paid employment. An estimated million unemployed workers were expected to benefit from this legislation. Training allowances, roughly equal to unemployment-compensation benefits in the particular states, are paid to heads of households accepted in the program who have had work experience of three years. Jobless youths, from ages 19 to 22, are also eligible for weekly training allowances, and subsistence and travel expenses are paid for persons undergoing training away from home. The program is jointly administered by the Department of Labor, which is responsible for selecting trainees and paying them, and by the Department of Health, Education, and Welfare, which manages the vocational-training aspects.

It should be said in passing that some state governments have acted independently and have already established their own retraining programs. California, which had been particularly hard hit by the shift from aircraft to missiles, is, again, a prime example.

Atomic Energy

Atomic energy has had an immediate and direct impact on government. The atomic bomb itself was developed by the War Department, but after the war the principle of civilian control was established with the creation in 1946 of the Atomic Energy Commission (AEC). Within the AEC, there is a Military Liaison Committee through which the Commission advises the Defense Department on matters related to the military application of atomic energy. This arrangement seems to have worked out well, and the issue of civil vs. military control has faded into the background.

The AEC has been criticized by those who believe that it has not moved fast enough to develop nuclear energy for domestic purposes at prices competitive with conventional fuels. Pressure for the AEC to accelerate this program, and to build reactors of its own, still continues. At the same time, the public is much concerned over radiation hazards, and the AEC has, on occasion, been charged with issuing public statements minimizing these dangers. Since it runs the atomic-energy program, some people feel that the AEC finds itself compelled to put out reassuring statements. For this reason, they have recommended that the Public Health Service, as a neutral body, be given complete responsibility for a comprehensive, nationwide program of radiation safety. Since 1959, there has been a Federal Radiation Council which advises federal agencies on the formulation of radiation standards and on the establishment and execution of programs of cooperation with the state governments.

Serious as fallout is after the testing of nuclear weapons, it is anticipated that the hazards of radioactive wastes from peacetime atomic energy will be far greater. These wastes are put in tanks which are stored underground, but this is only a temporary solution, because of the huge amounts of radioactive wastes which are expected to accumulate and the need to isolate them for hundreds of years. Experts reporting to the Senate Foreign Relations Committee made the sober statement that "the quantity of peaceful waste material will within 25 to 50 years become sufficient to endanger mankind unless reliably stored" and that "there is insufficient information about the reliability of existing waste storage techniques."[9] State and local governments need to protect citizens from sources of radiation in atomic plants and other places where radioactive materials are stored or handled. As the reader will have learned from the newspapers, several fires have already broken out in such places, and firemen are being trained in the special methods of fighting such conflagrations. Since we are only in the early stages of the "Atomic Age," the effects on public administration will be much greater in the future.

Missile and Space Technology

The government is also very much involved in missile and space technology. Responsibility for the military phases rests with the Defense Department—particularly the Air Force—while the National Aeronautics and Space Administration is in charge of the civilian space program. The military and civilian phases are not easy to separate, a problem which is discussed in Chapter 6. So long as the Cold War continues, budgets for military missiles will continue to be high. Possibilities in space exploration for peaceable purposes appear unlimited. Communications satellites, mentioned earlier, and weather satellites are already operational. In all, it is estimated that $50 billion will be spent before the end of the decade on the space exploration currently programmed.

ADVANCES IN SOCIAL INVENTIONS

The American environment has been radically transformed, by advances in not only physical but also *social* technology. The word *technology* means "a systematic body of methods for the achievement of human purposes in any field."[10] Man invents not only physical, but also social devices, and the latter have a great impact on public administration.

[9] *Possible Nonmilitary Scientific Developments and Their Potential Impact on Foreign Policy Problems of the United States*, Senate Foreign Relations Committee, 86th Congress, 1st Session, Washington, D.C.: Government Printing Office, 1959, p. 20.

[10] *Ibid.*, p. 9.

Government itself is an example of social invention, but we will concentrate instead on the institutions and devices which have grown up in the environment which surrounds it. A list of social inventions could be endless, for it might range from double-entry bookkeeping to international organizations like the United Nations. We will mention, therefore, only a few of the most important ones.

The Corporation

Let us put the corporation at the top of the list, as did John M. Gaus when he wrote his landmark essay on the "Ecology of Government." Gaus explains that, according to *Webster's Dictionary, ecology* is "the mutual relations collectively between organisms and their environment." Thus, to use Gaus' own words:

> . . . An ecological approach to public administration, builds, then, quite literally from the ground up; from the elements of a place—soils, climate, location, for example—to the people who live there—their numbers and ages and knowledge, and the ways of physical and social technology by which from the place and in relationships with one another, they get their living.[11]

The corporation is, of course, no recent social invention. Its great age has, however, in no sense destroyed its vitality; it still generally retains its character as an indispensable element in the large-scale production we take for granted in modern society. At the same time, we continue to find it necessary to the public interest to control its operations. Max Lerner comments:

> . . . A discerning anthropologist, studying characteristic American inventions, such as the dating pattern, the success system, and judicial review, might seize on the corporation as the most important of all. Reaching into every area of life, it has become the instrument by which Americans organize and project demanding group effort, impersonality, continuity beyond the individual life, and limited liability. It is striking that a highly individualistic people should accept a transformation of its life wrought by so impersonal a social invention.[12]

[11] John M. Gaus, *Reflections on Public Administration*, University, Ala.: Univ. of Alabama Press, 1947, pp. 8–9.

[12] Max Lerner, *America as a Civilization*, New York: Simon and Schuster, 1957, p. 284.

There is no need here to repeat the story of the battle against the "trusts" and the passage of the Sherman Act in 1890, and then, in 1914, of the Clayton Act. Important as this antimonopoly legislation has been, the problem of size still remains. Corporations have continued to grow, and the nation is still plagued by the dilemma of how to retain the advantages of large-scale operations and at the same time preserve competition and protect the smaller businessman and the consumer. The number of antimonopoly cases brought by the government in recent years is large enough to make clear that the threat of monopoly is very real. While eliminating the loopholes in the laws has been important, the real problem has always been in the area of administering the law. Before the Federal Trade Commission and the Justice Department can take action which they can reasonably expect to be sustained in the courts, they must collect much detailed information in complicated areas of the economy. The enforcement problem is staggering, and the budgets of the regulatory agencies, no matter how much increased, never seem to be equal to the task. The large-scale corporation does pose difficult problems for government, but, again, Lerner points out:

> The sharp question that might be put by the defenders of the corporate empires is: What was the historical alternative? Without the corporate form America could probably not have developed industrialism so rapidly or on so large a scale, nor could it have accumulated capital and plowed it back into industry as dramatically as it did. An economy of small firms was possible in Jackson's day but scarcely in ours. One alternative was national ownership with big-scale enterprise under government trusts. But this would have raised even more far-reaching issues of power than the corporate empires have done. Whatever group owns or runs the economic plant of a country has enormous power vested in it; that holds true also of the group that runs the trade-unions and even more of the group that runs the government. If the same group holds power in all three of these areas there is scarcely a crack possible in the combined monolith of power. What can be said of the American corporation as a power bloc is that, while it may sometimes control and even cow specific officials or agencies of the government, it is not in itself the government. Along with the other power institutions it presents on the American landscape a plurality of power groupings which are the better for their dispersal.[13]

[13] *Ibid.*, pp. 288–289.

Government officials wield great power when they award contracts to different corporations. If big business consistently comes out on top in these decisions, small businesses find it hard to survive. The now defunct Reconstruction Finance Corporation, which loaned billions before, during, and after World War II, was frequently charged with favoring the bigger companies, but even its operations are now dwarfed by the billion-dollar contracts let out by the Defense Department.

Of the total defense budget for the 1961 fiscal year, about $21 billion was spent on procurement. One hundred big corporations received, in all, 75 percent of these contracts. The top ten alone received $7.6 billion. Three corporations—namely, General Dynamics, Lockheed, and Boeing—each received just over $1 billion. Two others, General Electric and North American, were each granted over $900 million in defense business. Furthermore, 86.4 percent of these contracts were awarded without competitive bidding.[19] Could a larger share of this business have been given to smaller companies? Do the "giants" have too much power? Should both the Defense Department and Congress do something about curbing the influence of these "giants"? If so, what specifically should be done? How can the public be sure that military procurement officers are making fair decisions in awarding these contracts? Is it fair to refuse to give more defense business to efficient producers just because they already are so very large? These are among the controversial questions of public policy that the corporation poses.

Labor Unions

The union is another social invention now very prominent on the American scene. Previously weak in comparison with corporate power, the unions received a great boost with the passage in 1935 of the Wagner Act, which required employers to bargain collectively with the workers. Union power grew so greatly that, in 1947, Congress passed the Taft-Hartley law which sought to redress the balance and to curb certain labor abuses. The scandals of the International Teamsters and certain other unions led to the Labor Management

[14] See Fred J. Cook, "Juggernaut: The Warfare State," *The Nation*, **193**, No. 14 (October 28, 1961), 281.

Relations Act of 1959 which introduces government into unprecedented supervision of the internal affairs of the unions. Under this Act, all unions except those consisting entirely of government workers must submit reports to the Labor Department on their constitutions, bylaws, officers, loans, investments, and financial status. To process these reports, the Department had to create a new Bureau of Labor-Management Reports.

The government's role however, goes beyond the mere processing of reports. Under the "bill of rights" provision of the law, union members may complain to the Department if they feel that their privileges to vote, to run for office, and to speak up at meetings have not been respected by union officers. The law requires national or international unions to elect their officers at least once every five years, either by secret ballot or at a convention of delegates chosen by secret ballot. Local unions must elect their officers at least once every three years, also by secret ballot. The purpose of these requirements is to curb such abuses as rigging of union elections and punishment of members who defy dictatorial or corrupt leaders. The financial-reporting provisions are intended to prevent misuse of union pension funds and other resources. This brings the government directly into the management of union activities, just as it has been drawn into the vital role of making decisions affecting the corporations. In general, government today is as much concerned with the unions as a "power cluster" as it is with business.

Pressure Groups

Both business and labor are examples of pressure groups, the last itself constituting an important social invention. Pressure groups are of many different types—economic, social, professional, and philanthropic, but, in every case, they join together individuals who have a common interest and who want to influence public policy accordingly. Frequently, a tripartite alliance is formed, between an administrative agency on the one hand, a pressure group, and sympathetic legislators. If the administrative agency is big and powerful, the interest group equally so, and the legislators in question highly influential, such an alliance can wield tremendous power.

This was revealed during a House subcommittee's investigation of the Army-Air Force dispute over two antiaircraft missile systems: the Army's *Nike-Hercules* and the Air Force's *Bomarc*. Each service talked with members of Congress and backed the contractors who were prepared to build its system. On the side of the Air Force was the Boeing Company which was to produce the *Bomarc;* on that of the Army was the Western Electric Company. Both firms made no bones about the political contacts they had made.[15] They were, of course, justified in making such contacts, but it is this kind of alliance which may be said to represent the height of pressure-group activity, because it unites so much strength. Consequently, each of the services is capable of putting tremendous pressure on the Secretary of Defense and on the White House itself. The point should not be missed that administrative agencies themselves are pressure groups.

Whether or not we agree with the viewpoints of given pressure groups, the reality is that they exist, and that administrative officials are constantly dealing with them. As a social invention, the pressure group is now highly sophisticated and well organized. The problem of forward-looking policymakers, both in the legislative and executive branches, is how to piece together the public interest out of a welter of frequently conflicting private pressures. The very multiplicity of the power centers in our society, the point stressed by Lerner, seems to offer the best long-run protection to the public.

Technical-Assistance Programs

Turning to international relations, a social invention now much used is *technical assistance*. Throughout history, nations have borrowed from one another, taking advantage of significant discoveries and advances in other lands. Since World War II, the techniques for mutual cooperation have been refined in the form of extensive programs for the interchange of skills and knowledge between the peoples of the world.

The reasons for the "revolution of rising expectations," mentioned earlier in this chapter, have been most cogently propounded by Arnold Toynbee, the well known British philosopher and historian:

[15] See James McCartney, "Inter-Service Rivalry Creates Political Pressure on Pentagon," *St. Louis Post-Dispatch*, November 16, 1961, editorial section.

> The poor countries are prolific, not in cars, but in babies. The progress of public health measures and preventive medicine has been notably increasing a non-Western baby's once short expectation of life. In consequence, population, in the poverty-stricken two-thirds of the world, is now exploding. Even in economically backward countries where there is a moderate increase in production in absolute total figures, the average share available per head of the population is falling because population is now increasing at a rate with which the increase in production is failing to keep pace.
>
> If we succeed in getting rid of war, as we have already succeeded in getting rid of pestilence, the problem of the pauper two-thirds of mankind will become importunate. *If the impoverishment of this majority is not arrested and reversed, there seems bound to be a catastrophic collision between them and the increasingly affluent minority.*[16]

The people of the underdeveloped countries now know that they do not have to suffer this misery perpetually. The United States and the other nations of the Free World on the one hand, and the Soviet Union and its satellites on the other, are now engaged in a fierce competition in the field of technical assistance. Both blocs are sending technicians of many different kinds to these countries to help them in economic development and other programs intended to raise per capita incomes substantially. Such aid has been extended as a part of the Cold War, but, even if the Cold War ended, technical assistance would continue—probably on an even greater scale—because it is still only in its preliminary stages. Enlightened statesmen of the developed countries know that extremes of poverty in other parts of the world can no longer be dismissed as the responsibility of the peoples in question. A sense of world community is developing, and, with such a consciousness, the misfortunes of one nation are the concern of all.

The United States has been providing technical assistance on an increasingly wider scale ever since President Truman's announcement in the early 1950s of the Point IV program. We had previously operated such programs—in Latin America, for example, under the Institute of Inter-American Affairs—but on a much more limited basis than we now do. Technical assistance on a multilateral basis is of-

[16] *St. Louis Post-Dispatch*, January 3, 1960, editorial section. Contains article by Toynbee reviewing decade just ended. (Italics ours.)

fered by the United Nations. As an international agency, the United Nations has been able to call upon the skilled nationals of countries all over the globe, whether from large or small nations. Similar programs have long been offered by the specialized agencies with which the United Nations is associated, such as the International Labor Organization and the World Health Organization, to mention only two. The reader may find it a valuable exercise to prepare a more complete list of social inventions which have had a marked impact on government. Further reference will be made to technical-assistance programs in Chapter 3, which examines the question of "Administration and Culture."

THE IDEOLOGICAL ENVIRONMENT

The *ideological* environment refers to the ideas and beliefs of the American people. Government is what a people living in a particular place, with certain traditions and viewpoints, decide to make it. If this seems an overly simple statement, remember that people do not develop physical or social inventions unless they want them. The factors of human aspirations and preferences have thus been present in all of the developments already mentioned in this chapter.

Individualism

The American tradition of individualism has always been a principal element in this ideological background. During the colonial period, "government" was associated with British rule and "executive power" with the tyranny of the British Crown. When independence was achieved, those who drafted the state constitutions were anxious to protect the nation against abuses of government power. Although by the time of the Constitutional Convention in 1787, a counterreaction had developed, and there was much support for a stronger national union, the writers of the Constitution were, in general, believers in limited, not "big," government.

Political leaders in both major parties still find it necessary to disavow any belief in "big" government. This term generally refers to the building up of governmental power, particularly in Washington, presumably just for the sake of making government "big." Americans do not want that kind of government, but the real question is whether, in fact, the expansion of governmental power is the result of a conspiracy of the bureaucrats. Felix Frankfurter made a penetrating statement some 30 years ago:

> The paradox of both distrusting and burdening government reveals the lack of a conscious philosophy of politics. It betrays some unresolved inner conflict about the interaction of government and society. I suspect that it implies an uncritical continuance of past assumptions about government and society. We have not adjusted our thinking about government to the overwhelming facts of modern life, and so carry over old mental habits, traditional school-book platitudes and campaign slogans as to the role, the purposes, and the methods of government.[17]

In other words, government has expanded, not because of any movement for "big" government as such, but rather as a response to the demands of modern society. American individualism is not only derived from the ideology of the Revolutionary War, but also from the thinking of the frontier period, when everybody was supposed to help himself rather than to rely on the government. However, the frontier has long passed from the American scene, and in practice, it is increasingly recognized—even if still grudgingly by some—that, under conditions of modern living, many people cannot be expected to help themselves. The mythology of individualism and self-help still persists, however. No matter how big we have found it necessary to make government, we do not believe in "big" government. Extracts from an interview with John Galbraith when he was economic advisor to President-elect Kennedy are very revealing:

> QUESTION. Doesn't this all mean a larger role for the federal government?
>
> ANSWER. Yes, it could mean that. One tendency—in some ways, I think, the most unhappy tendency of the last 20 years—has been to take an ideological view of the role of the federal government, and to say that we must, by all odds and by any possible devices, minimize that role.
>
> This in turn leads others to defend the federal government for any and all functions. The argument, then, is not over the desirability of the individual functions of government but over government per se.
>
> QUESTION. Does it not come down to a question of how big the government should be?

[17] Quoted in Gaus, *op. cit.*, p. 1.

ANSWER. No. We must think of the issue in practical terms. If we're going to produce automobiles, we must produce roads, and we will get roads, as we have learned, only with a substantial federal subsidy.

If we're going to have better cities and fewer slums, then we must tear down the slums and redevelop the land, and we have learned that this happens only with federal financial assistance and federal leadership.

And so it goes. I regard these not as questions of ideology, not as matters of religion, but as essentially practical problems. How do we know what must be done? I'm constantly shocked that a nation which regards itself as inherently practical should endeavor to decide so many questions on such essentially theological grounds.[18]

Our Business Civilization

Our business civilization and its values have also greatly influenced our thinking about government. The example of business, with its machines and its efficiency, is constantly held up to the government official. So admired is the business example that, as Dwight Waldo believes, "probably the most pervasive and important model in American administrative study in the Twentieth Century is the *machine model.*"[19] Waldo points out that the scientific-management movement is based on a "cultural orientation toward the machine."[20] Did not this movement, which so quickly spread to government, arise at the same time as the development of the internal combustion engine and the "extensive mechanization of daily living?" In Waldo's words: "Achieving efficiency in administration is conceived analagously to achieving efficiency in machine performance. There must be good design—organization charts equal blueprints—parts must be adjusted properly to one another; friction must be reduced; power loss prevented, and so forth."[21]

Business itself has been anxious to see government become more efficient. This explains its financial support for municipal research bureaus and study groups created to make thoroughgoing studies of governmental administrative organization. Prominent businessmen usually participate in the work of such groups and are responsible for

[18] "Interview with John Kenneth Galbraith," *U.S. News & World Report,* November 21, 1960, p. 93.

[19] Dwight Waldo, *Perspectives on Administration*, University, Ala.: Univ. of Alabama Press, 1956, pp. 30–32.

[20] *Ibid.*, p. 30.

[21] *Ibid.*, p. 32.

many of their recommendations. Furthermore, some members of the business community accede to the government's pressure to accept temporary and sometimes indefinite assignments, despite the fact that in so doing they must make serious financial and other sacrifices. The practical—rather than theoretical—nature of Americans leads them to want to imitate the corporate executive. As Dahl and Lindblom state:

> . . . one reason for the speed with which the bureaucratization of social life proceeds is that to the modern mind no other way of looking at organization seems sensible. For example, a close correlation exists between the pragmatic attitude of Americans toward organization and their propensity for bureaucratizing social relationships. For bureaucracy is above all a triumph for the deliberate, calculated, conscious attempt to adapt means to ends in the most rational manner.[22]

Business, however, also drains talent away from government. To date, it has been the business career that has been preferred by college graduates and others with marketable skills or potentialities. This is dealt with in greater detail in Part IV, but it must be mentioned here as one of the negative consequences for government of our business civilization.

Peculiarities of the Political System

Certain peculiarities of the United States constitutional and political system have also shaped public administration in different ways. Since they reflect American thinking about government, they constitute an important part of the ideological environment.

There is, for example, the long-standing rivalry between the executive and the legislative branches. It is never clear just what the exact dividing line between the two branches really is. Both strive to lead—and frequently department heads and employees of the executive establishments in general are caught in the middle. They have not one "boss," but two—in fact, three, if we count also the element in the general public that seeks expression. There is nothing wrong in having so many "bosses," provided they speak with one voice, but often they do not. One consequence is that a chief executive cannot possibly maintain the same control over his subordinates as the general

[22] Robert A. Dahl and Charles E. Lindblom, *Politics, Economics and Welfare*, New York: Harper and Row, 1953, p. 245.

manager of a private company is able to do. This is not only true of the President, but—since separation of powers exists at all three levels of government—it is also the fate of state governors and municipal mayors. The gain in responsibility to the public may, in the long run, offset the damaging effect on administrative leadership, but the latter consequence is a very real one, nonetheless.

If we compare our system with that of the British, we will readily see the differences in the framework in which public administration operates in each country. In England, the legislative and executive powers are fused, while the Cabinet, as an inner committee of the Parliament, clearly exercises the leadership in defining public policies. Political parties, unlike those in the United States, are tightly disciplined and generally do what their leaders have first decided. As Dahl and Lindblom write, "the governmental policy is so organized that in so far as the cabinet itself can be coordinated, governmental policy can be coordinated, and against a unified cabinet there is slight opportunity for minority leaders to obstruct cabinet policy, exercise a veto, or compel bargains that seriously conflict with important cabinet policies."[23] It should be no surprise, then that, in England, the reverse criticism is frequently heard: The Cabinet leads too much and parliamentary control is too weak.

The divided leadership that is characteristic of the American system greatly facilitates the operation of pressure groups. If chief executives controlled disciplined party representatives in the legislatures, interest groups would not be able to exert influence at so many different points. Instead of being able to operate simultaneously on legislators, department heads, and lesser administrative officials, they would have to concentrate their attention on the chief executive and his principal advisers. This would not necessarily make them any less powerful, but it certainly would radically change their mode of operations.

The Great Burdens on Chief Executives

The great burdens placed upon chief executives in the United States, particularly upon the President, are another important aspect of our political system. Ceremonial, political, executive, and other

[23] *Ibid.*, p. 345.

responsibilities are combined in one office, whereas in other countries some of the load is carried by other officials and groups. The British Prime Minister is generally relieved of ceremonial duties by the Crown, and is greatly aided in political policymaking by the other members of the Cabinet. It is no wonder, then, that an appreciable part of the literature of public administration in the United States is devoted to the chief executive and his problems.

A Unique American Contribution—Federalism

The influence of another peculiarly American institution, judicial review, has already been discussed in Chapter 1. Federalism, however, has not been mentioned as yet. The system of the division of powers between the national government and the states has worked so well that some scholars consider federalism the unique American contribution to the science of government. To make this system function so well, Americans have devoted much thought and effort to perfecting devices for cooperation between administrative officials at all levels of government. This *cooperative federalism,* as it is frequently called, is another important part of the framework in which public administration functions, and will be discussed in detail in Chapter 5.

We have come to the end of this description of some of the principal elements—physical, social, and ideological—in the environment of public administration in the United States. As we have seen, physical change comes quickly, but against a background of certain enduring ideas and traditions. Certainly no one can doubt that public administration has an extremely important role to play in modern American society.

BIBLIOGRAPHY

Commager, Henry Steele, *The American Mind*, New Haven: Yale Univ. Press, 1950.

Dewey, John, *The Public and its Problems*, New York: Holt, Rinehart and Winston, 1927.

Frankfurter, Felix, *The Public and its Government*, New Haven: Yale Univ. Press, 1930.

Gaus, John M., *Reflections on Public Administration*, University: Univ. of Alabama Press, 1947. See Chap. 1, "Ecology of Government."

Gaus, John M., "American Society and Public Administration," in *The Frontiers of Public Administration*, Chicago: Univ. of Chicago Press, 1936.

Lepawsky, Albert (ed.), *Administration: The Art and Science of Organization and Management*, New York: Knopf, 1949. See Chap. 5, "American Administration."

Lerner, Max, *America As A Civilization*, New York: Simon and Schuster, 1957.

Senate Foreign Relations Committee, 86th Congress, 1st Session, *Possible Nonmilitary Scientific Developments and Their Potential Impact on Foreign Policy Problems of the United States*, Washington, D.C.: Government Printing Office, 1959. Study prepared by Stanford Research Institute.

Speroff, B. J., "Automation and Human Relations: Some Problems and Predictions," *Personnel Administration*, **XXV**, No. 2 (March–April, 1962).

Van Riper, Paul P., *History of the United States Civil Service*, New York: Harper and Row, 1958. A thoroughgoing analysis of personnel movement in the American environment.

Vieg, John A., "The Growth of Public Administration," in Marx, Fritz Morstein (ed.), *Elements of Public Administration*, Englewood Cliffs, N.J.: Prentice-Hall, 1959.

Waldo, Dwight, *The Administrative State*, New York: Ronald, 1948.

Waldo, Dwight, *Perspectives on Administration*, University: Univ. of Alabama Press, 1956.

White, Leonard D., *The Federalists*, New York: Macmillan, 1948.

White, Leonard D., *The Jeffersonians*, New York: Macmillan, 1951.

White, Leonard D., *The Jacksonians*, New York: Macmillan, 1954.

White, Leonard D., *The Republican Era*, New York: Macmillan, 1957.

CHAPTER 3

Administration and Culture

As we have seen, the cultural characteristics of the American people have left a deep imprint on government and public administration in the United States. For several reasons, however, the relationship between administration and culture should be explored further. First, each of the countries to whom the United States gives technical assistance has its own values and traditions, which are by no means the same as ours. While these countries generally want to "modernize" their economies and to utilize the skills and techniques of the developed countries, they frequently find this extremely difficult because of the natural persistence of time-honored traditions which resist sharp changes. If our technical-assistance programs are to be successful, they must be conceived and carried out with a full understanding of the culture of each recipient country. The problem is difficult, but not insoluble, as we shall see later.

Second, the need to adapt government programs and administrative techniques to the requirements of groups with different cultural backgrounds exists as well within the continental United States. Examples of such groups are the American Indians and the Mexican and Spanish Americans of the Southwest. These people, of course, are American, and they represent one of the greatest values in our society—cultural diversity. In order to serve them efficiently, public employees who have contact with them should understand why and how they are in some respects different from other Americans.

Third, the United States supervises the affairs of certain dependent peoples. A principal example here is the Trust Territory of the Pacific Islands, consisting of islands captured from the Japanese during World War II, and administered by the Interior Department. This trusteeship, held under the United Nations, includes all of the Marianas, Marshalls, and Carolines, except for Guam. In addition, Saipan was recently removed from Navy control and made a part of the Trust Territory. The inhabitants of these islands consist of various tribal groups whose culture, again, must be understood by the American officials who represent us there.

TECHNICAL-ASSISTANCE PROGRAMS

Why do we want to get involved in the domestic affairs of other nations, and, also, why do they ask us to do so? The Center for International Studies of the Massachussetts Institute of Technology answers these questions very well in a report it made recently to the Senate Foreign Relations Committee:

> It is important that the American diplomat consistently and clearly recognize that our primary interest in many parts of the world is not to develop conventional alliances or to protect conventional economic interests but to promote the evolution of societies capable of contributing to the spread of the democratic process and to an orderly world. This requires that the diplomat go far beyond conventional dealings with the foreign office and the government and that he enter deeply into the substantive objectives and problems of specific programs. He must project a steady and reliable vision of what the society to which he is assigned may become and of what might be its place in an orderly world system. He must be the leader in designing and carrying out a sustained program of action agreed on between the two countries and designed to bring this vision to life.[1]

The authors of this report explain that there is a conflict between the *traditionalists* and the *modernizers* in the underdeveloped countries. The traditionalists are those with vested interests in the existing society, while the modernizers are those who stand to gain from change. The former group might attempt to emerge victorious by using repressive measures against the impatient modernizers, while

[1] *Economic, Social, and Political Change In The Underdeveloped Countries and Its Implications For United States Policy*, 86th Congress, 2nd Session, Washington, D.C.: Government Printing Office, 1960, p. 75.

the latter may decide that the best way of obtaining their objective is through the quick change of a communist-type regime. Since today's international pressures do not permit the United States to be indifferent to what happens in the underdeveloped countries, a third choice is encouraged by the United States: the "gradual modification of the institutions, practices, and structure of the traditional society in the direction of modernization while retaining some of its traditional cohesive features."[2]

There are serious limits as to how influential we can be in this matter, however, since the host country retains its sovereignty and rightly plots its own destiny. Yet it is they who request our aid in improving their internal economies (as they sometimes do also of the Soviet bloc countries), and thus, though national sovereignties still remain, our foreign operations largely take place within the domestic structures of these nations.

Traditional Societies and the Problem of Change

The term *modernization* refers here to economic development and, in particular, to industrialization. Traditional societies, explain the authors of the MIT report, are characterized, by a very limited technology. There is no regular flow of inventions and innovations making for sustained economic growth. Agriculture is the principal economic activity, and most of the population is illiterate. The people live in close contact, family ties are strong, and generally there is a great emphasis on face-to-face contacts. What the sociologists call "static role conceptions" dominate the thinking of the people. They are born into their social roles; children are expected to live the same kind of existence as their parents. Social stratification and rigid class lines are outstanding characteristics of such societies. Pessimism or fatalism is another; that is, the view that there is no use trying to change things, because this is the way they have always been, or it is not in man's power to bring about such changes. "The government—and the nation itself—is likely to seem a remote and distant entity, associated with the extraction of taxes and the arbitrary recruitment of sons for military service."[3]

If modernization is to be achieved, says the MIT report:

[2] *Ibid.*, p. 61.
[3] *Ibid.*, p. 24.

In the end all this must alter. There must be a radical shift in balance to urban life; literacy must increase; agricultural methods must change; and the markets must widen and become increasingly commercial. Land tenure arrangements are likely to require alteration. The idea must spread that the physical environment can be understood and controlled in ways which permit higher standards of welfare. The government must come to be identified with activities and objectives which conform to popular interests. And in the end, if democracy is to emerge, the citizen must come to accept the responsibilities as well as the power to determine who shall rule and in what direction public policy shall go.[4]

In other words, the existing culture must be modified in important respects. Thus, in the last analysis, the foreign technician must also become an agent in social change. He must adapt his approach to the local environment, but if he yields on every point, he will have accomplished nothing. Above all, he must be skillful in changing rigid and reactionary psychological attitudes and breaking down resistance to his valid recommendations. Naturally, he can do this best only when he is intimately familiar with the nature of these attitudes and the reasons for their existence. If he does not even know that they exist—as has sometimes happened—he not only proves himself ineffective, but he also contributes to the reinforcement abroad of the caricature of the "Ugly American."

Culture and Public-Health Administration

Let us illustrate this principle with some of the efforts to establish modern public-health programs. In 1950, after eight years of cooperative health programs in Latin America, the Institute of Inter-American Affairs requested the Public Health Service to make a thoroughgoing evaluation of what had been accomplished. Cultural anthropologists were included in the survey team because of the conviction that "knowledge of the people is just as important in many aspects of a public health program as is knowledge of medical science."[5] The section of the final report containing the findings of these cultural anthropologists certainly bears out this thesis.

[4] *Ibid.*

[5] *10 Years of Cooperative Health Programs in Latin America; An Evaluation*, conducted by the Public Health Service for the Institute of Inter-American Affairs, Washington, D.C.: 1953. Findings and recommendations on "Cultural Aspects" appear in chap. 2, pp. 11–29.

Preventive and Curative Medicine

It was discovered from this survey that many Latin Americans were reluctant to present themselves for periodic check-ups in the health centers jointly maintained by the Institute and the host government. In their culture, to consult a physician was rare enough for most people; to do so before one became sick definitely broke with local habit. Thus, although the health centers offered both preventive and curative service, the survey team found that the average Latin American in most cases went to the centers, "not primarily to keep well, but to get well." The American health technicians, trained in a society which emphasizes the advantages of preventive medicine, could not understand this. Yet, significantly, it was found that, in those countries where the centers were operated with "frank recognition that for a long time to come curative medicine must be an integral part of any public health program," the relations between staff members and the public were good. In those places where curative services were provided only grudgingly, this was not the case, and the cooperative health programs were far less successful.

Folk Medicine

Latin Americans also cling tenaciously to their faith in folk medicine. The health center, with its physicians and other exponents of modern medicine, must compete with the native *curandero,* and the latter has a distinct edge in the esteem of the local masses. The people respect the *curandero* because they are impressed with his knowledge of the magical and other causes of illness as contained in the country's folk-lore traditions. He knows just which herbal teas and other folk-cure remedies to prescribe; and the people do not blame him if, as often happens, he fails to save the patient. They reason simply that the *curandero* was impotent against certain evil forces. The professionally trained doctor operates under a great handicap in such societies because the patients who do finally consult him are often in such advanced stages of illness that nothing can be done for them. When these patients die, the people become all the more convinced that the modern doctor is incompetent by comparison with the revered *curandero.*

Yet there are ways of utilizing these folk beliefs for the purposes of modern medicine. For example, in Chile, the health-center doctors had to treat many cases of infant diarrhea. Although they knew that the cause of these outbreaks was a contaminated water supply, they also knew that the mothers probably would not heed instructions to give their babies boiled water to drink. As a solution, they decided to use the stratagem of prescribing herbal teas. Since this was a familiar remedy to them, the mothers gained confidence in the doctors, and, at the same time, some of the cases of infant diarrhea were cured in this way.

Another example can be found in Mexico, where isolation of the sick is well established in the culture. Usually this is because it is feared that visitors might make the sick person's condition worse; a visitor might carry with him the evil effects of "aire" (bad air), of "strong body humors," or of "strong blood." The real source of contagion, the patient himself who coughs up germs and can infect someone in the same room, is given little thought. As the authors of the evaluation report write, "The nurse need not remark on the potential danger of 'aire,' but if she simply says that visitors are undesirable the chances are that the family will respect her recommendation, even though she is thinking in terms of contagion and they in terms of magic."[6]

These are happy examples, because it was possible to persuade the people to follow the treatments indicated by medical science. However, the impression should not be left that it is always possible to find a formula for converting folk beliefs into instruments of modern medicine; yet much more progress is usually made when the health technicians—whether they are United States advisers or Latin Americans—understand the intricacies of folk medicine and the nature of the remedies that make sense to the people.

Social Traditions and Medicine

Knowledge of the social organization of the family in a particular environment is another key to obtaining acceptance of modern health programs. In Xochimilco, Mexico, the bride typically lives in the home of her husband's family, where she is closely controlled by her mother-in-law. The health-center staff in this town noted that some of the pregnant women who visited the center either were not follow-

[6] *Ibid.*, p. 25.

ing their recommendations or were experiencing some difficulty in trying to do so. When they investigated, they found that the patient's mother-in-law was telling her to disregard the advice received at the health center. Obviously, in such a situation, there is nothing that any outsider can do, so we can understand the quiet comment that "recognition of these and similar problems makes more intelligible the response of the patients."[7]

Cultural Differences in Public Administration Programs

Another area in which technical assistance has been given for some time now is public administration itself. From the very start of the foreign aid programs, it quickly became evident that the countries receiving such help could not effectively utilize it unless they were also assisted in improving the quality of their public services. The governments of these countries direct economic development and similar programs, and it is exceedingly important that their administrative agencies be organized properly and that they function in an efficient manner. Yet, in practice, this has not been easy to accomplish. Furthermore, this has been the case even when groups of local nationals, inside and outside the government, have pressed hard for administrative reforms. The problem again is one of social change, with the ensuing conflict between the modernizers and the traditionalists.

People are efficiency-conscious only if their environment and traditions require them to be. An industrialized civilization creates the need for time schedules, elimination of waste, and everything experts from the developed countries associate with efficiency. Since the underdeveloped countries are, by definition, nonindustrialized, it is only natural that they do not think in these same terms. Americans believe that the government should employ only that number of persons which it actually needs to get its work done properly. Naturally, we sometimes slip and put too many on the payrolls, but it is significant how violently the public reacts when this happens. In the underdeveloped countries the situation is very different. A large part of the population may eke out a bare existence by tilling the soil, but thousands of others will congregate in the cities and towns where jobs are

[7] *Ibid.*, p. 28.

very hard to get. The convenient solution is to put as many of the jobless as possible on the government payrolls. This is long established practice in the Near East, Asia, and Latin America, and, of course, it means that the public agencies are often grossly overstaffed.

Iran is frequently cited, because its government has thousands of surplus employees, many of whom work only on payday. As the authors of *The Overseas Americans* point out, the American management experts made the mistake of approaching this as a problem in management—rather than social—analysis. They write:

> From the Iranian point of view, on the other hand, the surplus employee practice was not at all regarded as a problem. Payments to workers who do not work is the normal and economic equivalent, in underdeveloped Iran, for the more complex forms of transfer payments, agricultural price supports, and many, many others. . . . Until Iran develops a social security system and an economic development program that puts more of its trained people to work at useful jobs, it seems doubtful that any amount of administrative advice will solve the surplus employee practice.[8]

The Intense Competition for Government Jobs

Administrative experts from the developed countries are accustomed to the full employment which exists in their home environments, and they expect government jobs to be hard to fill. Yet the common situation in the underdeveloped countries is for there to be a large oversupply of manpower, even among professional and other white-collar workers. Furthermore, members of the educated classes compete, sometimes desperately, for government jobs. In the United States, many college-trained persons prefer industry. Actually, private employment is looked down upon in many of these countries. For example, one of the major problems India has had to face in its industrialization program is how to combat the prejudice among those with formal education against any kind of job associated with using one's hands.

Of course, there is nothing wrong with public service having high prestige in these countries, but the mere existence of numerous applicants for government jobs does not ensure the establishment of a merit system. Unfortunately, the pressures in some countries are to

[8] Harlan Cleveland, Gerald J. Mangone, and John Clarke Adams, *The Overseas Americans*, New York: McGraw-Hill, 1960, p. 164.

make job security, rather than merit, the central consideration. As Riggs describes the problem:

> In many countries bureaucracy seems to lay down its own terms for survival. Seniority, patronage, strict tenure rules, part-time employment, corruption—these are signs that the dominant pressures on administrators are not directed toward production. They suggest rather the importance of connections with individual families and cliques, of time serving, of catering to those with standing and money, and so forth.[9]

Recruit and promote people solely on the basis of their ability and performance? Give equal pay for equal work? How can this be done if local traditions require strong deference to age, seniority, and social position—as it does in Asia?

The Familistic Orientation

What Hauser calls the *familistic orientation*[10]—the practice of helping one's relatives—is also deeply entrenched in the traditional societies. This leads to nepotism in both private and public employment. Hauser had in mind the countries of South and Southeastern Asia, but family ties are also very strong in other areas, particularly Latin America.

Here again, American society is appreciably different, and this leaves us with a blind spot. We meet what we consider to be our family obligations, but our scale of values differs from that of these other cultures. In a book which has not been accorded the attention it deserves, Salvador de Madariaga[11] years ago explained what comes first to the Spaniard—his family—and this holds true for the Latin American. After his family come his friends, the Church, and then the state. With this kind of orientation, nepotism—far from being the evil many of us consider it—is only the natural development of the human personality. When the element of job scarcity enters the picture as well, it is not difficult to see why this familistic orientation

[9] Frederick W. Riggs, "Public Administration: A Neglected Factor in Economic Development," *Annals of American Academy of Political and Social Sciences*, CCCV (May, 1956), 78–79.

[10] Philip M. Hauser, "Cultural and Personal Obstacles to Economic Development in the Less Developed Areas," *Human Organization*, XVIII, No. 2 (Summer, 1959), 78–84.

[11] Salvador de Madariaga, *Englishmen, Frenchmen, and Spaniards*, New York: Oxford Univ. Press, 1928.

should be so strong. In both Latin America and Asia, the individual remains in close association with his relatives throughout his life. In the United States, people spend their formative years within the family unit, but, upon attaining maturity, generally leave it to lead a separate existence.

The Role of Friendships

Different ideas as to the treatment of friends also often produce problems. From what has already been said about the strength of family and personal ties in many countries, this should come as no surprise. As the authors of *The Overseas Americans* observe, while Americans tend to "subordinate personal relationships, [the people] in most parts of the world set a higher relative value than we do on the niceties of interpersonal relations."[12] Friendships are not unimportant in dealings in private and public agencies in the United States, but usually they do not play the same role as in many other societies.

Fayerweather[13] cites numerous incidents in Mexican subsidiaries of United States companies in which locally hired officials have baffled the American executives by allowing personal, rather than business, considerations to influence their decisions. In one case he reports, a Mexican in the job of purchasing agent in a United States subsidiary is very reluctant to take a firm stand with a local supplier whom the American representatives of the parent company consider unreliable. The purchasing agent never does clamp down on the supplier, because the latter is a friend of his. It is good business practice, he believes, to help one's friends; besides this is a good principle to follow in any kind of relationship with other people. Perhaps in this case the Mexican was also right in dollars-and-cents terms, since he knew the suppliers and local business practices much better than did the American executives. In the long run, keeping friends might be better for the financial position of the company as well as for the purchasing agent's peace of mind. In any case, the incident does illustrate how the thinking pattern of the foreign national may not jibe at all with that of the American.

[12] Cleveland *et al.*, *op. cit.*, p. 38.

[13] John Fayerweather, *The Executive Overseas*, Syracuse, N.Y.: Syracuse Univ. Press, 1959, pp. 1–9.

Edward T. Hall, too, has studied this question of friendships, and he makes some acute observations:

The American finds his friends next door and among those with whom he works. It has been noted that we take people up quickly and drop them just as quickly. Occasionally a friendship formed during schooldays will persist, but this is rare. For us there are few well defined rules governing the obligations of friendship. It is difficult to say at which point our friendship gives way to business opportunism or pressure from above. In this we differ from many other people in the world. As a general rule in foreign countries friendships are not formed as quickly as in the United States but go much deeper, last longer, and involve real obligations. . . .

Friends and family around the world represent a sort of social insurance that would be difficult to find in the United States. We do not use our friends to help us out in disaster as much as we do as a means of getting ahead—or, at least, of getting the job done. The United States systems work by means of a series of closely tabulated favors and obligations carefully doled out where they will do the most good. And the least that we expect in exchange for a favor is gratitude.

The opposite is the case in India, where the friend's role is to "sense" a person's need and do something about it. The idea of reciprocity as we know it is unheard of. An American in India will have difficulty if he attempts to follow American friendship patterns. He gains nothing by extending himself in behalf of others, least of all gratitude, because the Indian assumes that what he does for others he does for the good of his own psyche. . . .[14]

Cultural Differences and Administrative Relationships

Whatever the kind of technical assistance offered, difficulties often arise in the personal relationships between representatives of the cooperating governments. Friction of this sort can arise in any relationship, public or private, calling for frequent contacts between nationals of different countries. The problem is not one which arises only in the context of aid programs; the expansion of technical-assistance programs has simply served to bring to the fore many of the points of conflict.

[14] Edward T. Hall, "The Silent Language In Overseas Business," *Harvard Business Review*, XXXVIII, No. 3 (May–June, 1960), 91–92.

Hall, in his fascinating book, *The Silent Language,*[15] recounts some typical incidents. He tells one story about an American expert sent to Egypt to teach modern agricultural methods to the farmers of that country. This expert requested his interpreter to ask an Egyptian farmer how much he expected his field to yield that year. The farmer became very angry. The interpreter, anxious to smooth over the situation, told the American that the farmer had simply said he did not know. The real explanation was that the "Arabs regard anyone who tries to look into the future as slightly insane. When the American asked him about his future yield, the Egyptian was highly insulted since he thought the American considered him crazy. To the Arab only God knows the future, and it is presumptuous even to talk about it."[16]

Another revealing case has to do with the natives of a South Pacific island. In their hiring practices, the white supervisors had been employing too many natives from one segment of the island's population, unknowingly disrupting the power relationships between the different groups of natives. As a result, the whole island was infuriated. The head men of two factions met one night to discuss "an acceptable reallocation of the jobs." Finally, they reached a solution, and, accompanied by their followers *en masse,* woke up the plant manager between two and three in the morning to tell him what had been decided. The American, knowing "neither the local language nor the culture nor what the hullabaloo was all about, thought he had a riot on his hands and called out the Marines."[17] He did not know that, to the natives, being awakened in the middle of the night did not imply the extreme emergency it does in the American culture.

The tendency of the American to be frank in his statements also creates problems. The foreign national is not accustomed to such directness and is both taken aback and resentful. In Latin America, children are taught to demonstrate their *educación,* meaning good manners, and to be polite and deferential in their relations with others. To tell a virtual stranger just what you really think is not an accepted part of the culture pattern. So, to the American, Latin Americans may seem uncooperative and even evasive, while, he in

[15] Edward T. Hall, *The Silent Language,* New York: Doubleday, 1959.
[16] *Ibid.,* p. 15.
[17] *Ibid.,* p. 25.

turn, strikes them as someone who apparently could use some *educación.*

In this area of differing national characteristics, it is easy to make dangerous generalizations and to be unaware of one's own prejudices. A common blindness is to feel sure that the best attitudes and practices in one's own culture represent the national standards, and to assume that the worst cases in a foreign country are typical of that country's standards. Called by the sociologists "ethnocentric thinking," this clouds many of the discussions of administration and culture. Fortunately, much of this "ethnocentric thinking" is disappearing as nationals of different countries get to know one another better. On the question of frankness, anyone who has had really close contacts with nationals of other countries knows that they can, in time, be so frank as to be devastating. Their critical faculties may be held in reserve, but when released they have real force. Straightforward expressions of opinion, privately given to friends, are not as rare as some outsiders all too prematurely conclude. Indeed, Hall says that, in India, one sign of real friendship is "speaking one's mind." This bewilders the American who finds that, "as he gets to know people in India better, they may become more critical of him."[18] The price of becoming real friends is exposure to a good deal of blunt criticism, whereas when he did not have this status the foreigner was treated with polite formality.

The point still remains, however, that, while some of the dissimilarities are sometimes exaggerated, "the actual behavior of men is not the same the world over. For instance, a Japanese, when insulted, might behave differently from one of us. He might be less belligerent at the moment but much more concerned about 'losing face'."[19] Cultures differ profoundly, but only because the different societies of men possess "in different degrees characteristics that are present in all."[20] In other words, people around the world manifest the same qualities, but to a lesser or greater extent. Frankness in initial contacts is a characteristic of Americans, but frankness as a quality is far from nonexistent in other parts of the world.

[18] Hall, "The Silent Language in Overseas Business," *op. cit.,* 92.

[19] George C. Homans, *The Human Group,* New York: Harcourt, Brace, and World, 1950, p. 191.

[20] *Ibid.*

Atomism

Americans also deplore what Hauser calls *atomism*[21] in the underdeveloped countries. He means by this the loose structure of such societies, as manifested by such phenomena as the extreme competition for top positions in both private and public employment; the bitter feuds between rival factions; the tendency to "mind one's business" instead of cooperating together; the emphasis on personal rather than organizational ends; and, in general, the lack of discipline. While these are factors identified with countries in South and Southeast Asia, they are commonly found in most *traditional* societies.

Naturally, management experts from the highly developed countries find these serious obstacles to improvement, as they certainly are, yet each of these negative factors has a ready explanation in terms of the local environment. This does not mean that administrative reform is impossible in most of the underdeveloped countries, because the record shows that, when their own leaders will support such reform, it can be achieved. Latin America, Costa Rica, Panama, and Colombia have adopted civil service systems and other countries in the area have made significant improvements in both personnel practices and public administration in general. Progress has also been made in other parts of the world, particularly in the field of in-service training. Certainly it is true that this progress has been slow, but in areas of profound social change it generally is. Respect for "organizational ends" cannot realistically be expected in countries in which modern, large-scale organizations do not exist, and whose people, therefore, do not understand their advantages. As a start is made in the transition to a modern society, the culture itself begins to change, and some of these tendencies recede into the background. Thus, one of the keys to success in dealing with the peoples of other countries is to understand the relationship between these obstacles and the present state of their economies. Possibly some of the countries receiving technical assistance from the United States or another source will never modernize; the cultural and other barriers may prove too strong. On the other hand, there is no evidence that administrative reform

[21] Hauser, *op. cit.*, 82–83. See also Richard W. Gable, "Culture and Administration in Iran," *Middle East Journal*, XIII (Autumn, 1959), 407–421.

will be impossible in any of them, and generally speaking, experience so far strongly suggests that, in time, the obstacles can be surmounted.[22]

THE CULTURAL FACTOR IN DOMESTIC PROGRAMS

The same failure to take into account the cultural characteristics of the people being dealt with has occurred in the administration of the affairs of the American Indians. This is brought out very well by Laura Thompson in her outstanding book, *Culture in Crisis, A Study of the Hopi Indians*.[23] Miss Thompson served as coordinator of the Hopi project of the Indian Personality and Administration Research. This was a long-range program jointly sponsored by the Office of Indian Affairs and the University of Chicago's Committee on Human Development, the latter being succeeded by the Society for Applied Anthropology. Eleven communities in five Indian tribes (Hopi, Navaho, Papago, Sioux, and Zuni) were studied as part of this research program. Its purpose, as Miss Thompson explains, "was to study the Indians both as individual personalities and as tribal societies in order to discover, by scientific inquiry, how the effectiveness of Indian Service long-range policy and program might be increased from the standpoint of improving Indian welfare and developing responsible local autonomy."[24]

A Culture in Crisis

The Hopi, a tribe of several thousand Pueblo Indians inhabiting arid lands of the northern Arizona highland, were found to have a culture which was neatly balanced both internally and in its relations with the external environment. This balance, however, had been upset by patterns of conduct imposed on them by private groups such as the Mennonite missionaries and also by the Indian Service itself. The Hopi were suffering a crisis as the result of this imbalance, which

[22] For further discussion of this matter, see Felix A. Nigro, "Personnel Administration and Cultural Differences," *Personnel Administration*, XXIV, No. 5 (September–October, 1961), 34–41.

[23] Laura Thompson, *Culture in Crisis, A Study of the Hopi Indians*, New York: Harper and Row, 1950.

[24] *Ibid.*, p. xvi.

could only be corrected by allowing them to find their own solutions to their problems through the unhampered functioning of their culture. Miss Thompson explains, "exotic, arbitrarily imposed types of administration may be expected, in the long run, to be unsuccessful and psychologically unhealthy in human terms because they attempt to superimpose arbitrary, rigid, and foreign culture structures on the community and tend therefore to dislocate critically indigenous structures and to engender culture crisis."[25]

The Hopi had lived for centuries in a desert environment in which they had to struggle hard to survive. As a result, they had developed a highly cooperative form of social organization in which each individual clearly accepted the need to join efforts in the interests of the group. Far from finding individualism a virtue, the Hopi actually frown upon it. Unaware of this, school teachers and other white American personnel made appeals to the individualistic, competitive spirit which they assumed the Hopi would have. One teacher sent a group of Hopi children to the blackboard to do arithmetic problems. In order to stimulate them to do good work, she asked them to turn their backs to the board as soon as they had finished. To her surprise, the child who finished first waited and looked around furtively. He did not turn his back until one of the other children had done so. The teacher was forced to abandon this practice, just as she had to stop designating the bright children as leaders of the classroom. They just would not accept this "honor." Hopi children are not competitively inclined, to the point that they do not even keep score when playing basketball or other games.

We could not expect the adults to be any different; most Hopi men do not want to be foremen on construction and other projects on the reservations. They know that, if they accept such positions, they will be accused of thinking that they are better than the other Hopi working on the same project, and, consequently, they will be the object of disparaging remarks from their tribesmen. The individual workmen do not expect higher pay for more skilled work; a highly skilled stonecutter is content to get the same pay as an unskilled laborer.

Miss Thompson's essential thesis is that "each society molds the potentialities of its constituents, but it can do so to their full potentialities only if allowed cultural autonomy."[26] The policy of assimilation

[25] *Ibid.*, p. 181.
[26] *Ibid.*, p. 148.

by force was the direct opposite of permitting such "cultural autonomy," so Miss Thompson and her colleagues believed that the Indian Service had had a harmful effect on the Hopi. Forced assimilation was wrong, because, if the Hopi were not allowed to "remain essentially themselves," they could not be expected to retain "their integrity as individuals and as a group." This did not mean that the Hopi should not change their ways at all. To survive, cultures must adjust to new conditions. However, "every change adopted by the tribe must pass two tests: it must have survival value in the arid environment; and (2) it must be reconciled or rationalized in terms of Hopi traditional values and world view."[27]

Conflicts Between Generations

Alexander Leighton describes the administrative problems of one of the Relocation Centers to which the Japanese population of the Pacific coastal regions was evacuated shortly after the outbreak of World War II. The Center in question was the one at Poston, Arizona; interestingly enough, it was located on an Indian reservation and administered for the War Relocation Authority (WRA) by the Indian Service. Just as at the other Centers, the Poston evacuees consisted of Isseis, Niseis, and Kibeis. The Isseis were the old Japanese, born in Japan, who had originally come to the United States with the expectation of returning to their home country, but for various reasons had decided not to do so. They could not have become American citizens, because the law then did not permit it. They retained their status as citizens of Japan, and, when the war broke out, they were immediately classified as enemy aliens. The Isseis felt nostalgia for Japan, hoped it would win the war, but did not want to see America harmed. They had, after all, spent much of their lives in the United States, and had reared their children here. The Niseis were the American-born and American-educated Japanese, who, naturally, had largely adopted the ways of typical young Americans. Although the Niseis respected the authority of their parents and were drawn to them by strong emotional ties, they wanted to live as Americans, not as Japanese. Like the children of immigrants from Europe, many Niseis were ashamed of their parents' foreign ways and inability to speak good English. All this inevitably produced friction between the

[27] *Ibid.*, p. 187.

two generations. The Kibeis were American-born Japanese who had spent their formative years in Japan and who then returned to this country, sometimes with ideas that made their readjustment to the American pattern of living difficult.

In the Japanese culture pattern, elders are respected and wield the authority. Yet, during the early history of the Poston project, the administrators, following official WRA policy, gave ascendency to the Niseis. Specifically, only those Japanese who were American citizens were eligible to be elected to the Community Council which advised the Project Director on internal affairs. Since the Isseis were not citizens, they could not play a prominent part in the emerging structure of the self-government project. To make matters worse, they were placed in an inferior position to the Niseis as far as influence in the community power structure was concerned, thus reversing the traditional relationships. Consequently, the first efforts at self-government did not prove popular with a sizeable element in the community. This was later corrected by establishing an Issei Advisory Board whose members were elected by the residents of each block. Gradually the Isseis were given more to say in matters of project administration, and the Community Council and the Issei Advisory Board came, for all practical purposes, to be one. Leighton reports that, eventually, "both in general meetings and in committees, the Isseis and the Niseis worked together on equal terms and in most cases managed to reach mutual agreement."[28] Accordingly, he makes the following observation: "[the] *conflict between older and younger generations is characteristic of the organization of many societies and has important bearing on the patterns of leadership.*"[29]

Lack of Unity Within the Administration

Another difficulty in adapting governmental programs and administrative techniques to the needs of specific cultural groups is lack of unity within the administrative body itself. This was a serious problem in the Japanese Relocation Center; Leighton describes a situation

[28] Alexander Leighton, *The Governing of Men*, Princeton, N.J.: Princeton Univ. Press, 1945, p. 223.

[29] *Ibid.*, p. 339.

of "incoordination and disarticulation within the administrative structure"[30] of the Center, with the largest conflict occurring between the "people-minded" and the "stereotype-minded" staff members. To the first group, "evacuees were people first and Japanese secondarily."[31] These staff members were free of strong prejudices against the Japanese and viewed their job essentially as one of helping the project residents make as satisfactory an adjustment to living in the Centers as possible under the circumstances. Instead of becoming angry when the evacuees had complaints, they did their best to satisfy those complaints which seemed justified.

The "stereotype-minded" staff members, on the other hand, viewed the Japanese with suspicion; they were basically unsympathetic with the stated WRA policy of treating them as members of relocation centers, not of internment camps. They thought the evacuees should do what they were told without raising any questions and that if they did not obey they should be punished. As Leighton explains, "since the stereotype-minded staff members were thinking of their stereotypes, rather than of human beings, they gave little attention to the incentives of human behavior other than those concerned with fear of punishment."[32]

The "people-minded" group was numerically small, but it included the Project Director and most of the rest of the top staff. They proved generally effective in their relationships with the project residents, whereas the "stereotype-minded" did not. With few exceptions, the latter held the more routine-type jobs and generally had less education than the "people-minded" group. It is also significant that they had not had much of a chance to learn and to appreciate the reasons for the official WRA policy of encouraging project self-government.

Due to the opposition of these two groups, the project administration's relationships with the evacuees were not as a cohesive team. Just as tensions developed among the evacuees, so did friction arise between members of the administrative staff. This proved so serious an impediment to efficient operation that Leighton comments:

> By and large humanity has and is paying a heavy price for disarticulations of this sort. In the Center it cost the evacuees much suffering and

[30] *Ibid.*, p. 346.
[31] *Ibid.*, p. 81.
[32] *Ibid.*, p. 85.

it cost the members of the Administration themselves almost as much. For the Government and the American people, it cost the money that could have been saved by better operation and it cost something in democratic principles.[33]

Leighton emphasizes that every administrative undertaking "must meet the needs and fit the belief systems of its constituent members no less than the people being administered."[34] The technical features of costs, manpower requirements, and such things as equipment and supplies are important, "but so too are answers to the needs of the people, the adjustment of belief systems, and the adaptation of customs and practices which permit the collective efforts of administration and administered."[35] Among Leighton's specific recommendations are the following:

Keep out of the administrative group persons whose intelligence is below that required for the type of work they must do—this includes not only technical proficiency, but ability to grasp and act on general policies.

Keep out persons who have deeply ingrained systems of belief that are incompatible with their duties; for example, strong racial prejudice in people who are part of an administrative organization that will have jurisdiction over other races.

Make sure that members of the organization understand the main purposes and policies; use staff meetings and all educative methods possible in order to keep interest alive and thinking active.

Make sure that no member of the organization is placed unnecessarily in a position where he is exposed to excessive frustration, conflict, and uncertainty; have the right man in the right job.[36]

ADMINISTRATION IN TRUST TERRITORIES

Cultural differences also play an important part in the administration of trust territories, and the Pacific Trust Territory will serve well to illustrate the cultural factors which must be considered by the ad-

[33] *Ibid.*, p. 347.
[34] *Ibid.*, p. 348.
[35] *Ibid.*
[36] *Ibid.*, p. 349.

ministrative body.[37] Long before the World War II landings on the Marianas, the Marshalls, and the Carolines, the Navy Department had contracted with a number of anthropologists to prepare handbooks on the customs of the island residents. Later, when the islands were captured, these same anthropologists donned uniforms and became the nucleus of the military government units. Thus, from the very start there was awareness of the need to adapt administrative techniques to the characteristics of the natives.

After the war, the Navy established a School of Naval Administration at Stanford University, which was headed by an anthropologist and in which naval officers were given intensive training before being assigned to military government in the Trust Territory. Similarly, in 1947—also under Navy sponsorship—the Pacific Science Board of the National Research Council launched one of the biggest anthropological research projects ever to be attempted, for which more than 30 persons were sent to the islands. Later, anthropologists in civilian status were attached to military government units as advisers to the naval officers in charge. When, several years later, the responsibility for administering the islands was transferred from the Navy to the Department of Interior, these advisers were retained, although in recent years they have had less influence.

Naturally, there are differences of opinion between these advisers and the island administrators. The latter are sometimes unconvinced by the suggestions of the anthropologists as to how to deal with the natives, and some of the anthropologists feel that they should be in the administrative posts so that they could see to it that their knowledge of the local customs is actually applied. There are unresolved questions of just what the relationships between the social scientists and the administrators should be in these situations, but, clearly, the anthropologists make a contribution to more enlightened administrative policies. As just one example, it was discovered that on the island of Truk there was no precedent for filling positions of high rank through the appointment process. Instead of making the island's na-

[37] See Thomas Gladwin, "Anthropology and Administration in the Trust Territory of the Pacific Islands," in *Some Uses of Anthropology: Theoretical and Applied*, Washington, D.C.: Anthropological Society of Washington, 1956, pp. 38–65. See also H. G. Barnett, *Anthropology in Administration*, New York: Harper and Row, 1956.

tive chief an appointive official, as on the other islands, the decision was made to have him named through a secret election, because research showed that the Trukese did not trust in a mere show of hands, so strong was their desire to control their chiefs.

SUMMARY

In concluding this chapter, it should be pointed out that appreciation of cultural factors is really another application of the human-relations approach referred to in Chapter 1. In dependency government, this means treating the native peoples as human beings, not as inferiors. In technical-assistance programs, it means understanding the viewpoints of representatives of a different culture. In domestic programs, like those for the Indians and other ethnic groups, it means showing similar understanding. Just as the needs of individual personality must be considered in programs where the cultural background of the clients is the same as that of the administrators, so must they be respected in undertakings where the "administered" have different traditions.

BIBLIOGRAPHY

"Administration of Personnel Programs in Underdeveloped Countries, an Annotated Bibliography," *Public Personnel Review*, **XXII,** No. 2 (April, 1961).

Bock, Edwin A., *Fifty Years of Technical Assistance*, Chicago: Public Administration Clearing House, 1954.

Education For Social Change, Establishing Institutes of Public and Business Administration Abroad, Washington, D.C.: Brookings Institution, 1961.

Esman, Milton J., "Japanese Administration—A Comparative View," *Public Administration Review*, **VII,** No. 2 (Spring, 1947).

Fayerweather, John, *The Executive Overseas*, Syracuse, N.Y.: Syracuse Univ. Press, 1959.

Gable, Richard A. (ed.), "Partnership for Progress: International Technical Co-operation," *Annals of the American Academy of Political and Social Science*, **CCCXXIII** (May, 1959).

Glick, Philip M., *The Administration of Technical Assistance*, Chicago: Univ. of Chicago Press, 1957.

Hall, Edward T., *The Silent Language*, Garden City, N.Y.: Doubleday, 1959.

Interprofessional Training Goals for Technical Assistance Personnel Abroad, Report of an interprofessional conference on training of personnel for overseas service, New York: Council on Social Work Education, 1959.

Millikan, Max F., and Blackmer, Donald L. M. (eds.), *The Emerging Nations, Their Growth and U.S. Policy*, Boston: Little, Brown, 1961.

Paul, Benjamin D. (ed.), *Health, Culture, and Community*, New York: Russell Sage Foundation, 1955. Case studies of public reactions to health programs in different cultural settings.

Saunders, Lyle, *Cultural Differences and Medical Care*, New York: Russell Sage Foundation, 1954.

Senate Foreign Relations Committee, 86th Congress, 2nd Session, *Economic, Social, and Political Change in the Underdeveloped Countries and Its Implications for United States Policy*, Washington, D.C.: Government Printing Office, 1960. Study prepared by Center for International Studies, M.I.T.

Sharp, Walter, *International Technical Assistance*, Chicago: Public Administration Service, 1952. Contains valuable reference material on first years of post-World War II technical-assistance programs.

United States Papers Prepared For the United Nations Conference on the Application of Science and Technology for the Benefit of the Less Developed Areas, Washington, D.C.: Government Printing Office, 1963.

A Selected List of U.S. Readings on Development.

VII. Social Problems of Development and Urbanization.

VIII. Organization, Planning, and Programming for Economic Development.

IX. Scientific and Technological Policy, Planning and Organization.

X. International Cooperation and Problems of Transfer and Adaptation.

XI. Human Resources, Training of Scientific and Technological Personnel.

PART II

ADMINISTRATIVE ORGANIZATION

CHAPTER 4

Line and Staff Services

Few organizations today are so small that the head man can directly supervise every one of the subordinate employees. As Pfiffner and Sherwood define it:

> Organization is the pattern of ways in which large numbers of people, too many to have intimate face-to-face contact with all others, and engaged in a complexity of tasks, relate themselves to each other in the conscious, systematic establishment and accomplishment of mutually agreed purposes.[1]

Since organizations are typically large, the need for delegation is created; the top man cannot possibly do everything himself, so he must divide the work among assistants who, in turn, must allocate some of their responsibilities to those subordinate to them. There are two types of this delegation of responsibility: one to *line* officials and the other to *staff* officials.

The respective roles of each are perhaps best studied within the framework of city administration. In recent years, whole cities have sprung up, the administrative structures of which were developed virtually overnight. A good example is Oak Ridge, Tennessee, which was originally built by the War Department as the site for its Manhattan Atomic Bomb Project. Oak Ridge was constructed on a huge 59,000-acre tract from which some 3,000 farmers were removed. By

[1] John M. Pfiffner and Frank P. Sherwood, *Administrative Organization*, Englewood Cliffs, N.J.: Prentice-Hall, 1960, p. 30.

1944, it had a population of 75,000. With the completion of the Manhattan Project, the population declined, yet Oak Ridge continues to be a sizeable community, with a 1960 population of 27,169. Cases could also be cited of small cities which quickly grew into relatively large ones as the result of large influxes of government and defense workers.

Let us assume, then, that we have been asked to prepare the organization plan for a brand new city with an anticipated initial population of, say, around 50,000. In newly created agencies, the first act of delegation is the initiation of the organizational structure itself. We may suppose that the decision has been made to hire a city manager, and that the new city will be organized according to a typical council-manager form of government. The Manager, a professionally trained individual, is to develop plans for the rest of the administrative organization, and he is given the power to appoint all department heads. His first job is to prepare an *organization ordinance* for the approval of the City Council; the purpose of this ordinance is to create the departments and the other major organization units of the city government, and to define their responsibilities. The ordinance must take into account the different public services the municipality is expected to provide. Since cities vary somewhat in the kinds of services they make available to the community, there is no standard blueprint that can be applied, yet certain kinds of activities are generally considered essential. These can be divided into the two types of function mentioned above, line and staff.

LINE SERVICES

Line services refer to those activities which are *substantive* or *direct* in their contribution to the city administration's objectives, such as police and fire protection. The term *line* originated in the military, where it refers to the military commanders and other officers in direct charge of combat operations—those, in other words, responsible for the substantive work of the armed forces; the line, or chain of command, extends from the top-ranking officer down to the lowest ranking enlisted man. The police are responsible in this way for the maintenance of law and order and for the enforcement of the relevant ordinances. They will also have to administer the city jails. The fire department also functions substantively in a program of prevention and fire-fighting. Officials in this department are responsible for the enforcement of fire regulations, and for investigating the causes of fires.

Since the City Manager—as the executive head of the municipality—has the responsibility for providing general direction of all functions of the city government, he is the chief line officer. Yet he has neither the time nor the technical proficiency required for either police or fire work; therefore, he must delegate this line responsibility to qualified subordinates.

There are many other line services that must be instituted by the City Manager if the administration is to be effective in the community. For the development of the physical facilities of the community, the City Manager provides for a Department of Public Works. The responsibilities of this department will include construction and maintenance of the streets and the sewer and storm drain system; garbage and trash collection; installation and operation of street lighting and

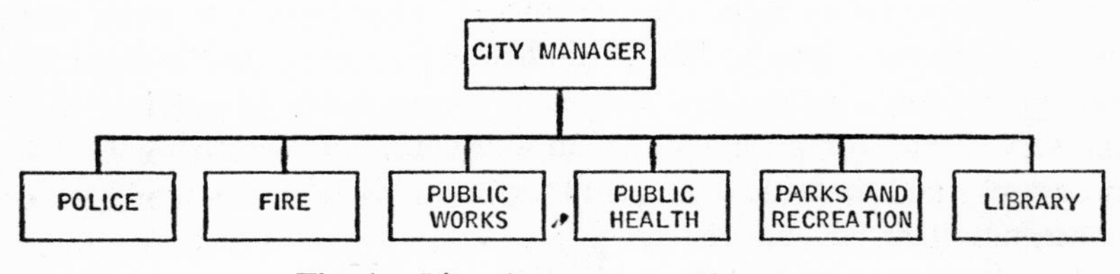

Fig. 1. Line departments, City of X.

other municipal electrical facilities; enforcement of building laws and regulations; maintenance and repair of public buildings; and traffic engineering. Similarly, to prevent outbreaks of disease and otherwise to protect the health of the city's residents, a Department of Public Health is essential. Still another direct service to the public is provision of park and recreation facilities, which makes necessary a Department of Parks and Recreation. Finally, since the City Council has decided that there will be a municipal library, the Manager provides for a Library Department.

All of these line departments are shown in Figure 1. The reader may have wondered if the City Manager expects the population to do without a water supply. Indeed, he does not; but since the city is in a large metropolitan bay area, the water is provided by a municipal utility district serving all the cities in the area.

STAFF SERVICES

Before the line units can begin to function, they need manpower, money, equipment, materials, buildings, and various services. As Pfiffner and Sherwood explain, these services are *adjectival* in nature, or *indirect* in their contribution to the administration's objectives. Again, the City Manager cannot personally undertake to provide all of these indirect services; he must also establish certain staff agencies —to be manned by specialists—in the particular fields concerned.

First, there is the task of finding qualified persons to fill the positions in the administrative branch. The basic employment policy will be outlined in a *civil-service ordinance* and approved by the City Council. A complete personnel program consists of various elements and requires a good deal of specialized knowledge; thus, a Personnel Department is the first staff agency to be instituted. Its function will be to advise the City Manager and the Council on personnel policies, and to help the line officials to find and retain good employees. It will give competitive examinations, both for original entrance into the service and for promotion, plan and carry out in-service training programs, and provide leadership in stimulating the employees to contribute their best efforts.

Nothing can be accomplished by the municipal government without money, so there must be some provision for a Finance Department. The various components of the finance function include:

1. Preparation and control of the budget
2. Receipt and safekeeping of all municipal funds
3. Assessment of real and personal property
4. Administration and collection of municipal taxes and license fees
5. Procurement of materials, supplies, equipment, and services
6. Supply, property and records management
7. Financial estimating and fiscal accounting

As chief executive, the City Manager himself will be responsible for financial planning, yet he will not have the time to exercise direct supervision over these tasks; he will need competent subordinates in immediate charge of each specialized function. Specifically, there should be a budget officer, a treasurer, an assessor, a tax collector, and a purchasing agent. Each official will, of course, have to be given the necessary complement of assistants and office help, and each will be performing a staff service in making it possible for the line departments to get their work done.

The City Council has also advised the Manager that it will create a Planning Commission. The Manager, however, is to appoint a director of planning and to exercise general administrative control over him, just as he does over other department heads. The Director of Planning and his staff are to provide professional advice to both the Manager and the Planning Commission on problems relating to the development of the streets, roads, park areas, bridges, and other physical facilities of the municipality. They will prepare master plans and other guides for the orderly growth of the city. Final adoption of these plans will be the responsibility of the City Council, after hearing the recommendations of the City Manager and the Planning Commission.

The planning staff itself will not assume direct responsibility for building these facilities. The Public Works Department will primarily be in charge of this, although with some participation by Parks and Recreation. The last department will have the responsibility for the construction and maintenance of roads, buildings, and other physical features of recreation and play areas.

The various departments of the government will need legal advice; the city must also have legal counsel to represent it in court, both as defendant and plaintiff. Expert legal assistance will also be required in the drafting of ordinances, resolutions, contracts, and other documents. The case then is complete for adding a fourth staff agency —the Legal Department.

It should be noted that each of these four units provides facilitating services for *all* the line departments. In other words, their scope of activities is citywide. They are not restricted to helping only the line agencies, but also mutually service one another, as when the City Attorney gives advice to the Personnel Director, and when the Finance Department purchases materials and supplies for all three other staff units, as well as for itself and the line agencies. Because they make their services available to the entire city government, they are known as *central staff agencies*. Figure 2 shows the proposed administrative organization for the municipality, with these central staff agencies now added.

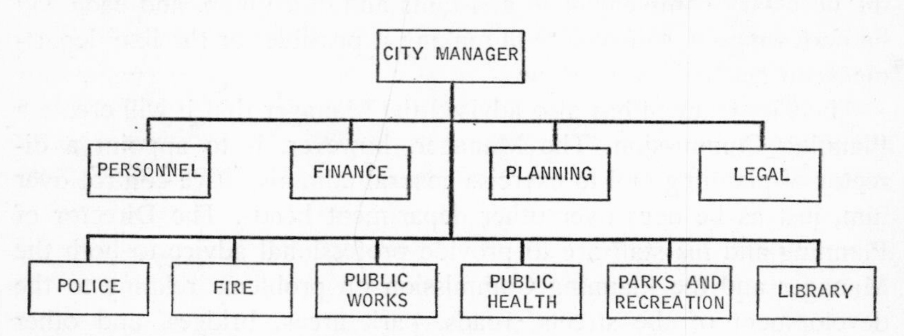

Fig. 2. Proposed administrative organization, City of X. Top row: staff agencies; bottom row: line agencies.

The City Manager must organize his own immediate office in such a way as to discharge his responsibilities with maximum efficiency. He has already delegated important line responsibilities, and also provided for central staff agencies which should give him invaluable help. But he will also need an Assistant City Manager—someone to represent him in contacts with all department heads and also to act for him in his absence. Such a person will be a full-fledged deputy, empowered to give orders to the department heads and to exercise any other powers delegated to him by the City Manager. This does not mean that the department heads will always have to deal with the Manager through the deputy, but that the Manager will designate certain kinds of business which they normally should first take up with the Assistant City Manager. This will free the Manager's time for meetings with the City Council, conferences with leaders of community organizations, and negotiations with federal, state, and other local officials in the area, and similar activities. Since the Assistant City Manager will be directly in the line of command between the Manager and the line department heads, he will be the number two line officer.

Having a deputy will help a good deal, but there will be some tasks that neither he nor the Assistant City Manager will have time to perform. Preparing drafts of speeches is one such task. Doing the same for press releases and keeping in touch with press representatives is another. Going over reports by the department heads and making preliminary comments is another. Looking up information and collecting data the Manager needs is still another. Sometimes the designation "leg man" is used to refer to aides who do such work. This, however, should not be interpreted to mean that the work itself is of an unimportant character. Whether or not the Manager makes a good speech is certainly not a minor matter. So, in our hypothetical example, the position of Administrative Assistant to the City Manager is also needed.

Will the person appointed to it be staff or line? On the basis of the duties described above, he will be staff. This is, however, a different

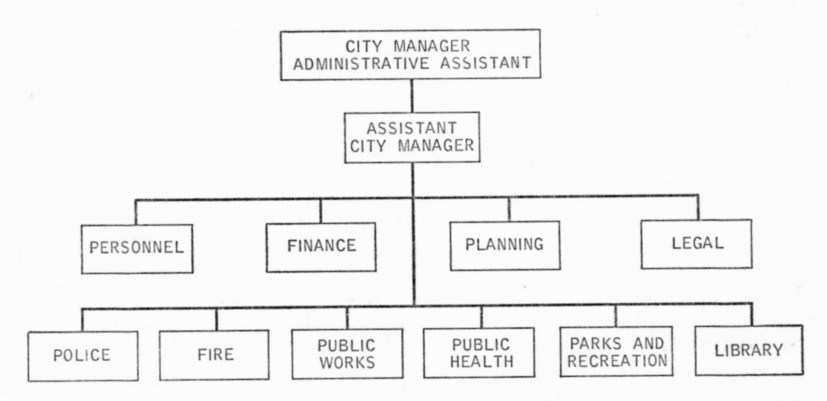

Fig. 3. Proposed overall administrative organization, City of X.

kind of staff activity than that carried out by the central staff agencies, which will handle routine functions of the organization; that is, they will regularly take action and make decisions in the name of the top line officer. The Administrative Assistant to the Manager is not expected to act for his superior—he is rather a personal aide and adviser. The City Manager will make some decisions partly on the basis of information and advice supplied by the Administrative Assistant, but he will not ask the assistant to act for him in getting these decisions executed.

Apart from clerical assistance, our City Manager now has all the help he needs in his immediate office. Figure 3 shows the overall administrative structure of the municipality as he has constructed it. The Commissions and Boards, such as those normally established by municipalities in such fields as parks and recreation, planning, and personnel are not shown, since this is not necessary for our purpose here.

Staff Officials Within the Line Departments

Let us turn our attention now to the internal organization of the line departments. Public Works will be quite large, combining as it does the responsibility for several different functions. Therefore, the position of Assistant Director of Public Works is authorized. This is a line position, because the Assistant Director will serve as a full-fledged deputy, second in the line of command. To continue, the department will need to keep cost figures on its various activities; in

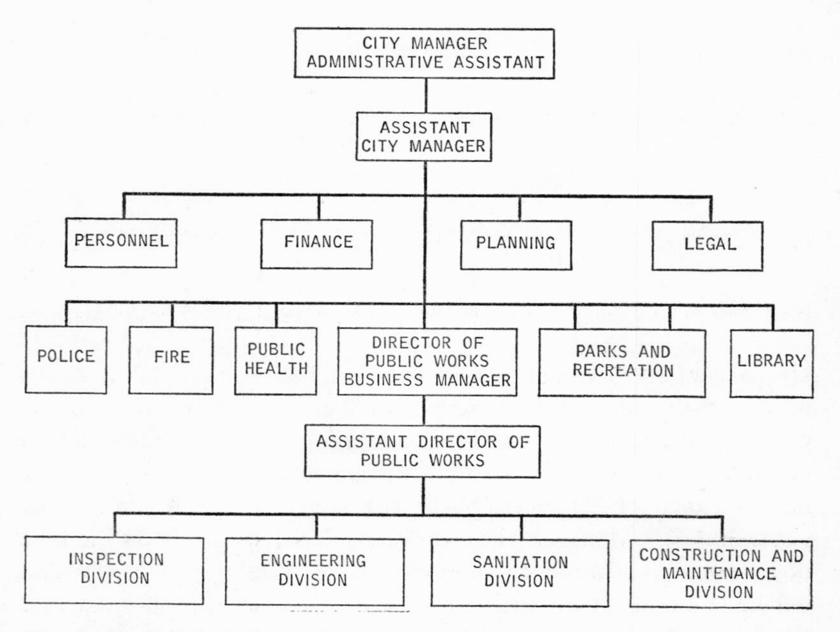

Fig. 4. Proposed administrative organization, City of X. Internal organization of one department.

addition, the Director of Public Works will need someone in his immediate office to be responsible for receiving complaints from the public. He will also require someone to act as liaison to the City Personnel Department. Clearly, then, there is enough work here for a departmental business manager, who would perform all of the abovementioned tasks, and assume responsibility for office-management functions in general, such as records systems and care of machine equipment. The objective here is to facilitate the work of the line supervisors in the Public Works Department.

Thus, we see that, besides the central staff agencies, there will be staff officers such as business managers carrying out the same adjectival functions within the line departments themselves. In fact, similar positions may be created even within subdivisions of these departments. Furthermore, more than one staff official may be needed at the departmental level and in each subdivision. Since our city will not be large, this is not likely, but it could happen in some departments. For example, perhaps in time the Public Works Department will require, in addition to the business manager, a full-time personnel officer. Establishment of such positions will not be limited to the office of the Chief Executive. Figure 4 shows how the Public Works Department, for example, would look in the framework of the total city government.

MISCONCEPTIONS ABOUT STAFF–LINE FUNCTIONS

Once the entire administrative branch has been organized and is functioning, the City Manager may hold regularly scheduled conferences attended by all department heads, both line and staff. One of the purposes of these meetings would be to obtain the advice of the group on proposed city-wide policies. At these meetings, the line department heads present would be performing the staff function of counselling the Manager on different problems, and would serve as members of a planning group for the Manager. In other words, line-and-staff duties may be performed by the same persons. This point is important to remember, because it has sometimes erroneously been assumed that line officials never perform staff functions. Furthermore, line and staff functions are also sometimes combined in the same agency. Suppose that the responsibility for operation and maintenance of public off-street parking facilities has been placed with the Finance Department. Provision of such parking facilities is a direct, rather than an indirect, service to the public. It is, therefore, a line, rather than a staff function. Such combinations of line and staff functions in the same agency are far from unusual.

Confusion has also resulted from the attempt to distinguish between the two functions on the basis of the *command* vs. *advice* criterion. If an official was empowered to issue orders binding on others, it was assumed that he clearly fell in the line category. If all he could do was proffer advice, he was "staff." That this is an incorrect distinction the reader already knows from the statement made previously that staff agencies, such as the Personnel Department, do take action. The Personnel Director does not simply advise the City Manager on personnel policies; he is expected to tell the line officials directly what is and what is not acceptable policy in the field of personnel. He must make decisions and give orders on his own, without having first to consult with the Manager. The Personnel Director, in making his decisions, will sometimes even derive his authority, not from the Manager, but from the law itself. Thus, he does exercise authority and he is far from limited to a purely advisory role.

Sometimes it is wrongly felt that the staff performs only an incidental function, with the line carrying out the really important tasks, but the fact that both line and staff services are found in all large modern organizations clearly indicates that both are essential. Time devoted to proving that one is more important than the other is as futile as that spent proving the rear wheels on an automobile to be more important than those in front. Best results are secured when both groups work together harmoniously, but unfortunately they sometimes do not.

STAFF–LINE CONFLICTS

Conflicts between individuals will arise in any organization, but the staff-line relationship does seem to be a natural breeding place for such clashes. Let us analyze the reasons for this, and then we will direct our attention to possible methods of controlling or averting such conflicts.

Specific Resentments of Line Officials

The line frequently resents the *controls* exercised by the staff officials. Line officials generally will not propose illegal or improper actions, but sometimes they make requests which, in the best judgment of the staff experts concerned, should be denied. Whether or not the purchasing agent's judgment is the best, the fact remains that, as the city's expert in this field, he is authorized to accept or reject requests made by line officials. The nature of the relationship, then, is such that the sensitivities of the line officials are easily offended. Obviously, the more tactful the staff expert is, the better his relationships with the line, but advising him to be tactful will not remove the source of the difficulty; so long as he exercises a veto over the line official, resentments of this type are bound to occur.

Line officials feel even more bitter when they reflect upon the recency of the creation of the staff units. In modern organizations, many of the staff units were established only in recent years. Line officers naturally do not like to receive orders from the representatives of these new staff units particularly if the latter are younger and have more education than those in the line group. In the past, many line supervisors started their working careers without extensive educational backgrounds, and, by dint of hard work, they gained posts of high responsibility. In many cases, their advancement was slow, something which they find hard to forget. Their resentment increases when they see college-trained youngsters recruited directly from school into well-paying jobs in staff departments, where promotion is often more rapid than it was for them when they started out. To cap it all, these young men are placed in positions where, despite their limited work experience, they can give the line men orders.

Line officials also sometimes fear that the staff man will discover deficiencies in their work or procedures. Since it is the nature of the staff's job to check on operations and to recommend improvements, the line naturally is afraid that the staff experts will succeed in effecting major changes in the accustomed ways of doing things. Since resistance to change is a human characteristic, it is not strange that the line should suspect the staff of being insensate "innovators."

Further, line officials are frequently jealous of the influence they believe the staff man has with the "boss." Individuals serving as assistant to an organization executive, as one example, arouse such feelings. The assistant functions as a personal aide to his superior, and thus he is in a strategic position to become influential with him. (Perhaps he may never become really close with him, but there is always that strong possibility.) Witness what Thomas L. Whisler says about the assistant:

> Seldom will any other executive in the organization spend as much time in the company of the chief executive as will that executive's personal assistant, provided that the assistant's role is conceived primarily to be that of communicator. . . . Such frequent interaction becomes generally known and is the source of the assistant's power, the cause of the others' interest and anxiety, and the best evidence of the tendency of the chief executive to convert himself into a two-man team. There are those who seek to disparage the assistant-to by calling him a satellite, but any system is the sum of all its parts. The significance of the satellite in the total system is becoming clear to us today in a number of contexts.[2]

Whisler means by "communicator" that the assistant reviews reports and other written communications prepared by line subordinates and interprets their point of view to the chief, and that he conveys to these same line men the thinking of the chief. A "communicator," therefore, is directly in the stream of things, with a real opportunity to gain power. No wonder that some line officials should worry about how much influence the assistant is developing with the boss.

Relationship Difficulties of Staff Officials

The power relationship is not one sided, however. Since frequently they are relatively new additions to the organization, staff men tend to be uncertain of their status. Indeed, they may even feel an inferiority in their relationships with the line. This may or may not be true of the assistants to the chief, but, on occasion, it has been the case with staff specialists in such areas as personnel, research, and planning. Staff men in these areas feel that they have to justify their existence, both to the management and to the line officers. While it is true

[2] Thomas L. Whisler, "The 'Assistant-to' in Four Administrative Settings," *Administrative Science Quarterly*, V, No. 2 (September, 1960), 213–214.

that, in government, staff activities are by now generally accepted, the services rendered seem intangible and are much harder to justify in terms of results than are those of the line departments.

For example, Public Works can point to the streets, roads, and sewers it builds and maintains. Parks and Recreation can cite impressive statistics showing the number of people in all age groups using its facilities. Public Health can demonstrate how its vaccination programs have reduced the incidence of such feared diseases as polio, and so forth. While the staff departments can also cite statistics, their figures have less force. If Personnel reveals that it administered so many examinations during a given period, someone may question why it was necessary to give that many. The City Manager may receive such good advice from the Legal Department that he considers its services indispensable, but he has no quantitative measurement to prove this. To refer to the number of legal opinions he has received from the city attorneys during a specific period does not prove anything. Furthermore, what evidence can he give to prove beyond the shadow of a doubt that he really needs to have an administrative assistant? And, does the Public Works Department really need a business manager?

Since the staff man renders a service which is indirect in its contribution to the agency's objectives, his job, naturally, is frequently more difficult to justify than those of line officers. While whole staff departments are usually not eliminated in budget reductions, the staff people often do suffer greater job insecurity than do line men during times of financial stringency. If cuts must be made, staff specialists may go first. Even if funds are not short, staff groups may still have reason to feel insecure, particularly if their function is brand new. A good example would be that of a recently established planning staff. How long should it take this staff to develop their plans? Are they inefficient if a few months pass and they still are in the process of preparing these plans? And how can it be proved one way or the other that these plans, when finally ready, are sound? It is no wonder that some staff men should feel uneasy about their status. Usually there are at least some line men who either opposed or were lukewarm to the institution of the new staff activity in the first place.

Because they are anxious to establish themselves, some staff men push too hard in their relationships with line officials. They put pressure on them to accept their recommendations, and they may not conceal their annoyance when the line men seem unconvinced. If these staff people felt more secure, some of their overaggressive conduct undoubtedly would disappear. It is up to the management of the agency to give the staff people the assurances which would reduce such psychological tensions.

Another area of conflict arises from the tendency of some staff officials to look down on the line men. If their educational background is superior, as it frequently is, some of them will develop a condescending attitude. Indeed, a few may even have the idea that they constitute the "brains" of the organization, by contrast with the line people who, from their viewpoint, are unimaginative, sometimes crude, and, in any event, indisposed to look ahead and to plan their work properly. This is a stereotype which has no basis in reality. There is no reason to believe that the staff experts have a monopoly on brain power. The line department head is not of feeble intellect simply because he needs help from staff advisers. Line officials are also decisionmakers, and to make good decisions requires a high level of intellectual ability. The best way for the condescending staff man to find this out is for management to place him in a line position for a while and let him make some of these decisions. He would then probably realize that he was grievously mistaken about the nonintellectual nature of the line function.

In Chapter 1, the tendency of some officials to cling to the rule book and to make the procedures ends in themselves was noted. Since many of the staff specialists do wield control, it is not surprising that some should become unduly negative and rigid in their outlook. A complaint often heard is that the staff is more interested in perpetuating itself and its paper work than it is in helping the line organization. Outright lack of sympathy with the line is rare, but lack of flexibility in dealings with them is frequent. The argument here is not that the staff should always cater to the requests of the line without regard to existing regulations; it is rather that staff specialists should maintain a positive attitude in considering a line officer's requests. Since the organization's regulations cannot cover every situation that arises, the staff man can, when appropriate, occasionally yield to a line request. The line is justifiably infuriated if it has cause to feel that staff units are predisposed to look disfavorably upon *any* request they might make. Unfortunately, some staff people are so minded; some may even themselves be unsure as to what the regulations mean, and may take the safe side in denying the line man. On the other hand, line officials frequently make sweeping condemnations of all staff agencies on the basis of only one or two negative experiences.

The conscientious staff officer faces a real dilemma. He wants to preserve his integrity and to be respected by his colleagues, such as those in personnel, finance, or planning. There is no quicker way to lose their esteem than to be seen constantly capitulating to indefensible requests of line officials. However, neither should he be so unbending as to impede the work of the line men. The problem, then, is how to achieve this happy balance.

Finally, the staff man is sometimes accused of living in an "ivory tower." The charge is that the staff specialists seem virtually to lock themselves in their offices, where, divorced from reality, they develop impractical plans. Unfortunately, some staff men do seem to isolate themselves from line officials. In some cases, this is attributable to the analytical nature of the staff work itself; the specialist wants a quiet atmosphere in which to develop his plans. Whatever the explanation, it is professional suicide for a staff official to maintain a posture of aloofness. A line man could hardly be expected to place his confidence in someone he does not know, and who apparently is not interested in knowing him. If staff units are to succeed, they must use "salesmanship" and persuasion in developing close working relationships with the line. The staff man who circulates freely throughout the line organization, who has numerous face-to-face contacts with operating officials, and who convinces them that he wants to help, is on much more solid ground than one who holds himself aloof.

These are some of the causes of the friction between line and staff. Numerous cases can be cited where the line man was at fault, but just as many can be described where the responsibility lay with the staff man. While these cases may be revealing as to the cause of the trouble, they tend to reflect the bias of the person who relates the "facts" as he sees them. A much more constructive approach is to explore the different proposals which have been made for improving staff-line relationships.

IMPROVING STAFF–LINE RELATIONSHIPS

First, the superior officer should make entirely clear to both staff and line subordinates the exact nature of their responsibilities. The staff specialist should not be given vague assignments, because this not only leaves him uncertain as to his duties, but is also apt to increase any resentment among the line men. We have seen that some staff men are overanxious to establish themselves. If their purpose is not specified, the danger is that they may go too far in pressuring the line to accept their recommendations. Conversely, line officials who refuse to cooperate with the staff men have no excuse if the chief has made clear that they will be expected to cooperate in certain clearly defined areas.

All too frequently, superior officers do not specify their subordinates' responsibilities, as shown in a recent study by the American Management Association (AMA) of the assignments given assistants to high executives in some 140 organizations. In situations where the assistant was not working out, it was found that one of the principal reasons was the failure of the superior to define his duties. "Just come into my office and see where you can be of help to me,"[3] the president had told him. Just how the assistant was to approach his relationships with other officials was also left in the air: "You may find Mr. Smith a little difficult, but you'll know how to handle him."[4] The two men who made this study for the AMA, Ernest Dale and Lyndall F. Urwick, use the sentences quoted to exemplify this kind of mistake. They interviewed the assistants and their superiors, and explored this whole question in workshop seminars with management groups. While their study deals with staff officials in industry, there is no reason to believe that similar mistakes are not made in government.

Second, Ross Pollock suggests that the chief should search his own mind to detect and eliminate any biases of his own. He should ask himself, "What are my own attitudes and beliefs about staff? What experiences have I had which make me feel this way?"[5] The back-

[3] Ernest Dale and Lyndall F. Urwick, *Staff in Organization*, New York: McGraw-Hill, 1960, pp. 166–167.

[4] *Ibid.*

[5] Ross Pollock, *The Leader Looks at Staff-Line Relationships*, Washington, D.C.: Leadership Resources, Inc., 1961, p. 15.

ground and past experiences of the executive may interfere with his objective use of staff assistants. Pollock cites the hypothetical case of Executive A who

". . . has always held line jobs. As he moved through supervision into management, he constantly fought staff for allocating him too little floor space, for overcontrolling his spending of company funds, and for limiting his hiring of the people he wanted. He arrives at a leadership post with negative feelings toward staff."[6]

Such an executive will tend to minimize his own need for staff help and to give the staff units only weak support, if that. He does not take an objective view of staff-line relationships, and since he has this prejudice, he fails to create an atmosphere in which his line and staff subordinates can work together harmoniously. By contrast, Pollock describes another type, Executive B., who "started his career as a supervisor on a small unit which grew explosively. As more and more people joined his organization, he was propelled into executive ranks. He feels strongly the need for staff assistance. He has positive, friendly feelings toward staff."[7] Executive B, we can assume, is not prejudiced against the line officers. After all, he is one himself.

Third, staff and line officers should be encouraged to become better acquainted, and absence of frequent contact between them should be an immediate source of concern to the agency head. We have already mentioned the tendency of some staff men to withdraw into an "ivory tower." Line supervisors, similarly, may not relish too much contact with the "college punks." The management of the agency should impress upon the heads of staff departments the need for their men to establish rapport with the line organization. Actually, the best staff director is one who does not need to be told this. So long as the agency management makes clear that this kind of close relationship between line and staff is desired, any number of methods of accomplishing the objective can be employed. The executive's own staff meeting provides him with an excellent opportunity to bring together staff and line subordinates at regular intervals and to encourage them to work together. It has been suggested that line heads invite representatives of the staff to their departmental conferences, and vice

[6] *Ibid.*, p. 3.
[7] *Ibid.*

versa. Informal luncheon meetings with members of both groups present have in the past also contributed to better mutual understanding. Efforts should also be made to provide travel funds and other inducements for staff officers to visit the actual sites of line operations. The line man may be on sound ground when he criticizes the staff specialists for infrequency of visits and for seeming to develop their recommendations in a vacuum. Impressions formed at headquarters may prove entirely erroneous when the true field situation is studied. The military discovered this a long time ago; Dale and Urwick write:

> Almost the first lesson taught to a young general staff officer serving with troops is to go and see for himself the conditions under which soldiers are living, to get to know personally the officers with whom he deals. . . . The only effective safeguard against "bureaucracy," the insidious breakdown of effective understanding which invariably ensues when officials rely on "paper" communications unsupported by personal contact, is for administrators of all grades to have or make time to go and see for themselves. The first sign that a general, or any other executive, is no leader is when he becomes "chair-borne." He is content to fall back upon penmanship about circumstances with which he has no direct experience, to rely on the written word to do duty for the deed undone.[8]

Fourth, rotation of staff and line assignments should be practiced. The objective is to assure that those in staff jobs at any particular time appreciate the point of view of the line men, and that the latter have the same tolerance for the staff specialists. People frequently change their outlook when they go into a different kind of job. The man who was bitter against the staff units when he served in the line organization suddenly starts to talk a different tune when he is rotated to a staff assignment. Similarly, the staff man who switches to a line assignment will grow to appreciate the reality of problems he once thought imaginary or highly exaggerated. Wherever possible, rotation should, in fact, be part of the individual's internship. Staff recruits in such fields, for example, as personnel, finance, and planning, can profitably be detailed to work in the line departments as part of their initial training. Similarly, arrangements could be made in some cases for line recruits to spend part of their learning period in one or more staff offices. At later stages in their careers, rotation can take the form of temporary details or of transfers for indefinite periods of time.

[8] Dale and Urwick, *op. cit.*, p. 101.

This brings us to the fifth and final point: that the character of the person's academic preparation is of great importance. Taking the staff men first—since many of them are trained for specialized assignments—there is a great danger that the programs of study they pursue may be too narrow. Since they will be dealing constantly with the line organization, they should not only be technically competent in their fields but also have a proper grounding in the substantive work of the organizations with which they are employed. Specifically, this means that those preparing to enter the service in such posts as personnel and finance should also receive appropriate training in the social sciences, such as economics, sociology, and anthropology. Without this kind of background, they will not fully understand the role of their employing organization in modern society. In this connection, it is well to remember that habits of thought, first developed as the result of inadequate university training, naturally carry over into the graduate's actual conduct on the job and become more deeply embedded in his outlook as the result of continuous contact with persons similarly trained. One of the damaging consequences is the failure of the staff man to become sufficiently interested in the details of line functions. Such a failure is particularly unstrategic for good relations with the line organization, for the easiest path to gaining the confidence of the line official is to demonstrate interest in, and the desire to learn more about, the program activities of which he is in charge.

Many line men enter the public service as economists, lawyers, medical doctors, social workers, engineers, and statisticians. In the past, quite a few have in time come to occupy the key program-administration posts, such as the positions of line department and division heads in our hypothetical city government. Although trained in one of these areas, they are placed in posts where their primary responsibility is for administration, not for the direct performance of professional tasks in the particular field. This, for example, has been true of engineering graduates for some time now. Consequently, some training in administration is also highly desirable so that they will not be completely at sea when they are later appointed to directive posts. Broad training is thus highly desirable for both staff and line workers. Basically, it is narrowness of viewpoint which has in the past made it so difficult for them to develop effective working relationships.

In concluding this chapter, another comment of Pollock's may be noted as particularly realistic:

An organization needs the *drive of line* and the *linking power of staff*. The chief executive must marry the two. Neither—no matter how good their will—can achieve union alone; their interests conflict. Good staff–line relationships are created by competent staff, competent line, and effective leadership of both by the chief executive.[9]

There is no cure-all for staff–line frictions, but the top executives can do a great deal to keep such conflicts to a minimum. This is one important test of their leadership qualities.

BIBLIOGRAPHY

Brown, David S., "The Staff Man Looks in the Mirror," *Public Administration Review*, **XXIII,** No. 2 (June, 1963).

Dale, Ernest, and Urwick, Lyndall F., *Staff in Organization*, New York: McGraw-Hill, 1960.

Dalton, Melville, "Staff and Line Relationships—A Study of Conflicts," in Dubin, Robert (ed.), *Human Relations in Administration*, Englewood Cliffs, N.J.: Prentice-Hall, 1961.

Dimock, Marshall E., *The Executive in Action*, New York: Harper and Row, 1945. Chap. VIII.

Gaus, John M., "A Theory of Organization in Public Administration," reproduced in Nigro, Felix A. (ed.), *Public Administration, Readings and Documents*, New York: Holt, Rinehart and Winston, 1951.

Gorlitz, Walter, *History of the German General Staff, 1657–1945*, Frederick A. Praeger, 1953.

Learned, Edmund P., Ulrich, David N., and Booz, Donald R., *Executive Action*, Boston: Harvard Graduate School of Business Administration, 1951. Chaps. X and XI.

Lepawsky, Albert (ed.), *Administration, the Art and Science of Organization and Management*, New York: Knopf, 1949. Chap. 10.

Nelson, Otto L., Jr., *National Security and the General Staff*, Washington, D.C.: Infantry Journal Press, 1946.

[9] Pollock, *op. cit.*, p. 14.

Pfiffner, John M., and Sherwood, Frank P., *Administrative Organization*, Englewood Cliffs, N.J.: Prentice-Hall, 1960. Chap. X.

Sampson, Robert C., *The Staff Role in Management: Its Creative Uses*, New York: Harper and Row, 1955.

Simon, Herbert A., *Administrative Behavior*, New York: Macmillan, 1957. Chap. II.

CHAPTER 5

The Geography of Organization

As organizations grow in size, it proves impossible—or at least undesirable—to administer all activities out of a single office; besides the headquarters location, field offices are also needed. Even in our city of 50,000, a few such branch offices will have to be established. The Public Health Department might have several district health centers, each serving residents of a demarcated zone in the city. This brings the service closer to the people, and also makes possible the provision of the special facilities which may be required in any one area. Similarly, park and recreational facilities will be constructed at different locations throughout the city, each such installation being manned by field representatives of the Department of Parks and Recreation. Other examples could be given, but let us now illustrate with two very large jurisdictions where the need for field offices is much greater. This will introduce an element in organization planning not yet treated: the geographic factor.

TWO EXAMPLES OF REGIONAL ADMINISTRATION

The Chicago Park District

In 1960, the population in Chicago was 3,550,404, which makes it 70 times larger than our hypothetical city, and, as anyone who has been in Chicago knows, its physical area is extensive; it should be no surprise, then, that the Chicago Park District should have many different field locations throughout the city.

First, a few words about the Park District's legal status are in order. Actually, it is a separate municipality, independent of the city government. Originally a number of park districts were established in different neighborhoods of the city, in accordance with the provisions of state law. Each had its own taxing powers and was governed by an elective board of commissioners. By 1934, 22 separate park systems of this type existed. In that year, various civic groups, anxious to simplify the complicated structure of local government, were successful in obtaining the passage of a Park Consolidation Act. Through this legislation, the Chicago Park District was created and the previously separate parks were placed under its jurisdiction. The Park District is governed by a five-man Board of Commissioners, appointed by the Mayor with the approval of the City Council. This is the only formal link with the city government, because the District still levies its own taxes and pays all charges for the operation, maintenance, and improvement of the parks.

Field activities are carried out at dozens of installations known as parks or playgrounds. The parks are bigger than the playgrounds and usually include sizeable buildings with separate gymnasiums for girls and boys, a swimming pool, game rooms, shops, and even auditoriums, in addition to outdoor facilities for sports. The playgrounds are smaller and usually have one or more small buildings with game rooms, plus the outdoor facilities and equipment for different kinds of recreational activities.

The Headquarters Staff

Responsibility for the general direction of recreation programs at all these field locations rests with the Recreation Division, located in the District's Administration Building in downtown Chicago, where the headquarters staff of the District is located. The Recreation Division is part of a Department of General Operations which also includes a Building Facilities Operating Section. The latter section is responsible for providing maintenance personnel and services at each of the parks and playgrounds. In other words, there is a division of responsibility in the Headquarters Office, with the Recreation Division responsible for the program activities in the field, and the Building Facilities Operating Section for the physical housekeeping services. There are several other departments at headquarters which need not be discussed here.

The headquarters—field office organization of the Recreation Division is shown in Figure 5. At the top, we have the director and two assistant directors who have responsibility in the headquarters office for the city-wide recreation program. This headquarters staff formulates the broad policies governing the kinds of programs to be offered throughout the city. The program-planning staff consists of experts in the different recreational specialties who make their skills and know-

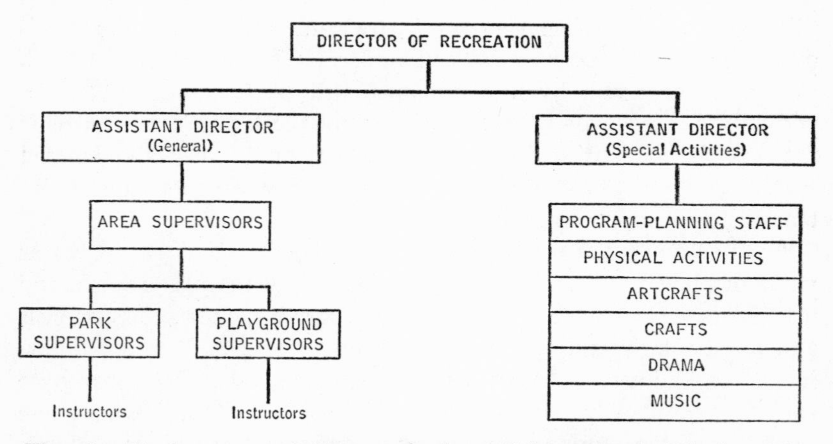

Fig. 5. Headquarters: field organization, Chicago Park District. The program-planning staff provides technical supervision of recreation activities in parks and playgrounds.

ledge available to the instructors at the field locations. For example, the program expert on artcrafts supervises, from a technical standpoint, the activities of the field artcraft instructors, and helps them to develop programs which will stimulate park patrons to do creative work in the manual arts, weaving, rug making, knitting, sewing, fabric decoration, and pottery making. Another expert similarly advises the crafts instructors who teach techniques of working with leather, wood, metal, reed, plastic, and other media. There is also a dramatics expert who helps the field instructors plan and direct dramatic programs at the local parks. Physical activities, including games and sports of various kinds, are so extensive that the Recreation Division requires more than a single program expert; a General Supervisor heads a staff of a dozen or so specialists who advise and instruct the physical-activity instructors in the field locations on how to organize and conduct indoor and outdoor physical activities and gymnastics.

As Figure 5 shows, the Recreation Division at Headquarters has divided the city of Chicago into a number of areas or zones. Since the Director of Recreation could not directly supervise each and every one of these zones, there are Area Supervisors who exercise administrative supervision over the parks and playgrounds in each zone. It is not necessary for these Area Supervisors to maintain offices in their areas; instead they have desks at the Headquarters office, but they do spend most of their time visiting the parks and playgrounds in their zones. The Area Supervisor serves primarily as administrative coordinator of the various parks and playgrounds in his area, and as liaison between them and Headquarters, rather than as the direct supervisor for each recreation center in the zone. To fill this last capacity, there is a Park Supervisor to oversee the various activities and programs offered at each park, and a Playground Supervisor with the same function at each playground. These officials are a part of the Field-Office Staff.

The Field-Office Staff

It is the Park Supervisor to whom the people of the local community look for the development of recreation programs that meet the needs of the neighborhood. It is his job to develop a balanced program of recreational activities in the park which he supervises. In this capacity, he exercises administrative supervision over all personnel assigned to the park, including both the professional staff and the building-facilities maintenance employees (these latter are not discussed here, since we are concentrating on the program itself). In other words, the Park Supervisor is a *generalist*; that is, one who integrates and coordinates the efforts of the *specialists*, or the individual activity instructors (Figure 6). For example, overzealous instructors may press for a disproportionate use of park facilities for their particular programs; two or more may try to reserve the same hours and space, leading to conflicts which can best be solved by a common superior. Thus, the Park Supervisor makes the final decisions as to the days,

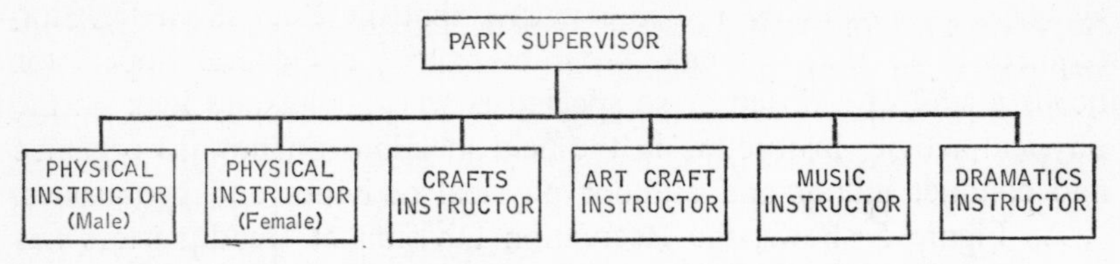

Fig. 6. Recreation staff, large park, Chicago Park District.

hours, and places that will be reserved for the different kinds of recreation programs. Some summers ago, this author spent several weeks visiting some of these Chicago parks, and he was impressed by the variety of roles played by the Park Supervisor: diplomat, interpreter of human wants and needs, psychologist, coach, disciplinarian, public speaker, bookkeeper, philosopher, showman, and—on occasion—janitor. The Park Supervisor's extensive contacts with parents, children, adult park patrons, and many different civic groups, combined with his responsibility for administrative direction of a variety of programs, make the position an unusual one. From the viewpoint of the Headquarters Recreation Division, the Park Supervisor is its representative with the local community organizations and the general public, and it relies on him for the implementation of the rules and policies instituted at headquarters. It also depends on him to submit periodically detailed reports covering the overall program at the individual park.

Although the Park Supervisor must know a great deal about the technical aspects of individual activities, he himself does not carry out or lead these activities. The professional or instructional staff already mentioned has this responsibility. Taking their direction from the Park Supervisor, these instructors also see to it that park property is properly taken care of, that park rules are followed by the public, and so forth. Of course, they keep detailed records of their activities for the Park Supervisor.

Relationships between the Headquarters and Field Staffs

Since the Area Supervisors are the liaison officers between the field staff and the officials at Headquarters, the Park Supervisors communicate their points of view to the Recreation Division through the Area

Supervisors, indicating the special needs and problems of the individual parks. In turn, the Area Supervisors transmit policy directives and instructions from the Director of Recreation to the Park Supervisors. This system does not obviate all direct contact between the Director of Recreation and the Park Supervisors, however. Certain urgencies necessitate dispensing with the formal, routine channels, and Headquarters officials—even the Director of Recreation, himself—may telephone the Park Supervisor directly, and vice versa. In fact, it has been increasingly recognized that too much rigidity in formal communication systems is undesirable. So long as normal situations flow through the Area Supervisors, flexibility of operations is encouraged.

A more direct channel operates between the program-planning staff at Headquarters and the instructional field staff. It is not the Area Supervisor—nor even the Park Supervisor—who gives the field staff technical guidance, but the program-planning staff. Each specialist on this staff must do his best to cover the entire city, visiting all of the field locations in their turn. This is no easy task, but with competent instructors in the field, there is usually little need for the specialists to consult with them with great frequency. During his visit at a field location, the program expert assists in every way possible, advising on technical problems and clarifying program objectives. This, naturally, also entails a review of the instructor's performance and his efficiency. Thus, the instructional staff is subordinate to two types of supervisory official: the Park Supervisor with his interest in overall program coordination and administration at the individual park, and the Headquarters program expert, with his interest in the particular activity specialty and the city-wide coordination of the particular specialty.

One of the alleged "principles" of administration—unity of command—postulates that no one should receive instructions from more than one person. So respected was this axiom at one time that dire predictions of failure were made for any organization which failed to observe it. On the contrary, as the example of the Chicago Park District shows, an organization which insisted on having each of its employees receive instructions from one, and only one, person would quickly get into difficulties. For example, the Park Supervisor might know a good deal about the physical-activity part of the recreation program. If time permitted—but, of course, it does not—he could exercise technical, as well as administrative, supervision over the physical-activity instructors at his park. It is very unlikely, however, that he could also give technical instructions to the park personnel in other fields.

The whole point, as Herbert A. Simon has so clearly shown,[1] is that unity of command is incompatible with the principle of specialization. No one can be a specialist in everything, and, since modern organizations are specialized, unity of command in this sense is not possible in them. Since the total job is broken down into various specialized parts, lines of responsibility are created in addition to the administrative chain of command. Indeed, as Frederick W. Taylor advocated many years ago,[2] it might be desirable for the individual to take orders, not from two people, but from several different functional specialists. Taylor recommended separate foremen for machinery, materials, speed, and other functional aspects of the work, with each authorized to give commands directly to the workmen. While these specific proposals are not followed to the letter today, it is unquestionable that multiple supervision is generally practiced. As we saw in Chapter 4, line officials are under the control of several different kinds of staff units, such as personnel, finance, and planning, who must be listened to every bit as much as the line supervisors. The program-planning group that we are now discussing simply represents another source of instructions. It is another kind of staff service.

Multiple supervision does, of course, lead to conflicts between the members of the program-planning staff and the line supervisors. Such conflicts should be resolved through referral to the appropriate higher-level administrative supervisor. Let us assume that the Park Supervisor believes that a program-planning technician from Headquarters has given the incorrect technical instructions to one of the park staff. He can discuss the problem with the Area Supervisor, who, in turn, can take it up with the Director of Recreation. The Director, of course, makes the final decision. It should not be assumed, however, that differences of this type need always go up to the top line officer

[1] Herbert A. Simon, *Administrative Behavior*, New York: Macmillan, 1957, pp. 22–26.

[2] Frederick W. Taylor, *Scientific Management*, New York: Harper and Row, 1947, pp. 99–109.

for final resolution. Perhaps the Park Supervisor can himself convince the program technician that he was wrong. If not, maybe the Area Supervisor will be able to do so. In other words, the incident need not develop into a major controversy.

Unity of command is really satisfied at the park by having all staff *administratively* responsible to one person, the Park Supervisor. This is where the strongest case can be made for unity—in the administrative direction. Two or more administrative bosses are likely to lead to trouble, because each may demand the attention of the subordinate at the same time. Furthermore, they may disagree and give conflicting orders, without any effective recourse of appeal by the worker.

The instructors at the parks are fortunately not in this position; by and large, they function independently of the Park Supervisor in carrying out the technical details of their work. In the unlikely event that the Park Supervisor did rescind an instruction given by a program-planning staff specialist, the instructor can promptly advise the staff specialist of his dilemma. The matter then will be resolved between the Park Supervisor and the program-planning staff specialist, or referred to the Area Supervisor—and, if necessary, to the Recreation Director—for final decision.

This, then, in general terms, is the Chicago Park District's solution of the age-old problem of how to administer functional programs over a large physical area. This observer's impression was that its technical and administrative staff worked together very well. Perhaps an important reason for this is the similar background of many of the Park Supervisors, instructors and Headquarters program technicians. Many Park Supervisors have previously served as physical-activity instructors or in specialized phases of recreation work. Their point of view is not apt to be out of line with that of the park staff or of Headquarters representatives; they are leaders of a professional group imbued with the same goals and possessing the same enthusiasms.

The Forest Service

Let us turn now to the national level for another illustration of the "geography of organization." Since some federal agencies are very large, this is where the greatest use is made of program experts in different specialties to help the line officials in the field. Several different examples could be given, but we will concentrate on the Forest Service.[3]

At the head of the Forest Service is the Secretary of Agriculture, followed in rank by the Chief of the Service, who, incidentally, is a civil-service appointee. Under the Chief, there are two main program subdivisions: one is for the administration of the national forests and for cooperative programs with state and local governments; the other is for research, with which we are not concerned here.

The Chief is assisted in Washington by a number of Assistant Chiefs, each of whom heads highly specialized staffs which are "supposed to be compilers of information, sources of ideas, and observers of field work."[4] In other words, they are not directly engaged in field operations.

The Forest Service has divided the country into ten regions, each headed by a Regional Forester. He is responsible for all Forest Service functions in his region, except for research. Figure 7 shows how

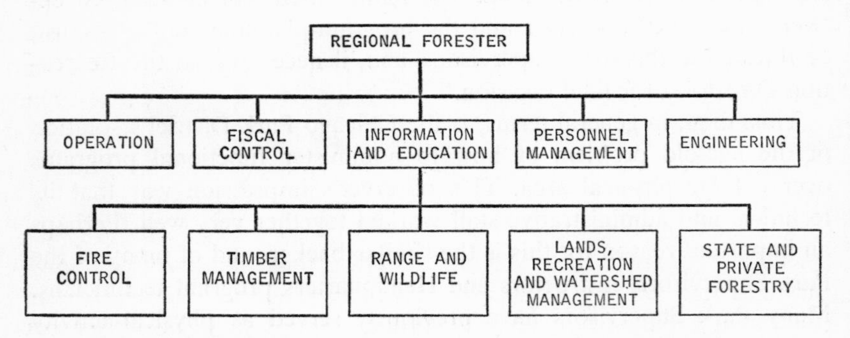

Fig. 7. Typical regional office, organization, U.S. Forest Service.

he is flanked by staff specialists in no fewer than ten fields, although, depending on the work load, some of these fields may be combined. Except for fiscal control, the title of Assistant Regional Forester is given to the heads of each of these functional divisions. It is in the regions, of course, that the forests themselves are located. Each forest

[3] For the following discussion the author is indebted to Herbert Kaufman for his excellent book *The Forest Ranger: A Study in Administrative Behavior,* Baltimore: Johns Hopkins Press, 1960.

[4] *Ibid.*, p. 43.

is under the control of a Forest Supervisor. He has the same responsibilities at his level as the Regional Forester, except for state and private forestry. Each Forest Supervisor, in turn, has a number of functional specialists under his administrative supervision. These are fewer in number than at the regional level, the exact number depending on the work load at the particular forest. At the bottom of the field organization is the Ranger. Every national forest is divided into Ranger districts which are, then, the smallest geographical subdivisions of national forest administration. The Ranger must be versatile, for he is responsible for all functions in his district except large construction or other special projects. He is usually assisted by one or more Assistant Rangers and by both permanent and seasonal labor forces, but he does not have any functional-staff specialists assigned to him. The Ranger *is* the Forest Service in the district.

Line–Staff Conflicts

The principal fields in which program specialists function are: timber management; range and wildlife; lands, recreation, and watershed management; and state and private forestry. Each program group naturally wants stressed the functions it represents. Kaufman describes the resulting conflicts:

> What creates a problem for the field man is the fact that the materials [written instructions] sometimes require mutually exclusive courses of action on his part. The specifications for roads, for example, are generally predicated on engineering premises alone, but roads built to those specifications may conflict with the demands of watershed management or recreation management or timber management specialists. Rigid adherence to timber management or range management program goals can generate public criticism that provokes objections from information and education specialists. Emphasis on recreation that gratifies recreation officers may disturb fire control officers. What looks like adequate concern for the grazing uses of the national forests may seem like indifference to wildlife from the perspective of those who specialize in this function. . . . Despite the general consensus on the desirability of multiple-use resource management, it is not always clear what this indicates in specific instances.[5]

How do the Rangers resolve these conflicts? If the Ranger does not agree with the advice of a program specialist on the Forest Su-

[5] *Ibid.*, p. 68.

pervisor's staff, the matter may end there if the specialist in question decides to withdraw his suggestions. He may, however, insist that his instructions should be followed. The Ranger can then protest to the Forest Supervisor who makes the decision. The same holds true if it is the specialist who makes the appeal to the Forest Supervisor. Significantly, Kaufman reports that the Rangers tend to accept advice from the staff experts and are reluctant to protest to the Forest Supervisor unless they consider the point at issue very important. "While the Rangers will not brook what they regard as interference in the administration of their districts, they also recognize that the shared contacts and vantage points of the line and staff officers at the higher level mean those officials are likely to see many things the same way —and for valid reasons."[6] Nor does this mean that the Rangers play a submissive role, but simply that they accept the logic of functional staff–line organization. Kaufman stresses that disputes of this type are not frequent, and that harmony, rather than conflict, is the keynote of operations. A principal explanation for this is what he calls the "homogenization" of the Forest Service personnel—that is their similar background—more than 90 percent of the professional employees are foresters. This is true not only of the line officers but also of the specialists in timber management, fire control, wildlife, and recreation. It is also true of the officials engaged in personnel, administrative management, information, and budgeting. While they are located at different levels of the organization and function in different fields, the common background of training of the organization's personnel cannot help but be a strong force towards harmony. It will be remembered that the same point was made about the professional staff of the Chicago Park District.

Headquarters–Field Conflicts

In organizations like the Forest Service, conflicts arise, not only between line and staff officers, but also between "headquarters" on the one hand and the "field" on the other. Indeed, some antipathy between headquarters and field staffs seems inevitable in agencies with field programs. The same hostility usually exists, to some extent at least, between employees of state governments stationed in the state capital and those in the branch offices throughout the state.

[6] *Ibid.*, pp. 106–107.

MISUNDERSTANDINGS IN THE FIELD. In general, the field people tend to feel neglected, particularly if they are situated far from headquarters. Lessened contact increases the possibility of misunderstanding. The field official easily convinces himself that headquarters does not understand the problems in his area and is insensibly trying to cast all field offices into the same mould. Although many field complaints are justified, some of the strong statements made by field officials should not be taken at face value. The understanding headquarters official knows that sometimes the irritations are minor and the agency management can eliminate them without too much difficulty.

The situation is much more serious when the field men are "captured" by the local population they serve and come to consider themselves representatives of these groups rather than of the headquarters office of the agency. As Kaufman stresses, such a danger is a very real one in a program like that of the Forest Service. Not only are many different activities carried on, but they all have ardent champions in the local communities. For example, grazing interests may try to influence the Ranger to apply headquarters' broad directives in such a way as to give this local pressure group favored treatment. Similarly, recreation enthusiasts, hunters, sportsmen, and bird lovers naturally want the Ranger to give special attention to their needs in the national forests. There is a certain area of discretion left to the Ranger; without violating national policies outright, he is in a position to modify them substantially in their actual application in his district. Yet, Kaufman tells us, the Forest Service has been generally successful in reducing the temptation for Rangers to become such "captives" of the local community. Even when they do yield to local interests, it is generally to protect the long-run interests of the Service, not simply to please the local citizens.

One technique that the Forest Service uses to maintain the Rangers' primary loyalties to it and not to the local community is the "preformed decision." Headquarters cannot predict all the sets of circumstances which will arise at particular locations but, profiting from past experiences, it can anticipate many of them and specify the course of action to be taken for each category of case. Accordingly, appropriate instructions for each type of anticipated field situation are incorporated in the manuals, directives, and other written instructions which are sent to each Ranger. Kaufman explains, "The field officers then need determine only into what category a particular circumstance falls; once this determination is made, he then simply follows the series of steps applicable to that category."[7] It is in this sense that his decisions are "preformed."

"Limitation of authorization" is another method for assuring field compliance. This refers to the controls exercised by higher level officials over the Ranger's actions. While the Ranger is the Service's link with the local people, there are few policy decisions that he can make on his own. He can complete small timber sales, issue permits of minor importance for the use of forest facilities, and hire laborers for continuing and emergency work. Practically everything else, although initiated by the Ranger, must be approved by higher officials.

"Dispute settlement" is a related technique. This refers to the procedure for resolution of the staff–line conflicts already described. Kaufman stresses that this procedure serves the constructive purpose of making the higher-level official aware of issues and of ambiguities in policies that otherwise would escape his notice. "Dispute settlement" thus "employs conflict for purposes of organizational integration."[8]

The Forest Service's policy on transfers also discourages resistance to headquarters' policies. Transfers of professional personnel from station to station are very frequent. While the principal objective here is to broaden the individual's work experience in the Service, the policy of frequent transfers also prevents him from becoming too attached to any one locality, and developing such strong ties with community groups that he loses his objectivity in pressing the local viewpoint upon headquarters.

The Forest Service's policy of promotion from within also encourages conformity. This is so uniformly applied that, when he conducted his research, Kaufman could not find a single Ranger who had been recruited from outside the Service. Furthermore, he found that almost all the Rangers' superiors had at one time or another in their careers themselves served as Rangers. Promotion is typically slow, so the individual has a good long time in each rank to absorb the Service's point of view, a process which Kaufman aptly terms "organization acculturation."

[7] *Ibid.*, p. 91.
[8] *Ibid.*, p. 105.

Another important way in which the Forest Service arouses this "will and capacity to conform" is by making positive efforts to ascertain the field staff's reaction before making policy and other changes. The techniques for accomplishing this are varied. For one thing, formal polls are conducted in which the men are asked their opinions on specific questions, such as the use of uniforms and personnel policies. Informal methods are also employed, such as when during field visits the superior officers invite the Rangers to make suggestions on how to improve conditions in the Service. If they have a voice in decisions before they are made, employees, whether in the field or at headquarters, will develop stronger organization loyalties.

MISUNDERSTANDINGS AT HEADQUARTERS. The foregoing has illustrated some of the misunderstandings among the field staff, the pitfalls to which they are vulnerable, and some of the policies that headquarters has initiated over the years to combat the resultant problems. There are also possibilities of misunderstandings at headquarters. For one thing, the headquarters staff may jump to the conclusion that the field staff is resisting central policy. Also, knowledge of field conditions may be somewhat limited among headquarters staff; on one occasion, when the forests were under the General Land Office of the Interior Department, a Washington official ordered a Forest Supervisor and his Ranger to purchase rakes to clear up dead wood on his reserve. The particular reserve happened to cover three and a half million acres, and fallen trees were often longer than a city block and too thick for a man to see over! While these misunderstandings by headquarters are to great extent overcome by the system of internal promotion just described, field officials could be at times frustrated by the policies established at headquarters.

CENTRALIZATION AND DECENTRALIZATION

A major aspect of regional organization deals with the question of centralization versus decentralization. An agency with many field offices and far-reaching jurisdiction must sooner or later come to grips with this question, for the larger the agency, the less direct control is it able to effect at the central office. This was clearly demonstrated in the discussion of the Forest Service, where official overall policy is one of decentralization—contrasted by the measures taken at headquarters to minimize this decentralization and to emphasize central control, as Kaufman's analysis reveals. Thus, the Forest Service is both centralized and decentralized; it has uniform national policies which the local officials cannot disregard, while specialized situations at each of the localities necessitate policy decisions made at the field level.

Strong prejudices frequently characterize any discussion of the centralization—decentralization issue. In the American environment, centralization is generally condemned and decentralization praised; political forms are decentralized and the virtues of local initiative and responsibility are emphasized. Witness the angry reaction of most Americans against tight control from Washington or from the state capital. Yet there are circumstances in which a policy of centralization is the more advisable, at least temporarily. As Paul Appleby,[9] once an Assistant to the Secretary of Agriculture, has wisely observed, nothing can be decentralized until it has first been centralized. Headquarters policies must first be defined, or there will be as many policies as there are field offices.

A case in point is that of the Veterans Administration (VA). Gladys Kammerer tells us that during the Harding administration—when the agency was known as the Veterans Bureau—it was discredited by major scandals.[10] In addition, many field officials had been appointed because of their devotion to veterans' problems, rather than for their administrative leadership and understanding. During this time, as might be expected, there was relatively little control from central headquarters. When General Frank T. Hines became VA administrator, he took strong measures to bring the field offices under strict controls to prevent further scandals and malpractices. Thereafter until 1945, all personnel activity, no matter how routine, was subject to Washington approval; the regional manager could not even authorize the purchase of a pair of scissors, nor could he shift offices from one corner of the building to another without headquarters' sanction. While this policy of centralization went to extremes, in view of the history of scandals in the field operations there were decided advantages. Besides, it was feasible, because at

[9] Paul Appleby, *Big Democracy*, New York: Knopf, 1945, p. 104.

[10] Gladys M. Kammerer, "The Veterans Administration in Transition," *Public Administration Review*, VIII, No. 2 (Spring, 1948), 104–106.

that time the "program of benefits administered by the agency, consisting primarily of insurance and pension benefits and hospitalization, required identical administrative decisions, case by case, which the administrator deemed could best be made in Washington to assure uniformity, fairness, and equity."[11] Since 1945, all of this has changed, for the VA has expanded its activities greatly and consequently devolved much authority back to its field offices, and the latter now can be trusted to bear a good deal of the load for administering this expanded program.

Centralization may also be a necessity during crises or other periods of stress. The crisis may occur when new activities are launched or when sharp changes in previous policies are made. Headquarters wants to hold the reins until the emergency is ended. This is explained by a British expert:

> When a ministry undertakes some new activity or adopts a substantial change in policy, it may be necessary, for a time, to retain complete authority and control at the centre. During this early period experience will be gained and precedents will be created which will enable top management to form and define its policy and intentions in more detail. When this point is reached, some measure of decentralization will become possible. At the start the delegated responsibilities may be limited but they will be increased as further experience and understanding of the subject is acquired throughout the ministry until, except for questions of the highest importance, decentralization of day to day administration is complete.
>
> This position may continue for some years, and then because the subject takes on a new importance, or attracts considerable political attention or possibly because public criticism reveals that conflicting or inconsistent decisions are being given, it becomes necessary to withdraw delegated authority and once more centralize decisions. After a further period of centralization when interest in the subject has abated or when the ministry has re-defined its policy or its aims, the process of decentralization will begin all over again.[12]

The increasing use of computers and data processing machines has a bearing on this question. One of the strongest arguments for de-

[11] *Ibid.*, p. 104.

[12] H. J. Kruisinga (ed.), *The Balance Between Centralization and Decentralization in Management Control*, Leiden: H. E. Stenfert Kroese N.V., 1954, p. 71.

centralization of decisionmaking is that only the field offices have the facts on which to make sound judgments. Headquarters just does not know enough to be able to decide correctly. The "information revolution," however, may well destroy this argument. As Dale points out, "if enough information can be brought to a central point quickly enough, there may no longer be a need to have problems settled at a point close to their source."[13] It has been predicted that, in both industry and government, the computers will routinize operations and eliminate the jobs of many members of middle management, or those occupying positions in the intermediate levels of the hierarchy. It is still too early to say whether this will happen; furthermore, it is not clear that the machines will be used principally to receive and to store data at the headquarters level. As Pfiffner and Sherwood state, they could just as easily be employed to build up information in the field offices. "Computer technology," they conclude, "seems to be in such a state of flux that, if decentralization has other enduring values, the communications system will be adapted to facilitate its advantages."[14]

Political factors also enter into the picture, as already revealed in the history of headquarters—field relationships in the Veterans Administration. The background of scandals largely explains the centralization policy in effect during the interval between the two Wars. Sometimes political pressures cause an agency to loosen, rather than to tighten, national controls. To illustrate, local politicians may ask national administrators to relax certain controls over field offices simply because these controls prevent political infiltration. If the pressure is severe, an administrator may agree to "decentralize." Decentralization, when it occurs for these reasons, may actually be a cloak for cowardice. Influential politicians will sometimes even try to dictate the field structure of an agency. For example, United States Senators prefer state to regional offices, because it is easier for them to control appointments to federal jobs in their own states. Having an office in each state may thus be justified as "decentralization" when a few regional offices would suffice and cost much less to maintain.

These points reveal that questions of political strategy and other

[13] *Ibid.*, p. 32.

[14] John M. Pfiffner and Frank P. Sherwood, *Administrative Organization*, Englewood Cliffs, N.J.: Prentice-Hall, 1960, p. 201.

external influences may well be more controlling than the pure logic of administrative efficiency. In the following chapter, we will elaborate this theme of the "Politics of Organization." The comments made here are but a prelude; yet they are necessary to draw attention to a frequently overlooked aspect of the centralization-decentralization controversy. Decentralization, then, depends on the circumstances. Too often this question is phrased as an "either-or" proposition, whereas, it is really more desirable if centralization of basic policy precedes delegation of authority to the field.

ADMINISTRATIVE RELATIONSHIPS AMONG LEVELS OF GOVERNMENT

So far we have discussed the geography of organization in terms of headquarters—field-office relationships of agencies at a particular level of government. The Chicago Park District is an example from the municipal, and the Forest Service from the federal level. However, this is only one aspect of the geographic factor in organization. Administrative relationships among levels of government are even more important in terms of total program activity and the number of public employees involved.

It has long been obvious that administrative activities in the United States are not compartmentalized by levels of government. National, state, and local governments do not occupy separate administrative bailiwicks. Our federal system, in which state and local governments play a strong role, continues to show great vigor, but many of the most important governmental activities today are the joint responsibility of all levels of government. The term *cooperative federalism* is now familiar in American government. A complete factual account of the numerous programs which fall under this umbrella is included in the standard American government texts; we will, therefore, concentrate on discussing intergovernmental cooperation in terms of the patterns of administrative behavior which have developed around it.

Grants-in-Aid

The grant-in-aid is the principal instrument of intergovernmental cooperation. While federal grants to the states and cities are more spectacular, involving as they do large sums for such programs as highways, airports, urban renewal, and public welfare, the states themselves also give substantial subsidies to local government units, as, for example, to school districts. Without the subsidy system the benefiting agencies could not provide urgently needed services. At the same time, the agency which makes the grants is able to insist that certain standards be met as a condition for receiving them. Its representatives inspect the work of the recipient agencies. For example, the Bureau of Public Roads in the Department of Commerce does not build the highways, anymore than the Federal Aviation Agency constructs the municipal and county airports; neither does the State Department of Public Instruction assume direct responsibility for giving classes in the local schools. The grants do not, therefore, result in centralized administration, but they do mean supervision from a higher level.

At first glance, it would seem logical that the need to accept subsidies of this kind would cause the recipient agencies to feel resentful towards the disbursing agencies. States-rights sentiment should make state officials hostile towards representatives of the federal agencies who supervise the way they use federal funds. Local government employees should feel the same way about state officials who check on them. On the contrary, officials participating in grant programs, both on the giving and receiving ends, usually work together very well. This is because of the strength of their professional ties and their mutual identification with the same functional programs. Professional workers cooperating in such fields as forestry, agriculture, public welfare, education, and recreation have a great deal in common—so much so that they identify more with one another than with the level of government as such. Federal, state, and local loyalties are minor compared to the ties binding individuals to their professional colleagues, even if these colleagues are employed at another level of government. In a significant study by Edward W. Weidner, entitled *Intergovernmental Relations As Seen By Public Officials*,[15] a series of questions was put to officials employed by the national, state, and local governments in Minnesota. The purpose was to elicit their views on various aspects of intergovernmental relations. As just one example, local government officials were asked, "Do you have less say-so

[15] Edward W. Weidner, *Intergovernmental Relations As Seen By Public Officials*, Minneapolis: Univ. of Minnesota Press, 1960.

about your function as a result of contacts of state administrators with you?"

Municipal officials participating in the survey were classified into three groups: (1) functional workers; (2) mayors, clerks, and managers; and (3) municipal councilmen. Most of those in these three groups rejected the idea that they or the municipality had less to say as a consequence of their relations with state officials supervising grant programs. Mayors, clerks, and managers were the least sure of this. Functional officials were much more confident that their influence had not been lessened. At the county level, an even higher percentage of the functional officials were of the same opinion. The replies to this and similar questions clearly indicated that professional workers were the most friendly to contacts with, and to supervision by, the professional representatives of the state government. Furthermore, state functional officials were found generally to be friendly towards professional agents of the national government; the great majority of them were of the opinion that the approach of the federal officials was essentially positive and helpful, rather than negative and mere inspection or direction. Significantly, Weidner also reports that, whereas the functional officials are "activity-minded," the general executive and governing personnel are "unit-of-government oriented." This should not be surprising; politically elected officials would naturally be more sensitive about supervision from *without* the community. To elected officials, the professional contacts the specialists enjoy can easily seem unwarranted interferences by "bureaucrats" of other levels of government.

Interstate Compacts

Interstate compacts are another example of "cooperative federalism," and, though they are not as important as grants-in-aid in terms of size and variety of programs administered, they have become an important element in the American federal system. Whereas the grant-in-aid represents a vertical relationship between levels of government, the compact is basically a horizontal one between two or more state governments.

Of the many dozen compacts which have been approved since 1789, 34 provide for the establishment of an interstate agency to administer a given program.[16] It is with these interstate compact agencies that we are concerned as examples of the "geography of organization." The compact agencies rely on education and persuasion to accomplish their purpose, because in very few cases do they have enforcement powers of their own. Typically, the agreements make clear that the findings of the compact agency will not be binding in the courts. Enforcement powers which do exist may only be exercised by the regular administrative machinery of the signatory states.

The water-apportionment commissions exemplify the use of persuasion. The responsibility of these commissions is to oversee the technical details of the allocation of water to the participating states. Stream-gaging stations are operated to obtain data for determining whether the states are keeping within the limits set by the compact as to the amount of water which may be stored or diverted. The commission cannot take action against a violating state; all they can do is report their findings to the appropriate state officials and try to convince them that they should take action to obtain compliance with the compact agreement within their state. As in the case of the other compact agencies, the members of the water-apportionment commissions argue their case before legislative and administrative bodies, and also conduct public relations programs to enlist the support of the public for making effective the compact agreement. Leach and Sugg comment that "public relations work has therefore assumed as much importance in compact agencies as it has in other segments of our national life."[17]

Even the New York Port Authority, the most successful of interstate-compact agencies, is without enforcement powers: The compact agreement states that the "two states shall provide penalties for violations of any order, rule or regulation of the Port Authority, and for the manner of enforcing same."[18] However, an interstate agency like the New York Port Authority is not impotent because, in general, the participating states do provide effective means of enforcement, and the agency itself uses powerful tools of persuasion. Even among the

[16] The factual information which follows is from Richard H. Leach and Redding S. Sugg, Jr., *The Administration of Interstate Compacts,* Louisiana State Univ. Press, 1959.

[17] *Ibid.,* p. 92.

[18] *Ibid.,* p. 96.

few agencies which do have enforcement powers, primary reliance has been placed on persuasion and public education.

The Metropolitan Problem

There is one final area which cannot be omitted in any thoroughgoing discussion of the "geography of organization." Note the following statement:

> At no point in the structure of the American federal system of government are problems of intergovernmental relations so marked, varied, and difficult as in the large metropolitan areas, where the activities of all three levels of government function in close proximity. Within such areas, federal, state, county, and municipal agencies, often supplemented by a small host of special purpose units of local government, must carry on their functions in close juxtaposition, subject to an extremely complicated framework of federal, state, and local laws and administrative regulations.[19]

As of 1960, there were at least 16,976 units of local government in the nation's 212 standard metropolitan statistical areas.[20] Within this mass of overlapping units, provision of public services to the residents of the areas on a unified basis is exceedingly difficult. The separate municipalities and other local government units tend to operate independently, failing to develop coordinated plans and programs for arterial roads and streets, traffic control, economic development, civil defense, police protection, and other services. Proposals have been made for the creation of metropolitan governments, that is, new political entities which would be equipped with the necessary powers for providing such area-wide services. Indeed, some of these proposals reflect great ingenuity in adapting existing political forms to meet, at least partially, the need for integrated administration.

For example, a recent report of the Advisory Commission on Intergovernmental Relations recommends passage of state legislation authorizing local governmental units to contract with larger units for the provision of specified public services. The smaller units of government frequently cannot provide certain services as economically

[19] *Government Structure, Organization, and Planning in Metropolitan Areas*, House Committee on Government Operations, 87th Congress, 1st Session, Washington, D.C.: Government Printing Office, 1961, p. 1.

[20] *Ibid.*, pp. 13–14.

or as efficiently as larger jurisdictions. Furthermore, if many smaller units enter into such contracts, this permits a large measure of uniformity in metropolitan administration. The Advisory Commission cites the case of Los Angeles County which, through contracts of this kind, provides municipal-type services to many cities in the County. The city of Lakewood, to illustrate, with a population of nearly 100,000, receives all its municipal services from the County. Other cities contract for particular services, such as public health.[21] Jamison and Bigger believe that Los Angeles County "may well be entering an era in which it will be the major administrative unit in the metropolitan area, while policies with respect to standards and kinds of local services will be set by city councils for the county departments to follow."[22]

Another device is joint provision by two or more units of government of a particular service, or the joint operation of a governmental facility. The Advisory Commission also recommends that legal authority for such arrangements be obtained. It cites the joint financing and maintenance of government buildings in Chicago, St. Paul, and Berkeley, California; the joint operation of hospitals in Louisville and Chattanooga, and of sewage disposal facilities in the Atlanta area.

Still another of its recommendations is for the states to authorize legislative bodies of municipalities and counties in metropolitan areas to make voluntary transfers of functions. The objective here is for the boards of county commissioners and the city councils to appraise critically the quality of the public services their jurisdictions are providing. Depending on the findings, they might then agree to relegate to the county the responsibility for such functions as water supply and sewage disposal. Conversely, they might even find that the county should cease providing the municipalities with certain kinds of services.[23]

The Advisory Committee makes many other proposals, but those mentioned illustrate the difficulties of providing administrative services in metropolitan areas. Problems bear little relationship to politi-

[21] *Ibid.*, pp. 24–25.

[22] Judith N. Jamison and Richard Bigger, "Metropolitan Coordination in Los Angeles," *Public Administration Review*, XVII, No. 3 (Summer, 1957), 164–165.

[23] *Government Structure, Organization, and Planning in Metropolitan Areas*, *op. cit.*, pp. 25, 30–31.

cal boundaries. Metropolitan residents are confused by the bewildering pattern of local government, but as yet no firm sense of identification with the metropolitan community as such has developed. Thus, local government officials must do what they can to provide efficient public services—a difficult task.[24]

The "geography of organization" is thus more than a consideration of headquarters–field-office relationships alone. There is also the much bigger problem of how to pool the efforts of many different political jurisdictions, and this undoubtedly will require very serious attention in the coming years.

BIBLIOGRAPHY

Commission on Intergovernmental Relations, *A Report to The President for Transmittal to The Congress,* Washington, D.C.: Government Printing Office, June, 1955.

Fesler, James W., "Field Organization," in Marx, Fritz Morstein (ed.), *Elements of Public Administration,* Englewood Cliffs, N.J.: Prentice-Hall, 1959.

Gant, George F., "The Southern Regional Education Program," *Public Administration Review,* **XII,** No. 2 (Spring, 1952).

Goodrick, M. George, "Integration vs. Decentralization in the Federal Field Service," *Public Administration Review,* **IX,** No. 4 (Autumn, 1949).

Hebal, John J., "Generalist Versus Specialist in the Bureau of Indian Affairs," *Public Administration Review,* **XXI,** No. 1 (Winter, 1961).

House Committee on Government Operations, 85th Congress, 2nd Session, *Federal-State-Local Relations (Federal Grants-In-Aid),* Washington, D.C.: Government Printing Office, 1958.

Intergovernmental Relations Subcommittee of the House Committee on Government Operations and the Senate Committee on Government

[24] See also Victor Jones, "Associations of Local Governments: Patterns for Metropolitan Cooperation," *Public Affairs Report,* Berkeley, Cal.: Bureau of Public Administration, 3, No. 2 (April, 1962).

Operations, 86th Congress, 1st Session. *To Establish An Advisory Commission on Intergovernmental Relations.* Washington, D.C.: Government Printing Office, 1959.

Keenan, Boyd R., "The Midwest's CIC: Experiment in Regional Cooperation," *Public Administration Review*, **XXIII,** No. 1 (March, 1963).

Kruisinga, H. J. (ed.), *The Balance Between Centralization and Decentralization in Managerial Control,* Leiden: H. E. Stenfert Kroese N.V., 1954.

Lepawsky, Albert (ed.), *Administration, The Art and Science of Organization and Management,* New York: Knopf, 1949. Chap. 12.

Metropolitan California, Sacramento, Cal.: Governor's Commission on Metropolitan Area Problems, 1961.

Metropolitan St. Louis Survey, *Path of Progress for Metropolitan St. Louis,* 8124 Delmar Boulevard, University City 24, Mo., August, 1957.

Organization and Management in The Forest Service, Washington, D.C.: Government Printing Office, 1962.

Outdoor Recreation for America, A Report to the President and to Congress by the Outdoor Recreation Resources Review Commission, Washington, D.C.: Government Printing Office, 1962.

Penniman, Clara, "Reorganization and the Internal Revenue Service," *Public Administration Review,* **XXI,** No. 3 (Summer, 1961).

Redford, Emmette S., "Problems of Mobilization Agencies in Establishing Field Organizations," *Public Administration Review,* **XII,** No. 3 (Summer, 1952).

Stein, Harold (ed.), *Public Administration and Policy Development, A Casebook,* New York: Harcourt, Brace, and World, 1952. See cases on federalism and regionalism.

Willbern, York, "Professionalization in the Public Service: Too Little or Too Much?", *Public Administration Review,* **XIV,** No. 1 (Winter, 1954).

CHAPTER 6

The Politics of Organization

Many people believe that building an organization structure is strictly a question of logic, that no matter what the purposes of the organization, there are certain principles which must be followed. Such people profess to see no relationship between the technical questions of organization and disagreements over objectives. Such an approach is unrealistic, to say the least. In the first place, there is the inevitable controversy over whether there is or is not a need for a given organization *to exist* at all. Second, policy disputes may arise over the *formation* of the structure itself; one form may promote one purpose, whereas another might hinder the achievement of this purpose. These disputes originate in differences of opinion as to *which purpose* or purposes the organization is supposed to serve. One group may stand to gain from one set of goals; another group may have quite different objectives in mind. Further, political battles center around the question of who will have *jurisdiction* over the organization, or which agency will ultimately be responsible for its administration. Once an organization has been established, there is the continuous debate over its reorganization, political overhauling, revision of goals and objectives, and whether or not the responsibility for its administration should be shifted to a different governing body.

Consider, for example, the proposed creation of a Department of Urban Affairs, which has been suggested as a federal solution to urban problems across the nation. Those in favor of setting up such an agency argue that this additional executive department would bring long overdue attention to the growing problems of the cities; those opposed believe either that state and local governments are doing well enough, or that existing federal arrangements are adequate (at the time of this writing, this last view has prevailed in Congress). Or consider the controversy which surrounds the determination of responsibility for the Forest Service; there are those who would find it more desirable for this agency to be located in the Department of the Interior, while others favor the present arrangement under the Department of Agriculture. Clearly, then, there can be no question as to the political nature of organization problems.

As might be expected, very few of the controversial aspects of organizational planning and administration are clear-cut, yes-or-no issues. There may be several factions arguing any particular issue, and the real and ostensible reasons behind each interest are highly complex. Probably the best way to present this complexity of the politics of organization is to discuss in detail specific examples taken from the national scene. Three particularly illustrative cases are the creation of the Federal Aviation Agency (FAA) and the National Aeronautics and Space Administration (NASA) and the struggle over administrative control of the Forest Service, to which we have already referred.

THE CASE OF THE FEDERAL AVIATION AGENCY

Originally, the operational, economic, and safety aspects of civilian and commercial aviation were all combined in a single agency—the Civil Aeronautics Authority—as provided in the Civil Aeronautics Act of 1938. In 1940, Congress approved Presidential reorganization plans which provided for two separate entities, a Civil Aeronautics Board (CAB) and a Civil Aeronautics Administration (CAA), the latter being placed in the Department of Commerce. The purpose was to divide the quasi-legislative and the quasi-judicial functions from the day-to-day management of the airways. The responsibility of the CAB was the economic regulation of the commercial-aviation industry, in much the same way as the Interstate Commerce Commission controlled the railroads. The CAB was also responsible for making air-safety rules (quasi-legislative function) and for investigating accidents (quasi-judicial role). The new CAA took over the responsibility for the operations of civilian aircraft, and generally managed the airways, including enforcement of the safety rules.

At the outset, this division of responsibilities seemed to be a decided advantage, for it allowed the CAB to focus entirely upon the economic and regulatory aspects of commercial aviation, while a single agency would similarly be responsible solely for the important task of controlling the air routes. As events soon proved, however, this division of authority was not sound, for the CAA had been given limited powers and comprised only one of the many responsibilities of the Department of Commerce. The latter was in itself a handicap because "buried deep in the Department of Commerce, a conscientious administrator's pleas for even a minimum of urgently required improvements were too often ignored or overruled by disinterested or preoccupied departmental superiors or by economy-minded budget officials."[1] More importantly, the CAA could not on its own assign the use of airspace to all planes in service, especially the military; nor did it have the authority to establish or to supervise a system of air traffic control and navigation aids common to both commercial and military aviation.

The boom in air travel that followed the close of World War II quickly revealed a need for more effective control of the skyways, so, in 1946, an interagency Air Coordinating Committee was established, on which all federal agencies with any interest whatsoever in airspace utilization were represented. The purpose of this Committee was to coordinate the allocation of airlanes to the numerous aircraft and to the agencies responsible for them. Further, in 1947, a House subcommittee had recognized the need for a system of air navigation and traffic-control aids to apply to both civilian and military planes, and thus another interagency body was created, the Air Navigation Development Board, which was composed of representatives of the Departments of both Commerce and Defense. In the Air Coordinating Committee, however, decisions could only be reached by unanimous agreement of its many member agencies, and the conflicting interests of the military and civilian users of airspace had sad consequences

[1] *Federal Aviation Act of 1958*, Senate Report No. 1811, Committee on Interstate and Foreign Commerce, 85th Congress, 2nd Session, Washington, D.C.: Government Printing Office, 1958, p. 6.

for air safety. In the Air Navigation Development Board, each of the departments had the power of veto, which seriously hampered any resolution of the conflicts between civilian and military air interests, and which ultimately resulted in the waste expenditure of millions of dollars in the development and production of navigation devices and equipment.

A major example of the latter problem is the famous TACAN—VOR/DME controversy. VOR/DME refers to the technical navigation and air control devices developed and installed by the CAA as approved by Congress. The military, however, found these unsuitable for their specific needs, and proceeded to develop their own system known as "tactical air navigation," or TACAN. The respective systems of commercial and military aviation were left uncoordinated until each interest had spent much time, effort, and money in completing its projects. As a House Committee emphasized, "the TACAN controversy, no doubt, contributed to delay in the development and installation of a short-range air navigation system to meet the needs of jet-age aviation."[2] The Senate Committee on Interstate and Foreign Commerce was even more frank; referring to the Air Navigation Development Board, it said:

> One of the chief results of this type of 'coordination' was the now famous TACAN–VOR/DME fiasco which involved the expenditure of millions of dollars for the planning and development of a military air-navigation system that was essentially incompatible with the system being developed by civil authorities. As a direct result of these circumstances, the bleak fact is that our airways-control system is largely inadequate for present civil and military needs. This is the price we are now paying for years of diffusion, confusion, and a bargain-basement approach to the problems of aeronautical development.[3]

More disastrous, however, was the lack of coordination of air use between the civilian and military agencies. Existing methods of skyway administration proved hopelessly obsolete in the face of greater and greater numbers of aircraft flying at greater and greater speeds, resulting in a number of mid-air collisions. One of these occurred

[2] *Federal Aviation Act of 1958*, House Report No. 2360, Committee on Interstate and Foreign Commerce, 85th Congress, 2nd Session, Washington, D.C.: Government Printing Office, p. 5.

[3] *Federal Aviation Act of 1958*, Senate Report No. 1811, *op. cit.*, pp. 6–7.

during 1955 between a United Airlines DC-7 and a TWA Constellation over the Grand Canyon, killing all 128 aboard the two planes. Two similar collisions took place early in 1958: An Air Force jet fighter rammed into a United Airlines DC-7 over Las Vegas, Nevada, and all 47 aboard the airliner perished in the crash; a month later, a National Guard jet trainer hit a Capital Airlines Viscount near Brunswick, Maryland, killing an additional 12.

A probe into the Grand Canyon tragedy revealed that "establishment of an airway over the heavily traveled route over the Grand Canyon was being delayed by objections of the military made through an Air Coordinating Committee panel."[4] An investigation into the Las Vegas incident found that a commercial-airway route passed directly over the Nellis Air Force base and as many as 60 commercial flights a day were being made over the base. The supersonic jet trainer was operating under a "local clearance" issued by the base without the knowledge of the nearest CAA control tower.

The Movement for a New Agency

We see, then, that the history of air administration had been riddled with political conflict between military and civilian interests long before the Federal Aviation Agency was created. Additional political pressure was brought to bear on the issue by what John Dewey calls a "new public."[5] By "new public," Dewey means the emergence of definite sentiments by groups of citizens arguing for recognition of new needs for governmental action. Inflamed over the series of air collisions and reports of a host of near misses, this "new public" was no longer satisfied with governmental arrangements for dealing with aviation problems. Pressed by this public outrage, Congress quickly took action on the matter. There were those who believed that the solution lay in the creation of an altogether new agency. These people felt that air transportation had grown enough in volume and importance to warrant a separate and independent agency of its own, rather than to remain among the various responsibilities of the Department of Commerce. Senator Monroney of Oklahoma—Chairman

[4] *Federal Aviation Act of 1958*, House Report No. 2360, *op. cit.*, p. 4.

[5] See John Dewey, *The Public and Its Problems*, N.Y.: Holt, Rinehart and Winston, 1927.

of the Senate Subcommittee on Aviation—was such an advocate. During the hearings held early in 1958 he said:

> An independent agency is absolutely indispensable for the situation that we face in the air traffic control today. It must have its right to present its problems to the Bureau of the Budget or the President, it must have its right to present its problems to the President, and to testify on its own behalf as to aviation's needs without screening by any department that might be its organizational superior. The independence of the new aviation authority is absolutely necessary with the problems that aviation has today. . . . Aviation, which is perhaps the most dynamic element of our economy today, has grown with such great speed and has assumed such stature that only a new organizational structure will completely meet the challenge which we face in the jet age.[6]

The outcome of this movement was the formulation of a Federal Aviation Act of 1958, which provided for a Federal Aviation Agency, and called for the abolishment of the CAA. As outlined in the bill, the new agency would be headed by an administrator who would be appointed by the President, subject to Senate confirmation. Thus, the FAA Administrator would report directly to the President, in the same way as the cabinet secretaries and the heads of other large agencies do. As Senator Monroney has said, the "heart" of the bill is in a section which reads:

> The Administrator is authorized and directed to develop plans for and formulate policy with respect to the use of the navigable airspace; and assign by rule, regulation, or order the use of the navigable airspace under such terms, conditions, and limitations as he may deem necessary in order to insure the safety of aircraft and the efficient utilization of such airspace. He may modify or revoke such assignment when required in the public interest.[7]

The bill also proposed that the FAA be responsible for developing and maintaining a unified system of air navigation and traffic aids, in order to prevent such conflicts as the TACAN fiasco. Originally, the bill gave the FAA the authority to formulate the air-safety rules, but permitted the airlines to appeal to the CAB if a rule promulgated by

[6] *Federal Aviation Agency Act*, hearings before Senate Subcommittee on Aviation, 85th Congress, 2nd Session, Washington, D.C.: Government Printing Office, 1958, pp. 39, 232.

[7] *Federal Aviation Act of 1958*, Senate Report No. 1811, *op. cit.*, pp. 14–15.

the FAA seemed to them to impose an unnecessary economic hardship. This right to appeal, however, was deleted when persons testifying at the Senate and House hearings argued that such potentially numerous appeals would weaken the main objective of the proposed agency.

Reactions to the Proposed Legislation

Both the Defense and Commerce Departments supported these measures; in fact, Malcolm A. MacIntyre, then Under-Secretary of Defense, said he thought the bill represented "an excellent balancing of the civil and military interests involved in national aviation, with the objective of achieving joint planning and greater safety and efficiency in the use of airspace."[8] However, since the proposed agency severely limited its powers, the CAB—as represented by its Chairman, James R. Durfee—protested vehemently. Although Durfee favored the creation of a "single aviation agency responsible for the research, development, installation, maintenance, and operation of aviation facilities and services relating to air traffic control. . .,"[9] he strongly opposed the authority that would be given to the FAA both to formulate and to enforce air safety rules. Durfee argued that the rulemaking involved questions which were better resolved by the five-man CAB than by any single administrator, as called for in the proposed bill. Further, there were the economic considerations previously mentioned; the FAA would be given the power to make and to enforce safety measures that could impose financial hardships on the commercial airlines. Durfee stressed, "it is obvious that standards could be established which would further enhance safety but at a price that few could afford to fly."[10] Here he was arguing for the provision of right of appeal to the CAB. Durfee failed to convince Congress, however; the Senate Committee's counter was that:

> The theory that rulemaking is to be done only by a body of judicially minded, disinterested laymen applies well in the field of economic regulation. There the problem is one of balancing competing business interests; technical problems, if existent, are largely incidental. The theory tends

[8] *Federal Aviation Act of 1958*, House Report No. 2360, *op. cit.*, p. 23.
[9] *Ibid.*, p. 24.
[10] *Ibid.*, p. 26.

to break down, however, when applied to the promulgation of minimum aviation standards. Here, the competition, if any, is between men and machines; the standard to be applied being principally determined by existing technical considerations. Competing economic interests may indeed be involved, but here it is that they are incidental.[11]

Finally, on August 23, 1958, the Federal Aviation Act was approved. Thus, we see in the creation of the FAA, and in the background which led up to it, a good example of the politics of organization. Not only did the conflicting interests of civilian and military aviation comprise a substantial political difficulty, but we see also how the concerns of the public are involved in a greatly influential way. The "old public" had, prior to the series of air disasters, been content to leave the situation to those already entrusted with air administration—namely, the CAB and the CAA—and to separate the military arrangements. The widely publicized hazards of the existing situation and the famous TACAN controversy effected a sizeable change in the public mind, however, and gave rise to the "new public," which brought pressure upon Congress to reevaluate aviation administration and to take corrective measures. Those persons who still resisted the innovations, such as the Chairman of the CAB, represented the "dying public."

THE CASE OF THE NATIONAL AERONAUTICS AND SPACE ADMINISTRATION

The history of the National Aeronautics and Space Administration provides another very good example of the power struggles which underlie decisions on organizational questions. As in the foregoing illustration, military interests conflict with civilian interests in this case; these conflicts are further compounded by rivalries *within* the military. But here, too, public pressures on space issues have played a dominant role in influencing governmental action. As we have seen, mid-air collisions spurred Congress into action which led to the creation of a new aviation agency; similarly, the two Russian Sputniks, successfully launched in late 1957, startled the American public—accustomed to seeing its country first in scientific advances—out of its relative complacency into a new and active interest.

[11] *Federal Aviation Act of 1958*, Senate Report No. 1811, *op. cit.*, pp. 10–11.

Although the United States had maintained a space program, it obviously had not been pushed fast enough. All three branches of the Defense Department—the Air Force, the Navy, and the Army—had been doing research and development in the space field, and were preparing to launch satellites. On the civilian side, the National Advisory Committee for Aeronautics (NACA) had also been active. But the spectacular successes of the Sputniks clearly revealed that these space programs were lagging in comparison with Russian plans, and a chagrined Congress quickly resolved to change the situation.

The problem—one which opened the path to political rivalries—was where to allocate the responsibility within the administrative branch for space problems. Should the Defense Department be placed in charge of both the military and the civilian aspects, or conversely, should the whole space effort be placed under a civilian agency? If the latter, there was still the question of whether to turn space issues over to the existing NACA or to create a new agency for the purpose. Answers to these problems were particularly difficult since it is hard to draw a line between peaceful and military uses of outer space: "Practically every peaceful use of outer space appears to have a military application. For example, the military establishment is concerned with weather control, all forms of communication, reconnaissance satellites for mapping; and even medical research on weightlessness has implications for satellite weapons."[12]

As a purely temporary solution, Congress passed legislation giving the responsibility for both civilian and military aspects of space exploration to the Defense Department for a period of one year. This left the permanent allocation of responsibility wide open to competitive bidding among various interested agencies. Through its chairman, James H. Doolittle, NACA "made a strong bid in January [1958] to assume responsibility for space programs. So did the Pentagon, the National Science Foundation, and the National Academy of Science."[13] In addition, Senator Anderson of New Mexico, then Vice Chairman of the Joint Congressional Committee on Atomic Energy, had already introduced a bill to put the space program under the Atomic Energy Commission. The battle was on.

[12] *National Aeronautics and Space Act*, Part 2, hearings before Senate Special Committee on Space and Astronautics, 85th Congress, 2nd Session, Washington, D.C.: Government Printing Office, 1958, p. 383.

[13] *New York Times*, March 30, 1958.

Thus, while we shall not endeavor to discuss the details of the arguments put forth by these competing agencies, we see that the very nature of space problems helped to create strong political issues. The central question with which Congress was concerned, however, was that of military vs. civilian control. Members of Senate and House committees questioned leading scientists and others prominent in the space field as to the dividing line, if any, between military and civilian applications. A characteristic exchange occurred between Senator Lyndon B. Johnson and Roy W. Johnson, Director of the Advanced Research Projects Agency (ARPA) in the Defense Department.

SENATOR JOHNSON: The Atomic Energy Commission is given by statute the power to develop research in atomic weapons for the Department of Defense, is it not?

MR. JOHNSON: That is correct.

SENATOR JOHNSON: Would you agree to a change in the act transferring this power to the Department of Defense?

MR. JOHNSON: I would not, sir.

SENATOR JOHNSON: Would you recommend giving the space agency [proposed in a Senate bill] the power to do all the research and development of weapons for the Department of Defense, then?

MR. JOHNSON: I would not, sir.

SENATOR JOHNSON: How do you reconcile those two positions?

MR. JOHNSON: I think we have two quite different problems.

SENATOR JOHNSON: Would you elaborate on that?

MR. JOHNSON: I think we have in the space situation many more complex things that we do not know about and we must learn more about. I think we have in outer space a new possibility of attack from an enemy. I think that in space we are involved not only with a new atmosphere to work in, we are involved with a whole new system of transportation, and I think in nuclear energy we have a narrower, a much narrower thing to deal with.[14]

It should be made clear that the head of the ARPA was not advocating complete military control of the space program, but only that if a new agency were created, nothing should be done to interfere with the military's research and development efforts in the space field.

[14] *National Aeronautics and Space Act,* Part 1, hearings before Senate Special Committee on Space and Astronautics, *op. cit.*, pp. 149–150.

The National Aeronautics and Space Act of 1958

In the end, Congress decided on a compromise solution. In July, 1958, NASA was created. Although it was to be under civilian direction, it was clearly stated that the Defense Department would continue to be responsible for "activities peculiar to or primarily associated with the development of weapon systems, military operations, or the defense of the United States (including the research and development necessary to make effective provision for the defense of the United States)."[15] Like the FAA, NASA was to be an independent agency, reporting directly to the President. At the same time, a National Aeronautics and Space Council was also established, the principal membership of which consisted of the President (now replaced by the Vice President), who served as chairman, the Secretaries of Defense and State, the NASA Administrator, and the Chairman of the Atomic Energy Commission. The legislation instructed the Space Council to "provide for effective cooperation" between NASA and the Defense Department, and to specify which space activities could be "carried on concurrently by both such agencies notwithstanding the assignment of primary responsibility therefor to one or the other of such agencies."[16]

Space Rivalries

Such "effective cooperation," however, was difficult in practice. Not only was there competition between NASA and the military, but there also were internal rivalries in the Defense Department between the Army, the Navy, and the Air Force. Each wished to pursue space projects on its own: the Army fought to keep control of its rocket team at the Huntsville, Alabama missile agency, and its contracts for space and missile research with the Jet Propulsion Laboratory at Pasadena; the Air Force pressed for the dominant role within the Defense Department in space activities; and the Navy was loath to relinquish its various satellite projects. The services quickly began to

[15] Public Law 85–568, 85th Congress, H.R. 12575, July 29, 1958. See Section 102 (b).
[16] *Ibid.*, Section 201 (e).

duplicate one another's efforts. Both the Army and the Air Force proceeded with work on communications satellites, an area the Navy was also pursuing in addition to its development of a navigation satellite. The Navy was also planning to put up a reconnaissance satellite which would compete with the Air Force's *Samos*. Further, not only was each military branch competing with the other two, but all three were overlapping the activities of NASA. The Navy, for example, was working on a weather satellite which would directly vie with NASA's *Tiros*.

For a few months after the creation of NASA, the Army was successful in keeping its Huntsville missile agency. However, NASA maintained that this facility, as well as the Army's contracts with the Jet Propulsion Laboratory, should be transferred to its own jurisdiction, arguing that the military could afford to have only one service with a "space mission," and that the Air Force was virtually assured of that role. When the Air Force exercised the dominant role within the Defense Department, the Army could be expected to run out of big missile and space projects. Therefore, it was logical to transfer the rocket team to the civilian space agency where it would have greater scope. Late in 1958, President Eisenhower ordered a compromise, letting the Army keep the Huntsville facility for the time being, but giving NASA control over the Jet Propulsion Laboratory.

The picture changed when, in 1959, Secretary of Defense Neil McElroy issued an order giving the Air Force the primary responsibility for military space activities. Specifically, this directive provided that, eventually, the Air Force would have complete responsibility for the launching of all military research and test vehicles into space, which meant that the Army could no longer make a strong case for retaining the rocket team. Late in 1959, by a presidential reorganization plan approved by Congress, Eisenhower transferred the rocket team to NASA. One big chapter in the power struggle over space had ended. The Air Force and NASA were the joint victors over the Army.

However, McElroy's order was not so tightly worded as to terminate all duplicating of space activities within the military. Before taking office as the new President, Kennedy appointed an *ad hoc* committee to report on the space problems he would confront in office. Among the statements this committee issued in January, 1961, was that "each of the military services has begun to create its own independent space program. This presents the problem of overlapping programs and duplication of the work of NASA."[17]

The new Secretary of Defense, Robert S. McNamara, issued an order in March, 1961 making more definite the Air Force's control over military space development. It provided that, "except under unusual circumstances [all] space development programs and projects" were to be assigned to the Air Force. It was made clear, however, that the Navy would keep its transit navigation-satellite program and the Army its *Advent* communications-satellite project. Shortly thereafter, McNamara assigned to the Air Force the responsibility for developing and operating all reconnaissance-satellite systems. In June, 1962, the Army *Advent* project was shut down, and the Air Force directed to take over development, production, and launching of a new, lighter, communication satellite. Finally, much of the duplication in space activities within the Defense Department was thus eliminated.

Some military men still insist that the Defense Department should have the entire space program. Major General J.B. Medaris of the United States Army told members of a House committee early in 1960, "We are trying, gentlemen, to divide the indivisible." In his opinion, there was ample precedent for the military to be in charge of civilian as well as military programs. How about the activities of the Army Corps of Engineers in improving navigation and in building flood control works? And was it not true that the Signal Corps had operated the communications system in Alaska? Further, had the committee forgotten that the Army was in charge of civilian administration of the Panama Canal?[18]

On the other hand, Dr. William H. Pickering, Director of the Jet Propulsion Laboratory, expressed concern that there was "an increasing tendency for military applications to dominate the space picture."[19] He felt that NASA and the military were competing "for relatively scarce manpower and facilities as well as dollars." The re-

[17] *Ad Hoc* Committee on Space, "Report to the President-Elect," January 12, 1961, p. 3.

[18] *Review of the Space Program,* (No. 3, P. 2), hearings before House Committee on Science and Astronautics, 86th Congress, 2nd Session, Washington, D.C.: Government Printing Office, 1960, pp. 811–812.

[19] *Ibid.,* (No. 3, P. 3), pp. 898–899.

sulting "duplication and competition" could prove very costly to the nation. He argued that the NASA should be in charge of a unified program, with complete responsibility for all basic space research, both for civilian and military purposes. Pickering maintained that a civilian agency with these powers would not neglect military security needs, and that the efficient way of organizing the space program was to put NASA in complete control, with the military applications evolving out of the accomplishments of the civilian space effort. Furthermore, he was skeptical that in future warfare, space weapons could be fired effectively from satellites.

Congress could not agree with the points of view as expressed by either General Medaris or Dr. Pickering. In the case of the latter, they were particularly concerned about putting all space research into the hands of a civilian agency when the Russians might be planning to establish battle stations in outer space. Yet, every time the Russians achieve new space successes, the military becomes restless, and argues that the United States military space program is inadequate without greater military control. President Kennedy flatly refused to grant a larger role to the military, however, and thus, Congress decided to continue the system of shared responsibility, hoping for greater cooperation between the military and NASA.

Considering the circumstances, the relations between NASA and the military are now generally cooperative. Technical committees on which both are represented attempt to eliminate duplication of effort in specific project areas. In addition, NASA has recently come into its own, having a much bigger share of the space budget as compared to its early days, and enjoying far more publicity of a favorable nature. Some overlapping of efforts continues, naturally, since a single space agency was never approved. Both NASA and the Defense Department carry out basic space research and satellite programs, but this is inevitable due to the previously mentioned lack of clear demarcation between military and civilian applications of space exploration. Conflicts, too, still exist, occurring primarily between the Air Force and NASA. But many observers believe that this competitive situation in space efforts has actually been beneficial to the nation's overall progress. Even the history of duplication of activities, they feel, has promoted rather than retarded progress, for suppose the country had looked to a completely unified program administered by a single agency—and the agency had failed in its goals? The many different groups of scientists, these observers suggest, have served to correct one another in scientific experimentation.

THE CASE OF THE FOREST SERVICE STRUGGLE

As we noted at the start of this chapter, the political struggle over the Forest Service that took place between the Departments of Agriculture and Interior is another excellent example of the politics of organization, and particularly reveals the tactics frequently employed by opposing interest groups. It also demonstrates the role sometimes played by strong individual leaders in administrative politics; that is, when an individual has a personal interest at stake, he can sometimes win a great deal of political support by capitalizing on the public issues and utilizing the interest groups in the field of national policy concerned. Although the Forest Service issue has been dead since 1940, the political war waged by the two Departments covered a span of about 60 years. A key figure in the struggle during most of this period was Gifford Pinchot, whose personal interest in forest conservation was a dominant factor throughout the controversy.

Even as late as 1891 there were no national forests. Ten years earlier, Congress had established a tiny unit, called the Division of Forestry, in the Department of Agriculture as a result of a detailed report on the nation's forests, but it had not authorized national forest reserves. In 1891, Congress finally gave the President authority to set aside 13 million acres of forest land for such reserves, but it made no "provision for administering the reserves or for keeping them in good shape."[20] Unrestricted grazing was allowed, and "thieves often found it easy to cut and remove some of the finest timber."[21] Pinchot was among those who urged that this situation be corrected, arguing that even more timber land should be set aside, and that a plan should be developed for the efficient management of all the reserves. In the subsequent years, the nation's reserves were expanded, but in 1897 Congress passed legislation giving Interior, not Agriculture, essential control over all the reserves.

[20] M. Nelson McGeary, *Gifford Pinchot: Forester, Politician*, Princeton, N.J.: Princeton Univ. Press, 1960, p. 36.

[21] *Ibid.*, p. 37.

Pinchot was hired by the Secretary of Interior to make a study of the reserves, and to prepare a detailed proposal for organization of a national forest service. At first, Pinchot was not particularly concerned with the question of which department should have the responsibility for the timber lands; his primary concern was only that conservation measures be fully implemented. His experience in the Department of Interior, however, soon convinced him that this was not the place for his beloved forests. McGeary relates that the more Pinchot "learned about the Department of Interior, however, the more distrustful he became of the general philosophy of its personnel. As the months and years passed he became convinced that, with exceptions here and there, the Interior Department tended to be more interested in methods of giving away government land than in protecting it for the general use and welfare."[22]

Shortly after Pinchot completed his report in 1897, a vacancy developed in the position of head of the still existing Division of Forestry in the Department of Agriculture, and the Secretary of Agriculture promptly offered the post to Pinchot. Pinchot accepted and immediately began a campaign to get the forest reserves transferred to the Department of Agriculture. Although he was successful in enlarging the Division and in increasing its budget appropriations, Pinchot was at first frustrated in his attempts to obtain control of the forests. Powerful interests opposed to conservation wanted the Interior Department to retain control over the reserves. Interior had the legal authority to prevent "timber grabbing and forest devastation," but it was lax in the enforcement of the law. As McGeary describes the situation, "those who stood to gain by unmolested sawing and cutting and grazing, sensing that forests under Pinchot would be more vigorously protected than forests under the General Land Office, strained every muscle to defeat the transfer."[23] The General Land Office was the unit in Interior which had been placed in charge of the reserves.

Undaunted, Pinchot and his followers devoted their efforts to convincing dozens of different associations to pass resolutions which recommended the transfer of the reserves to Agriculture. Although these attempts met with increasing success, the picture brightened

[22] *Ibid.*, p. 44.
[23] *Ibid.*, p. 52.

considerably when Theodore Roosevelt became President. Not only was Roosevelt an ardent conservationist himself, but he was also an intimate friend of Pinchot. Even before Roosevelt moved into the White House, Pinchot went to see him, urging him to recommend to Congress that the Forestry Bureau (the title had been changed from Division to Bureau, due to its increased size) be given full responsibility for managing the government's forests. Roosevelt obliged, but Congress was not yet ready to act. Planning his moves carefully, Pinchot sought more allies for his point of view. In 1900, he organized the Society of American Foresters, whose meetings proved to be a "major factor in developing a sense of comradeship and an *esprit de corps* among the foresters attached to the Bureau of Forestry."[24] Further, now well practiced in legislative contacts, Pinchot sought out key members of Congress.

Roosevelt cooperated at every turn. On one occasion, he invited some Congressmen to lunch at the White House in order " 'to give [Pinchot] a chance at them on the transfer bill'. " On another, he invited one of the wealthiest lumber barons in the country to confer with him at the White House, with Pinchot present. This meeting was deliberately scheduled to take place one month before a convention of the National Lumber Manufacturers' Association. Roosevelt's plan was to get the movement for forest conservation to come from the lumbermen themselves, and he succeeded in persuading his guests to support the reserve policy.

Pinchot was astute in using support wherever he could get it. Bitter disputes frequently broke out between the different private interests using the national forests for grazing purposes. Land feuds, sometimes terminating in shooting or other forms of violence, were not uncommon. The cattlemen resented "encroachments" on their holdings by sheepmen and by small homesteaders. They erected fences to keep out the invaders and resorted to other strong measures, all of which shocked the public and led to a movement to stop all grazing in the national forests. Playing his cards carefully, Pinchot "joined in publicly denouncing big stockmen, but at the same time sought and obtained their support for the transfer."[25] Pinchot had never believed that the forest lands should simply be set aside and

[24] *Ibid.*, p. 57.
[25] *Ibid.*, p. 59.

not used in any way by private interests. Since he favored continuation of grazing and even the legalizing of fences, "the cattle barons" now decided that it would be politic for them to support him in the transfer issue.

The high point in Pinchot's campaign came in 1905 when he organized a meeting of the American Forest Congress in Washington, D.C. McGeary explains Pinchot's real purpose as follows:

> Billed as a kind of parliament for representatives of groups interested in forests, the Congress convened for five days. Among the delegates were influential foresters, lumbermen, miners, railroad men, wool growers, and men representing the grazing and irrigation interests. Pinchot, designating Roosevelt as honorary president of the Congress, induced his boss, Secretary of Agriculture Wilson, to act as president, and his father, James Pinchot, as first vice-president. The meeting, packed with persons favorable to forest conservation, was primarily a propaganda device for demonstrating to Congress and the country the sizable amount of support that had been built up for practical forestry.
>
> With the aid of the astute publicity unit of Pinchot's Bureau, news releases concerning the meeting were circulated throughout the nation. The *Brooklyn Daily Eagle*, for example, on the day before the Congress met, devoted an entire page to the meetings and to the general subject of forestry. Readers of the *Eagle* and of many other newspapers were reminded that if the current rate of timber cutting continued, the nation's forests would be exhausted in about sixty years.[26]

The Forest Congress passed a resolution favoring the transfer, and victory was finally at hand for Pinchot. Less than a month later, the transfer bill was passed in both houses of the United States Congress and quickly signed by President Roosevelt. Overnight Pinchot "was transformed from a man with some foresters but no forests, into a man with 86 million acres of forest land." Shortly thereafter, the title of the Bureau was changed to United States Forest Service, and the reserves were designated as "national forests."

The Later Revival of the Controversy

This was not to be the end of the issue, however; years later, in the 1930s, it was revived, when Franklin D. Roosevelt named as his

[26] *Ibid.*, p. 60.

Secretary of Interior Harold Ickes, a man of strong opinions and many enemies, but whose personal integrity was above question. Ickes was determined to erase the public image of Interior as a venal department; a hard worker, he set high standards for his subordinates and was strict in holding them to account. Under Ickes, Interior became a respectable department. In the process of building it up, Ickes became convinced that it should become a Department of Conservation, with complete responsibility for all federal natural resource programs. Schlesinger writes, "the keystone for such a department, as he saw it, had to be the Forest Service. From his first days in Interior, Ickes therefore embarked on an interminable campaign of intrigue, persuasion, and pressure designed to recapture Forestry from Agriculture."[27]

At this time, Pinchot was still very active in public life; in fact, when FDR became President, Pinchot was the Republican Governor of Pennsylvania. Ickes and Pinchot were good friends, but as soon as Ickes' plan to take over the Forest Service became clear, the personal relations between the two men deteriorated. Pinchot never questioned Ickes' integrity, but he reasoned that Ickes could not live forever—and then what would happen to the Forest Service in an Interior Department so tarnished with past history of scandals? After all, Harding's Secretary of Interior, Albert B. Fall, had "auctioned off some of the nation's prize oil reserves" to private interests. Fall had tried to "recapture the Forest Service from Henry C. Wallace in order to increase the available loot."[28]

Ickes argued that this was all part of the past and should be forgotten. He felt strongly that so many programs had been taken away from Interior that few of its "vital organs" remained. A real fighter, he even proposed a trade of bureaus with Agriculture Secretary Henry A. Wallace. He was ready to cede to Agriculture such bureaus as Reclamation, General Land Office, Grazing, Soil Erosion, and Subsistence Homesteads in exchange for Forestry, Roads, and the Biological Survey. Schlesinger writes that for a time in March, 1934, Wallace was inclined to agree to this most unusual proposal, but the Forest Service objected so strenuously that Wallace "turned against

[27] Arthur M. Schlesinger, Jr., *The Coming of the New Deal*, Boston: Houghton Mifflin, 1959, p. 346.

[28] *Ibid.*, p. 344.

the package deal."[29] Pinchot, it should be mentioned, was doing his best to help the Forest Service in this fight. He completed his second term of office as Governor of Pennsylvania at the end of 1934. Defeated in his bid for the Republican nomination for the Senate, he had retired to private life, but still maintained his old interests. In June, 1935, Pinchot wrote in his diary: "Saw Harold who is red hot to get Dept. Cons. I'm again (*sic*) it strong." Back to work he went, trying to arouse the country against the Ickes' plan. In a letter to the newspapers, he warned that "the National Forests are again in danger." Before mailing the letter, he explained to Ickes that he "hate(d) like the devil" to be against him, but that he had to follow his conscience. However, as Ickes persisted in his plan, Pinchot dropped the amenities, and Ickes responded in kind. In a speech given in April, 1937, at the national convention of the Izaak Walton League, Pinchot charged that Ickes had allowed his ambition to impair his good judgment and that it was his desire for more power that made him want the Forest Service.[30] Ickes inveighed against Pinchot as " 'the self-anointed Messiah of conservation' who had posed too long 'as the infallible, the impeccable, and the omnipotent conservationist of all time'."[31]

FDR's attitude during this controversy was basically to keep out of it. In principle, he seems to have supported Ickes' side of the argument, but he did not think the matter important enough to make a major issue of it with Congress. In FDR's opinion, Interior had been created to take care of the public lands and Agriculture to help those farming privately owned lands; logically, this placed the Forest Service in Interior. The President did not think that anybody could any longer say that the Interior Department was "utterly black and crooked."[32] FDR appeared undecided for a long time, but as Schlesinger noted: "Yet, for all the troubles this competition created, it also spurred each Department to redouble its efforts in the conservation cause—a fact which may too have entered into Roosevelt's calculations."[33]

[29] *Ibid.*, p. 347.
[30] McGeary, *op. cit.*, pp. 410–411.
[31] Schlesinger, *op. cit.*, p. 347.
[32] *Ibid.*, p. 349.
[33] *Ibid.*

In 1938, Congress shelved a bill pushed by Ickes which would have converted Interior into a Department of Conservation and Works. The battle was almost over, but not quite, since in 1939 Congress passed a Reorganization Act under which the President could make the switch by proposing a reorganization plan to Congress. In January 1940, the President wrote Pinchot a letter suggesting that he might be leaning towards Ickes' point of view. FDR was irked because Pinchot had inspired faculty members of forestry schools to send the White House a batch of antitransfer letters.

Pinchot showed FDR's letter to Supreme Court Justice Felix Frankfurter "who agreed that the President was angry but doubted if he would take any action. To make doubly certain, however, Pinchot addressed an antitransfer letter to every congressman and senator." Finally, in February, 1940, newspapermen could assure Pinchot that the transfer move was dead.[34]

Today the Forest Service is securely in Agriculture, but disputes of this kind involving other agencies still remain a commonplace of the national scene. In a letter written to a friend in 1904, Pinchot himself made this revealing comment:

> So much of my time is necessarily given to the political side of the subject, to looking after the appropriations of the Bureau, trying to convince Senators and Representatives that forestry is to their advantage, and addressing public meetings of lumbermen and others, that I am almost beginning to fear that I may cease to be a forester altogether.[35]

The "politics of organization" is also very much in evidence in state and local governments. The same alliances and conflicts exist among administrative agencies, pressure groups, individual legislators, and interested citizens. As Wallace S. Sayre has summarized this so well: "Organization theory in public administration is a problem in political strategy; a choice of organization structure is a choice of which interest or which value will have preferred access or greater emphasis."[36]

[34] McGeary, *op. cit.*, pp. 411–412.
[35] *Ibid.*, p. 60.
[36] Wallace S. Sayre, "Premises of Public Administration: Past and Emerging," *Public Administration Review*, XVIII, No. 2 (Spring, 1958), 104.

BIBLIOGRAPHY

Aviation Facilities Planning, Final Report by the President's Special Assistant, Washington, D.C.: Government Printing Office, 1957.

Dalton, Melville, *Men Who Manage*, New York: J. Wiley, 1959. Analyzes power struggles in a private company.

House Committee on Interstate and Foreign Commerce, 85th Congress, 2nd Session, *Federal Aviation Act of 1958* (Report No. 2360), Washington, D.C.: Government Printing Office, 1958.

House Committee on Science and Astronautics, 86th Congress, 2nd Session, *Review of the Space Program* (No. 3, Parts I, II, and III), Washington, D.C.: Government Printing Office, 1960.

House Subcommittee on Interstate and Foreign Commerce, 85th Congress, 2nd Session, *Federal Aviation Act* (Hearings on HR. 12616), Washington, D.C.: Government Printing Office, 1958.

Long, Norton E., "Power and Administration," *Public Administration Review*, **IX**, No. 4 (Autumn, 1949).

Millett, John D., "Concepts of Organization," in Marx, Fritz Morstein (ed.), *Elements of Public Administration*, Englewood Cliffs, N.J.: Prentice-Hall, 1959.

Pfiffner, John M., and Sherwood, Frank P., *Administrative Organization*, Englewood Cliffs, N.J.: Prentice-Hall, 1960. Chap. 17, Power and Politics.

Rourke, Francis E., "The Politics of Administrative Organization," *Journal of Politics*, **XIX**, No. 3 (August, 1957).

Senate Committee on Interstate and Foreign Commerce, 85th Congress, 2nd Session, *Federal Aviation Act of 1958* (Report No. 1811), Washington, D.C.: Government Printing Office, 1958.

Senate Special Committee on Space and Astronautics, 85th Congress, 2nd Session, *National Aeronautics and Space Act* (Hearings on S. 3609, Parts I and II), Washington, D.C.: Government Printing Office, 1958.

Senate Special Committee on Space and Astronautics, 85th Congress, 2nd Session, Report No. 1701, *National Aeronautics and Space Act of 1958*, Washington, D.C.: Government Printing Office, 1958.

Senate Subcommittee on Aviation, 85th Congress, 2nd Session, *Federal Aviation Agency Act* (Hearings on S. 3880), Washington, D.C.: Government Printing Office, 1958.

Somit, Albert, "Bureaucratic Realpolitik and the Teaching of Administration," *Public Administration Review*, **XVI,** No. 4 (Autumn, 1956).

Stein, Harold (ed.), *Public Administration and Policy Development, A Casebook*, New York: Harcourt, Brace, and World, 1952. See "The Transfer of the Children's Bureau," "The Office of Education Library," "The Air Search and Rescue Program," and "The Kings River Project."

CHAPTER 7

Informal Organization

An organization is more than its structure and its official relationships as spelled out in its organization charts and manuals. The basic units of any human organization are the individual and the groups with which the individual is associated; thus, every organization is also a social system in which its members develop patterns of behavior which actually may deviate from official directives. This is called the "informal organization," and an appreciation of its role is indispensable to the understanding of the functioning of any agency, public or private. The following distinctions should be made:

The Human Organization: refers, on the one hand, to the concrete individual with his rich personal and social background, and, on the other hand, to the intricate pattern of social relations existing among the various individuals and groups within the [agency].

The Individual: refers to the sentiments and values which the person is bringing to the work situation because of his past social conditioning and present social situation outside of the [agency]: i.e., the past and present patterns of interaction in which he has participated or is participating outside of work.

Social Organization: refers to the actual patterns of interaction existing within and between employee groups, supervisory groups, and management groups in an [agency] here and now. It will include those relations that remain at a common human level (friendships, antagonisms, etc.), those that have been built up into larger social configurations (social codes, customs, traditions, routines, and associated ideas and beliefs), as well as those patterns of relations formally prescribed by the rules, regulations, practices, and policies of the [agency].

Formal Organization: refers to those patterns of interaction prescribed by the rules and regulations of the [agency] as well as to the policies which prescribe the relations that obtain, or are supposed to obtain, within the human organization and between the human organization and the technical organization.

Informal Organization: refers to the actual personal inter-relations existing among the members of the organization which are not represented by, or are inadequately represented by, the formal organization.[1]

The formal organization prescribes what interpersonal relationships *ought to be*; the informal organization tells us what they *actually are*. The former can tell us nothing about the activities of the small groups to which the individual workers attach themselves, yet it is in these groups that resistance to the edicts of administration sometimes develops. The formal organization applies rational criteria in terms of work goals and methods, and it places emphasis on efficiency, reduction of costs, and increase of worker output.

DISPARITIES BETWEEN FORMAL AND INFORMAL ORGANIZATION OBJECTIVES

With the help of Harvard University, the Western Electric Company in the late 1920s and early 1930s conducted extensive research in order to identify the factors in the work situation which affected morale and efficiency. The results of these experiments revealed essentially that management had been making too many assumptions about how the workers ought to react. In one experiment, the activities of a small group of men engaged in making parts of telephone switches were observed. In order to increase production, these men were compensated in accordance with a piece-rate system which management considered fair to the workers, without imposing upon them undue physical strain; if they cooperated in the logical terms set by management, their own best interests would be served. (At the time this research was conducted, it was common practice to try to

[1] F. J. Roethlisberger and William J. Dickson, *Management and the Worker*, Cambridge: Harvard Univ. Press, 1939, pp. 565–567. The word *agency* has been substituted for the words *plant* or *company*.

increase production by making fatigue studies and introducing such correctives as rest pauses and economic incentives.) Yet these men refused to increase their production, but, rather, agreed among themselves to set output at a certain daily level which, in their judgment, was entirely adequate. If, on any one day, one of them did happen to exceed this group-determined norm, he simply failed to report the excess, reserving it—frequently with the tacit approval of the foreman—for a future report. The men's attitude was based on a strong feeling that if production went up, some jobs might be eliminated, or wage rates cut—despite the fact that management had assured them that this would not happen, and that there was no previous evidence to indicate that it would. The foreman, although his position represents management, must associate with the workers, and he is doomed to an uncomfortable existence if he provokes their scorn. Therefore, he is inclined to keep much from management.

Management was using logical arguments in an area where the workers, members of a small, closely knit group, were typically ruled by sentiments. In effect, management had been making decisions with no real awareness of the existence and the strength of these sentiments. Specifically, the researchers discovered that the members of this small group were governed by the following code:

1. You should not turn out too much work. If you do, you are a "rate buster."
2. You should not turn out too little work. If you do, you are a "chiseler."
3. You should not tell a supervisor anything that will react to the detriment of an associate. If you do, you are a "squealer."
4. You should not attempt to maintain social distance or act officious. If, for example, you are an inspector, you should not act like one.[2]

The significant fact behind item 2 was that the group was compensated as a unit for the pieces of equipment it produced. If any one worker slackened up on the job, this could reduce the earnings of all members of the group. So, while the group resisted management's desire for increased output, it also acted to stabilize production at existing levels. Item 3 illustrates the group's function in protecting itself against the management. "Squealers" were ridiculed and ostra-

[2] *Ibid.*, p. 522.

cized. Item 4 can be explained by the fact that the very essence of a small group is that its members can freely mingle with one another without any consciousness of social barriers or other distinctions separating them from one another.

Social distance measures the closeness of the relationship, not only between the individual employees in a group, but also between the different kinds of workers that make up the entire organization. If someone holds himself aloof from the rest of the group, he is in effect breaking with them and consequently becomes disliked by them. Social distance separates shop from office personnel, junior from senior executives, and so on. In this social stratification, status symbols —such as desirable office space, handsome desks, and other evidences of the worker's importance in the organization—play an important part. All this characterizes the organization as a social system, and thus, changes in work procedures made by management which disrupt the existing social relationships between the workers, or which make them feel less important, will not produce the desired result. No matter how sensible piece-rate systems may seem to the management, they often have an inherently disadvantageous impact on the informal organization. Because they apply for the most part to the lower echelons, they "tend to subordinate the worker still further in the company's social structure."[3] In general, then, this experiment revealed that the management had erred in assuming that the worker responded to economic incentives only, and that the only limitations on his output were physiological.

In another experiment, a group of five girls engaged in assembling telephone relays were placed in a special test room, apart from all other workers. The job of these girls was to remove 40 tiny parts from trays and put them together. For a period of two years, changes were deliberately made in the physical conditions under which they worked to note the effect on their rate of production. Sometimes the lighting was improved or made worse; rest pauses were introduced and then eliminated. Yet, even when working conditions were changed unfavorably, production did not go down; in fact, it increased.

This reaction was baffling; it seemed as though the company could

[3] *Ibid.*, p. 546.

make almost any kind of change in the conditions under which the girls worked without their reacting negatively. This was just the opposite from the experience the management had with the men operating under the group piece-work system referred to above, in which it seemed that the company could make no change without arousing opposition. It was only when the role of the informal organization in each group had been accurately diagnosed that the picture became clear. Because the girls had been selected for an important experiment and been given special status by being placed in the test room, they felt much more important; they were glad to cooperate with a management which treated them with such consideration. The informal organization of this group functioned in harmony with the formal organization. The Hawthorne researchers had found the key to the problem: in the future, management would have to weigh proposed changes, not only in terms of their technological soundness, but also of their impact on the informal organization.

At this point, the question may be asked, "Is not the case of government different? Why should there be conflicts between the formal and informal organization in public agencies?" It is true that the Western Electric Company exists to make profits, while the government does not; it is also true that few government operations are of an assembly-line nature. Just as in business, however, the top managers of government agencies apply rational considerations in defining work objectives and methods. Yet they may not, in fact, be as rational as they think they are in establishing standards for the workers. Management applies its own logic and its edicts may conflict head on with the values of the informal organization. Changes in office space, layout, or in the arrangements for employee parking space, the introduction of automated equipment—all may be desirable from an administrative view, yet opposed by the employees. As one example only, a prison warden may want to emphasize rehabilitation of the inmates. This approach may seem strange to those prison guards who feel strongly that the inmates should be treated with an iron hand. To be successful, the management of any enterprise must be aware of possible resistance by the informal organization and do what it can to cope with such resistance. It must also know how to make the fullest possible use of the forces in the small work groups which can promote agency objectives.

CHARACTERISTICS OF SMALL GROUPS

In addition to an awareness of worker resistances and the particular forces among the various segments of the organization's employees that can be used to management's advantage, the administrative structure and policy should take into consideration the basic dynamics of any small group, which we shall define as follows:

> A small group is composed of the interrelationships of a limited number of people—with no firm upper limit on the number of members—who have developed shared ways of perceiving their environment and of behaving within it.[4]

These interrelationships and shared perceptions lead to common experiences, friendships, reciprocal favors, and stratification, each of which reinforces the other three: "Men who share meaningful experiences get to know each other and tend to form into cliques. The integration of these cliques is maintained through further shared experiences and through exchanges of favors. The places of individuals in hierarchies of stratification limit and condition their relationships with each other."[5]

The *frequency* with which men interact, of course, is directly related both to the ease with which a clique is formed, and to its cohesiveness once it has been established. If the clique is to be based on friendship, these relationships must prove pleasant to its members, but there is every indication that "if the frequency of interaction between two or more persons increases, the degree of their liking for one another will increase, and vice versa."[6] To remain strong, friendships must be based on continued close contact. Conversely, where relationships are only sporadic or infrequent, cliques generally either do not form at all, or never become very strong. Job similarity tends to reinforce friendships, not only because individuals with identical

[4] Robert T. Golembiewski, *Behavior and Organization: O & M and the Small Group*, Chicago: Rand McNally, 1962, p. 89.

[5] Richard L. Simpson, *Friendship Cliques in United States Air Force Wings*, Technical Report No. 3, Air Force Base Project, sponsored by Human Resources Research Institute, U.S. Air Force, and executed by Institute for Research in Social Science, University of North Carolina, mimeographed, p. 4.

[6] George C. Homans, *The Human Group*, New York: Harcourt, Brace, 1950, p. 112.

or similar jobs are likely to be located geographically adjacent to one another, but also because men like to "talk shop," and similar interests tend to draw together men of similar jobs.

Naturally the closer the similarity of social and educational backgrounds among members of the group, the more cohesive is the group likely to be. Similar personal interests—as well as job interests—tend to draw individuals together. Such like interests may even lead to off-the-job relationships and mutual recreational pursuits, creating even greater frequency of interaction. Social position, too—as defined by rank in the organization—tends to increase the degree of contact among certain members of a division or department, especially since there is likely to be a greater similarity of work assignments in each rank. This leads to the stratification mentioned above, and divides the larger group into smaller subgroups.

The exchange of favors among the members of the group also serves to reinforce the friendships. Lending money, assisting in various personal tasks, exchanging work details, lending personal equipment, and even giving someone else the credit for one's own accomplishments if one feels he needs the recognition, all represent the sort of on-the-job favors reciprocated among the individuals. Again, if job relationships are extended into the private lives of the workers, the degree of these amenities is likely to increase all the more. These exchanges generally take place quite spontaneously, not as shrewd trades or as the result of the cautious weighing of advantages.

Another important factor that contributes to group cohesiveness is the degree to which team work is required. Workers are less likely to form into closely knit groups if they are involved in separate, self-contained work units. This is due not only to the fact that team efforts are likely to center around related work assignments, but also due to the very cooperation that is required of the members. While most humans have a strong need for affiliation and affection—and the small group, wherever it is found, contributes greatly in meeting this need—the intense sense of identification that is evoked through cooperative effort has a considerable effect on the formation of friendship cliques. If one individual is lax in his efforts, group pressure from the other members of the team serves to keep him in line. The cooperative effort required by the nature of the work comprises an "organizational reality," as does the prestige value of equipment or office space provided by the organization. Such visible signs of status, when they are shared by all members of the group, also contribute to group solidarity. If other divisions or departments are not so outfitted, the prestige value goes up further, and reinforces the group image among those who enjoy these visible status symbols; conversely, among those who do not, group solidarity comes about from a defensive point of view—the members become friendly and present a solid front of opposition to those with the higher status. This leads us to still another organizational reality, one in which administrative policy represents a threat to the workers. As demonstrated earlier in this chapter, the piece-rate system of increasing output at the Hawthorne Plant seemed to be such a threat to each worker, and to the group as a whole, that the workers agreed upon their own private rate of production.

Types of Friendship Cliques

Group cohesiveness is likely to exist among workers of the same organization unit and rank for the reasons cited above, but this does not by any means preclude the formulation of friendship cliques between members of different organization units or ranks. Consequently, we can classify informal organization relationships into the following types: *Horizontal intra-unit groups,* composed of members of the same organization unit and whose ranks are all identical or very similar; *Horizontal inter-unit groups,* composed of members whose positions are on about the same levels, but who are located in different organization units; *Vertical intra-unit groups,* composed of members of the same organization unit, but who are of different rank; and *Vertical inter-unit groups,* whose members are from different organization units and of different ranks.

Horizontal Intra-unit Groups

As indicated earlier, these groups are apt to comprise much of the informal organization. Organizational rank sets boundaries to men's interaction, and, individuals of the same or similar rank are likely to identify with one another more closely than with individuals of much higher or lower positions in the organizational structure. Moreover, their geographical proximity keeps them in constant contact with one another; they "see each other repeatedly in their work, and thus are apt to become friends."[7] They are together for long periods during the day, and frequently socialize during lunch—if not during other occasions away from the job as well. As one example, taken from the military, reveals:

> During temporary duty, barracks rooms serve as important social centers. The men gather in their rooms to play cards, drink, or simply talk. When hard liquor is present, it is freely shared with friends. An airman who walks into a friend's room and finds a group drinking customarily helps himself to the bottle without asking permission or receiving a prior offer. Much of the visiting, however, takes place not among immediate neighbors but among men who work together and live within reasonable proximity.[8]

Of course, the military situation is atypical of organization in general, since the men not only work together, but usually live in the same quarters and spend much of their recreational time together. Yet this illustrates even more cogently how constant proximity forces the likelihood of friendship cliques in the horizontal intra-unit group.

The atmosphere engendered by group solidarity tends to promote fine outlets for personality expression and general well-being. The group protects and gives support to its individual members when they are in trouble, as for example, covering up for a friend when reporting certain information to a superior, or helping him out if he is particularly overloaded with work assignments. The group also provides a basis for comparison of individual performance. If one is praised by his fellow workers, he gains an incentive for doing even better; if he is criticized, as can happen just as easily, he knows where he stands with the group and what he must do to recoup his standing in it. Similarly, the determination not to let one's buddies down is frequently a principal motivation for the group's members. In other words, the group creates the "social reality" in which the members can function with a better sense of purpose. Whether this purpose is to the advantage of the formal organization or not will be discussed in subsequent sections of the chapter.

[7] Simpson, *op. cit.*, p. 10.
[8] *Ibid.*, p. 6.

Horizontal Inter-unit Groups

Sometimes clique relationships also develop among individuals located in different organization units. One way this can come about is from a natural working relationship between two or more units, such as supply departments with production or operating divisions. For example, a friendship sprang up in the Air Force between a gunner and a mechanic who serviced the gunner's aircraft. If certain individuals have been designated as liaison officers between organization units, chances of friendships are greater, but even the occasional meetings of the members of one division with those of another can flower into cohesive relationships. Similar work and/or personal interests can greatly contribute to these alliances, which often comprise a significant part of the informal organization. Another way horizontal inter-unit groups can form is if two or more individuals of more or less equal rank join forces to accomplish a common organizational objective. "Horizontal defensive" and "horizontal aggressive" cliques, as termed by Dalton, are two examples.[9] The former is an alliance based on a common threat, such as those frequently found in government bureaucracies, where threatened budgetary reductions, or proposed reorganization plans which call for lesser autonomy of the divisions, induce even competing divisions to pool their efforts against the action. The latter is formed "to effect changes rather than to resist them."[10] The members may be the very same as those previously associated in horizontal defensive cliques. However, alliances of these types are generally temporary, and disintegrate once the issue which united them has passed unless there are other factors strong enough to generate a more enduring friendship.

Another kind of horizontal inter-unit group is the "random clique," so termed by Dalton because its members come from many different parts of the organization, and generally do not share any common work goals. They are united essentially by friendship and social attraction. "From the cafeteria to the showers they meet and gossip about their home departments and their dissatisfactions."[11] While

[9] Melville Dalton, *Men Who Manage*, New York: Wiley, 1959, p. 61.
[10] *Ibid.*
[11] *Ibid.*, pp. 63–65.

sometimes these "random cliques" involve individuals of differing organizational ranks, they usually tend to involve workers from essentially similar echelons.

Vertical Intra-unit Groups

The case of the relationship of the Hawthorne workers with their foreman, cited in the beginning of this chapter, is a good example of a vertical intra-unit relationship. The foreman—of higher rank and a representative of management—nonetheless spent most of his time with his subordinates, and thus was more favorably disposed toward the values of this group than toward the aims of management. Here again, proximity is a strong factor in the formulation of these friendships, but similarity of personal and vocational interests serves to reinforce them. However, since rank differences tend to separate workers, there generally must be a strong personal need for unity between higher- and lower-ranking officials. This is exemplified in what Dalton refers to as "vertical symbiotic" cliques; the word *symbiotic* derives from the biological term *symbiosis,* meaning "a mutually beneficial internal partnership between two different kinds of organisms."[12] Thus, a superior and certain of his subordinates form a mutually beneficial partnership within the organization unit. The subordinates aim to protect their superior by keeping him informed as to any real or rumored threats to his position and other useful bits of information they might pick up. He, in turn, protects the group, recommends wage increases, and, where necessary, covers for the members in his dealings with management.

Another example of this sort of relationship can be seen in a situation that occurred when an Air Force Reserve captain was given the job of intelligence officer in one of the squadrons. The captain was not up-to-date with Air Force operating procedures and "had little desire to learn his job well enough to perform in the most efficient manner."[13] The sergeant, on the other hand, was very familiar with these procedures, and the captain, who was not lacking in resourcefulness and diplomacy, told the sergeant, "I will take orders from you." The captain followed through and signed papers brought to

[12] *Ibid.*, p. 58.
[13] Simpson, *op. cit.*, p. 17.

him by his subordinate without even so much as reading them. The sergeant was happy with this arrangement and reciprocated by saving the captain from embarrassment whenever his lack of knowledge was in danger of being exposed. The two men soon became good friends off as well as on the job.

It should be pointed out here that vertical intra-unit relationships sometimes have adverse consequences for the organization unit as a whole. If a friendship exists between only one or two subordinates and their superior, the other subordinates may become suspicious of their coworkers, and exclude them from the horizontal cliques. If, for example, they believe that the superior's friends are carrying tales to him, they are likely to do their best to keep information from them, and the whole relationship of the chief with his staff is poisoned. Or it can happen that a friendly superior gives more to his subordinates than he receives from them, because for one reason or another he wants to protect them. Dalton calls this a "vertical parasitic" relationship, and it, of course, also damages the standing of the superior officer with the rest of the subordinates.

Vertical Inter-unit Groups

One way individuals of one rank can become friendly with those of another in a different organization unit is through the "random" process described earlier. Another is through the promotion of a member of the unit to a higher position in a different unit. Purely social friendships, formed outside a unit, are still another way these relationships are established.

The chief value of participating in one of these groups is the influence wielded with the "contacts" in higher positions. Such contacts can be helpful in gaining status with one's own superior, or, as one example, if the superior is slow or uncooperative in obtaining important information or "clearance" from another division, one can merely avoid the formal channels by going directly to his contact in the other division. Such contacts are an indispensable element in the informal organization of government agencies, and often expedite what would otherwise involve an undue amount of red tape. Further, an individual in a high position in the agency is often rewarded by his lower-ranking friend who sends him various bits of useful information.

THE ADVANTAGES OF INFORMAL ORGANIZATION TO THE FORMAL ORGANIZATION

It has been said that "cliques sometimes devise their own ways of accomplishing work which, while not strictly in accord with the regulations, are more efficient than officially established standard operating procedures."[14] In other words, in practice, the formal organization is not always as logically practical as it attempts to be, and the informal organization often compensates for this deficit. We have already seen how the relationship between the Air Force captain and his sergeant led to greater efficiency for the total operation; the formal organization put the captain in command according to official hierarchical procedures, yet clearly not he, but the lower-ranking sergeant was the right man for the job. Further, we have alluded to the slowness and uncooperativeness on the part of some officials, whom it is sometimes advantageous to by-pass in the interests of greater efficiency. The only way this can be accomplished satisfactorily is through friendly contacts in other areas of the organization. And we have seen how positive horizontal or vertical relationships can contribute substantially to work incentives and pleasant associations within the organization. Such pleasant identification promotes internal harmony and smoothness of operation. As Simpson puts it, "it is safe to assume that this heightened feeling of well-being . . . is beneficial for role performance and thus is indirectly functional for the system."[15] Indeed, Dalton believes that the vertical symbiotic clique is "the most common and enduring clique in large structures."[16] Even "random" cliques can play a valuable role in the organization. As Dalton expresses it, random cliques are "small unattached gossip groups moving freely around the firm." As such, they "intensify informal activities in the plant" by providing an alert member of some functional clique with valuable information.

Group solidarity within the informal organization is particularly helpful as an administrative aid, since pressure from the members of one's friendship clique tends to carry more weight than do dictums from management. In the Air Force, for example:

[14] *Ibid.*, p. 16.
[15] *Ibid.*, p. 14.
[16] Dalton, *op. cit.*, p. 59.

One sergeant advised another, "Never volunteer information to the chief about where a man is until he asks." He explained that a man may have sneaked off without the chief's finding out. During a flight mission one of the gunners performed poorly, causing some of the guns to jam. For this the other airmen on the aircraft criticized him bitterly, but when reporting the incident to the aircraft commander they said nothing to indicate that the gunner had been at fault. After the same mission the flight engineer carefully waited until no officers were in the vicinity before reprimanding some of the men who had neglected to pull the battery wires before leaving the aircraft.[17]

There is good reason to believe that the flight engineer's way of handling the situation was far more effective than it would have been had he had the men called out on the carpet officially. The importance of group ties to efficiency is brought out strikingly in the comparison of two combat situations described by Marshall.[18] In one case, individuals who had no previous acquaintance with one another were inducted into a strange outfit; their combat value turned out to be almost nil. In the other, gun crews, squad groups, etc. had been separated from their parent unit and also sent to a strange company, yet they fought vigorously on the battle scene. The explanation, of course, is that, in the second case, the small group remained intact despite their transfer from the larger company.

DISADVANTAGES OF INFORMAL ORGANIZATION TO THE FORMAL ORGANIZATION

Apart from work restriction which has been previously mentioned, the informal organization can have other harmful effects on the administrative structure. For one thing, friendship cliques have a habit of circulating among themselves bits of unofficial information which can create difficulties for the formal command. Information is sometimes "leaked" about some plans considered by the higher echelons which are not for official distribution. For example, suppose the administration is planning to transfer an employee; the "grapevine" can disseminate such information in an amazingly short period of time to

[17] Simpson, *op. cit.*, pp. 19–20.

[18] S. L. A. Marshall, *Men Against Fire*, Infantry Journal, Washington, D.C., and William Morrow and Co., New York, 1947, p. 151.

the man involved, and he may be able to use his contacts to block the transfer. Ugly gossip can also circulate in this manner concerning the private lives of other employees and administrative officials. Whether true or false, such gossip can serve detrimentally to the general morale and harmony of the operation. Rumors can also be spread, needlessly arousing other groups to unrest and putting management in a difficult position. However, a wise management will keep attuned to this grapevine, recognizing in it the real needs and attitudes among the personnel, and, where necessary, acting—before it is too late—on any false rumors and ugly gossip.

A much more insidious consequence of friendship cliques is the prevalence of favoritism in making promotions. It has been found that "shop talk" frequently centers around politicking on behalf of personal gains. The right treatment of the "right" people can lead to one's personal benefit, whether or not the benefit is truly merited. This, too, can serve to downgrade morale, for the other workers can acquire an unfavorable image of management policy.

The vertical parasitic clique described earlier is another example of an undesirable effect of informal organization. A superior who allies himself with a few favored subordinates can damage the efficiency of the department's overall operation, and can seriously impair what might otherwise be valuable leadership on his part.

CONTROLLING THE INFORMAL ORGANIZATION

The administration that is aware of the dynamics of informal organization and of small groups in general, as well as of the particular nature of the cliques and alliances within its own organization, can do much to minimize the harmful effects of informal organization and to maximize its potential advantages. As Dalton writes:

> Cliques are the indispensable promoters and stabilizers—as well as resisters—of change; they are essential both to cement the organization and to accelerate action. They preserve the formalities vital for moving to the goal, and they provoke but control the turmoil and adjustment that play about the emerging organization.[19]

Dalton noted that when cliques start to get out of hand, managements generally take the following steps:

[19] Dalton, *op. cit.*, p. 68.

1. Guarded attacks on the clique, such as hints by superior officers at formal meetings that "not all sins are pardonable."
2. If these evidences of disapproval prove ineffective, taking positive action to hold the clique at least at its existing strength. This is the policy of "containment."
3. If containment fails, transfer or even promotion of the leader of the clique.
4. Dispersal of the clique by assigning its members to different work locations in the plant.
5. Instead of dispersal through permanent assignment to separate work locations, a system of rotating clique members from one part of the firm to another.
6. Changing work procedures and the duties of the jobs to "disrupt clique routines and thus weaken it."
7. Discriminating against clique members in different ways, in order to force them to resign or ask for transfers.
8. If the clique member is expendable, formal action demoting him, with the hope that he will desist from his activities or else quit the firm.[20]

On point 2, Dalton mentions an interesting technique: set up a new committee with a bona fide mission and assign one or more members of the troublesome clique to work with this new group. This steers the clique members into more useful activities, exposes them to the values of teamwork, and at the same time removes them from the influence of the other clique members. On point 3, Dalton describes how the management may suddenly discover new abilities in the clique leader. Anxious to put him in a job where he can do less harm, it may even be glad to promote him if that is the only way to accomplish the objective. Although we are reserving for Chapter 12 a discussion of the characteristics of *informal leaders,* we wish to note here what can happen if top officials decide that one of the informal leaders has become a menace and that his power must be broken. Correctives 3, 4, and 5 can be applied when the members of the "deviant clique" are too valuable to be subjected to the humiliation of formal disciplinary action. The same is true of 6, the purpose of which is so to change the work routine as to lessen the rate of interaction and therefore the sense of solidarity between the clique members. Some work procedures facilitate interaction, others do not. As

[20] *Ibid.*, p. 65.

to 7, sometimes the stratagem used is to deny the individual information or help that he needs in order to do his work properly. For example, he can be given an assignment which proves impossible for him to execute. There are many different ways of putting obstacles in his path and of driving him to the point of desperation. Item 8 represents the extreme punishment, but note that, even here, the clique member is not dismissed outright. Dalton is of the opinion that "almost never would an able executive be dismissed for clique activity. Higher managers value these skills as necessary for cutting a way through or around chaotic situations."[21]

In any kind of organization, then, cliques have their desirable and undesirable aspects. Any one clique can be broken up, but cliques as such cannot be abolished. The informal organization cannot be legislated out of existence; nor can it be ignored, for, as we have seen, it can greatly influence the success or failure of the agency mission. Thus, it is to the administration's advantage that all supervisors and technicians have a full understanding of informal organization and its operation. Unfortunately, the small group has received all too little attention in management circles. Future improvements in management effectiveness in both the public and private sectors will depend greatly on the progress made in harmonizing the formal and the informal organizations.

BIBLIOGRAPHY

Argyris, Chris., "The Individual and Organization: Some Problems of Mutual Adjustment," *Administrative Science Quarterly,* **II,** No. 1 (June, 1957).

Argyris, Chris., "Some Problems in Conceptualizing Organizational Climate: A Case Study of A Bank," *Administrative Science Quarterly,* **II,** No. 4 (March, 1958).

Cartwright, Dorwin, and Zander, Alvin (eds.), *Group Dynamics, Research and Theory,* New York: Harper and Row, 1960.

[21] *Ibid.,* p. 67.

Dalton, Melville, *Men Who Manage*, New York: Wiley, 1959.

Dubin, Robert (ed.), *Human Relations in Administration*, Englewood Cliffs, N.J.: Prentice-Hall, 1961. Chap. 5.

Golembiewski, Robert T., "The Small Group and Public Administration," *Public Administration Review*, **XIX,** No. 3 (Summer, 1959).

Golembiewski, Robert T., "O & M and the Small Group," *Public Administration Review*, **XX,** No. 4 (Autumn, 1960).

Mansfield, Harvey C., and Marx, Fritz Morstein, "Informal Organization," in Marx, Fritz Morstein (ed.), *Elements of Public Administration*, Englewood Cliffs, N.J.: Prentice-Hall, 1959.

Mechanic, David, "Sources of Power of Lower Participants in Complex Organizations," *Administrative Science Quarterly*, **VII,** No. 3 (December, 1962).

Odiorne, George S., "The Clique—A Frontier in Personnel Management," *Personnel*, **XXXIV,** No. 2 (September–October, 1957).

Pfiffner, John M., and Sherwood, Frank P., *Administrative Organization*, Englewood Cliffs, N.J.: Prentice-Hall, 1960. Chap. 6.

Roethlisberger, F. J., and Dickson, William J., *Management and the Worker*, Cambridge, Mass.: Harvard, 1939. Chaps. XXIII–XXVI.

Simpson, Richard L., "Friendship Cliques in United States Air Force Wings," Technical Report No. 3, Air Force Base Project, Sponsored by Human Resources Research Institute, U.S. Air Force and executed by the Institute for Research in Social Science, University of North Carolina. Project Directors: Gordon W. Blackwell and Nicholas J. Demerath. AF–HRRI Project No. 505–037–0001. (Mimeographed).

Studies in Social Psychology During World War II, prepared and edited under the auspices of a special committee of the Social Science Research Council, Princeton, N.J.: Princeton, 1949. Four volumes:

- v. 1. *The American Soldier: Adjustment During Army Life*, by S. A. Stouffer and others.
- v. 2. *The American Soldier: Combat and its Aftermath*, by S. A. Stouffer and others.
- v. 3. *Experiments on Mass Communication*, by C. I. Hovland and others.
- v. 4. *Measurement and Prediction*, by S. A. Stouffer and others.

Walker, Nigel, *Morale in the Civil Service: A Study of the Desk Worker*, Edinburgh: Edinburgh Univ. Press, 1961.

PART III

BASIC PROBLEMS OF MANAGEMENT

CHAPTER 8

Decisionmaking

Part III of this book deals with the "Management Function," which is "To determine what you want people to accomplish, to check periodically on how well they are accomplishing it, and to develop methods by which they will perform more effectively."[1] *Deciding* what to do, and how to do it, is, then, the heart of the management function; accordingly, in this opening chapter of Part III, we will make some general observations about decisionmaking in administration.

Analysis of decisionmaking is understandably a central point of concern in the human-relations approach to management. Decisions control behavior; at least, that is the intention. What really takes place in an organization cannot be understood if one does not know what kinds of decisions are made, who participates in making them, and what their exact role is. Increasingly, this subject is given a good deal of emphasis by students of administration, reflecting a movement away from preoccupation with mechanical questions of work efficiency and organization structure to a much greater interest in the human beings who make up the organization and how they interact.

THE DYNAMICS OF DECISIONMAKING

According to Robert Tannenbaum, decisionmaking "involves a conscious choice or selection of one behavior alternative from among

[1] Lawrence A. Appley, *Management in Action*, New York: American Management Association, 1956, p. 323.

a group of two or more behavior alternatives."[2] Much of decisionmaking is of course concerned with questions of policy; the basic question is what *ought* to be done, and obviously this is something which entails subjective judgments and individual preferences, which make a decision seem rational to some people and irrational to others. Indeed, sometimes the official is forced to make a decision which appears illogical but which solves the particular administrative problem. Yet some discussions imply that decisionmaking takes place in an orderly sequence of steps as follows: (1) recognition of the problem; (2) collection of data; (3) classification and analysis; (4) inventory of means; (5) listing of alternatives; (6) evaluation of alternatives; (7) decision; (8) implementation; and (9) follow-up and feedback. Recent research reveals that in many actual cases the process begins with consideration of a proposed solution, in other words with step (6).[3] Essentially, however, there are three steps in the decisionmaking process. First, the individuals concerned must become aware of as many of the different behavior alternatives available to them as possible. Second, they must analyze each alternative in terms of the possible consequences if adopted. Third, after weighing the advantages and disadvantages of the possible courses of action, they must choose one of them—in other words, make the decision.

Each of the three steps frequently involves some very complex determinations, making direct participation in the decisionmaking process a difficult task, for one must accept the responsibility for proceeding successfully from steps one to three. If such and such a course is followed, certain results may be achieved—but there is no certainty that they will be. As Tannenbaum writes:

> In the first place, an individual never has the knowledge to make it possible for him accurately to determine the nature of the consequences which will follow upon the choice of a given behavior alternative or their probability of occurring, assuming that all other related elements remain constant. And because he does not have knowledge of the future, he

[2] Robert Tannenbaum, Irving R. Weschler, and Fred Massarik, *Leadership and Organization: A Behavioral Science Approach*, New York: McGraw-Hill, 1961, p. 267.

[3] John M. Pfiffner, "Administrative Rationality," *Public Administration Review*, XX, No. 3 (Summer, 1960), 129.

must use imagination in attaching values to the consequences, which values may not obtain when the consequences are actually experienced. In the second place, all other related elements will not remain constant.[4]

Still, while the administrator does not collect and order his data in the same way that experimental social scientists do, he is very much aware of the "probable human reactions to his decisions and actions."[5] In other words, he does know how to make decisions which take into account the power relationships between people affected by his determinations, and he can make intelligent decisions by carefully weighing all the elements in a particular situation. This means that he relies to a great extent upon his past experience. As a practical man, he applies "common sense," meaning what his personal judgment tells him is correct.

There is a natural reluctance on the part of those who hope for the development of a true administrative science to rely on this personal judgment. They are convinced that the best hope for progress is to continue the search for more rational ways of making decisions. Further, they argue that the record shows very clearly that, when primary reliance is placed on administrators' subjective judgments, the net result is the statement of alleged principles which have never been substantiated by empirical research.[6] Granted that the administrator's judgment cannot meet the test of complete rationality, some observers believe that preconceived notions dictate decisions all too frequently, without any real consideration of the facts. Alexander Leighton is among those critical of the failure of the administrators to make proper use of social-science data already available. When the scientific approach is employed, says Leighton, "facts, observed events, and ascertained information play a dominant role."[7] By contrast, in administrative policymaking "conclusions are supported by a structure of logic that extends dangerously high on its mixed foundation of facts and basic assumptions. It is vast in proportion to the facts employed. Frequently the facts are insufficient to form

[4] Tannenbaum *et al., op. cit.*, p. 268.

[5] Pfiffner, *op. cit.*, p. 131.

[6] See Donald C. Rowat (ed.), *Basic Issues in Public Administration*, New York: Macmillan, 1961, pp. 75–91.

[7] Alexander Leighton, *Human Relations in a Changing World*, Princeton: Princeton Univ. Press, 1949, p. 152.

any part of the foundation, and are fastened on the superstructure here and there for illustration."[8] Leighton states that the decisionmaker makes it appear that he has proceeded in an orderly way from consideration of the facts to conclusions logically derived from them. Actually, he feels, the conclusions come first, and then facts are found to justify them.

Of course, the administrator may not be a free agent in his determinations. His superior officers may expect him to decide questions in certain ways, no matter what the facts may be. They may have preconceived ideas to which they expect him to conform. Public opinion is also an important factor because the mood of the people may make it impossible to obtain community acceptance of certain decisions, even if they are well reasoned. Furthermore, once a major decision is made, there is often a strong compulsion to stick with it. Doubts may arise as to its soundness, but the administrative agency, perhaps the entire government, is already committed. Vast sums of money may already have been spent, and rather than lose this investment, the natural tendency is to suppress these doubts and make day-by-day decisions which are consistent with the original basic policy determination.

THE ROLE OF THE DECISIONMAKER

It is often said that the managers or executives are paid to make good decisions. In determining and weighing the alternatives, however, the executive usually has the help of other people, and may even depend so much on some that, in effect, he is merely endorsing their decision, rather than making his own. The responsible executive alone can make it official, but it is frequently others who really decide. The executive's own immediate subordinates are among those who share in the decisionmaking process. Their job is to help him to define problems and to find solutions. The executive also obtains valuable information and suggestions from the heads and staff of other parts of the organization. Further, he frequently consults with representatives of outside organizations before making final decisions. "Lateral" clearances of this type are very common in govern-

[8] *Ibid.*

ment, where one agency must check with another and where consultation with various private groups is essential. Thus, as Harlan Cleveland writes, "No one person 'decides' anything; each 'decision' of any importance is the product of an intricate process of brokerage involving individuals inside and outside the organization who feel some reason to be affected by the decision, or who have special knowledge to contribute to it."[9] Cleveland does not believe that, in large-scale organizations, the individual's opportunity to participate in decisionmaking is sharply limited, but rather that:

> A large and powerful organization has so many more important decisions to be made that there is proportionately more, not less, decision-making authority to go around. The larger the organization and the wider its reach, the more lateral contacts it has to make and maintain, the more complexities must be sorted out by experts on complexity—which is to say leaders. . . . The nearer you get to the top of the hierarchy the fewer unreviewed decisions you make. The man who buys writing pads and pencils for a government agency is virtually his own boss, but the President of the United States has to operate in a world peopled with countervailing organizations in and out of government which believe his every move is of concern to them, and must therefore be cleared with them. The more countervailing organizations have to be consulted, the more members of the internal staff must be assigned to deal with them—and must therefore "participate in major decisions."[10]

While responsibility for decisionmaking is widely diffused, "the types of decisions as well as the conditions change in character as we descend from the major executive to the non-executive positions in organization."[11] The top executives concentrate their attention on decisions relating to ends rather than means. Middle-level executives break these broad purposes into more specific ends. At the lower levels, the emphasis is on making decisions which effectively implement the policy directives received from above. This is of great importance despite the fact that the responsibility for it rests in the

[9] Harlan Cleveland, "Dinosaurs and Personal Freedom," *Saturday Review*, February 28, 1959, 38. See also Herman M. Somers, "Organization—Door to Opportunity," *Civil Service Journal*, III, No. 1 (July–September, 1962), 5–8 and 15.

[10] *Ibid.*, 14.

[11] Chester I. Barnard, *The Functions of the Executive*, Cambridge: Harvard Univ. Press, 1956, p. 192.

hands of the low-level personnel. If the wrong decisions are made at this point, the basic plans established by the top managers will prove to be failures:

> From the point of view of aggregate importance, it is not decisions of executives but of non-executive participants in organization which should enlist major interest. . . . It is here that the final and most concrete objectives of purposes are found, with the maximum of definiteness. There is no further stage of organization action. The final selection of means takes place at this point.[12]

Factors which Influence the Decisionmakers

Thus, whoever he may be, the decisionmaker usually depends upon others for his factual information. Sometimes these others provide him with very sound and valuable data, but sometimes they can or do not. Because of the kinds of problems being dealt with, they will frequently also present the administrator with conflicting recommendations, which makes his decision even more difficult. Therefore, access to relevant information is of great importance in decisionmaking. If he is strategically placed in the communications network, the official is in a better position to obtain the facts he needs in order to make sound decisions. Supervisors can also help subordinates to make good decisions by providing them with necessary and useful information. The subordinate is very much dependent on the initiative of the superior officer in this respect, because he cannot demand this information. Chiefs who keep their subordinates in the dark make it impossible for them to make correct determinations. Mere possession of the facts does not, of course, ensure good decisions, and then it usually is impossible to obtain all of the facts. But certainly the decisionmaker is handicapped to begin with if he is denied access to important information.

The personalities and prior backgrounds of executives also influence their decisions. The executive is above all an individual who has his own sentiments and values which he brings to the "work situation because of his past social conditioning and present social position outside the agency."[13] His very identification of problem areas is de-

[12] *Ibid.*

[13] F. J. Roethlisberger and William J. Dickson, *Management and the Worker*, Cambridge: Harvard Univ. Press, 1939, p. 566.

pendent on his individual value system, meaning his conceptions of what is desirable public policy and appropriate behavior.

The individual's previous training may also influence *the way in which he makes decisions.* For example, the man who is a "bundle of fears," about both himself and others, is prone to keep a tight control on everything. He is suspicious that subordinates may abuse any authority he delegates to them. On the other hand, they might perform so well as to outshine him, so why should he give away his job? Possibly it is simply a peculiar tendency: he has to dot every "i" and cross every "t" in the correspondence that goes out of his office.[14]

The individual's previous work history in the agency also has a direct bearing on the decisions he makes. In Chapter 5, reference was made to the possibility that the Forest Ranger might become a "captive" of the local community in which he is stationed. Because he has such frequent contacts with the citizens of the community, he may come to identify with their interests and to champion their point of view. Conversely, because of his remoteness from the scene of operations, a headquarters officer may make decisions which are unrealistic in terms of the situation in the field. This is why efforts are often made to put men with field experience in headquarters jobs, and vice versa. Job rotation can be justified as an excellent means of broadening the experiential base upon which decisions are made. "Balanced decisions" are made by persons with "balanced" backgrounds.

In choosing the members of the work team, the administrator is really, to some extent at least, controlling the kinds of decisions the group will make. If he selects only persons with the same ideas, he reduces the possibilities of friction but he also creates the conditions for "conformism." The sage statement has been made that "when everyone in the room thinks the same thing, no one is thinking very much."[15] This is why some organizations avoid rigid "promotion from within" policies. If individuals are to be creative, the work atmosphere should be one in which new ideas can be freely presented. Choosing persons with a diversity of backgrounds is an important factor in creating such an atmosphere. It means that a wider range of possibilities is considered in reaching organization decisions.

[14] See Marshall E. Dimock, *The Executive in Action,* New York: Harper and Row, 1945, pp. 83–84.

[15] Tannenbaum *et al., op. cit.,* p. 108.

Community mores also influence the administrator's decisions. As a member of the society in which he lives, the official shares its moral and other views. Administrative decisions made in one cultural setting may not make sense to people living in a different environment.

Authority and the Decisionmaking Process

Grants of particular kinds of decisionmaking responsibilities measure the power an individual or group has in the organization, as was indicated in Chapter 6. *Power* has been defined as "the capacity to secure the dominance of one's values or goals."[16] Typically, when changes are proposed in the formal organization, a struggle takes place to gain strategic positions in the decisionmaking nexus so as to be able to exert this power.

The traditional approach to administration put great stress on formal authority and the individual's place in the official hierarchy, and assumed that such authority, which necessarily flowed from the top to the bottom of the organization, naturally controlled the workers. It was felt that the workers could be manipulated at will by those who had the right to give them orders. The key to improvements in management, it was moreover assumed, was to make changes in the assignments of formal authority to the heads of the different organization units. What was overlooked was the fact that the principal source of difficulty often was inability to obtain the cooperation of the workers, not incorrect allocation of responsibilities to the supervisors.

As we saw in Chapter 7, power is not measured by position in the formal hierarchy alone. One who holds a high position on the organization chart may actually have very little influence in the organization. Membership in the cliques of the informal organization may be a much better measure of the individual's real standing in the structure. The name of an official's secretary may not appear on the organization chart, yet, in reality, she may be far more influential with him than are some of his fellow executives, and she may even participate in making decisions which are not at all a part of her job

[16] John M. Pfiffner and Frank P. Sherwood, *Administrative Organization*, Englewood Cliffs, N.J.: Prentice-Hall, 1960, p. 77.

description. Conversely, some of the responsibilities spelled out in the job descriptions of other employees may never be exercised. In other words, what the formal organization prescribes, the informal organization can modify or eliminate.

Thus, the holders of formal authority in the organization must cope with the power centers represented by the small groups described in detail in the previous chapter. As we have already seen, the soundness of their decisions will depend on their understanding of the characteristics of these groups; and whether their decisions will actually control the behavior of the workers will depend on their skill in dealing with the members of these groups and their leaders.

Formal authority must not be confused with power, because, clearly, the right to issue commands does not ensure that the commands will be heeded, while evidence of power is "to influence someone to behave in a particular way or to make decisions."[17] For the same reason, Tannenbaum makes a distinction between *formal* and *effective* authority. Further, Simon writes:

> Authority may be defined as the power to make decisions which guide the actions of another. It is a relationship between two individuals, one "superior," the other "subordinate." The superior frames and transmits decisions with the expectation that they will be accepted by the subordinate. The subordinate expects such decisions, and his conduct is determined by them.
>
> The relationship of authority can be defined, therefore, in purely objective and behavioristic terms. It involves behaviors on the part of both superior and subordinate. When, and only when, these behaviors occur does a relation of authority exist between the two persons involved. When the behaviors do not occur there is no authority, whatever may be the "paper" theory of organization.[18]

Sometimes those with the right to give orders may prefer to put their requests to the subordinates in the form of suggestions, a wise approach in gaining acceptance of authority, since a succession of formal orders may produce resistance. Too much ordergiving may in fact be evidence that the supervisor is having difficulty in exercising effective authority. He fails to get the desired response, and makes

[17] *Ibid.*, p. 25.

[18] Herbert A. Simon, *Administrative Behavior*, New York: Macmillan, 1957, p. 125.

the situation worse by seeking to compel compliance by reasserting his authority.

The worker may even exert effective authority over his formal superior. In Chapter 7, the case was described of the Air Force captain who found it convenient to "take orders" from the sergeant who was familiar with the details of intelligence work in the squadron. This is the unusual situation of a virtually complete reversal of roles, with the formal superior becoming the subordinate for all practical purposes.

Normally, supervisory officers will depend a good deal on trusted subordinates and accept their judgments on many matters simply because they have developed confidence in them. Subordinates become "specialists" in the detailed responsibilities they have exercised over long periods of time. Their great familiarity with the problems encountered in carrying out their assignments leads the chief to believe they are in the best position to "know." In some areas, then, these subordinates hold the real authority.

The Reluctance to Make Decisions

No discussion of decisionmaking would be complete without a frank statement of the reluctance of many humans to make decisions. Even when in possession of very adequate facts, some people will try to avoid making a decision. In fact, Chester I. Barnard speaks of the "natural reluctance" of men "to decide." He explains:

> The making of decisions, as everyone knows from personal experience, is a burdensome task. Offsetting the exhilaration that may result from correct and successful decision and the relief that follows the terminating of a struggle to determine issues is the depression that comes from failure or error of decision and the frustration which ensues from uncertainty.[19]

Some people believe that the environment in the government is such as to discourage the executive from making decisions. So many clearances with other officials and agencies are required that he finds it easier to "pass the buck." Businessmen who enter the government service complain bitterly about the red tape. Accustomed to being able to take quick action in their companies, it is a frustrating experi-

[19] Barnard, *op. cit.*, p. 189.

ence for them to have to await approval of proposed actions by finance officers and others as prescribed in the laws and regulations. They are annoyed by the career government official's apparent unconcern over these delays, and they may even come to the conclusion that far too many of them are experts in escaping responsibility.

"Passing the buck" is, of course, a practice which exists in private companies as well. Both in government and industry, evading responsibility is the mark of the poor, rather than the good, official. Furthermore, there is no reason to think that any but a very small minority of public employees behave in this way. Yet the government environment is different, since it is the taxpayers' money that is being spent. Fear of public criticism may discourage the official from making certain decisions; sometimes the irresponsible nature of some of the criticism leads him to withdraw from the government decisionmaking scene. He prefers to make his decisions elsewhere. Others adapt to the government environment and find it both possible and exciting to participate in the formulation and implementation of public policies. However, Dahl and Lindblom point out that "passing the buck" is not necessarily undesirable:

> Reluctance to render a decision combined with an effort to push the decision on to someone else—what Americans call "passing the buck"—is also inherent in bureaucratic structures. Specialization helps the specialist to make competent decisions within his domain of enterprise, but it also means that he may be incompetent outside it. What appears to be a weak-kneed refusal to come to the point may actually be a healthy limitation of the specialist's power. Hierarchy operates in the same direction, for one of the major purposes of hierarchy is to *prevent* subordinates from making decisions they ought not to make. In a complex organization, coordination would be impossible if the members did not know when to "pass the buck."[20]

While this is true, subordinates sometimes try to "pass the buck" upward, that is, have their superiors make the decisions for them. In the discussion of delegation, it is sometimes overlooked that subordinates themselves sometimes resist the chief's efforts to get them to make some of the decisions. As Lawrence Appley points out, it is

[20] Robert A. Dahl and Charles E. Lindblom, *Politics, Economics, and Welfare*, New York: Harper and Row, 1953, p. 249.

easy for someone to sit back and do nothing, because a situation has arisen which is not covered by an existing delegation of authority from his superior officer. Sometimes what needs to be done is prohibited by the official policies in force at the time. That makes it even easier for the subordinate to decide that there is nothing that he can do. Appley condemns such inaction:

> If the action which his best judgment tells him should be taken is one that is expressly forbidden by policy or instruction from higher management, then the executive tries to get clearance to make a change. When there is not enough time for the clearance to come through, he has to take action and explain or defend it afterwards. When there is no policy or higher management guidance on the question, he tries to sell his viewpoint to those above him; but if time runs out he still must act.[21]

Although some people will think this is going too far, Appley feels that, just as the manager must sometimes make decisions on the basis of inadequate facts, so must he sometimes act "with inadequate clearances." Whether or not one agrees with him on this, certainly the least that the subordinate can do is to exercise the decisionmaking power which has been delegated to him. The superior's ability to get him to do so is one of the evidences of his leadership qualities.

Acceptance of Authority by Subordinates

The fact that acceptance by subordinates is far from guaranteed is well worth exploring in some detail. There are a number of positive reasons why the individual may be willing to do as the superior requests.[22] First, he may follow instructions not because he is personally convinced of their soundness, but because he believes in the overall purposes of the organization and does not want to place obstacles in the way of their attainment. It is loyalty to the organization that really inspires his acceptance of authority. The significance of this is that if the organization is able to convince the worker of the importance of its program, it will be in a better position to obtain the worker's cooperation. Second, there are situations in which, if he is to retain his standing in his own work group, the employee must cooperate with the formal organization. We saw in the preceding chap-

[21] Appley, *op. cit.*, pp. 102–103.
[22] See Tannenbaum, *et al.*, *op. cit.*, pp. 272–273.

ter how failure to perform well exposes the individual to the censure of the other members of the group. Of course, the reverse situation can also exist, as when the group puts pressure on the individual to resist the authority of management in favor of the authority of the group. Third, the individual may cooperate because he has been promised certain rewards. The incentives offered may be economic, such as salary increases and bonuses, or nonpecuniary in nature, such as more prestige. The trouble here is that not all workers respond to these incentives. They are satisfied with their existing pay and privileges, perhaps because they feel that they could obtain these same advantages in another organization. In any case, there is a limit to the rewards that any organization can offer any one worker, and the worker may feel he has already gained such high status as to be indifferent to appeals for further efforts on behalf of the organization. Fourth, with some workers it is a matter of moral conviction that they should respect the authority of formal superiors. In fact, some people prefer authoritarian to democratic supervision, as we shall see in Chapter 12. The cultural pattern also has its influence here. In some societies, respect for authority is so deeply ingrained that subordinates are not even supposed to make suggestions to superiors. The socially accepted role of subordinates is to follow orders without question. "Two-way" communications, now emphasized so much in the United States, is too radical a concept to be accepted in environments where deference to superior formal position is great. Fifth, the individual may do what the superior asks simply because he respects him for some personal quality. This, again, ties in with the culture pattern. In some parts of the world, as we saw in Chapter 3, the respected quality may be superior age; it may be the reputation which the superior enjoys in his profession. The possibilities are many, but, in any event, the willingness to follow is based on a favorable personal reaction to the chief, without any critical examination of his requests.

EXPERIMENTATION IN DECISIONMAKING

As we approach the end of this chapter, it might be well to stress that experimentation is a form of decisionmaking. Here there is frank admission at the start that the solution is not known. The decision is to try and find one by making an assumption and then seeing if it can be proved to be true. The assumption may deal with basic policies or with detailed work procedures. In either case, there is a willingness to make mistakes and to take risks. These risks may be great or small, depending upon the particular innovation. Franklin D. Roosevelt did not hesitate to experiment with different programs for ending the depression. The critical nature of the times encouraged such boldness, but so did his temperament. Sometimes, however, experimentation does not mean trying spectacular things. Leonardo da Vinci is quoted as having said: "The men who have come before me have taken for their own all useful and necessary themes." Picking up their leavings, he made numerous experiments, some of which proved highly successful, including a machine which could sharpen 40,000 needles an hour, "probably the first mass production machine in history."[23]

It has been stated that "a clerk keeps records; the executive grounds himself on the clerk's collected facts; he goes on to imagine new combinations of facts, and he experiments in search of new results."[24] Certainly, in a world in which experimentation in the physical sciences has produced so many benefits, more creativity in administrative decisionmaking should be encouraged.

BIBLIOGRAPHY

Barnard, Chester I., *The Functions of the Executive*, Cambridge, Mass.: Harvard, 1956.

"Decision-Making in Defense: The Role of Organization," a symposium. *Public Administration Review*, **XVIII,** No. 3 (Summer, 1958).

Dubin, Robert (ed.), *Human Relations in Administration*, Englewood Cliffs, N.J.: Prentice-Hall, 1961. Chap. 15.

[23] *The Royal Bank of Canada Monthly Letter*, Montreal, 40, No. 7 (September, 1959), 4.

[24] *Ibid.*

Durisch, Lawrence L., and Lowry, Robert E., "The Scope and Content of Administrative Decision—The TVA Illustration," *Public Administration Review*, **XIII**, No. 4 (Autumn, 1953).

Glover, John Desmond, and Hower, Ralph M., *The Administrator, Cases on Human Relations in Business*, Homewood, Ill.: Irwin, 1963.

Griffiths, Daniel E., "Administration as Decision-making," in Halpin, Andrew W. (ed.), *Administrative Theory in Education*, Chicago: Midwest Administration Center, Univ. of Chicago, 1958.

McCamy, James L., "Analysis of the Process of Decision-making," *Public Administration Review*, **VII**, No. 1 (Winter, 1947).

Peabody, Robert L., "Perceptions of Organizational Authority: A Comparative Analysis," *Administrative Science Quarterly*, **VI**, No. 4 (March, 1962).

Pfiffner, John M., "Administrative Rationality," *Public Administration Review*, **XX**, No. 3 (Summer, 1960).

Pfiffner, John M., and Sherwood, Frank P., *Administrative Organization*, Englewood Cliffs, N.J.: Prentice-Hall, 1960. Chap. 21.

Shartle, Carroll L., *Executive Performance and Leadership*, Englewood Cliffs, N.J.: Prentice-Hall, 1956.

"Should Decision-Making be the Basis of Organization Theory?" in Rowat, Donald C. (ed.), *Basic Issues in Public Administration*, New York: Macmillan, 1961.

Simon, Herbert A., *Administrative Behavior*, New York: Macmillan, 1957.

Stein, Harold (ed.), *Public Administration and Policy Development, A Casebook*, New York: Harcourt, Brace, and World, 1952.

Tannenbaum, Robert, "A Look at Formal Organization: Managerial Decision Making," in Tannenbaum, *et al.*, *Leadership and Organization: A Behavioral Science Approach*, New York: McGraw-Hill, 1961.

CHAPTER 9

Communications

Communications has been defined as "that process whereby one person makes his ideas and feelings known to another."[1] However, experience has shown time and time again that more is required than the desire to communicate. One must be able to adjust to situations and personalities. Any organization relies on at least a fair degree of harmonious interaction among its employees in order to achieve its objectives, and, wherever there is friction, there will be a block at that point in the communications network. Yet, even when people enjoy good working relationships, successful communication is not easy. Also needed is the ability to make one's thoughts entirely clear to the other person, and for this to be possible, the individual's own thinking must be absolutely clear. Vague instructions reflect cloudy thinking; "If an executive cannot shape up in his own mind a clear concept of policies, objectives, programs, and organization structure, and cannot produce a clear picture in the minds of others, he is seriously handicapped."[2]

Decisions must be explained properly to those who are to put them into effect. The individual may know exactly what he wants to say but is unable to express himself clearly. Yet, if a sound decision is communicated poorly, the desired results will not be obtained. Decisions themselves are based on communications received from different sources, and subordinates present their recommenda-

[1] Lawrence A. Appley, *Management in Action*, New York: American Management Association, 1956, p. 182.
[2] *Ibid.*, p. 186.

tions and progress reports to their superiors in the form of communications, both written and oral. In written communications, the individual may use the wrong words or employ expressions that cloud his real meaning, and similar confusion results from lack of clarity in oral communications. Sometimes, too, a cause of the difficulty is failure on the part of one or both of the communicators to listen properly. All of these aspects are vital in the decisionmaking process discussed previously, and for this reason, it is frequently stated that communications and decisionmaking are inseparable.

Further, power in the organization is measured by the respect commanded by an official's communications. Since communication is basically interaction, study of the communications pattern in an organization will reveal the role of each of the participants:

> Let us suppose that a man is foreman in a factory, and that we are watching him at work. What do we see and hear? We watch him, perhaps, overseeing a battery of punch presses, going from one man to another as they tend the machines, answering their questions and showing them, if they have made mistakes, where they have gone wrong. We see him also at his desk making out records. That is, we see that he has a certain kind of job, that he carries on certain activities. We see also that he deals with certain men in the plant and not with others. He goes to certain men and talks to them; others come to his desk and talk to him. He gets his orders from a boss and passes on the orders to members of his own department. That is, he communicates or, as we shall say . . . interacts with certain persons and not with others, and this communication from person to person often takes place in a certain order—for instance, from the boss to the foreman and then from the foreman to the workers—so that we can say . . . that the foreman occupies a position in a chain of communications.[3]

TYPES OF COMMUNICATIONS

From the standpoint of the direction in which communications flow, three types can be distinguished: (1) downward; (2) upward; and (3) lateral. Let us discuss each of these in turn.

[3] George C. Homans, *The Human Group*, New York: Harcourt, Brace, and World, 1950, pp. 11–12.

Downward Communication

Downward communication refers to the directives and other messages which originate with the officials at the top of the organization and are transmitted down through the hierarchy—through the intervening levels of supervision—until they reach the lowest-ranking worker in the chain. The traditional approach to administration concentrated on this kind of communication and pretty much ignored the other two. It was assumed that the management was in a position to make decisions which were in the best interests of the workers. Once made, these decisions could be "dropped in the chute," so to speak, and be expected to slide smoothly down the hierarchy. If any hitch developed in the implementation of the decisions at any point in this downward chain, it was attributed to the shortcomings of the workers concerned. Furthermore, top management held the ultimate authority, so it could invoke means to force compliance with its instructions.

The Hawthorne experiments, referred to in Chapter 7, showed that downward communication was not so simple. Management could not make decisions which would be accepted at lower levels without first encouraging upward communication, that is the transmission of information and opinions by the workers up the same hierarchy, in other words, travelling the reverse route. In large organizations, downward communication is difficult enough to begin with, because orders must descend through numerous intermediate levels before the point of execution is reached. Misunderstandings can easily occur when instructions pass through so many people. If little upward communication exists, the difficulties are multiplied, because the orders themselves are apt to be unrealistic and to meet with worker resistance.

Upward Communication

Many years have passed since the Hawthorne experiments, but few organizations have been able to develop really effective systems of upward communication—that is, messages that are passed from the lower levels of the hierarchy up to the management. Earl Planty and William Machaver identify a number of barriers to upward communication:

1. Physical distance or inaccessibility
2. Dilution or distortion at each level
3. The attitude of the supervisor
4. The inferior status of the subordinate
5. Tradition.[4]

Workers separated by great distances from the source of authority at the top of the organization have difficulty in communicating upward. A field worker, for example, may have relatively infrequent contact with the head of the field office. The latter in turn may have only limited opportunity to see, and therefore to express his ideas fully to his superiors at headquarters. The same is true even when all the workers are located in the same area. The larger the organization, the greater the number of links in the supervisory chain, and the principle of "following channels" requires that no link in this chain be bypassed; everyone must deal through his immediate chief. It is not surprising, then, that few messages that are voluntarily initiated by the lowest worker ever travel upward until they finally reach the desk of the top executive. Reports required by the top management must traverse this route, but they do not have the spontaneity that ideally should characterize the system of upward communication.

As information is passed up the hierarchy, it is subject to a filtering process at each level. Some of this is deliberate; a good deal is unconscious. The picture of operations as described by a subordinate may not square with the superior's conception of the situation, particularly when the subordinate reports that some things are not going well at all. "Problems" are disturbing, and a typically human reaction is to refuse to believe that they exist or are as serious as they are painted to be. (Good news ascends the hierarchy much more easily than bad news.) The tendency is to "edit" the reports to present a brighter picture. An agency head can sometimes appear to be unbelievably blind as to what is really going on in his agency; yet based on the reports he gets everything *is* fine: these reports sim-

[4] See Earl Planty and William Machaver, "Upward Communications: A Project in Executive Development," *Personnel*, XXVIII, No. 4 (January, 1952), 304–317.

ply do not present him with all the facts. Consequently, the upwards reporting system is often of very limited value in locating trouble spots in the agency's operations.

In theory, when a man becomes the head of an organization, he acquires a vantage point which gives him a broader view of operations. In practice, however, the executive who is not afraid of problems and who wants the true picture is still apt to be the victim of what Appley calls "the conspiracy of smoothness,"[5] or the tendency of his assistants to "protect him against discomforts and to shield him from unpleasantness." As Appley writes:

> . . . Though his vision is broadened, he is less able to see what is going on at his very feet. Again it is the old story of his old associates and his intimates insisting on treating him differently. Somehow information does not get to him in the usual way; suddenly he does not know what the grapevine is saying; suddenly he isn't one of the old gang; suddenly he is wrapped in cellophane, insulated against certain realities, and, unless he works to prevent it, given special information in specially prepared forms. Various leaders who have told me of being victims of this process come from such widely separated walks of life as the church, business, government, and labor unions.[6]

The executive represents to the subordinate someone who wields power and could damage the subordinate's prospects for advancement. This creates a communications block, for the subordinate is wary even though the superior may urge him to be frank. Subordinates who, for one reason or another, feel secure in their positions tend to express themselves the most frankly to their superiors. For example, a characteristic of colleges and universities, in the opinion of Harlan Cleveland, is that the firmly established professor is free to express himself: "From the very moment he assumes office, the dean will find a disarming and sometimes jarring frankness on the parts of those faculty members who are secure in their outside positions."[7] If the professor has published and enjoys high prestige in his field, he will normally receive job offers from other institutions and other invitations attesting to his value. Since his reputation is based prin-

[5] Appley, *op. cit.*, p. 195.
[6] *Ibid.*, p. 196.
[7] Harlan Cleveland, "The Dean's Dilemma: Leadership of Equals," *Public Administration Review*, XX, No. 1 (Winter, 1960), 25.

cipally on his outside standing, he does not have to worry too much about the reaction of his immediate superiors. There are limits to this, of course, but, in general, upward communication is not as inhibited in the academic world as it is in many other environments.

If the chief is not interested in hearing about problems, he in effect shuts off upward communication. There are some supervisors who sincerely want to encourage at least some upward communication, but who unwittingly discourage it. Their errors are of several different kinds. One possible difficulty is that they are not good listeners in any relationship, with subordinates or otherwise. These individuals are so tied up with their own problems and personalities that they find it difficult to concentrate on what the other person is saying. Either they interrupt to express their own viewpoints—sometimes abruptly changing the subject—or they give the other person little chance to say much. The net result is that there may be a good deal of communication of the superior's feelings, but little or no upward communication of the subordinate's views to him. In recent years, there has been a sprouting of books and articles in the management field on "listening." Belatedly, there is awareness of this previously neglected aspect of communications. Then, too, the superior may not know how to arrange his time so as to create the relaxed setting that will encourage the subordinate to speak up. Constant interruptions to take telephone calls and frequent glances at one's wrist watch make the subordinate feel ill at ease. He came in with something important to discuss, but somehow he never gets a chance to introduce the subject. The pity is that the superior officer may really have been interested in hearing about the problem.

The subordinate is handicapped at the outset of any upward communication, because he is not free to break in on the superior and intrude on his time. If the chief has something on his mind, he can, at any time, ask the subordinate to see him as soon as possible. In a sense, he controls their time; they in no sense control his. They must, rather, petition an audience with him. There are usually several who want to see the chief at the same time, and he is very busy as it is satisfying the other demands on his time. Further, the status symbols which set off the superior officers tend to discourage subordinates. The chief may be surrounded by personal aides and secretaries who are anxious to conserve his time; indeed, his secretary can function as a powerful obstacle to easy contact with him. Many are the subordinates who meet with so many obstacles when trying to see the chief that they decide to drop the matter altogether.

Upward communication is in a very important sense "unnatural." It is like rowing upstream, against the current. Downward communication has the great force of tradition behind it. There is nothing at all unusual about communications originating at the top of the hierarchy and being routed downward. By contrast, upward communication is unconventional. In most organizations, it is not established procedure for the employees spontaneously to direct upward any large numbers of communications. The employee who attempts to do so may even take a risk. Further, the management that genuinely wants to encourage upward communication will have difficulty because the upward route will generally have been used so rarely in the past that the employees will remain reluctant to use it.

All of these obstacles are formidable, but the very awareness of them constitutes the first step in a program of improving upward communication. If it is so aware, management can embark on a program to stimulate upward communication. The management should not expect such communication to be spontaneous with the employees, nor is it enough simply to tell the workers that upward communication is desirable. Most of the employees will require clear evidence that the management really is interested in their opinions. Since an important change is being made in the worker's accustomed role, he understandably needs help and encouragement in making the shift from mere cog to full participant in the aims of the organization. Some workers may be so used to playing an insignificant role that they have become quite indifferent to the future of the organization. Thus, the management must change the whole outlook of these workers if it is to succeed in getting them to participate in any system of upward communication.

Superior officers should follow a consistent policy of listening to their subordinates. This may involve adapting to a willingness to face bad news. The management should encourage its supervisors to do this, and the example set by the agency head in this respect will normally have a great influence on the other executives. If he encourages communications from below, and accepts even negative reports, his key assistants are likely to do the same with their subordinates.

The most unfriendly atmosphere for upward communication is one in which the management seems to isolate itself, keeping information to itself and considering many matters "confidential" and not to be revealed outside the inner circle. A management which practices such limited downward communication automatically inhibits upward communication, and, in effect, builds a wall between itself and the rest of the organization. For subordinates to initiate upward communication in such an atmosphere would be almost tantamount to defiance. Fortunately, such an attitude by the management is now considered old fashioned and tends to be the exception rather than the rule.

The supervisor should exercise care in selecting his "communicators"—that is, those who provide him with information—and make sure that these communicators are not merely "reflectors" of what he is predisposed to seeing. Some executives make a point of surrounding themselves with at least one or two "no" men in a conscious effort to avoid the "conspiracy of smoothness" mentioned earlier. For example, Attorney-General Robert Kennedy acted as a "communicator" in his brother's Cabinet. Some newspaper reports indicated that as the President's brother the Attorney-General was able to be far more blunt with the Chief Executive than any other member of the administration, and this bluntness may explain why the late President depended so much on his younger brother. Selecting the "communicators" on the basis of pure convenience is a common mistake by superiors. The foreign national who knows English, for example, is easy to communicate with, but what he relays may be unrepresentative of the predominant beliefs in his society. The executive who obtains most of his field information from headquarters makes the same kind of mistake, even though it may be convenient for him to talk with the headquarters staff but inconvenient to visit the field offices for first-hand information.

The superior officer should also strive to correct those of his personal habits which prevent the subordinate from speaking to him freely. Again, the superior must first be aware of these mannerisms, and humans are typically blind when it comes to personal failings.

Yet some self-prompting is possible once the supervisor has become aware of these tendencies and has really decided to encourage the subordinate. It should be pointed out here that superior officers frequently feel a compulsion to demonstrate their superiority to their subordinates. With some, this is a protective device; if they *appear* to know more than their subordinates, they can feel they are living up to their official roles in the organization. Other supervisors are vain and would in any case treat their subordinates with condescension. While the supervisor must never forget his responsibilities as a superior officer, his position hardly means that he is always better apprized of all the facts than is the subordinate. Once the supervisor recognizes that his subordinates are likely to possess information that he does not, he is much more apt to encourage subordinates to communicate with him freely.

Another common mistake is for the superior to state his own position before he listens to the subordinate, rather than inviting the subordinate to give his opinions on the particular problem. There may be no intention on the part of the superior to force his views on the subordinate, but the latter is quickly placed in a difficult position: he must agree with the boss. Few people will want to challenge the chief so openly. Encouraging one's subordinates to express their views holds another advantage. As noted in the previous chapter, some workers prefer to leave all decisions to someone else in order to avoid the responsibility. Such an attitude generally serves to impair the caliber of the individual's work, which ultimately reflects on the supervisor, as well as adds to his load of decision-making. If however, the supervisor encourages free expression of ideas from his subordinates, he is likely to lead this sort of individual to develop his capacity for greater responsibility. The supervisor will never succeed in this if he merely asks his subordinates for reactions to his own ideas.

Where it is indicated and feasible, the superior officer should *use* the information given to him by his subordinates. Nothing is more destructive of free expression—and of upward communication—than the chief's failure to act upon the ideas and problems reported to him. The subordinates are led to believe that they are wasting their time, and may even wish that the superior had not gone through the formality of listening. The purpose of communication is to achieve organizational objectives. Action at some point is essential if subordinates are to continue to feel motivated in contributing to these objectives by communicating significant information to their superiors.

Lateral Communication

Lateral communication is that which takes place among workers of the same level in the hierarchy, or among individuals of different levels who are not in a superior-subordinate relationship. Lateral relationships will frequently go from one agency to another, and are not restricted to intraagency relationships. We use the term *lateral* instead of *horizontal* in order to be able to include *all* across-the-organization contacts.

Traditional organization theory is based on the organization chart and the system of *scalar* authority it depicts. The scalar principle means that the different positions of authority are shown in descending order of importance. The limitations of the chart give the clue to the inadequacies of traditional theory, as is so well revealed in the following statement:

> The relation between the scheme of activities and the scheme of interaction in an organization is usually represented by the familiar organization chart, which shows the organization divided into departments and subdepartments, the various officers and subofficers occupying boxes, connected by lines to show which persons are subordinate to what other ones. Every such chart is too neat; it tells what the channels of interaction ought to be but not always what they are. The pyramid-type chart is particularly misleading because it shows only the interaction between superiors and subordinates, the kind of interaction that we shall call, following Barnard, *scalar*. It does not show the interaction that goes on between two or more persons at about the same level of the organization, for instance, between two department heads. . . .
>
> This kind of interaction we shall call lateral interaction, though we must remember that there are borderline cases where the distinction between scalar and lateral interaction disappears. The conventional organization chart represents the scalar but not the lateral interaction. *If it were not for the unhappy association with predatory spiders, the facts would be much better represented by a web, the top leader at the*

center, spokes radiating from him, and concentric circles linking the spokes. Interaction takes place along the concentric circles as well as along the spokes.[8]

Lateral communication is of great importance in assuring coordination of organizational objectives. The members of the organization should work together as a cohesive unit, but, if they are to do so, they must communicate their plans and intentions to one another clearly. Traditional organization theory has emphasized coordination through command; that is, through the downward communications of the superior. As Thompson explains: "each person's behavior is considered to be determined by the commands of his superior. If every superior is able to give integrated, rationally consistent commands, the organization will automatically be a coordinated system of behavior."[9] The fallacy in this reasoning is that the superior officer is not in a position to give subordinates these "integrated, rationally consistent commands."[10] The subordinates are likely to know the details of operations in their bailiwicks better than he can be expected to know them. Thompson continues:

> Specialization has long outrun human ability to coordinate in this fashion. Not only is the person in the command position increasingly dependent upon subordinates for the interpretation of incoming data and the initiation of activities, but interdependencies far beyond command jurisdictions have developed. Consequently, most coordination is programmed, built into routines.[11]

The concept of coordination by command is basically authoritarian in nature: The way to get the subordinates to work together is to order them to do so; if they fail to obey, punitive corrective measures should be taken. Overlooked is the fact that there are serious limits to the coordination which can be imposed on the employees from above. Such coordination tends to be nominal, simply because it is forced on the worker, and, at best, he only grudgingly complies. Real

[8] Homans, *op. cit.*, pp. 104–105. Italics ours.

[9] Victor A. Thompson, *Modern Organization*, New York: Knopf, 1961, p. 181.

[10] *Ibid.*

[11] *Ibid.*, p. 183.

teamplay is characterized by spontaneity. The individual wants to cooperate because he derives *personal* satisfaction from functioning as a member of the team.

In the previous chapter it was stated that, in modern organizations, decisionmaking is not monopolized by just a few top people. Management depends on the specialized skills and knowledge of its subordinates and modern administrations recognize this. Today, they invite workers to participate in the decisionmaking process. Logically, this requires the encouragement of both upward and lateral communication. The wise superior finds it advantageous to encourage his subordinates, not only to express their ideas to him freely, but also to settle as many problems as possible among themselves. If they are to cooperate in this manner, they must obviously be in close contact with one another.

Obstacles

Just as in the case of upward communication, the lateral pattern of interaction presents its difficulties. In some respects, effective lateral communication is even more difficult to achieve. In upward communication, the subordinate must adjust to only one person—his immediate supervisor. In lateral communication, workers must deal with several coworkers, and any one department head must try to work together harmoniously with all other department heads; he must also develop effective working relationships with department heads and other officials of outside agencies. These are the "countervailing organizations" referred to by Harlan Cleveland. Suffice it to say that, since cooperative relationships must be established with many different officials—with the usual variation in personalities and modes of behavior—lateral communication is far from easy.

The very division of an organization into specialized parts creates barriers to lateral communication and coordination. Specialists typically develop strong loyalties, not to the organization as a whole, but to their own areas of interest. The tendency is for them to regard members of other specialized groups as threats to their own positions in the organization. The members of each specialized group think its function is the most important in the agency. Furthermore, specialized professions have their peculiar frames of reference and technical language. The members of each can communicate among themselves effectively, but they frequently have difficulty grasping the point of view of outsiders.

That specialists in different fields can clash has been revealed in disagreements between members of the Atomic Energy Commission. John F. Kennedy was convinced that there should be more scientists in policymaking positions in the government, and, shortly after he became President, he named two outstanding scientists as AEC commissioners. Since there was already one scientist, named by Eisenhower, on the five-man Commission, this placed the scientists in the majority. The two other members, lawyers, finally resigned in July, 1962, after months of difficult relations with the scientists. The following excerpt from a newspaper article illustrates this friction and its cause:

> Underlying the division was a clash of philosophies between the two professions, between scientists and their dedication to the pursuit of scientific truth and lawyers and their dedication to the principle of government of laws.
>
> Illustrative of this clash of philosophies was an argument which went on for months over renewing the contract with the University of California for running three of the Commission's national laboratories. The scientists argued that in line with the principle of freedom of scientific research, a minimum of controls should be imposed on the University. The lawyers contended that if the Commission was going to give the University $300,000,000 a year, the Government should exercise tighter controls over how the University and laboratories chose to spend the money.
>
> Another illustration was the debate last fall over the size of the Commission's budget for the coming fiscal year. The two lawyers fought against any increase in the budget. The scientists are reliably reported to have expressed amazement that the lawyers should question the proposition that an ever increasing amount of money should be spent on scientific research.[12]

The article goes on to tell how the lawyers united their efforts and skillfully argued their point of view. They were far from lacking in verbal talents, and they won some significant victories in their attempts to tighten controls on spending for atomic weapons. Not

[12] *St. Louis Post-Dispatch*, July 1, 1962.

merely lateral communication, as measured in words, but a real meeting of minds was missing between the two factions. The incident illustrates how the vision of members of a professional group is limited by the "blinders" the members wear.

The horizontal cliques mentioned in Chapter 7 also provide the clue to much of the difficulty in lateral communications. Besides the frictions between specialists, there are rivalries and consequent tensions between the different organization units. Departments compete with other departments for bigger appropriations and more prominent roles in the total government program. Similarly, within any one department, the bureaus and other subdivisions fight for special status. The rival organization units eye one another with suspicion and sometimes with considerable hostility. Instead of freely exchanging information on operating plans, they may try to keep one another in the dark. Deviousness, instead of open discussion of mutual problems, may characterize the conversations between their respective personnel. The principal officials in each department may play their cards close to their chests, always afraid of being out-maneuvered by the other party.

The very complexity of modern organization also creates difficulties, just as it does in the case of downward and upward communications. The more persons an official must consult, both within and outside the agency, the more complicated the process of lateral communication becomes. Often he is uncertain as to whom he should consult, because the lines of responsibility within the agency are not that clearly defined. If he must check with another agency, his problem becomes even more difficult, for he may be unfamiliar with the work assignments of the officials in that agency. Valuable time is lost before he can identify the particular individual with whom he should deal. Furthermore, both in intra- and interagency contacts, physical separation may delay and impede communications, as is illustrated in communications between widely separated field offices. Merely looking at the organization chart of a large public agency will give some idea of the complexities of lateral communication. Although the interaction between the numerous departments, divisions, and organization units is not shown on the chart, the very number of these horizontally placed units suggests the intricate pattern of interrelationships necessary for efficient operation. Naturally, the red tape increases as documents and other communications are directed laterally from points inside and outside the agency.

An example of confused lateral communications comes from the history of the United Nations Relief and Rehabilitation Administration (UNRRA). Innumerable copies were being made in its headquarters office in Washington, D.C., of cables as they were received from field officials stationed abroad. The so-called "action copy" of each incoming cable was routed to the headquarters division which was considered to be the most concerned with the subject dealt with in the message. The jurisdictions of the different divisions had been defined so vaguely, however, that in many cases there was much uncertainty as to which headquarters official was supposed to receive the action copy. Accordingly, the duplicating machines were kept busy making countless copies of all cables so that each division could get a copy of every incoming and outgoing communication—just in case the subject matter might be of interest to it. This illustrates how, when organization responsibilities are so poorly defined that anyone's business is everyone's business, the communications channels become hopelessly clogged.

A further difficulty arises from the fact that the person initiating a lateral communication usually cannot exert the same pressure as can a supervisor on his own subordinates. In dealing with coequals, representatives of other agencies, or even the subordinates of others, the official must usually rely on persuasion. This may mean far more delay in lateral than in downward communication, where the traditional flow of authority does give the communication at least some ring of urgency.

Improving Lateral Communication

The first step in developing efficient communications is to build a sound organization structure and to make clear everybody's responsibilities. As to achieving coordination, George F. Gant stresses what he calls "unity by agency objective."[13] By this he means that employees at all levels will work together better if the leaders of the agency clearly explain the importance of the agency program and of their own particular contributions to it. Many different techniques

[13] George F. Gant, "Unity and Specialization in Administration," in Felix A. Nigro (ed.), *Public Administration, Readings and Documents*, New York: Holt, Rinehart and Winston, 1951, pp. 126–135.

can be employed in this effort, but obviously a very superior quality of leadership is required if the employees throughout the agency are to be induced to work together as a team. Furthermore, there may be important limits to the degree to which any individual may be expected to identify with the organization with which he works. Thompson writes:

Although some individuals undoubtedly give considerable loyalty to their bread-and-butter organization, it is only one loyalty among many. If the organization becomes the only object of one's loyalty, then the organization becomes a totalitarian state. Most people probably give their first or primary loyalty to their primary groups—the family, the informal work group, etc. The sharing of values and reality perceptions throughout the larger organization is, therefore, an illusion.[14]

One need not wholly agree with Thompson, but there must be some realization of the limitations to employee identification with organizational goals. Yet we saw in Chapter 5 how professional ties improve communication in grant-in-aid and other intergovernmental programs. It was pointed out then that individuals within the same profession could get along well, despite the fact that they were of different governmental levels, due to their professional loyalties.

Apart from vocational specialization, there is another important way in which the members of modern organizations are specialized; they are "socially specialized," that is, they have become specialized in working with one another. In efforts to improve lateral communication, it must be recognized that it takes a good deal of time before individuals can become specialized in this way:

We understand people easily through our experience with them, which teaches us their special use of words, the meaning of intonation and gestures, whether they are matter of fact or emotional, given to exaggeration or understatement, are reticent or voluble, and many other subtle characteristics of communication. Without the confidence that accompanies this kind of understanding, reticence, hesitation, indecision, delay, error, and panic ensue.

"Know your people" is nearly as important as "know your language" in the communication upon which organized effort depends. The difficulty of communication on matters of concrete action between individuals who have not known each other is a matter of common experience, but

[14] Thompson, *op. cit.*, p. 185.

its importance with respect to organization seems to be forgotten because the organizations we know have, in fact, developed usually through long periods. At a given time nearly everyone has habitual relationships with most of those with whom he needs to communicate regularly.[15]

The agency head naturally wants his subordinates to cooperate and to pull together; yet it takes a real effort to get even the heads of organization units to work together properly. Above all, the agency head must be aware of the probable existence of at least some sensitive relationships between them. With this awareness, he is in a much better position to induce coordinated efforts. The staff conference is frequently mentioned as a valuable tool for achieving coordination, yet the experienced executive knows that some of his subordinates may come to these meetings determined to conceal their real thoughts and plans from the others. He will also be well aware that some of the positions taken may be reactions to certain individuals and their personalities, rather than to the objective situation. Subordinate A may react negatively to suggestions made by subordinate B simply because it is B who makes them. If C were to make them, his reaction might be different. Thus, if the executive is to be successful in improving lateral communication, he must first be effective in improving the interpersonal relationships among his subordinates. Unless he understands his role in this way, the kinds of communications he evokes from them will likely consist of mere words unsupported by any real desire to cooperate. Surface appearances of harmony may be maintained during the conference—polite words may be exchanged —but, as a coordinating device, the meeting will have been a failure. Obviously, there are limits to what the executive can do to promote better personal relationships between his subordinates. It is a certainty, however, that he will have very little success unless he is first able to interpret accurately the feelings behind the communications they initiate, both when in a staff conference or when conferring with him individually.[16]

[15] Chester I. Barnard, "Education for Executives," in Robert Dubin (ed.), *Human Relations in Administration*, Englewood Cliffs, N.J.: Prentice-Hall, 1961, p. 20.

[16] An excellent treatment of this problem is Warren H. Schmidt and Robert Tannenbaum, "The Management of Differences," in Tannenbaum, Weschler, and Massarik (eds.), *Leadership and Organization: A Behavioral Science Approach*, New York: McGraw-Hill, 1961, pp. 101–118.

It has been suggested that in committee meetings no one comment on what someone else has said until he has first satisfactorily repeated what he understands as the other person's meaning. This, of course, has only limited application in direct operations, since the time usually is not available to go through such a procedure. But the subordinate should give some positive indication that he understands the assignment. In administration, the communicators do not have to be polished speakers or great writers, but they do have to make themselves understood. In general, it can be said that too few supervisors in government have developed really satisfactory communications skills. Fortunately, current training programs give the subject a good deal of emphasis.

In assuring proper clearance, one technique is to require those who originate the action copies of outgoing letters and documents to obtain the initials of certain officials on the file copy. These officials have been designated by management as those who should be consulted on the specific matter. The UNRRA example warns us that this list of officials should include only the names of persons with a *legitimate* interest in the particular communication. No purely mechanical procedure will solve this problem of lateral clearance before outgoing communications are finally dispatched. The originating official must finally use his own judgment in deciding whose initials should be obtained. If the correspondence is prepared for his own signature, the official should examine the file copy before he signs the original. In this way, if other important initials are missing, he can return the correspondence to the originator with instructions to obtain the necessary clearances. The repeated failure of a subordinate to forward correspondence which contains all the required initials will warrant the superior official to investigate.

This coordinating technique is effective because it provides a system of double checking. However, it is neither practicable nor desirable to have all outgoing letters signed by a higher official. Many will be signed and sent out by the originating officer. In such case, only a post-control can be exercised, as by reviewing files of correspondence already dispatched. In the final analysis, however, no matter what the procedural manual says, the effectiveness of the system of clearing correspondence will basically depend on the desire of the officials concerned really to cooperate.

INFORMAL COMMUNICATIONS

As we saw in Chapter 7, the formal communications network will always be supplemented by an informal one. If clearances are difficult to obtain through the formal channels, contact can be made informally with a friend who can expedite things. The "grapevine" can damage the organization by carrying ugly gossip and false information, but it also can play a constructive role. Valuable information that an individual will normally not be willing to communicate through the official channels is often transmitted to superior officers very rapidly through the grapevine. For instance, John Jones may be unhappy about a certain condition in his office, but he is not inclined to "jump" channels and complain to the management. He expresses himself freely to his friends, one or more of whom may have an "in" with the top officials in the agency. They informally communicate John Jones' dissatisfactions, whereupon management can look into a situation of which it had not been aware. Thus, the friendship ties characteristic of the informal organization remove some of the communication blocks in upward communication. They perform the same function in facilitating lateral and even downward communication: the superior officer may want to give a subordinate personal advice, but he feels that his official capacity does not permit it. He talks freely to another employee who is in a position to pass the advice on to the person concerned. Obviously, considerable skill must be developed in utilizing these informal channels if the desired results are to be obtained. The dangers are great, because information which is fed into the gossip mill can easily be distorted and do more harm than good.

Eugene Walton observes that the "organization's informal communications network begins to hum whenever the formal channels are silent or ambiguous on subjects of importance to its members."[17] This indicates that the management stands to profit from knowing what kind of information is being transmitted through the grapevine. Walton has investigated the means by which employees learn of significant organization developments. In cases where the employees

[17] Eugene Walton, "How Efficient is the Grapevine?" *Personnel*, **XXXVIII**, No. 2 (March–April, 1961), 45.

have heard about these developments mostly through the grapevine, there is a clear indication that the official channels were not functioning as efficiently as they should have been. Of course, no matter how good the formal system of communications, the grapevine will still exist, but it should not have to do the job of advising employees of management policies. This is the responsibility of the formal organization.

In closing this chapter, the following words of Herbert A. Simon are very much to the point:

> No step in the administrative process is more generally ignored, or more poorly performed, than the task of communicating decisions. All too often, plans are "ordered" into effect without any consideration of the manner in which they can be brought to influence the behavior of the individual members of the group. Procedural manuals are promulgated without follow-up to determine whether the contents of the manuals are used by the individuals to guide their decisions. Organization plans are drawn on paper, although the members of the organization are ignorant of the plan that purports to describe their relationships.[18]

It is with this question of "follow-up" that the next chapter, which deals with "Control," is concerned. Decisions must be communicated effectively and their execution properly controlled.

BIBLIOGRAPHY

Dorsey, John T., Jr., "A Communication Model for Administration," *Administrative Science Quarterly*, **II,** No. 3 (December, 1957).

Gouldner, Alvin W., "Cosmopolitans and Locals: Toward an Analysis of Latent Social Roles," I and II, *Administrative Science Quarterly*, **II,** No. 3 (December, 1957) and **II,** No. 4 (March, 1958).

Kriesberg, Martin, and Guetzkow, Harold, "The Use of Conferences in the Administrative Process," *Public Administration Review*, **X,** No. 2 (Spring, 1950).

[18] Herbert A. Simon, *Administrative Behavior*, New York: Macmillan, 1957, p. 108.

Landsberger, Henry A., "The Horizontal Dimension in Bureaucracy," *Administrative Science Quarterly*, **VI,** No. 3 (December, 1961).

Mortensen, Vivika, "Are Status Symbols Inevitable?" *Personnel Administration*, **XXVI,** No. 3 (May–June, 1963).

Pfiffner, John M., and Sherwood, Frank P., *Administrative Organization*, Englewood Cliffs, N.J.: Prentice-Hall, 1960. Chap. 16.

Redfield, Charles E., *Communication in Management*, Chicago: Univ. of Chicago Press, 1958.

Schmidt, Warren H., and Tannenbaum, Robert, "The Management of Differences," in Tannenbaum, Robert, Weschler, Irving R., and Massarik, Fred, *Leadership and Organization: A Behavioral Science Approach*, New York: McGraw-Hill, 1961.

Simon, Herbert A., *Administrative Behavior*, New York: Macmillan, 1957. Chap. VIII.

Simpson, Richard L., "Vertical and Horizontal Communication in Formal Organizations," *Administrative Science Quarterly*, **IV,** No. 2 (September, 1959).

Strauss, George, "Tactics of Lateral Relationship: The Purchasing Agent," *Administrative Science Quarterly*, **VII,** No. 2 (September, 1962).

Walton, Eugene, "How Efficient is the Grapevine?" *Personnel*, **XXXVIII,** No. 2 (March–April, 1961).

Walton, Eugene, "Motivation to Communicate," *Personnel Administration*, **XXV,** No. 2 (March–April, 1962).

Walton, Eugene, "A Study of Organizational Communication Systems," *Personnel Administration*, **XXVI,** No. 3 (May–June, 1963).

CHAPTER 10

Control

As has so often been said, it is easier to give an order than it is to get it carried out properly. Broadly speaking, *control* is the process which assures that individuals are meeting their responsibilities in the organization. This is accomplished in three ways: through the *social* control of the informal organization; through the *external* control of the legislature or other governing body and of the public in general; and through *management* control, or the system of followup implemented by the administrative hierarchy to see that policies and orders are executed with maximum effectiveness. As noted in Chapter 7, the pressure exerted by the informal group in the organization upon its members to observe the group's norms is often a more effective means of control than the formal edicts of management:

> Wise men have often noticed how powerful control can be in the small group, what a high degree of conformity often exists, though legal machinery is lacking. . . . The intelligent leader of a group will give less heed to inflicting punishment for the infringement of norms than to fostering the conditions under which the group can discipline itself. He will not neglect punishment, but it is ineffective unless supported by informal controls.[1]

Since this aspect was amply discussed in the earlier chapter, however, there is no need for further elaboration here. Suffice it to say that the wise official utilizes the potential for social control that exists among his subordinates to accomplish management objectives. External con-

[1] George C. Homans, *The Human Group*, New York: Harcourt, Brace, and World, 1950, p. 289.

trol is far too broad a topic to discuss here; it is considered in detail in Part VI. This leaves us with management control, the amplification of which is the concern of this chapter, but the reader is reminded that, in practice, any such separation of the three aspects of organizational control is purely artificial, if possible at all.

BASIC ELEMENTS OF MANAGEMENT CONTROL

Considered in this sense, control is simply an elaboration of management's policy directives and work instructions and, as such, is an integral part of administrative leadership. Most management-control systems include two fairly standard procedures: periodic, *written reports*, and *inspections*. In recent years, a third element has come to be emphasized in some forward-looking organizations, although it is by no means in general use: this we shall call—for lack of a better term—the *social audit*. While the first two aspects are self-defining, it is perhaps in order to explain briefly what we mean by the "social audit."

The dictionary meaning of *control* emphasizes the idea of "check" or "restraint," and, surely, this is necessary in any system of control. As noted in earlier chapters, however, the traditional approach to administration tends to accent the restraining element and to view control in the mechanistic terms of production standards, measuring individual performance solely in relation to these standards. Wittingly or no, this approach places a negative value on the worker, and implicitly assumes that the individual is more likely to act against organizational objectives than he is to strive toward their attainment. A forward-looking management, on the other hand, views the controls it establishes from a positive standpoint, and, while it makes clear to the employees what should not be done, it uses the control system basically as a means of coordinating efforts toward common organizational objectives. This approach is based on the assumption that the major part of control should be self-control, and its procedures are designed as much to check up on the wisdom of its own decisions as it is on the performance of its workers. Inherent in this approach, also, is the understanding that, if the individual is to use self-control in meeting the needs of the organization, the organization must meet the human needs of the individual. The purpose of the social audit, then, is to determine whether or not, and to what degree, the organization is satisfying the human needs of its employees.

The difference between these two philosophies can have a great bearing on the achievement of organizational objectives. Workers tend to resent constant subjection to numerous checks and restraints, and, while negatively oriented control can produce conformance with specific instructions, it also serves to inhibit worker initiative. Further, it fails to provide a means of appraising management's own policies. The social audit, on the other hand, recognizes the importance of worker initiative, and strives to measure *total* organizational health.

THE WRITTEN REPORT

Periodic, written reports are a vital part of any control system. First, they commit to permanent record the operational data needed for making evaluations and comparisons with previous or future reports. Obviously, while oral reporting is useful, it must rely on human memory and thus cannot be substituted for the written record. Second, written reports are more economical in terms of time. An official could not possibly review work results if these results were reported orally from each of his principal assistants, nor would these assistants have the time to report to their superior if, in turn, they had to schedule conferences with each of their own subordinates. Third, to some extent, written reports can be standardized for easy summary and compilation into single reports to the agency head. Clearly, the results of numerous conversations among many levels of superiors and subordinates could hardly be so conveniently summarized. Fourth, the data contained in reports frequently must be circulated among a number of different officials, and the written record can be dispatched to all simultaneously. The difficulties inherent in communicating this information orally to all those involved are too obvious to warrant discussion.

The nature and content of written reports will, of course, depend on the operations of the department from which they issue. Budgetary data, cost-accounting, personnel statistics and evaluations, production levels, purchasing data, inventories, proposed projects and plans, project progress or status—all these and more comprise the subjects that circulate in the typical organization's reporting system. The frequency of any one of these varies according to what is considered appropriate; a monthly requirement is quite common, but in some cases weekly and even daily reports are required. In the Forest Service, for example, Rangers must keep diaries which show to the nearest half hour how they spend each work day.

Although it would not serve our purposes to go into detail on each of these kinds of reports, a distinction should be made between *quantitative* or statistical reports and *qualitative* reports. In production-type activities, such as the assembly line, quantitative measures of work results are appropriate and relatively easy to use. In government, quantitative measurements are available in such areas as miles of roads paved, cubic feet of sweepings removed from the streets, number of job applicants interviewed, hired or placed, number of unemployment or social security checks mailed, and so forth. In these cases, the government is able to compare the labor and other costs per work unit, and to relate these data with similar figures for previous periods. These statistics are very useful, but there are serious limitations to purely quantitative evaluations. They effectively measure the work load, but they tell us nothing about the *quality* of the work produced. For example, the personnel office can report on the number of recruitments, but this says nothing of the quality of the hirings. Further, where the organization or one of its departments is performing a service—particularly an intangible service—work-unit measurements are difficult to devise. A group of researchers, for example, may issue numerous reports of their findings, but these give no indication that the group is performing a valuable service. On the other hand, too much emphasis on qualitative analysis can result in an overabundance of highly subjective reports which have little or no factual value. An efficient management, therefore, will include in their reporting system both quantitative and qualitative reports.

Common Errors in Reporting Systems

While an adequate reporting system is essential to an organization's effective operation, there are many ways in which it can serve to defeat its own purposes. The first error commonly made by management is to fail to consult with employees before putting a system into effect. What management considers to be a sound reporting system may, in fact, be a poor one, or at least one which could be improved substantially. The men on the "firing line," so to speak, are often in a better position to determine which data are significant and which are not. Those actually concerned with the specific details on which a report is to be based are familiar with the total picture of the operations at their end, while management officials can hardly be so knowledgeable. Consider the following example, taken from private industry:

> For instance, in a paint company, top sales executives at the home office required consolidated sales figures primarily by geographical areas. For control purposes they watched the trend of sales by regions. When sales declined in a region, they might increase expenditures for advertising in that area. Intensified advertising in such circumstances did not always make sense to the regional supervisory sales executives. For their purposes, they maintained records by size of containers sold, since these records reflected activity in the commercial, institutional, and home markets. They redirected selling effort in accordance with trends shown by these data. The sales supervisors carefully compiled their work notes for their own use and generally paid no attention whatsoever to the reports which they were required to forward to the home office. Thus there was wasteful creation of two sets of sales records from which further confusion might well result.[2]

In addition to causing duplication of effort, possible confusion, and lack of coordination, management's failure to discuss reporting systems with the particular employees involved can also serve to alienate the employees. The report does not solve the problem of control; it is only a tool for improving operations and individual performance. If the workers are alienated, their full cooperation and initiative will suffer, and, with these, the objectives of the organization. Thus, to the extent possible, the reporting system should be cleared by both management and the workers who are specifically involved.

This, of course, applies also when systems of reporting are evaluated and revised. The unfortunate fact is, however, that managements too frequently fail to evaluate and to revise existing systems. Supervi-

[2] Edmund P. Learned, David N. Ulrich, Donald R. Booz, *Executive Action*, Boston: Graduate School of Business Administration, Harvard Univ., 1951, pp. 123–124.

sory officials are sometimes simply unaware of how cumbersome the reporting system has become. What may have been an economical and efficient requirement at first, becomes, with the passage of time and its accompanying changes, an outmoded, time-consuming burden to all concerned. In this connection, note the following comment:

> Another way in which Washington can assist Ambassadors is to liberate them from the demands of unnecessary labors. A vast amount of time, for example, is devoted to extremely detailed reporting, especially in the commercial and economic fields. Staffs in Washington are overworked reading the reports which staffs in the field are overworked producing. On top of this is a welter of administrative paper. It is doubtful that any other government requires so detailed a record of its doings as does ours; few could afford it. No doubt a case can be made for each report. But, in the aggregate, the mass of reporting seems excessive. The best way to demonstrate the superfluity of some of the flow of paper would be to appraise samples of reports over a period of years to see what concrete return they produced. This is a field in which lessons might be learned from other governments.[3]

Sometimes, however, management places emphasis on such superficial aspects as the number, frequency, and length of reports, rather than upon the data contained in each report. The theory here seems to be that the more reports the employee is required to make, and the more time he must spend preparing them, the more effectively he is controlled. Some officials who pay scant attention to the content of reports submitted regard as a serious offense any delay by the subordinate in submitting them. Obviously, this attitude leads to an impossibly unwieldy reporting system which seriously hinders the organization's objectives. One unfortunate result of such a system is that a backlog of reports are piled high on a harassed official's desk awaiting review. In some cases, these reports are merely scanned—if read at all; in other cases a subordinate is assigned to the monotonous chore of reading them—a futile waste of valuable manpower. Further, while the employees may have met the superficial requirements of reporting, in doing so, they have not been effective in improving operations. Overburdened with an unrealistic quota of reports, the employee may resort to falsifying at least some of the data; this becomes particularly easy for him to justify to himself if he knows that

[3] *The Formulation and Administration of United States Foreign Policy*, Senate Foreign Relations Committee, 86th Congress, 2nd Session, Washington, D.C.: Government Printing Office, 1960, p. 114.

management doesn't really read the reports or care what goes into them. An earnest and diligent worker may be all too willing to sacrifice factualness in a report that no one will read in favor of doing a better job at his operational level. Another worker, though he may be eager enough, might not have the proper grasp of his field of operation or of the data he prepares for his report. Such an individual needs closer supervision and guidance; yet his ineffectiveness goes unnoticed as a consequence of the cumbersome report system. Still another individual may be somewhat lazy, yet remain undetected as long as he submits on time the impressively lengthy but meaningless reports required of him. Thus, a reporting system which is left unevaluated and unrevised can serve purposes quite opposite from those of control.

Another common error made is that too few supervisors discuss the contents of their subordinates' reports with them. Many of the difficulties described above could be eliminated if supervisory officials would take this responsibility. No report is entirely self-explanatory, and some questions, at least, should be asked; further, this may be exactly what the subordinate would welcome. He may find it impossible to maintain interest in the reporting system if his efforts are never commented upon. Yet, if he is given the opportunity to discuss his reports with his superior, he is likely to understand better the purpose they are intended to serve and the kinds of information he is supposed to include. The supervisor, on the other hand, would be in a better position to coordinate the efforts of his staff. He can compare the reports of each with one another, and question any inconsistencies among them. Although few people see things in exactly the same light, some data might deliberately have been falsified. Reviewing reports is as integral a part of the control system as report writing, yet in a cumbersome reporting system this aspect is all too likely to be overlooked.

Still another frequent error is the failure to create the conditions favorable to meeting the work goals called for by the reporting system. Adequate manpower and physical facilities must be available, and proper administrative support should be forthcoming. In practice, however, these are too frequently lacking. The numerous clearances required before personnel can be hired, and money can be spent to improve operations, place severe limitations on the achievement of prescribed goals. In addition, it is the all-too-common tendency of supervisory officials to be overgenerous in assigning responsibility but overconservative when it comes to delegating authority. Such officials expect a good deal from their subordinates, although they are reluctant to hand them the prerogatives to match. They may put too much pressure on their subordinates to meet work targets, and this will be reflected in the reporting system. An illustration from the military is worth noting: A superior officer during World War II was constantly on the field telephone demanding that the soldier in charge of the detachment take a certain hill. Wearied by this pressure, the soldier finally decided to report that the hill had been taken. He reasoned, "I'll have that position in another hour, so I'll tell them that I have it now and get them off my back."[4] It is in circumstances like these that some workers may try to beat the system by falsifying reports. The control system will not succeed if the workers do not believe that the standards established by the management are fair.

Of particular importance is the attitude of the supervisory official when the subordinate tells him he needs his help. Perhaps new equipment or more satisfactory office space is urgently needed. Maybe some worker poses a serious disciplinary problem, a typical situation in which support by the higher official is necessary before the immediate supervisor can safely take action. If the higher official seems annoyed that these problems are referred to him, or otherwise appears unsympathetic, the subordinate may be forced to conclude that he is being expected to accomplish the impossible.

The supervisor who delegates adequate authority to his subordinates gives nothing away. On the contrary, he helps himself by making it possible for them to carry out their assigned work satisfactorily. Furthermore, he is on much sounder ground if he later has to call their attention to shortcomings in their performance, since they cannot say that their reasonable requests for help were ignored.

INSPECTIONS

Reports, of course, should be supplemented by personal observations. In some cases, all that the superior official finds necessary is to make a brief visit himself to the different offices and work sites. In

[4] S. L. A. Marshall, *Men Against Fire*, Infantry Journal, Washington, D.C. and William Morrow and Co., New York, 1947, pp. 94–95.

other cases, a program of full-scale investigations is required. These may be made by a separate corps of inspectors who work full time on such assignments, or by members of the line and staff departments who suspend their regular duties temporarily in order to make the inspections.

Since the organization of the Forest Service has already been described (see Chapter 5), its inspection system can be used conveniently to illustrate several different kinds of inspections.[5] There is the General Integrating Inspection, made by headquarters of the regional offices and of the forest supervisors' offices by the regional offices; in turn, the forest supervisors make General Integrating Inspections of the individual Ranger districts. This is the most thorough kind of investigation, the purpose being to evaluate as a whole the activities conducted at the particular field location. Since the General Integrating Inspection is the most time consuming, it is made less frequently than the others. Regions are inspected at least once every five years, the forest supervisors' offices once every four years, and the Ranger districts once every three years. The inspection of a regional office is usually made by one of the Assistant Chiefs of the Service from headquarters, accompanied by another central office official known as the General Inspector, plus appropriate representatives of the Washington office divisions. The inspection of a forest supervisor's office is normally made by a two-man team headed by an assistant regional forester and aided by specialists from the various regional office divisions as needed. Finally, Ranger districts are inspected by the forest supervisor's office, with the help of appropriate staff assistants.

A second kind of inspection is called *functional*. It concentrates on individual functions, like timber management, engineering, information and education, and the others shown in Figure 7 (see page 112). Since it is narrower in scope, it is more detailed than the General Integrating Inspection. Two kinds of functional inspections are made: general and limited. The general type covers all facets of the particular function; the limited type concentrates on a specific activity or project within the particular functional field. For example, timber sales, one aspect of timber management, may be singled out for in-

[5] Herbert Kaufman, *The Forest Ranger, A Study in Administrative Behavior*, Baltimore: Johns Hopkins Press, 1960, pp. 137–140. See also *Organization and Management in the Forest Service*, Washington, D.C.: Government Printing Office, February, 1962, pp. 31–38.

vestigation. Functional inspections are generally made by teams from the appropriate functional division of the level in the organization which is conducting the investigation, i.e., headquarters, regional, or forest supervisor.

Fiscal-administrative inspections are also made regularly, which include essentially the fiscal operations and administrative housekeeping functions. In addition, special investigations are made of unusual problems, such as huge fires and charges of alleged misconduct on the part of forest officers.

Since it is a large organization, with numerous field locations, the Forest Service has a fairly elaborate system of inspections. Other public agencies do their inspecting on a less formalized basis. Suffice it to say that headquarters personnel make field trips from time to time to examine branch office operations, and that employees, both at headquarters and in the field, are subject to the scrutiny of various kinds of inspectors. There is no typical scheme of inspections for all organizations, since so much depends on the size of the agency and the nature of its activities. There are, however, certain common problems which arise in planning and administering any inspection system.

Problems in Developing Inspection Systems

First, there is the question of whether advance warning of the inspection should be given. The argument in favor of making surprise visits is that employees are prevented from making special preparations to deceive the inspectors. Once the inspectors leave, they will revert to their old habits and let things slide. Unquestionably, there are circumstances when the element of surprise is essential. If, for example, the purpose is to find out whether certain employees are really on the job, it would make no sense to advise them in advance of the visit. However, if there is no reason to think that the employees cannot be trusted to meet their minimum responsibilities, there should be no need for a surprise visit.

Again, the basic philosophy of the management of the agency dictates the use which is made of inspections. In the Forest Service, the management believes that the purpose of the inspection is not to try to catch someone at fault but rather to help him to do his job better.

When inspections are viewed in this way, they become a part of the agency's in-service training program. Kaufman makes this abundantly clear in his analysis of the role inspections play in the Forest Service. The inspectors pull no punches in criticizing the Ranger; but they concentrate on corrective measures. Indeed, after-dinner meetings are scheduled in which Forest Service policies and activities in general are discussed between "professional equals" rather than "supervisors and subordinates, or inquisitors and defendants."[6] Before leaving, the inspector tells the employee what is planned for the inspection report. This gives the employee a chance to answer any criticism, and sometimes he succeeds in getting negative aspects eliminated from the report. If the inspector remains unconvinced and is unwilling to strike the criticism from his report, the employee has recourse through a written protest to the Forest Supervisor. The inspection system is administered with such fairness that most Rangers are satisfied despite the "painful candor" of some of the inspectors' reports.

From the administrative standpoint, inspecting without advance notice may also result in no inspection, for the employees may be out in the field or otherwise unavailable when the inspectors arrive. The inspectors will then have to wait for the employees to return to the administrative offices or give up the inspection. They may even find that the head of the field office is away on vacation. To conduct the inspection in his absence would probably be meaningless; the head should be there to answer questions and to see to it that the inspectors receive the help they need. Also there are peak periods of work during which an inspection would only be inexpedient. Inspections should be made at more convenient times when work would not be impeded. Inspections take time. The inspectors have a right to expect the employees to give them their undivided attention, but they defeat their own purposes when they choose the wrong time for the inspection. This is one of the common points of friction in both headquarters-field and staff-line relationships. Field officials sometimes seem to feel that headquarters representatives conspire to take up too much of their time. Line officials make the same complaint about staff specialists. Better scheduling of the visits could eliminate some of this friction.

[6] Kaufman, *op. cit.*, pp. 140–150.

A second problem is the duration of the inspection. A frequent complaint is that the inspector does not stay long enough, and there is a tendency for some officials to make superficial inspections. Naturally, they do not deliberately make superficial inspections, but they feel compelled to stay in one place for no more than two or three days. If this is all that is required, then there is no legitimate complaint: too often, however, the official is on a "swing," meaning that he has left his normal post to make one of his occasional visits to the field, and he wants to include as many different field locations as possible. There is also pressure for him to return to his office, and most likely travel funds are running low. Thus, he may not be responsible for the shortness of his stay. Legislators look suspiciously at the budget requests for travel: Because a few administrative officials do like to "junket,"—meaning travel just for the fun of it—the legislator fears that allocations will be misused. In the main, this fear is unfounded, but the legislators, unsure of which officials they can trust, sometimes conclude that the safest policy is to trust none. There is good reason to think that higher travel budgets would, in the long run, bring sizeable economies made possible by more thorough inspections. Up to now, however, it has not been possible to convince the majority of legislators of this.

A third problem is the lack of thoroughness of the inspector. He leaves, believing he has all the facts when, in truth, he has only begun to scratch the surface. This is sometimes due to clever individuals who arrange matters so that the inspector is never able to make a real investigation. For example, a field-office head may know that some of his subordinates are anxious to mention to the inspector certain conditions which, in their opinion, require correction. The field officer may meet the inspector on arrival and prevent the rest of the local staff from seeing either of them during the inspector's visit. This kind of stratagem is apt to prove successful if, as is so frequently the case, the inspection lasts only two or three days or so.

Few officials are guilty of this kind of deceit, but "wining and dining" the inspector as a means of influencing him is an ancient technique that is still practiced frequently. Naturally, it stands its best chances for success when the inspectors are somewhat naive. "Wining and dining," as employed in modern times, is a highly sophisticated technique. Bribes are not offered, but subtle efforts to please are made. The employee invites the inspector to dine with him or to have a few drinks in some attractive setting. He may even reach into his pocket and "discover" that he has "extra" tickets for an important local function. Of course, if the inspector's wife is travelling with him, an "extra" ticket can conveniently be found for her as well! More commonly, the inspected officials have nothing in particular to hide but a good many points with which they want to impress the inspector. Accordingly, they monopolize his time and are impatient when their subordinates want to say something. This shows how important it is that the inspector have his own plan for conducting the investigation. The best inspector is one who politely but firmly indicates that he has his own ideas about the places he should visit and the people with whom he should speak. It goes without saying that an official with "junketing" tendencies makes the worst inspector.

The system of inspection should never become one of espionage, and this is a fourth problem area in administering the inspections. Some officials will make the mistake of thinking that any method of seeking information is justifiable if it proves successful. Encouraging employees to inform on others is reprehensible, yet some supervisors do so simply by listening to this kind of talk. If the subordinate employee is associated with his superior in a vertical clique relationship, it is easy for him to carry tales. This control is at the expense of alienating the other employees. The management will lose the respect of the workers if it uses, or countenances the use of, such underhanded ways of obtaining information. Eschewing any type or form of espionage may mean losing the opportunity to find out about some real worker deficiencies, but in the long run it makes for more effective control. The chances are that, sooner or later, the employee who cheats will be discovered anyway. Further, as we have already noted, it is much wiser to give the informal work groups the opportunity to discipline their members.

Some officials, though they may not make use of espionage, betray a singular lack of confidence in their subordinates. No sooner do they assign work to one employee than they ask another one to do exactly the same job. Their theory is that the first employee may fail to do the job or do it poorly, and that they are showing foresight by taking no chances. Their notion of control is to fortify their peace of mind with numerous checks on their subordinates. Fortunately, this kind of supervisor is quite rare. Most supervisors know that the greatest mental security comes from assigning work to trustworthy employees; if a subordinate cannot be trusted to do his work properly, the solution is to replace him with one who can command confidence. When two employees find that the chief has asked them to carry out the same assignment, they naturally form a low opinion of him, and feel as though they have been used as pawns in a game the superior may even find amusing. If this kind of system must be used to get the employees to do the work, something is radically wrong and the irresponsible employees should be dismissed. It is possible in such a situation that the supervisor is prey to far too many worries, possibly even to hallucinations, and that it is he who should be removed.

In view of these common errors, great care should be exercised in the selection of the inspectors. From what has been said, it is already clear that they should be persons who are thorough, sincere, and knowledgeable. Anyone with a tendency to be naive about people obviously should not be in the job of inspector. At the same time, the inspector should be fair and considered in his judgments. Theoretically, this is elementary, but, in practice, people have sometimes been employed as inspectors who lack the ability to make rational judgments. The job of any inspector carries with it a certain amount of authority, sometimes a good deal. Unless the individual has a balanced personality, there is real danger that he may abuse this authority. The test of an inspector's competence is his ability to make a thorough, impartial investigation without frightening people. Some inspectors cannot resist the opportunity to cow the employees they investigate. Persons with sadistic tendencies are dangerous as inspectors, and the selection process should be good enough to screen out all candidates with these inclinations.

THE SOCIAL AUDIT

As we stated earlier, the traditional concept of control has been one of measuring performance against standards fixed by the management. In industry, production goals have been emphasized; in government, the effort has been to evaluate the worker's performance in terms of his contribution to the attainment of organization objectives. What the individual has done for the organization has been the central consideration, not what the organization has done for him. It has been assumed that the organization must be a healthy one if the workers meet the production or other standards set by management. Now a different concept of organization health is beginning to appear, which holds that measurement of production and other visible output is not necessarily an indication of a basically healthy organization. There must also be evidence that the organization is satisfying the basic human needs of its employees. If it is not, in the long run it will decline. This is the thesis of Rensis Likert. What he calls "pressure oriented, threatening supervision"[7] may drive up production for a time, but only at the cost of damaging the human assets of the organization. When they are put under too much pressure, the workers become hostile to the management. Some will quit; others will lose interest in cooperating with the management. From the standpoint of its human resources, the organization will have deteriorated. This situation is not healthy, no matter what the production figures show at a particular time.

Accordingly, the control system should include an evaluation of the degree to which the organization is satisfying the basic human needs of its employees. Such an evaluation or "social audit,"[8] asks: How high is the level of worker motivation? are the employees able to feel loyal to the management? do they believe that they are respected as persons and not simply used like tools of production? are they convinced that the organization is doing something positive to satisfy their needs as humans? There is no standard way of making such a study, but usually the workers are asked to fill out questionnaires, and personal interviews are held with as many of them as possible. A careful review is also made of management's policies. All reliable indices of the effect of management practices in human relations terms are studied. The concept of control has obviously broadened considerably when one prominent businessman can argue that a yearly audit of "progress in human relations" is as worthwhile as

[7] Rensis Likert, "Measuring Organizational Performance," *Harvard Business Review*, XXXVI, No. 2 (March–April, 1958), 41–49.

[8] See Fred H. Blum, "Social Audit of the Enterprise," *Harvard Business Review*, XXXVI, No. 2 (March–April, 1958), 77–86.

the annual financial audit.[9] There are important implications for personnel practice when this broader view of control is employed. Likert suggests that "measurements and compensation formulas are needed which will penalize managers financially and otherwise when they permit the quality of the human organization under them to deteriorate, and reward them when they improve the quality of this organization."[10]

Government traditionally has lacked the flexibility of industry in fixing pay rates, but even with this limitation, it can find ways of rewarding the manager who builds up, rather than breaks down, the human resources of the organization. Of course, there already is awareness in both industry and government of the need to maintain and enhance the human values of the organization along with meeting work objectives. But the social audit incorporates into the control system a periodic review of the human assets of the organization. When this is done, the final judgment as to whether management has succeeded or not will depend not only on its technical efficiency, but also on its human-relations score sheet. Nothing could be more calculated than the social audit to induce the management to practice, as well as to preach, good human relations.

BIBLIOGRAPHY

Blum, Fred H., "Social Audit of the Enterprise," *Harvard Business Review*, **XXXVI**, No. 2 (March–April, 1958).

Dimock, Marshall E., *The Executive in Action*, New York: Harper and Row, 1945. Chap. XIX.

Dubin, Robert (ed.), *Human Relations in Administration*, Englewood Cliffs, N.J.: Prentice-Hall, 1961.. Chap. 18.

Follett, Mary Parker, "The Psychology of Control," in Metcalf, Henry C. and Urwick, L. (eds.), *Dynamic Administration*, New York: Harper and Row, 1940.

[9] *Ibid.*, pp. 77–78.
[10] Likert, *op. cit.*, p. 49.

Learned, Edmund P., Ulrich, David H., and Booz, Donald R., *Executive Action*, Boston: Graduate School of Business Administration, Harvard Univ., 1951. Chap. VIII.

Likert, Rensis, "Measuring Organizational Performance," *Harvard Business Review*, **XXXVI,** No. 2 (March–April, 1958).

Likert, Rensis, *New Patterns of Management*, New York: McGraw-Hill, 1961. Chap. 5.

Organization and Management in the Forest Service, Washington, D.C.: Government Printing Office, 1962.

Walton, Eugene, "Gauging Organizational Health—A Questionnaire Study in a Government Laboratory," *IRE Transactions of the Professional Group on Engineering Management*, EM–8, No. 4 (December, 1961).

CHAPTER 11

Public Relations

Lawrence A. Appley writes: "Whatever an organization does that affects the opinions of its various publics toward it is public relations."[1] Appley's definition of public relations is admirable for several reasons. First, it makes clear that every organization has public relations, because it is dealing with groups of people who will have opinions about it. A given organization may not employ a public relations director or have any formal program for developing favorable public attitudes, yet it will elicit some kind of response on the part of the people who have contact with it: thus it has public relations, "good, bad, or indifferent." A distinction should be made between *public relations* itself and *public relations administration.* If an organization is aware of the importance of its publics' opinions and develops a positive program intended to influence these publics intelligently and constructively, it has public relations administration. The purpose of public relations administration is to make sure that the agency's relations with its publics are good, rather than bad or indifferent.

Second, Appley refers to *publics,* plural, because modern organizations are constantly dealing with many different groups. This makes public relations administration difficult, since favorable relations may be enjoyed with one group, but often at the expense of another.

[1] Lawrence A. Appley, *Management in Action,* New York: American Management Association, 1956, p. 53.

MULTIPLE PUBLICS

A private company's publics include not only its customers but also its stockholders, labor unions, trade associations, suppliers, and the other organizations with which it has contact. In government, the specific nature of an agency's publics will depend on the kind of programs for which it is responsible. The Department of Agriculture's publics, for example, include numerous commodity groups, large and small farm operators, manufacturers of agricultural machinery, owners of grain elevators, the starving peoples of the world, and even the American housewife. As we saw in Chapter 1, in many important fields of government activity great discretion must be entrusted to officials in the administrative branch. These officials must define the "public interest." When Newton Minow, former Chairman of the Federal Communications Commission, called television a "wasteland," he did not endear himself to one of his publics—the broadcasters. On the other hand, he won the admiration of another—namely, numerous parents who were very disturbed by the emphasis on violence in television programs. The ideal situation, of course, is to enjoy reasonably good relations with all or the majority of the agency's publics. This is difficult to accomplish, particularly when agency objectives are described vaguely or inconsistently in the authorizing legislation. Legislators hope that a bill will satisfy as many different groups and individuals as possible. Enforcement officials are faced with the formidable task of accomplishing this in practice. Legislators themselves constitute one of the most crucial publics for administrative officials. If it is displeased, the legislature can reduce the agency's budget and even abolish it. The agency typically has many publics within the legislative body. These are the appropriations and other committees which review its activities and pass upon its requests for additional funds and approval of new programs. Each member of the legislature is by himself a potential public, depending on where his interests lie.

DEVELOPING THE PUBLIC RELATIONS PROGRAM

The management of any public agency should not only employ competent *media specialists*—those who handle press contacts, prepare news releases, write radio scripts, and carry out other information activities—but it should also create a favorable image of itself, both inside and outside the agency.

Media Specialists

Care should be exercised to keep the media specialists in their proper sphere. For the most part persons with backgrounds in journalism, these men and women have contributed a great deal to the success of the programs of many public agencies. Using their special skills, they have often achieved excellent results in interpreting the agency's program to the citizenry. Department heads and other top officials usually do not have the time to write their own speeches, so every day in government talented members of the information staffs prepare drafts for them. The director of information has shrewd comments to make to the agency head about how to obtain public support for a proposed course of action.

But with few exceptions, these media specialists are not qualified to participate in the formulation of the agency's policies as such. Some people believe that this is a proper and necessary activity for the information staff; their argument is that no public relations program, no matter how artfully conceived, can remedy deficiencies in the agency's basic policies. Accordingly, they argue, the information specialist should play a leading role in the development of the substance or content of the agency program. Logically, this position means that the information head should have much the same abilities as the agency head. What else if he is to have such an important role in the formulation of agency policies? It is here that the argument falls down. Most newspapermen do not have a broad enough background to qualify as agency policymakers. They are neither trained administrators nor experts in the content of government programs. Furthermore, in most cases they themselves do not aspire to such a role; they are content to function as information specialists. Realistically speaking, if the management of an enterprise is incapable of developing policies which produce good public relations, it should be changed. The solution is not to cede the policymaking function to the information staff. In fact, there may be a tendency for an organization to think that it has done all it can do in the field of public relations when it hires a staff of public relations experts.

Nothing that has been said above should be interpreted to mean that it is unnecessary or undesirable for the management to have a close relationship with the information staff. Public relations is a management tool, and this means that the information director should be fully advised of management plans and the reasons for new agency policies. Unless he is thoroughly familiar with the thinking of the management, he and his staff will be unable to do a good job of interpreting these policies to the agency's publics. Furthermore, while the information director may not qualify as a policymaker, he is equipped to give expert advice on probable public reactions to proposed policies and on how to present new policies with maximum effectiveness.

Employee Morale and Public Relations

Above all, the agency management should understand the relationship between the morale of all its employees and effective public relations. Dissatisfied employees are by no means an internal problem only. They live in the local community; their neighbors identify them with the agency. If they seem little interested in their work or, with apparent justification, are even critical of their superiors, these neighbors and friends will form an unfavorable impression of the agency. The relationship between internal personnel management and the agency's reputation in the community is very close. A high "quit" rate makes people wonder what goes on in the agency. Evidence of patent failure to impress upon the employees the need to deal courteously with local citizens will reinforce the notion that the government bureaucracy does not really care about the people. Some private companies have long recognized this relationship; the example comes to mind of the restaurant which prominently displays a sign, "This is a good place to work." The customers presumably are much more interested in the quality of the restaurant's food than in its personnel policies; but, of course, a place that can keep good employees is also one which takes pains to treat the customers well. This again demonstrates the breadth of the public relations field. In addition to its many other facets, it encompasses the important field of personnel administration, which is presented in detail in Part IV of this book.

Although the employees should be trained generally in public relations, a particular need is to develop their communications skills. Communications bears upon public relations in several important ways. For example, employees should be able to write intelligible letters in response to inquiries from the public. Also, the agency should have at least a few officials who are good speakers and who can explain its program to local groups. As we saw in Chapter 9, employees will be more likely to cooperate with the management if barriers to upward communication are removed. Inside and outside the organization, the agency will suffer if its personnel does not have some degree of competence in the area of communications. As Victor A. Thompson states: "If all people in a given situation had the same perception of the situation, there could be no conflict."[2] Good communications improve the possibility of avoiding conflict, but this, of course, is a difficult problem, because internally and externally the typical agency has a great many contacts producing many different kinds of situations. Suffice it to say that this again demonstrates why public relations is such a vital part of the management responsibility.

Community Relations Programs

A perceptive agency management knows that *systematic community relations programs* aid greatly in building public support. The purpose of such programs is to improve the agency's standing in the community, and to gain acceptance as a desirable element in the local picture.

In planning such programs, efforts are made to obtain answers to such questions as these:

Does the average citizen know what the agency's objectives are? Do leading citizens? Do the agency's own employees?

Are there any things for which the organization is generally criticized by members of the community? Do employees voice the same criti-

[2] Victor A. Thompson, *Modern Organization*, New York: Knopf, 1961, p. 126.

cisms? What identifiable expectations of the community are not being met by the organization?
Are the achievements of the individual employees in carrying out the work of the agency fully publicized?
Are local citizens aware of employee contributions to various community causes?
Is the local population aware of the benefits it derives from the location of the agency in the community?[3]

Once it has the answers to these and similar questions, the agency will know what it must do to make itself better liked in the community. Particularly important is the establishment of contact with "local thought leaders." These are the leading citizens of the community, such as prominent businessmen, heads of civic organizations, newspaper editors, radio and television officials, and school authorities. If the support of these people is obtained, it is very likely that the community as a whole will develop a favorable image of the agency.

The kinds of community relations projects that should be undertaken, of course, depend on local conditions, but the following are some possibilities:

1. Establishing a speakers' exchange with local groups. After a member of the agency's staff has spoken before one of these groups, such as the Lions, Rotary, or Kiwanis, the organization in question has one of its representatives speak at a meeting of the agency's own personnel.
2. Participating in community campaigns, such as the United Fund drive and the American Red Cross Blood Bank program.
3. Making buildings and other facilities available for meetings of civic groups which lack adequate accommodations of their own.
4. Holding "clinics" and arranging open houses in order to explain the agency's program to the users of its services and the public in general. Examples are the Post Offices' "rate clinics" for large users of the mails and similar meetings of the Veterans Administration with builders and others to explain its loan guaranty program.
5. Encouraging employees to be active in the local chapters of professional organizations, and in general giving the agency's support to such organizations.

[3] See "Community Relations For Government," Management Forum, *Public Administration News*, Chicago: American Society for Public Administration, VIII, No. 9 (November, 1958).

6. Making the outstanding achievements of the employees known to the community by holding special ceremonies and by appropriate publicity.

7. Sponsoring special events, such as anniversary observances, parades and pageants, demonstrations, special days and weeks, and similar programs for building good relations with the community.

8. Being sensitive to the needs of the community and endeavoring to satisfy reasonable requests for the improvement and extension of the agency's services.[4]

This is by no means a complete list, but it will suffice to explain what is meant by community relations programs. The need for such activities is undeniable, because so often local sensitivities are injured. In some university and college communities, there is animosity between the town folk, on the one hand, and the teachers, administrative staff, and students, on the other. The teachers may offend the local merchants by preferring to shop in a nearby big city where they find the prices more reasonable. In supporting causes like city-manager government, they may incur the displeasure of local politicians who want to preserve the status quo. And, just as private firms do their best to keep on good terms with the local citizens, so must government agencies.

U.S. military commanders abroad face a particularly difficult problem in trying to maintain friendly relations with the local populations. Foreigners are hard to understand in the first place, and they are resented even more when they happen to be members of the armed forces of another country. If ever a community relations program were needed, it is in circumstances like these. It is only because positive efforts have been made by the Defense Department to remove points of friction that one military analyst could say recently that "relations between the United States garrisons in Europe and the local civil population are, in general, better than they are in the United States."[5] The approach used has been twofold. On the one hand, the American soldiers and their families have been instructed in how to make a better impression with the local residents. Such training stresses much the same points as those made in Chapter 3. On the other hand, efforts are made to get the local people to

[4] *Ibid.*

[5] Brig. Gen. Thomas R. Phillips, "Army Working Long and Hard to Promote Good Will Abroad," *St. Louis Post-Dispatch*, June 7, 1959, editorial section.

understand the Americans better. In such efforts, the help of leading local figures has been enlisted with very good results. For example, in Germany a large number of community advisory councils, composed of German and American officials, have been established. These councils plan cultural activities and bring Germans and Americans into closer contact.

Making Effective Use of Press Outlets

Finally, in developing its public relations program, a good agency management makes effective use of press and other outlets. It is well aware that bungling in contacts with newspaper reporters and other representatives of the mass communications media can do great damage to its program. An information director with an extensive background in journalism understands the point of view of the press and knows when it is apt to be offended by officials who are well meaning but who have no "public relations sense." We will soon be discussing a very sensitive area as far as the press is concerned: withholding of information by government officials. This is where a good information director can save the management from making serious mistakes.

Thus, press relations must be managed well, and an agency management which underrates the importance of this may quickly find itself in publicity difficulties. Like any other chief executive, President Kennedy had his critics, but on one aspect of his performance, Democrats and Republicans alike rated him high: public relations. Through artful use of his televised press conferences and other techniques, he quickly succeeded in developing a favorable public image of himself and his family. While any President is in a good position to get favorable publicity, Presidents can make serious mistakes in the area of public relations, and not all are equally successful in their efforts to develop wide popular support.

LEGITIMATE INFORMATION VS. PROPAGANDA

In a democracy—indeed, in any kind of government—it is necessary that the people be well informed, and they cannot be unless the government tells them what it is doing and how the citizenry will be affected. Yet there has been no general agreement as to exactly how much and what kinds of information should be released by the various agencies. Legislators distinguish between "legitimate" public information activities and "propaganda." However, the difficulty lies in defining whether or not something is legitimate. Furthermore, what one brands as propaganda, another may sincerely argue as essential for developing public understanding and support of his agency's programs.

Obviously, political biases color the viewpoints expressed on this matter. Recently, a newspaper correspondent in California criticized the public relations activities of the State Water Resources Department for requesting budget appropriations to create three additional positions for photographers, as well as to purchase new photographic equipment.[6] The agency's justification for these proposed expenditures was that it needed photographic records of its construction program. The correspondent believed that the real aim was to impress the public with the achievements of the Democratic administration under Governor Brown. If the intention was purely to provide personal publicity for the top staff of the Water Resources Department as members of the Brown administration, the correspondent's complaint was justified. Realistically, however, it must be recognized that any administration, Democratic or Republican, will want to inform the public about its accomplishments, crediting the party in power for them. In addition, "The more efficient the official information services are in facilitating administration and increasing popular understanding of government policies the more they will add to the reputation of the administration of the day."[7] The California legislature not only rejected the request for additional positions and photographic equipment, but also eliminated two existing information positions in the Water Resources Department.

Thus, how much public information activity should be allowed often depends upon the political affiliations of the person who expresses his opinion. The correspondent believed that there was only "a legitimate, small-scale necessity to help newspaper reporters tell the people what various departments are doing."[8] The meanings

[6] *San Diego Evening Tribune*, April 4, 1962, editorial page.

[7] J. A. R. Pimlott, *Public Relations and American Democracy*, Princeton, N.J.: Princeton Univ. Press, 1951, pp. 96–97.

[8] *San Diego Evening Tribune*, *op. cit.*

of these terms are difficult to pin down: When is the public information activity "legitimate"? When is it "small-scale"? Not only will members of the different political parties disagree about this, but so will political neutrals.

Legislation and Information Release

The legislature actually defines the responsibilities of some agencies in such a way as to make "large-scale" information programs necessary. The Department of Agriculture was established in 1862 "to acquire and diffuse among the people of the United States information on subjects connected with agriculture in the most general and comprehensive sense of that word." The statute creating the Office of Education in 1867 requires it to "diffuse such information as shall aid the people of the United States in the establishment and maintenance of efficient school systems, and otherwise to promote the cause of education."

Disseminating information and enlisting public support is one of the functions of many executive agencies at all levels of government. Health departments could hardly function effectively without programs of health education; the public must be educated to recognize health hazards and to cooperate in governmental programs to reduce the incidence of disease. In other programs, paid advertising and other forms of publicity must be used if the legislative mandate is to be carried out successfully. Public agencies responsible for promoting tourism place such advertisements and make the same appeals to the spending public as private entrepreneurs. Similarly, state and local development commissions carry out systematic promotional efforts to attract new industries. Anyone who makes even a passing examination of the advertisements that appear in magazines and the Sunday issues of the newspapers will have no trouble finding some which describe the advantages of a particular state or locality as a place in which to start a business.

Sometimes it is said that government information programs should be limited to disseminating factual information, and that efforts to *persuade* should not be permitted because they are *propaganda.* The examples given above show clearly that it is impractical to try to make such a distinction. The public-health department cannot consider its job ended when it advises the public of an outbreak of disease; it must also *persuade* the citizen to take certain action, such as participating in a mass immunization program. Federal and state officials in agricultural programs similarly try to convince the farmer to use the technical advice which they give him. Diffusion of information, in and of itself, could hardly be considered sufficient, particularly when success in obtaining the desired results depends on the cooperation of a large number of citizens.

If the governmental activity meets with general public approval few people could question the need for persuasion. It is only when an element of controversy is injected into the picture, that the cry of propaganda is likely to be heard. Suppose that there is an alarming increase in the number of polio cases. Appeals in the newspapers, on radio and television, and in leaflets urge those who have not yet done so to obtain polio shots—these activities by the public-health authorities are considered proper. Suppose, however, that a group of citizens is urging the local government to fluoridate its water supply. How far can the health department go in urging public support for obtaining the legal authorization to provide for fluoridation? Some people are strongly opposed to fluoridation, but practically everybody is in agreement with immunization against polio. It is when people are against a program that they complain the most about propaganda.

Some recent scientific studies have shown a definite relationship between cigarette smoking and lung cancer and heart disease. In 1959, the Public Health Service made its stand on this question when the Surgeon-General, Dr. Leroy E. Burney, said that the weight of the evidence indicated that cigarette smoking was the principal cause of the increased incidence of lung cancer. He also stated that "no method of treating the tobacco or filtering the smoke"[9] had been discovered which materially reduced the hazard of lung cancer. He therefore concluded that "unless the use of tobacco can be made safe, the individual person's risk of lung cancer can best be reduced by the elimination of smoking."[10] Since this is the considered opinion of the Public Health Service, should the government launch a public-information program to dissuade people from smok-

[9] James Deakin, "Economic Factors Believed Delaying Tobacco Crackdown by Kennedy," *St. Louis Post-Dispatch*, July 8, 1962, editorial section.

[10] *Ibid.*

ing? This is an example of the most difficult kind of public relations problem that can confront government officials. Reporters pointedly put this question to President Kennedy during a press conference in May, 1962, shortly after the precipitous drop in stock-market values. Not only is the eight-billion-dollar-a-year tobacco industry one of the biggest in the country, but it also provides the federal government with $2 billion in tax revenues annually. Kennedy frankly said, "That matter is sensitive enough and the stock market is in sufficient difficulty to prevent my giving you an answer which is not based on complete information, which I don't have."[11]

Kennedy requested that the Public Health Service arrange for another, more comprehensive study of the problem. The results were made known early in 1964,[12] but, although the Public Health Service strongly supported the findings—that cigarette smoking was harmful—the new President, Lyndon B. Johnson, did not immediately call for a strong government anti-smoking campaign. However, in June, 1964, the Federal Trade Commission (FTC) issued a regulation which would require a prominent warning as to the health hazards of cigarette smoking on all cigarette packs, boxes and cartons sold, beginning January 1, 1965. A similar warning would be required in advertising, beginning July 1, 1965. The tobacco industry indicated that it would challenge the FTC's authority to issue such a regulation, and the FTC conceded that it might be as long as 4 years before the legal question was decided in the courts.

The administrative branch plays a leading role in initiating new policies and in obtaining public approval of new government programs. The record of recent years shows clearly that the White House must frequently make direct appeals to the public if it is to stand any real chance of getting its legislative proposals approved by a balking Congress. Here again, how far it can go depends a good deal on the degree of controversy attaching to the particular proposal. Efforts by the Kennedy administration to obtain public support for medical insurance under social security were labelled *political propaganda* by those opposed to the program. Distribution of printed materials,

[11] *Ibid.*

[12] *Smoking and Health*, Report of the Advisory Committee to the Surgeon General of the Public Health Service, Washington, D.C.: Government Printing Office, 1964.

speeches by federal officials urging the program's adoption, and similar efforts to persuade the public were assailed as unjustifiable use of public funds and improper activity by the public employees concerned.

On the other hand, when a proposal commands wide support, among adherents of both major parties and with many segments of the population, considerable public relations activity in the government is tolerated. A good example here was the Kennedy administration's trade-expansion program, approved by the Congress in October 1962. After submitting this program to Congress, the President said in a press conference early in 1962 that a large-scale educational effort would be needed to explain its advantages to domestic manufacturers. The White House itself was not equipped financially or otherwise to carry on this kind of public relations activity, so help was obtained on an unpaid, voluntary basis from private companies that were anxious to see the program become law. The services of three, high-priced industry executives were secured on this basis. In addition, four different public relations firms whose client corporations favored the trade bill contributed their services to the efforts to obtain passage of the legislation.[13] Although the government was getting the services of the industry executives free, they were functioning under White House auspices. Yet this public relations activity did not lead to a public outcry about government propaganda. The explanation is that Republicans and Democrats, conservatives and liberals, business and labor were generally united behind the trade bill as a necessary measure to protect America's foreign markets. A comparable consensus by no means existed with respect to medical insurance for the aged.

Political policymaking officials must decide for themselves in each case how far they can go in using government funds and personnel for developing support for new legislation. Not only in Washington but also in the State Capitals, the legislators do their best to see to it that no large sums of money are available which the administration in power can use for this purpose. Legislative controls on expenditures of this type have in the past been so strong that there seems to be little danger of an all powerful "government propaganda machine." Pimlott makes the following astute comment:

[13] *Los Angeles Times,* April 2, 1962.

The Executive is bound to be under a constant temptation to err in the direction of laxity, and its opponents to be unreasonably strict. Every administration will be tempted to "sell" itself and its programs to the people with the aid of the official publicity machine: the most conscientious official may be led astray by an excessive zeal for the public welfare which blinds his sense of constitutional niceties, the less conscientious may be influenced by personal ambition or outside pressures. Legislators and political opponents, even if they try to be dispassionate, start with a predisposition to suspect any activity which may strengthen the Executive: where they are less careful, their judgment may be warped by particular motives or influenced by outside interests which are not seriously exercised about constitutional propriety.[14]

WITHHOLDING INFORMATION

On the other hand, there has been much criticism in recent years of the tendency to *withhold* information from the public. Specifically, the complaint has been that some administrative officials refuse to release information which ought to be made known to the public. How can we say that we have a truly democratic system if the people are denied the facts needed for making intelligent judgments about government policies? The very idea of secrecy in the government is repugnant to most Americans.

The press has been much concerned because "freedom of information" is the very basis of its operations. It naturally becomes concerned when government officials appear unjustifiably to deny them access to important information. Such organizations as the American Society of Newspaper Editors, the American Newspaper Publishers Association, and the Associated Press Managing Editors Association have protested the withholding of information. Most of this criticism has been leveled at the federal government, and sometimes at the President himself. State and local officials have not escaped similar criticism. The problem is complex, because, although the public agency sometimes seeks to withhold information which would show it in an unfavorable light, in some circumstances it is justified in refusing to divulge certain data.

This situation has existed throughout American history since George Washington's administration, but since World War II the

[14] Pimlott, *op. cit.*, p. 94.

issue has arisen more frequently due to the increasing complexity of our society:

> What is distinctive about government secrecy today is the vast range of information that is now subject to laws preventing the disclosure of official data. Apart from the classification system in national defense, which attempts to conceal a wide variety of military and diplomatic secrets from foreign espionage, there have been a great number of statutes enacted and executive regulations promulgated which attempt to prevent the unauthorized release of non-defense but nevertheless confidential information. And in areas where secrecy is not sanctioned by such specific legal safeguards, presidents can always invoke their executive privilege to withhold information when they choose to do so. As a result there is virtually no area of the administrative process that has been left untouched by the claims of secrecy in modern American government.[15]

Congress, although it has certainly been concerned over this situation, is responsible for the very laws referred to above. The explanation is that Congress has had to safeguard the interests of private individuals who might suffer if the confidential files of the government were opened to public inspection. As one example, regulatory agencies such as the Federal Trade Commission and the Securities and Exchange Commission obtain much information about the internal affairs of private businesses in the course of their work. If they were required to disclose this data, they might injure a company's economic position. Similarly, to require that a regulatory agency make public any suspicion of a given company would be unwise until it has been proven that the company has violated the law. Much information in government files is purely personal; individual income taxes are a good example. The government needs this information, but its disclosure to the general public could both injure private interests and impede government enforcement efforts. Accordingly, Congress has worded the laws so as to permit administrative officials to keep this information confidential. That these laws are valuable no one would deny, but they also can be used to promote unnecessary and even dangerous secrecy. For example, the Housekeeping Act of 1789 authorized ". . . the head of each department to prescribe regulations, not inconsistent with law, for the government of his

[15] Francis E. Rourke, *Secrecy and Publicity*, Baltimore: Johns Hopkins, 1961, p. 11.

department, the conduct of its officers and clerks, the distribution and performance of its business, and the custody, use, and preservation of its records, paper, and property appertaining to it." This simple statute has been invoked frequently over the years by various administrative officials to justify keeping confidential any sort of information if it suited their purposes. So much use of this statute was made that the House Subcommittee on Government Information, established in 1955, became convinced that it was largely responsible for an alarming increase in executive secrecy. Representative Moss in the House and the late Senator Hennings in the Senate led the fight in Congress to amend it to prevent its misuse. This amendment was passed in August, 1958, and simply states: "This section does not authorize the withholding of information from the public or limiting the availability of records to the public." Before the bill was passed, however, Moss had to

> ". . . assure his congressional colleagues that passage of his amendment would not endanger the secrecy of military and diplomatic records, income tax returns, trade secrets received by the government in confidence, Federal Bureau of Investigation reports, or information that could be withheld legitimately under other laws enacted by Congress."[16]

In a report issued in 1960, the Subcommittee admitted that the amendment had not proved an effective check on secrecy.

Changes in the laws are thus not likely to provide a satisfactory solution to this problem. The really constructive role of the Subcommittee and of the Congress in general has been in maintaining so close a watch on executive officials as to deter them from declaring as much information confidential as they might. The Subcommittee has a good record of success in bringing pressure upon the administrative agencies to release information which they originally refused to disclose.

Further, under the doctrine of executive privilege, Presidents have refused Congress unrestricted access to documents and records of administrative agencies. President Kennedy himself invoked this doctrine when he refused to release the names of those in the Defense Department responsible for deleting passages from military speeches. The President felt that, as head of the executive branch, he should

[16] *Ibid.*, pp. 59–60.

accept full responsibility for any decisions these officials had made; the principle of separation of powers would be undermined if he allowed Congress to hold administrative officials directly responsible to it.

Many people feel that this doctrine of "executive privilege" is legitimately needed to protect the executive branch from encroachment on its powers by the legislature. Others, however, have severely criticized the President and department heads for making what they considered to be unjustified use of this doctrine.

In 1957, the late Senator Hennings of Missouri requested of Attorney-General Brownell a detailed justification of presidential rights to withhold information in order to see how the executive branch was construing the doctrine of executive privilege.[17] The Attorney-General flatly stated that executive privilege gave the President and his administration an "uncontrolled discretion" to withhold information in the public interest:

> While Congress passed the laws creating the executive departments, that does not mean that the heads of those departments are subject to the orders of the House of Representatives or of the Senate. Congress can, by a law, duly passed and signed by the President, add to or change the duties of a particular department, or even abolish it altogether. But that is all it may do. *It may not use its legislative power to compel a head of a department to do an act which the President must disapprove in the proper discharge of his executive power, and in the public interest.* And any law passed by Congress, designed to compel the production of papers by heads of departments would necessarily have to comply with the constitutional requirement that the President is as supreme in the duties assigned to him by the Constitution, as Congress is supreme in the legislative functions assigned to it. In other words, Congress cannot, under the Constitution, compel heads of departments by law to give up papers and information, regardless of the public interest involved; and the President is the judge of that interest. Such a law would render the President powerless in a field of action entrusted to his complete care by the Constitution.[18]

These, of course, were the opinions of one Attorney-General, based on his own analysis of the historical evidence. Many thought that

[17] *The Power of the President to Withhold Information from the Congress*, Senate Judiciary Committee, 85th Congress, 2nd Session, Washington, D.C.: Government Printing Office, 1958.

[18] *Ibid.*, pp. 3–4. Italics ours.

Brownell had gone too far when he said that the President had "uncontrolled discretion" to withhold information. Hennings' opinion was that the claim of executive privilege had to be weighed against a fundamental constitutional protection—the people's "right to know."[19] This right, he believed, was protected by the First Amendment, along with the guarantees of freedom of speech and thought. Further, Hennings was confident that the Supreme Court would interpret the First Amendment in this way. Only if the government could prove a clear and present danger would the Court sustain depriving the people of its "right to know." Hennings held that the President's power to withhold information was indeed a "privilege," not a right. Instead of being uncontrolled, it was subject to "relatively narrow limits." Even in the field of foreign affairs, this privilege existed "only to the extent that the effective and proper exercise of the President's power to conduct the foreign affairs of the nation requires it."[20]

Hennings' arguments are theoretically sound, but it seems unlikely that the federal courts would accept jurisdiction in so huge an area. A Supreme Court decision of this kind would almost certainly mean that a great number of requests would be made to compel public officials all over the country to release information.

Examples of Information Withheld

The kinds of information that administrative officials have unjustifiably tried to hold from the public are various. J. R. Wiggins cites a few:

1. For years after the inauguration of the Agricultural Adjustment program, the names of the recipients of Federal payments were kept secret.
2. Names of persons getting drought aid were kept secret under Department of Agriculture regulations until December 1953 when new regulations were adopted.
3. Information on loans by the Reconstruction Finance Corporation were secret until the disclosure in Congressional investigations in 1950–1951, after which a "goldfish bowl" policy was announced.
4. For three years the Public Housing Administration refused to give out the names of its employees.

[19] See *Executive Privilege (General Accounting Office)*, Senate Judiciary Committee, 86th Congress, 1st Session, Washington, D.C.: Government Printing Office, 1959, pp. 106–117.

[20] *Ibid.*, p. 116.

5. Applications for tax exempt status were concealed by the United States Treasury until amendments adopted in 1957 compelled disclosure.
6. The Treasury Department only recently agreed to abandon a policy of keeping secret the administrative settlement of fines, penalties, and forfeitures for import law violations.
7. The Panama Canal Administration withheld the names of Congressional personnel who had travelled without charge on its shipping line.[21]

Wiggins, like many others, believes that the Defense Department has placed a security classification on much information that could safely be made public. The House Subcommittee on Government information has reported the following:

Suppression of a list of military installations which sell packaged liquor to servicemen.

Classification of a report on the use of shark repellents, in which were detailed 69 cases of shark attacks, 55 between 1907 and 1940.

Description of a bow and arrow was classified during the war and kept classified as "confidential" until after hearings in 1958.

The Office of Security Review in the Defense Department solemnly reviewed for security clearance a review of a Civil War book entitled *Destruction and Reconstruction*, written by a Confederate Army General and first published in 1879.[22]

Further, despite efforts by the Defense Department within the past few years to reduce overclassification, the House Subcommittee on Government Information reported in 1960 that the "Pentagon was wielding secrecy stamps at a rate which created each week a stack of classified documents higher than the Empire State Building."[23] Senator Clinton P. Anderson of New Mexico has recommended that there be just as "severe penalty on those placing a restricted tag on unrestricted information as is now provided for those revealing secret data."[24] As it now stands, if those responsible for classifying data fail to restrict certain information and its disclosure later adversely affects the nation's security, they will be punished, but if

[21] *Ibid.*, p. 170.
[22] *Ibid.*, p. 171.
[23] Rourke, *op. cit.*, pp. 76–77.
[24] Clinton Anderson, "Top Secret—But Should it Be?," *The New York Times Magazine*, May 3, 1959, p. 14.

they overclassify, the only consequences are that they may be criticized outside of the military.

Congress is particularly irked when a civilian agency refuses to release important information under the pretext that the public does not need the information. An excellent case in point is the controversy over Project Mohole, which will undertake to drill a hole thousands of feet through the ocean floor in order to discover what sources of mineral and other wealth lie underneath the earth's crust. The National Science Foundation (NSF) has been assigned responsibility for this project. The controversy arose in June, 1962, when the NSF declined to make public the cost estimates submitted by bidding contractors. Newsmen requested this information when the NSF awarded the contract for the second phase of the project to a Houston, Texas, firm which had not been the lowest bidder. The General Accounting Office reported that the Texas firm submitted an estimate of $35 million, while a company which had performed preliminary work on the project had offered to do the work for $23 million. The director of the NSF argued that there was no point in disclosing the costs estimates, since no one knew how much the project would actually cost when finally completed. Congress, led by Representative Moss, protested. At first, the White House supported the NSF; an assistant special counsel to the President wrote to Representative Moss advising him that the NSF's position "makes sense." In the end, however, the White House decided that it did not make sense. Moss and his Subcommittee continued their protests, and finally President Kennedy ordered the NSF to establish "general public information procedures" on contracts and research grants, and, in a letter to Moss, said:

> Your point is valid that the circumstances surrounding any negotiated contract require even greater concern than usual that there be full understanding of the basis upon which such contracts rest . . . the people have an interest in, and a right to know about, the negotiations leading up to an agreement to spend huge amounts of tax funds on a scientific project for which no claims of military secrecy can be made.[25]

Thus, the strong desire of some officials to withhold information can lead to public criticisms of them. The best agency management

[25] *Los Angeles Times,* August 19 and 21, 1962.

is one which fully respects the public's "right to know." Of course, some matters must be kept confidential, but no government official should have the right to withhold information simply on his whim. The agency's public relations suffer whenever its procedures are enveloped in secrecy. Another recent example is that of the Municipal Airport Commission of St. Louis, which has been criticized for failing to open some of its meetings to the public. The results of closed meetings have been given to the press by the Commission's Chairman. The *St. Louis Post-Dispatch* believes that the people have a right to know the details of the Commission's procedures since "it is their business that is being transacted."[26]

Inevitably, when details that concern the public are hidden from it, questions are raised in the public mind: What is the agency afraid of? What devious procedures are taking place? Just how much is the agency acting in the public interest?

TRUTHFULNESS IN PUBLIC RELATIONS

In evaluating information for release, then, the agency should consider whether or not the release of it is purely a matter of propaganda in its own behalf, and, on the other hand, whether or not the withholding of it is purely a matter of fear of public criticism. The agency must ask itself, is this information—whether it is favorable or unfavorable—*really* in the public interest? In order to do this, the agency should be willing to recognize its own shortcomings and to make whatever improvements are necessary. Where it is failing, chances are that attempts to hide its faults by withholding information or to offset them by releasing propaganda publicity will only add to its poor public image. Yet, once the agency has completed an honest self-examination, it is in a position to improve its operations and, consequently, the image the public has of it. As Appley puts it, "Knowing what we are, we next want to know what we ought to be; how to get there; and how to get people to believe it."[27] This philosophy is also reflected by MacNamara in connection with police administration:

[26] *St. Louis Post-Dispatch*, April 20, 1962, editorial page.
[27] Appley, *op. cit.*, p. 54.

The best public relations program for a police department is to do a day-to-day, month-to-month efficient police job, keep the public informed of police problems, maintain strict and uncompromising internal discipline, and build up among the citizenry a sense of security of person and property. All the techniques of mass communication, all the baseball teams, police picnics, and similar claptrap will never convince the public that its police department is a fine one. The ruthless elimination of grafters, sadists, bigots, and blunderers from the police ranks (and their number is not legion in any department) will prove far more effective.[28]

Too frequently such frank and honest appraisals are not made, however, and agencies try to compensate with intensive public relations campaigns. Sometimes agencies are even said to have released false information. One recent example is the Atomic Energy Commission, which has, on occasion, been accused of giving out misleading statements about the radioactive hazards created by its atomic testing. Such a charge was made after completion of a small underground atomic energy test in Nevada in the summer of 1957.[29] Although the AEC reported that the explosion had not been detected at a range of more than 250 miles, Senator Humphrey learned that Coast and Geodetic Survey stations all over the continental United States had recorded shockwaves from the test. The AEC then publicly admitted that the test had been recorded at least 2,300 miles away in Alaska, but it claimed that it simply had made a mistake. This explanation never convinced parts of the press and some members of Congress.

And then in May, 1960, there was the famous U-2 plane incident. The Russians announced they had shot down the plane on a spy mission, but the United States at first said the plane was on an innocent weather-observation mission when the pilot's oxygen supply failed, and he accidentally flew over the Turkish-Soviet border. When Khrushchev announced that the pilot had been captured and had confessed to carrying out a "spy" operation for the Central Intelligence Agency, the Eisenhower Administration had to admit that its

[28] Donal E. J. MacNamara, "American Police Administration at Mid-Century," *Public Administration Review*, X, No. 3 (Summer, 1950), 188.

[29] See *Nomination of Lewis L. Strauss*, Senate Committee on Interstate and Foreign Commerce, 86th Congress, 1st Session, Washington, D.C.: Government Printing Office, 1959, pp. 441–442.

original accounts were falsehoods. As Rourke comments, in the furor over the U-2 incident, it was difficult to say just what the American public thought of that part of the affair which "involved the deliberate misrepresentation of facts by high government officials." He writes: "It is too early to say that the public is prepared to give unqualified acceptance to governmental falsehoods as long as they seem to serve the security interests of the United States, but the U-2 affair certainly presents the possibility that this is now the case."[30]

Intelligence activities present a very special case. In the case of domestic programs, there is no indication that the public will tolerate false statements. Sometimes a flat lie is not told, but the statement consists only of half-truths. Devious conduct of this type in the long run gives the agency a bad reputation. Although many people will not see through the half-truths, some of the press and the discerning element in the citizenry will not be fooled.

The related point is that the agency management should see to it that conflicting information is not given out to the public. Nothing annoys the citizen more than when he reads one public announcement one day, and the next he is told exactly the opposite. Fortunately, this does not happen very often, but, of course, a single mistake of this type can expose the agency to ridicule. One of the advantages of having a separate information staff is that it serves as the main channel for relations with the press. When most public announcements are released by the information office, the possibility of inconsistent statements is greatly reduced.

Sometimes officials will make "off-the-cuff" remarks to reporters which later prove embarrassing. When later policy contradicts what they have told the press, an awkward situation is created. The agency itself must also carefully think through its policies before it makes any public announcements. Inefficient management practices are likely to be reflected in poor public relations, since the public can only judge the agency on the basis of what it knows about it. If the agency's announcements seem to suggest that its operations are confused, it has only itself to blame.

Sometimes the nature of the agency's program puts it in a position where it is blamed for quick changes in government policy. The experience of the Selective Service System during World War II

[30] Rourke, *op. cit.*, p. 6.

is an excellent case in point. On numerous occasions, its Director, General Lewis B. Hershey, released statements about draft policies which he later had to change. Married men and fathers were told that they would not be drafted for some months to come, but then read in the newspapers that they should get ready for relatively quick induction into the armed services. On other occasions, men, certain they would be drafted based on the latest public announcements, suddenly found that the policy had been altered again and that they were not needed. Of course, as the picture changed on the fighting fronts, the armed forces kept revising the estimates of their manpower needs. General Hershey and the Selective Service System could only interpret draft requirements in terms of the latest statement by the military as to the number of new inductees they needed. Perhaps General Hershey was sometimes overly optimistic as to the chances men in certain categories had of not being called, but, basically, he was not himself at fault. The armed forces originally assumed that the military manpower pool was virtually inexhaustible and used strict standards in examining men for possible induction. Later these standards had to be relaxed as it became clear that the manpower pool was not unlimited.

It is easy to exercise hindsight and to say that, when the future picture is subject to so many uncertainties, public officials should not make statements which may create undue public optimism. Many citizens prefer to hear an opinion and are irked when government spokesmen refuse to commit themselves. If the official appears to be pessimistic, then he can be accused of unnecessarily alarming the public.

EVALUATING THE PUBLIC RELATIONS PROGRAM

In concluding this chapter, it should be stressed that a discerning management is well aware that the *quantity* of the publicity it receives is not necessarily related to success in its public relations program. Naturally the agency hopes that the press will publish its news releases and not neglect to report its accomplishments. Counting up the inches of space that it has received in the newspapers, however, does not, in and of itself, prove anything. Newspapers are swamped with requests to publish different material. Generally speaking, they ward off the publicity seekers and try to print only that information which is genuinely newsworthy. Usually, then, efforts to get into the newspapers every day or with great regularity do not meet with success anyway, and even if the agency does get better than average coverage because of its persistence, this does not mean that the reading public necessarily pays any attention to the articles in question. Discriminating readers come to identify the "blurbs" from the items with real substance. Then, again, mere publicity seeking can boomerang. By being in the public eye too much, the agency may find itself criticized all the more severely when something goes wrong with its programs. "We are not getting enough publicity" is a common complaint. Perhaps the reverse question should be asked, "Are we seeking too much publicity?" One of the valuable services that the information director can perform is to caution the management about placing too much emphasis on the quantity of publicity as such. The real test of success is the agency's skill in dealing with its various publics, and this will be measured in terms of the reactions of these publics, rather than the volume of information releases.

BIBLIOGRAPHY

Carlson, Eric, "Public Relations in International Technical Assistance," *Public Administration Review*, **XVI,** No. 4 (Autumn, 1956).

Cox, David M., "How Much Public Relations in Government?" *Public Administration Review*, **XXI,** No. 3 (Summer, 1961).

Dimock, Marshall E., *The Executive in Action*, New York: Harper and Row, 1945. Chap. IX.

Lepawsky, Albert (ed.), *Administration, The Art and Science of Organization and Management*, New York: Knopf, 1949. Chap. 17.

Levy, Sidney J., "The Public Image of Government Agencies," *Public Administration Review*, **XXIII,** No. 1 (March, 1963).

Long, Norton E., "Popular Support for Business Policy, The Bell System as a Case Study," in Long, Norton E., *The Polity*, Chicago: Rand McNally, 1962.

Pimlott, J. A. R., *Public Relations and American Democracy*, Princeton, N.J.: Princeton, 1951.

Rourke, Francis E., "Administrative Secrecy: A Congressional Dilemma," *American Political Science Review*, **LIV**, No. 3 (September, 1960).

Rourke, Francis E., *Secrecy and Publicity*, Baltimore, Md.: Johns Hopkins, 1961.

Rowat, Donald C. (ed.), *Basic Issues in Public Administration*, New York: Macmillan, 1961. Chap. VIII.

Senate Subcommittee on Constitutional Rights, 85th Congress, 2nd Session, *The Power of the President to Withhold Information From the Congress*, Washington, D.C.: Government Printing Office, 1958.

Senate Subcommittee on Constitutional Rights, 86th Congress, 1st Session, *Executive Privilege* (Parts I and II), Washington, D.C.: Government Printing Office, 1959.

Senate Committee on Government Operations, 86th Congress, 2nd Session, *Refusals To The General Accounting Office Of Access To Records Of The Executive Departments and Agencies*, Washington, D.C.: Government Printing Office, 1960.

Stein, Harold (ed.), *Public Administration and Policy Development*, New York: Harcourt, Brace, and World, 1952. See Part III.

CHAPTER 12

Leadership

Frequently the complaint is heard that an organization "lacks leadership." What is meant is that action of some sort should have been taken, but no one assumed the initiative in trying to get others to see the need for action, and thus nothing was accomplished. In other cases, the criticism is that the organization does not have "good leadership." Decisions are made and action taken, but those responsible for persuading others to accept their ideas led them in the wrong direction. These statements reveal both the *nature* and the *importance* of leadership. The essence of leadership is influencing the actions of others. Where the attempt to exercise such influence is not even made, there is a default of leadership. Where the attempt is made and others are persuaded to agree to certain action but the anticipated results do not materialize, the consequences may be serious for the organization.

APPROACHES TO LEADERSHIP

The Trait Approach

Not too long ago even learned, as distinguished from popular, discussions of leadership had a certain mystic quality. The leader was conceived of as someone blessed with certain qualities which made it relatively easy for him to bend others to his will. Nobody was really sure of the exact complement of leader personality traits, but it was generally assumed that many of these characteristics were inherited.

Today most social scientists are convinced that the trait approach to leadership is fallacious, because those conducting research on the qualities of leaders have been unable to agree on what those qualities are. In 1940, one scholar compiled a long list of traits which were identified in one or more studies as distinguishing characteristics of leaders as opposed to nonleaders. Only about five percent of these traits, however, were common to four or more of the studies. Such a low percentage of agreement could hardly substantiate the claim that leaders basically have the same personality characteristics. Examination of the research conducted since 1940 has shown the same lack of consistency in the findings on leadership qualities.[1] Cartwright and Zander summarize the present state of knowledge as follows:

> On the whole, investigators in this field are coming to the conclusion that, while certain minimal abilities are required of all leaders, these are also widely distributed among non-leaders as well. Furthermore, the traits of the leader which are necessary and effective in one group or situation may be quite different from those of another leader in a different setting. This conclusion, if adequately substantiated, would imply that the selection of leaders must consider a man's suitability for the type of functions he is to perform in a given situation and it would raise questions about the desirability of formal arrangements which maintain the responsibilities of leadership in the same person regardless of the changing task of the group and the changing requirements upon leaders.[2]

The Situational Approach

Accordingly, most writers now support this situational approach, although actually it is not new. Long before the term "situational approach" came into usage, Mary Parker Follett was calling attention to the emergence in American life of "leadership by function." In the late 1920s, this wise lady, whose writings are classics in management literature, gave several lectures on leadership.[3] In these lectures, she

[1] Dorwin Cartwright and Alvin Zander (eds.), *Group Dynamics, Research and Theory* (2nd ed.), New York: Harper and Row, 1960, p. 490.

[2] *Ibid.*, p. 491. See also Robert G. Wall and Hugh Hawkins, "Requisites of Effective Leadership," *Personnel*, **XXXIX**, No. 3 (May–June, 1962), 21–28.

[3] See Mary Parker Follett, "Some Discrepancies in Leadership Theory and Practice," in Henry C. Metcalfe and L. Urwick (eds.), *Dynamic Administration*, New York: Harper and Row, 1940, pp. 270–294. See also in this same collection of her papers the essay, "Leader and Expert," pp. 247–269.

noted that in scientifically managed organizations three types of leadership could be distinguished: the leadership of position, of personality, and of function. There was nothing new about the first two, because they represented the accepted views on leadership. The man holding a position which gave him formal authority over others obviously could make himself a leader. If he had a forceful personality, he could do this much more easily. This kind of individual combined the leadership of position with that of personality.

Something was absent, however, in such a conception of leadership. It failed to take into account the possibility that some persons, in fact quite a few in modern specialized organizations, exercised leadership because of their expert knowledge. The organization depended on them to give sound technical advice to their superiors. In many situations these experts actually did the "leading," because others were influenced by their judgments. Miss Follett stressed that "we have people giving what are practically orders to those of higher rank. The balance of stores clerk, as he is called in some places, will tell the man in charge of purchasing when to act. The dispatch clerk can give 'orders' even to the superintendent. The leadership of function is inherent in the job and as such is respected by the president of the plant." She noted that "the man possessing the knowledge demanded by a certain situation tends in the best managed businesses, and other things being equal, to become the leader at that moment."[4]

In Chapter 8 of this book, a distinction was made between *formal* and *effective* authority. Formal authority is the basis for what Miss Follett called leadership of position. Sometimes someone in a position of formal authority is unable to persuade others to accept his ideas. He lacks effective authority. The explanation for this may very well be that he does not possess "the knowledge demanded by the situation." In any event, we saw in Chapter 8 that not all effective authority is concentrated in the hands of a few persons at the top of the organization. Subordinates frequently exercise effective authority because they "know best" about a particular operation. Harlan Cleveland's excellent analysis was cited to show how specialization has diffused decisionmaking throughout modern organizations. The reader will remember Cleveland's statement that the real leaders are the "experts on complexity," in other words, the persons who understand what is needed in a particular situation.

[4] *Ibid.*, p. 277.

It should be made clear that Miss Follett did not consider that the leadership of function and the leadership of personality could not be combined in the same person. Nor did she deny that personality played a very large part in leadership. She did believe, however, that leadership of function was becoming more important than leadership of personality. She felt that the success of an organization depended a good deal on its being "sufficiently flexible to allow the leadership of function to operate fully—to allow the men with the knowledge and the technique to control the situation."[5] Miss Follett makes an interesting point about Joan of Arc. This great woman possessed leadership of personality because of the "ardour of her conviction and her power to make others share that conviction." Yet it is also related that "no trained artillery captain could excel Joan of Arc in the placement of guns."[6]

What are some of the other factors which affect the requirements for leadership, apart from expertise in a particular subject matter field? A change in the nature of the situation which confronts the group may call for a different kind of leader. The pilot in a bomber crew may be an excellent leader while the plane is in flight, but prove a very poor one if it crashes "and the crew is faced with the task of surviving or finding its way to safety."[7] The qualities needed to keep the crew working together efficiently in the air are not necessarily the same as those required when the men are afoot in a desperate situation for which advance planning was not possible. Similarly, the kind of activity influences the leadership requirements. The competent head of a public agency might be unsuited for a leadership role in a church group, yet a minor employee in the same public agency might be admirably equipped to lead the church group. Within the church, one person might be excellent for work with preschool children, another for youth activities, and so on. Thus, the characteristics of the followers obviously constitute an important variable in the situation. It takes one kind of person to lead a labor gang, another to direct professional activities. Within the professional ranks, supervisors lacking certain formal qualifications deemed essential by the subordinates, will prove ineffectual; a dean without the Ph.D. will not command the respect of many of the university professors.

[5] *Ibid.*, p. 278.
[6] *Ibid.*, p. 172.
[7] Cartwright and Zander, *op. cit.*, p. 495.

If the leadership assignment requires conciliation of various groups, the individual's personal background can eliminate him from consideration, as in an international agency, where the person's nationality might make him unacceptable to one or more parties to a dispute. These are only a few of the ways in which the situation can vary, thus altering the requirements for leadership. Readers of this book will probably be able to supply other examples.

HUMAN MOTIVATIONS AND LEADERSHIP

Before discussing in specific terms the kinds of leadership techniques which should be used in given circumstances, it is advisable to make a brief exposition of some of the theories as to human motivation. Depending on their concepts of worker motivation, one person may select one leadership pattern, another may choose a very different one. Anyone who seeks to lead others must be concerned with such questions as: What are the desires of people who work in organizations? what do they want from the management and its representatives? how do they want their superiors to treat them? what causes them to respect or not respect the management? what are the needs of human personality anyway? As we shall see, we have various theories but no agreement on the answers to these questions.

Different Theories of Motivation

Without any pretense of being exhaustive in the treatment of this profound subject, we will present here the opinions of three outstanding young scholars: Chris Argyris, Robert Dubin, and Robert Presthus. Illustrating the common interest in this subject of researchers in many different disciplines, Argyris is on the staff of the Yale University Labor and Management Center, Dubin is a sociologist, and Presthus a political scientist.

The Views of Chris Argyris

In one of his earlier writings, *Personality Fundamentals for Administrators,* Argyris makes a thorough review of the findings of the psychologists on human personality. Summarizing these findings, he states:

"At this time we can say, therefore, that man in his need-fulfilling behavior is to some extent:

like all other men
like some other men
like no other men."[8]

Argyris explains that man is like *all* other men "because some of his personality is derived from common biological roots," because "he experiences both gratifications and deprivations," and because he must adjust to the "traditionally defined expectations of the culture." Man is like *some* other men, because "he shares common experiences with his own work group, social class, sporting club, or other cultural organizations." The social pressures exercised by the groups with which he associates function to make him like the other members of these same groups. Man is *unlike any other* man, because he has his "own personal, private way of seeing and experiencing the world," and because "he behaves, feels, thinks in certain patterns which are unique to himself."

Based on his studies of the development of the human personality, Argyris believes that "people, in our culture, develop from a state of high dependence on others as an infant, to a state of independence, and finally, to a state of interdependence in their society as an adult," and that the individual enters the world of work just when he feels a strong desire to be self-reliant and to obtain the free expression of his personality. He wants to have something to say about the work situation, not simply to be the passive agent of others. He wants to be able to express his "needs, sentiments, and personal goals."[9]

The tragedy is that most modern organizations require the worker to be passive and dependent upon the management's wishes. In Argyris' opinion, it is the immature, not the mature, person who can find happiness in the modern organizations, because they are built upon the basis of scientific-management concepts which require the adjustment of the worker to the job, not the other way around. The worker is regarded pretty much as a tool of production, to be manipulated as the management sees best. The scientific-management point of view takes into account "primarily the physical and biological

[8] Chris Argyris, *Personality Fundamentals for Administrators*, New Haven, Conn.: Labor and Management Center, Yale University, 1953, pp. 10–12.
[9] *Ibid.*, pp. 46–47.

properties of man," and in many respects is even "diametrically opposed to the development of a healthy personality in our culture."[10] Argyris believes that most workers today are permitted "little control over their work-a-day world. [The] developmental processes and end result of the individual and organization are, at crucial points, fundamentally different and even antagonistic."[11] The individual seeks "self-actualization," that is, to be able to satisfy the needs of his personality, whereas the management is obsessed with trying to make the worker behave rationally. It even assumes that "individual differences in the human personality may be ignored by transferring more skill and thought to machines."[12] The task specialization of scientific management permits the individual to use only a fraction of his abilities. New work procedures based on even greater specialization, which management hails as a great improvement, make the workers feel even more frustrated. They find their role in the organization narrowed even more.

Argyris' analysis is disturbing, because he places the responsibility for this situation on the very nature of modern organization. It is not that the managers are responsible because of the mistakes they make in dealing with the employees, although such mistakes do make matters worse. It is that the typical organization is so constructed as to require that the employees be submissive and dependent, rather than active and interested participants. What, then, if anything, can be done to correct this situation?

Argyris does believe that something can be done. The organization might be altered in certain ways so that the personality of the worker can obtain "greater self-actualization on the job." Agreed, no attempt should be made to change the organization so that it meets the personal requirements of each and every worker. Formal organization as such is not "bad." Twisting it to meet the whims of every worker would produce chaos or at least a situation in which self-actualization could not take place in an orderly way. The worker can be given more to say without weakening the formal organization;

[10] *Ibid.*, p. 46.
[11] *Ibid.*, p. 48.
[12] Chris Argyris, "Personal vs. Organizational Goals," in Robert Dubin (ed.), *Human Relations in Administration*, Englewood Cliffs, N.J.: Prentice-Hall, 1961, p. 72.

in fact, this will strengthen it. The leader should not assume that, simply because the formal organization shows him at the top, he can make all the decisions for the workers without consulting them first. He should allow them to be real participants in the organization and give them some measure of control over their work environment.[13]

In general, Argyris believes that modern organizations should be altered so as to permit the individual to express his personality and play an active, rather than a passive, role in the work situation. Sometimes this need is referred to as "job enlargement," that is, building up the job so as to make it more satisfying to the worker. Argyris does not present a blueprint to follow in any program of job enlargement; this will depend on the organization and the particular situation. He is mostly concerned with calling attention to the conflict between formal organization and the individual's need for self-actualization. He makes clear that fundamental modifications, not mere tinkering, are needed if the formal organization is to be adapted to meet human needs and replace worker apathy with real involvement.

The Views of Robert Dubin

Dubin does not deny the individual's need for self-actualization; he questions, rather, whether people in general look to their jobs to provide it. He believes that all too often the assumption is erroneously made that the individual seeks a maximum of satisfaction from *all* the organizations in which he participates. This mistaken assumption leads to the view that man is the captive of his employing organization, because it denies him these satisfactions. The trouble with this theory is that it ascribes desires to the workers that many of them do not have. They are not that much interested in what the work situation can do for their personality fulfillment needs. Indeed, Dubin believes that probably for the majority of workers, including some management personnel, the job is not a central life interest. He thinks that it is in the voluntary kind of activity that most individuals look for their greatest satisfactions. They are much more interested in their after-hours' activities as members of clubs and other social groups. Far from feeling tyrannized by the work situation, they tolerate it and even perform efficiently despite their general apathy. So

[13] Argyris, *Personality Fundamentals for Administrators, op. cit.*, pp. 46–49.

long as the management makes clear what is expected of them and provides the requisite financial incentive, they can be counted on to do satisfactory work. This, to Dubin, is the "magic of social organization—the ability to sustain required behaviors even when the institution is not central to the actors' interests."[14] Dubin's view, then, is that most workers simply are not in the unhappy situation portrayed by Argyris and others. They never really become so involved in their jobs as to experience the frustrations they are supposed to have.

It must be made clear, however, that Dubin does not deny that some people do make work a central life interest. Any activity, whether it be required—such as working for one's livelihood—or voluntary—such as participation in a church group—can become an individual's most absorbing interest. Dubin's point is, rather, that the most absorbing interest does not have to be the work situation, and that probably for most people it is not. Accordingly, looking at our society as a whole, he finds, "nothing about the organization of productive work, or the supervision of people while doing it, that is so antithetical to human personality needs as to result only in frustration and disappointment."[15]

If Dubin is correct, "job enlargement" in many cases may not be necessary. Why try to make the job more interesting to someone who basically seeks his satisfactions elsewhere? Since there are limits anyway to making more interesting the narrow kind of assignment that has evolved through specialization, such efforts can easily boomerang. The leader should understand worker apathy for what it is and not expect total involvement in their job by the majority of the workers. After all, he has the "magic of social organization" on his side. On the other hand, Dubin's analysis does not mean that the management need not concern itself with making *any* of the jobs challenging, apart from the financial inducements. While the great bulk of the production line and clerical personnel may not be concerned on this score, those in professional and executive jobs often are. The professional typically is absorbed in his specialty and reacts as a distinctive individual with definite needs which he feels the organization should satisfy. The executive, whether the junior just start-

[14] Robert Dubin, "Persons and Organization," in *Human Relations in Administration*, Englewood Cliffs, N.J.: Prentice-Hall, 1961, p. 80.
[15] *Ibid.*, p. 79.

ing or the senior man seeking to cement his position, is typically concerned with the image of himself as a "success." For him to feel that he is such a "success" or on the road to becoming one, he looks to the organization to satisfy his psychological needs.

The Views of Robert Presthus

As to Presthus, he bases his interpretations on the interpersonal theory of psychiatry of Harry Stack Sullivan, according to which the human personality develops mainly as the result of social interaction. The individual's personality forms in definite ways as he reacts to the pressures of those with whom he comes in contact. From childhood on, he seeks to release tension by deferring to certain "authority figures," such as parents, teachers, and, in later years, the supervisor in a work situation. The cause of the tension is anxiety: he is anxious to obtain the approval of these authority figures. Presthus quotes Sullivan as saying: "I believe it fairly safe to say that anybody and everybody devotes much of his lifetime, and a great deal of his energy . . . to avoiding more anxiety than he already has, and, if possible, to getting rid of some of this anxiety."[16]

Argyris posits an individual who wants to be independent, rather than dependent on others. The culmination of personality development is that the mature person does not relish having to defer to authority figures. He wants to be able to behave like an adult, not an infant. Presthus passes no judgments on what is "adult" or "childlike" behavior, but simply accepts Sullivan's theory and is thus led to believe that many adults accept a status of dependency on their superiors as a means of relieving their anxieties. Presthus does not challenge the view that, to be effective, the superior's authority must be accepted by the subordinate; what he does question is the implication that the subordinate has much choice in the matter. As he sees it, the subordinate must relieve his anxiety tensions by bowing to the wishes of his superior officer, just as all through his life he has sought inward peace by yielding to other authority figures.

Some Other Views of Motivation

Others besides Presthus have stressed how some workers seek a status of dependency on their superiors as a means of relieving their

[16] Robert Presthus, *The Organizational Society*, New York: Knopf, 1962, p. 104.

tensions. Robert N. McMurry believes that the banking industry prefers the passive type individual who can be expected to conform in every way with his superiors' concepts of how he should behave. The preferred kind of addition to the staff is often someone who as a child was never completely weaned emotionally from overprotective parents. Sometimes he is someone who grew up in a "loveless and threatening environment [and] never dared to become self-reliant."[17] When he enters the world of work and gets a job where he is expected to accept responsibility, he is terrified:

> On reaching late adolescence or adulthood, he suddenly finds himself isolated from those who formerly provided love and reassurance. The prospect of facing a strange, formidable, and threatening world alone overwhelms him with anxiety.
>
> Some young people react to shock by becoming mentally ill; they become schizophrenic or make use of some other flight mechanism, for example, narcotic addiction. Most, however, respond by seeking to regain the lost security of childhood. They look for parental surrogates among persons who have power, strength, and authority and attempt to establish the same type of relationship—attachment, dependence, and submission—which they enjoyed with their parents. In most cases they earned the support and approbation of the latter by being "good" boys and girls, industrious, conscientious, and docile. As employees they repeat their childhood behavior pattern; they become the "good soldiers," the loyal, conscientious workers.[18]

Such persons, McMurry believes, react very well to the authoritarian kind of supervision practiced in some banks. They are relieved to be in a position where they need take no risks and can depend on others to worry about what should be done. In fact, in McMurry's opinion, they make excellent employees in such a setting, because they "personify bourgeois, copybook virtues."

McMurry describes a conformist type of individual especially desired by some banks to suit their conception of the "right type" of employee. In other situations, however, there is no attempt to employ the submissive type of person only. The employing organization

[17] Robert N. McMurry, "Recruitment, Dependency, and Morale in the Banking Industry," *Administrative Science Quarterly*, III, No. 1 (June, 1958), 92–93.

[18] *Ibid.*

wants individuals with initiative, but the employee, for one reason or another, lapses into a passive state.

Harry Levinson of the Industrial Health Division of the Menninger Foundation calls attention to the "male menopause." He is referring here to the period of middle age which for many men is one of "acute psychological loss" and thus really a "change of life." At 45, a man realizes that very likely he has fewer years ahead of him than behind him. Usually he must realistically anticipate that in all probability he will remain in much the same economic and social position for the rest of his life as he occupies in middle age. Levinson writes:

> Given the long period of dependency on parents in our culture, everyone struggles with the wish to become independent versus the pleasure of remaining dependent. This is particularly the struggle of the adolescent. When one becomes an adult he asserts his independence, but few of us can altogether give up our wishes to be dependent. When one feels less an adult, his dependent wishes come more to the surface. But, since he is in fact physically an adult, it is difficult for him to face the existence of such wishes.[19]

Some executives at this stage in their life build a "psychological cocoon" about themselves. They lose their old fight and fall into a rut. They fear younger men as threats to themselves and may even refuse to train them. Instead of continuing as assets to the organization, they become a drag on it. Levinson explains that these are not aberrations of weak individuals but common experiences of men who have reached middle age. Understanding this, the management can deal sympathetically with executives who suddenly seem to have lost their vitality and, by providing them with new challenges, it can help them regain their confidence.

Implications for Leadership

The reader, however, may likely raise the query, "Where has this analysis of theories of human motivation taken us? Is it not inconclusive, in view of the differences of opinion between such writers as

[19] Harry Levinson, "The Executive's Anxious Age," Management Forum, *Public Administration News,* **XII**, No. 3, Chicago: American Society for Public Administration (August, 1962).

Argyris, Dubin, and Presthus?" First, let it be made clear that the basic purpose was to indicate the complexity of the problem of human motivation. A subject which has so many ramifications cannot honestly be painted as relatively simple. It would be marvellous to be able to say, categorically, what all or most members of any organization can be expected to want in terms of leadership behavior by their superiors. It would simplify matters enormously if Argyris, Dubin, Presthus, and all the others espoused identical theories. The fact, however, is that they do not. From one standpoint, it is well that they do emphasize different needs of the human personality. People are different; no one person is exactly like another. All kinds of people will be found in any one organization: Some may feel the strong yearnings for independence described by Argyris and experience the frustrations he believes inevitable in modern organizations; others may be dominated by strong feelings of dependency, as depicted by Presthus and McMurry. Some may lapse into temporary feelings of dependency, as during the male menopause, while some may not care particularly about their experiences during the workday, as emphasized by Dubin; they may experience their joys and miseries after hours.

Actually, Argyris, Dubin, and Presthus do not claim that their theories apply to all individuals. Argyris admits that some workers have no desire to feel independent. Such workers, he states, must be classified as "not mature." He does not attempt to tell us what proportion of the working population is "mature" or "immature" in these terms[20] for the simple reason that he cannot. No statistical measures are available of the psychological make-up of millions of workers. Furthermore, as indicated, no one can predict exactly how many "mature" and "immature" workers will be found in any one organization. Similarly, Dubin does not say that all individuals look for their satisfactions off the job; and at no point does Presthus say that all employees feel the same strong urge to satisfy their anxiety tensions by deferring to the authority of others. The point, rather, is that each has a general theory of human motivation, which amounts to no more than an expectation as to what may probably be found in dealing with large numbers of workers. None denies that the supervisor must adapt his leadership pattern in accordance with the kinds

[20] Argyris, *Personality Fundamentals for Administrators, op. cit.*, pp. 47–48.

of subordinates he has under him. Treatment that satisfies one employee may offend another. General theories are helpful, but they can never relieve the supervisor of the need to understand the variations in human personalities.

LEADERSHIP STYLE

Usually three types of leadership styles or patterns are identified: authoritarian, democratic, and laissez-faire. Because democracy is so important a value to Americans, it will disturb some people that democracy may not be feasible with some work groups and in some work situations. Therefore, it is advisable to make clear at once in any discussion of leadership style that, as Golembiewski states, "the research literature does not consistently support any one leadership style."[21] On the other hand, while Pfiffner and Sherwood also recognize this to be so, their analysis is that "most of the research has seemed to support the desirability of moving toward the democratic type."[22] At this point, it seems wise to refer to some of these research studies.

Research Findings on Leadership

One of the most famous of these experiments was conducted with a group of ten-year-old boys at the University of Iowa in the late 1930s.[23] Four adult leaders were "trained to proficiency" in the three different leadership styles, authoritarian, democratic, and laissez-faire. The specific leadership behavior under each style is shown in Figure 8. Each of these adult leaders was assigned to direct the activities of a boys' club consisting of five boys who met after school to engage in hobby activities. The boys in each of the four groups were roughly similar in terms of social and economic background and

[21] Robert T. Golembiewski, "Three Styles of Leadership and Their Uses," *Personnel*, XXXVIII, No. 4 (July–August, 1961), 35. See also Erwin S. Stanton, "Which Approach to Management—Democratic, Authoritarian or . . .?" *Personnel Administration*, XXV, No. 2 (March–April, 1962), 44–47.

[22] John M. Pfiffner and Frank P. Sherwood, *Administrative Organization*, Englewood Cliffs, N.J.: Prentice-Hall, 1960, p. 364.

[23] The description of these experiments which follows is from Ralph White and Ronald Lippitt, "Leader Behavior and Member Reaction in Three 'Social Climates'," in Cartwright and Zander, *op. cit.*, pp. 527–553.

Authoritarian	Democratic	Laissez-faire
1. All determination of policy by the leader	1. All policies a matter of group discussion and decision, encouraged and assisted by the leader	1. Complete freedom for group or individual decision, with a minimum of leader participation
2. Techniques and activity steps dictated by the authority, one at a time, so that future steps were always uncertain to a large degree	2. Activity perspective gained during discussion period. General steps to group goal sketched, and when technical advice was needed, the leader suggested two or more alternative procedures from which choice could be made	2. Various materials supplied by the leader, who made it clear that he would supply information when asked. He took no other part in work discussion
3. The leader usually dictated the particular work task and work companion of each member	3. The members were free to work with whomever they chose, and the division of tasks was left up to the group	3. Complete nonparticipation of the leader
4. The dominator tended to be "personal" in his praise and criticism of the work of each member; remained aloof from active group participation except when demonstrating	4. The leader was "objective" or "fact-minded" in his praise and criticism, and tried to be a regular group member in spirit without doing too much of the work	4. Infrequent spontaneous comments on member activities unless questioned, and no attempt to appraise or regulate the course of events

Fig. 8. Characteristics of the three treatment variables. From Ralph White and Ronald Lippitt, "Leader Behavior and Member Reaction in Three 'Social Climates'," in D. Cartwright and A. Zander (eds.), *Group Dynamics, Research and Theory*, New York: Harper and Row, 1960, p. 528.

mental, physical, and personality characteristics. The adult leaders were shifted every six weeks from one club to another, and every time they switched to a new group they changed to a different leadership style. All the boys' clubs met in the same places and carried out the same activities under the same conditions. During these meetings, observers were present to study the boys' behavior in detail. The boys themselves were later interviewed to determine their reaction to each leadership style. Home visits were also made to the parents to discover what the impact of each leadership pattern had been on the boys' conduct at home.

The basic findings were as follows:

1. Under laissez-faire supervision, the boys proved less efficient. Furthermore, they did not like the club activities as much as when they were treated democratically. They did less work and poorer work than when under democratic supervision. The complete freedom they had under laissez-faire conditions led them to play more than when under either democratic or authoritarian supervision.

2. If efficiency is evaluated both in terms of work production and social satisfactions, democracy was clearly superior to both laissez-faire and autocracy. The boys worked as efficiently under authoritarian as they did under democratic supervision, but they enjoyed themselves more under democracy.

3. There was a significant difference in the boys' behavior when a democratic, as contrasted with a dictatorial, adult leader temporarily left the room. The boys in democracy kept right on working, but those under iron rule "stopped working as if glad to be relieved of a task which they 'had' to do." Work production went down precipitously during leader-out periods under autocracy whereas the decline was only slight under democracy.

4. The boys showed more originality and creative thinking under democracy than under either laissez-faire or autocracy, for "there was a larger amount of creative thinking about the work in progress than in autocracy, and it was more sustained and practical than in laissez-faire."[24]

5. Autocracy can create much hostility and aggression, including aggression against scapegoats. "Dominating ascendance," meaning imperious treatment of one boy by another, illustrated by such language as "shut up," took place much more often in the autocratically managed groups. Real hostility between the boys and aggressive demands for attention were also more characteristic of the autocratic groups. Destruction of work materials and property was not unusual

[24] *Ibid.*, p. 541.

when the meetings of the autocratic groups ended, but it did not take place at all in the democratic groups.

As to scapegoat behavior, it was evidenced in the autocratic, but not in the democratic, groups. Held down by the adult leader when he was playing the authoritarian role, the boys vented their spleen on some innocent member of the group. They took out on him their accumulated resentments against the adult leader. They could not openly defy the leader, so they directed their "aggressions" against other club members who had done nothing to them.

Upon return to democratic or laissez-faire treatment after autocracy, the boys sometimes released their "bottled-up tensions." The change to relative freedom after repressive control resulted in their breaking loose and engaging in much aggressive behavior, with the democratic adult leader now the scapegoat. The boys appeared to say to themselves, "Aha! *Now* I can do what I've been wanting to do in this club!"[25] After a couple of days, however, the "thrill of new-found freedom" wore off and the boys again exhibited the "spontaneous interest" characteristic of democracy.

6. There was more group-mindedness and friendliness in democracy. The pronoun "we" was used much more often in the democratic than in the autocratic groups. The kinds of remarks made by the boys in the democratic groups indicated the existence of greater group cohesion than under autocracy. "Friendly playfulness" was more pronounced, and there was a greater readiness to share group property.

A number of studies made with adult workers have also shown that democratic supervision produces better results. Frequently cited are those of the Institute for Social Research of the University of Michigan. The major finding was that work output was directly correlated with the amount of freedom the supervisor gave the worker. A comparison was made between the production achieved by groups of clerical workers functioning under "close" or "general" supervision. Close supervision meant that the supervisor "watched" the subordinates and checked constantly on how they were carrying out their tasks. Under general supervision, the supervisor put the workers on their own and employed an honor system. It was found that production was highest in work units headed by supervisors who prac-

[25] *Ibid.*, p. 545.

ticed general supervision. Furthermore, the high supervisors, in terms of production, in most cases themselves received general, rather than close, direction from their own superiors. Finally, the high supervisors were generally content to leave the detailed performance of the work to their subordinates, and to concentrate on their supervisory responsibilities. In this respect, they were "people-oriented." The low supervisors tended to neglect their supervisory responsibilities and to spend too much time actually trying to do a share of the production job themselves. Accordingly, they were considered to be "work-oriented."[26]

Later studies at Michigan and elsewhere, however, showed that employee-centered behavior by the supervisor did not necessarily result in increased production. They showed that "all kinds of combinations may occur—high morale and low production, low morale and low production, high morale and high production—which indicates the lack of any fixed and clear-cut relationship."[27] For this reason, Golembiewski argues that it is a mistake to try to answer the question, "Which kind of leadership should we use?" The really pertinent question he feels is, "Which kind of leadership *when*?"[28]

Selecting the Appropriate Leadership Style

Robert Tannenbaum and Warren H. Schmidt take up this problem in a most stimulating essay.[29] Their analysis is particularly valuable because they organize it around the central question of decision-making. Figure 9 reproduces a continuum which they have prepared showing the range of possible leadership behavior available to the manager. They explain each of the "behavior points" shown on the bottom line of the continuum as follows:

1. *The manager makes the decision and announces it.* Here the executive gives his subordinates no opportunity to participate directly in the decisionmaking process. He decides what the problem is, determines the

[26] Daniel Katz, Nathan Maccoby, and Nancy C. Morse, *Productivity, Supervision, and Morale in an Office Situation*, Ann Arbor, Mich.: Survey Research Center, Institute for Social Research, 1950.

[27] Pfiffner and Sherwood, *op. cit.*, p. 415.

[28] Golembiewski, *op. cit.*, 35.

[29] Robert Tannenbaum and Warren H. Schmidt, "How to Choose a Leadership Pattern," *Harvard Business Review*, XXXVI, No. 2 (March–April, 1958), 95–101.

possible courses of action, selects one of them, and then tells the subordinates to carry it out. In making his decision, he may or may not take into account how the employees will react to it. He may or may not use coercion in getting them to do as he says.

2. *The manager "sells" his decision.* There is no difference between this and 1., except that the manager does try to persuade the subordinates to accept the decision. He recognizes that some employees may not like the decision and may try to resist it, so he is careful to make clear what they will gain by accepting it. Note that the area of authority exercised by the manager remains large.

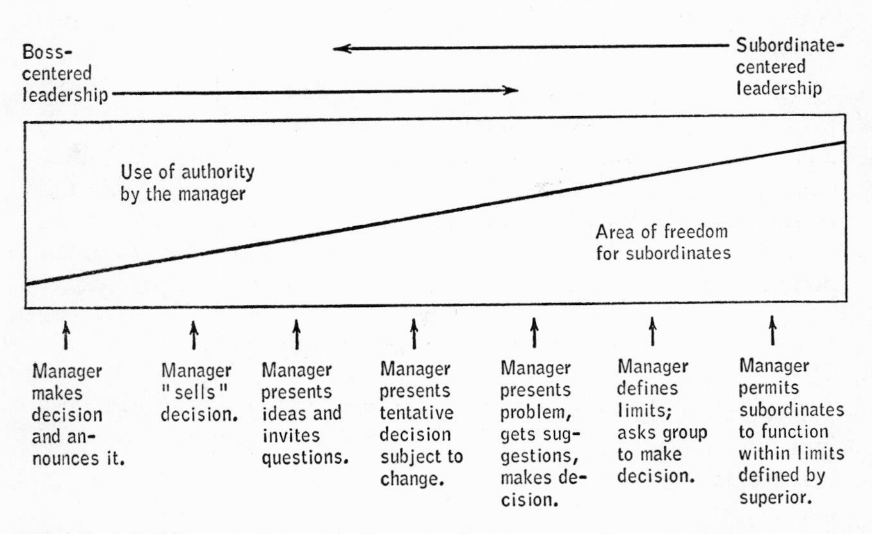

Fig. 9. Continuum of Leadership Behavior. From Robert Tannenbaum and Warren H. Schmidt, "How to Choose a Leadership Pattern," *Harvard Business Review*, **XXXVI,** No. 2 (March–April, 1958), 96.

3. *The manager presents his ideas and invites questions.* The difference between this and 2. is that the manager gives the subordinates the opportunity to explore with him the implications of the decision. Instead of simply explaining why they should accept it, he invites them to ask questions, and he takes the time to go into some detail about "his thinking and his intentions." At this point on the continuum, the "area of freedom for subordinates" begins to look significant.

4. *The manager presents a tentative decision subject to change.* Here for the first time, the subordinates are allowed to have some influence on

the decision. The executive retains responsibility for identifying the problem and developing a proposed solution, but only on a tentative basis. Before making a final decision, he asks the subordinates to give their frank reactions, but he also makes clear that he is retaining the right to decide the question as he sees fit.

5. *The manager presents the problem, gets suggestions, and then makes his decision.* In 1. through 4. above, the manager in every case makes the decision himself, although in 4. it is a tentative one. In 5., he asks the subordinates for their opinions before he makes any decision, final or tentative. He respects their knowledge of operating problems and knows that they may be able to suggest solutions that would not occur to him. After evaluating their ideas, as well as his own, he "selects the solution that he regards as most promising."

6. *The manager defines the limits and requests the group to make a decision.* Here the manager delegates to the subordinates the authority to make a certain decision. He states exactly what the problem is and makes clear the restrictions on what the employees can decide. As a hypothetical example, the manager tells the subordinates that a new parking lot will be built for the use of the employees. A ceiling figure of $100,000 for the construction costs has been fixed. So long as this figure is not exceeded, the group can decide to build whatever kind of lot it wants, an underground one or a surface one with multilevel facilities. The management may not like the employees' decision but will accept it within the financial limit.

7. *The manager permits the group to make decisions within prescribed limits.* The difference between 6. and 7. is that in 7. a general grant of decisionmaking power is made, not limited to any one problem. The example given is of teams of managers or engineers whose responsibility is not only to identify problems but also to decide what to do about them. The only limits on what the group can do are those specified by the official to whom the team leader reports. This leader may or may not himself participate in the making of the decision. If he does, he has no more authority than any other team member. He commits himself in advance to support whatever decision the group makes.[30]

Under 6 and 7, the subordinates' "area of freedom" widens greatly. The question remains, however, as to which of the leadership behaviors shown on the continuum is appropriate at a particular time. Tannenbaum and Schmidt identify three sets of factors which bear upon this question:

[30] *Ibid.*, 97.

Forces in the manager
Forces in the subordinates
Forces in the situation.[31]

Forces in the Manager

By "forces in the manager" Tannenbaum and Schmidt mean his own preferences, based on his past history and experiences. Is he the type who strongly believes that people should participate in decisions which affect them as individuals? Or is he someone who has long been convinced that the supervisor must stoically assume the burden of making the decisions himself because he is paid to do so? How much confidence does he have in other people in general and in his present subordinates in particular? Some managers are so constituted that they become uneasy if there appears to be an element of risk and uncertainty in the operations they supervise. This kind of executive is better off if he frankly acknowledges to himself that he is not the person to make delegations of authority as broad as those shown on behavior points 6. and 7. of the continuum.

Forces in the Subordinates

"Forces in the subordinates" refers to the expectations of the employees as to how the supervisor should behave in his relations with them. It also means the personality requirements of each individual in the group as these bear upon the question of the kind of direction he responds to best. The executive can allow greater freedom to subordinates under the following conditions:

1. The subordinates have relatively high needs for independence.
2. They *want* to assume responsibility, rather than to avoid it.
3. They have a "relatively high tolerance for ambiguity," meaning they would rather receive broad instructions than to be tied down by clear-cut instructions.
4. They are interested in the problem and believe that it is important.
5. They understand the goals of the organization and identify with them.
6. They have the necessary knowledge and experience to be able to deal with the problem.
7. They are accustomed to sharing in decisionmaking. This is what they expect and are prepared for, rather than being denied such a role.[32]

[31] *Ibid.*, 98.
[32] *Ibid.*, 99.

If these conditions do not exist, there may be no alternative to running "a one-man show." Depending on his assessment of these factors, the executive may on one occasion decide to make the decisions himself, on another to let the subordinates participate. If the manager has the respect of the subordinates, they will understand why in the one case he brings them in and in the other he does not.

Forces in the Situation

"Forces in the situation" refers to the "critical environmental pressures" which surround the manager, stemming from "the organization, the work group, the nature of the problem, and the pressures of time."[33]

As to the organization, it has values and traditions which condition the manager's behavior. Someone newly appointed from the outside "quickly discovers that certain kinds of behavior are approved while others are not." There is a great compulsion for him to select that kind of behavior on the continuum which conforms to his superiors' concepts of how he should conduct himself. Sometimes this is referred to as the "management climate" in the agency; in other words, the lower ranking executives tend to imitate the behavior of the higher ones. The latter are a very important part of the "situation."

Other organizational factors influencing the extent of employee participation are: the size of the organization units; their geographical distribution; and whether or not information about work plans must be kept confidential. In a very large and dispersed organization, it may be impossible to have as much employee participation as the management would like. If the activity is one involving the national security, work plans and other information obviously cannot be communicated as freely to the employees.

"Group effectiveness" is another consideration. Before he gives a problem to the work group to solve, the manager must be convinced that it is equal to the task. Has the group functioned effectively in the past? Does it seem confident of its ability to cope with this kind of assignment?

The "nature of the problem" also sets limits on the extent to which the manager can safely delegate. Perhaps the problem is one with

[33] *Ibid.*, 100.

which the work group is not familiar, so he must handle it himself. There is no virtue in asking any one subordinate or a group of workers to take on responsibilities they are not ready to assume. Yet the executive wants to be sure that he is making full use of the special knowledges and abilities of his staff. Tannenbaum and Schmidt suggest that the manager should ask himself, "Have I heard the ideas of everyone who has the necessary knowledge to make a significant contribution to the solution of this problem?" If he asks this question and answers it honestly, he is more likely to select the most appropriate leadership pattern.

"Pressure of time," meaning the need to act quickly, may force the manager to make the decision himself, without consulting with his subordinates. Leisurely consideration of every problem is not possible in the swift-moving environment of government. The manager does not by any means have full control of his time schedule; his own supervisors set deadlines for him. Unforeseen situations arise which make it necessary for him to make the best decision possible in a very short period of time. Under such circumstances, all he can do is consult with as many subordinates as possible, assuming that he even has time to do this.

The great value of the preceding analysis is that it makes clear the different considerations which should influence the decision as to leadership style. If the "boss-centered" type is used on occasion, this does not mean that the managers in question must be tyrants at heart. Of course, some may have such tendencies, evidenced by their use of "boss-centered" leadership even when it is not necessary. The point is that the manager should use the leadership pattern which is called for by the particular situation.

INFORMAL LEADERSHIP

Before ending this chapter, we feel it important to include a more detailed discussion of the nature of informal leadership. Both students and practitioners of administration should have a clear understanding of the source of power of informal leaders. They are not visible on the organization chart, but their presence is felt in any organization, and to give them inadequate attention may mean leaving out a very important part of the picture. In Chapter 7, it was described how a person without formal authority sometimes is the one really in charge. The example was cited of the Air Force captain who decided to "take orders" from a sergeant who knew much more about the details of intelligence operating procedures. As a result, the sergeant informally took over the leadership in the air squadron as far as intelligence work was concerned. This is not the typical kind of informal leader, however; in the usual situation, the work group has an informal leader, but he enjoys no clique relationship with the formal leader. Sometimes the happy situation exists of a formal head who is also accepted by the group as its informal leader, but this tends to be rare because much social distance normally exists between those holding positions of formal authority and the workers.

Characteristics of Informal Leaders

What is it that makes a group of workers accept one of its members as their leader? George C. Homans provides us with a very clear explanation. "The leader," he writes, "is the man who comes closest to realizing the norms the group values highest."[34] The norms are the ideas the group has about how its members should behave. They make up the group code referred to in Chapter 7. The individual who best lives up to this code comes to be accepted as the leader.

The qualities looked for in the leader vary in accordance with the kind of activities in which the group engages. In a street-corner gang, proficiency in the favorite sport of the group, like bowling or boxing, may be essential. As Homans comments: "The norms may be queer ones, but so long as they are generally accepted by the group, the leader, in that group, must embody them." The paradox is that, while the leader "controls the group, yet he is in a sense more controlled by it than others are, since it is a condition of his leadership that his actions and decisions shall conform more closely than those of others to an abstract norm."[35] Knowing *why* someone is the informal leader of a work group should prove helpful to the management. Since he best represents the way the group thinks and feels, by coming to understand him the management should be better able to deal with the group as a whole.

[34] George C. Homans, *The Human Group*, New York: Harcourt, Brace, and World, 1950, p. 188.
[35] *Ibid.*, pp. 188–189.

GUIDES TO LEADERSHIP

Homans presents a number of points about informal leaders practically all of which in our opinion apply equally well to formal leaders. Before presenting Homans' points, however, we should make clear that he does not intend them as inflexible rules; rather, he puts them forth as "convenient guides," to be applied by the leader "only within limits determined by the situation that faces him." Unfortunately, in the past, attempts have been made to develop "cookbook recipes" for leadership, consisting of listings of certain "principles." The fallacy in this approach is that "there are no rules for human behavior that apply in every situation without limit or change."

Following are Homans' "convenient guides" for leadership, presented with our own comments as to their bearing on the role of the formal leader as well:[36]

First, *the leader must establish his own position.* He should not attempt to lead the group until he has cemented his position in it. In the case of a formal leader, the problem is initially easier. His appointment to a position in the hierarchy automatically gives him the badge of authority. As we saw, his effectiveness in practice as a leader is another matter. The informal leader does not have this head start, so to speak. He must first gain status in the work group as the person who best embodies its ideals.

Second, *the leader must live up to the norms of the group.* At first glance, this appears a repetition of the first point. Homans, however, has some specific comments to make about how the leader should interpret this general requirement: He should practice what he preaches; he should set the example (anyone whose attitude is, "Do as I say, not as I do," is patently unqualified for a leadership role); he should abide by the actual norms of the group, not what he personally thinks they should be; and finally, the leader should concern himself with the matters that the men think important, not with those he thinks *ought* to be important to them. If he decides for himself what their best interests are, he indulges in paternalism. If he is guided by what they feel is important, then he really identifies with the group.

Third, *the leader must lead.* The leader must take the initiative in

[36] *Ibid.*, pp. 423–440.

seeking to resolve the problems which confront the group. Because he is the leader, he cannot sit back and expect someone else to assume this responsibility. This is exactly why so many people prefer to be led rather than to lead. They want no part of the responsibilities of leadership, and that is why they have made someone else the leader. They want him to tell them what to do. If he fails to do so, their respect for him lessens, and he may have to give way to someone else the group decides would make the better leader. Homans makes clear that he does not mean that the leader must make all the decisions. He can and should delegate the responsibility for some of them. What he cannot do is play a generally passive role and let the others take charge. In such case, he abdicates his leadership role. This point holds equally well for formal and informal leaders.

Fourth, *the leader should only give orders that will be obeyed.* If he insists on issuing an order that the men cannot or will not carry out, he loses status in their eyes. A formal leader can invoke sanctions and punish those who fail to comply with the order, but this is not the best way to get workers to cooperate. Chester I. Barnard supports Homans on this, saying that issuance of such orders can only be calculated to destroy "authority, discipline, and morale." Much better results are achieved if orders are given which the workers feel they can accept. The informal leader can successfully punish only when the group is with him.

Fifth, *in giving orders, the leader should use established channels.* A kind of hierarchy develops in informal groups, very much resembling that in formal organizations. The leader is surrounded by subleaders or lieutenants who serve as a channel between him and the other members of the group. This does not mean that the leader has no direct contacts with the men at the bottom of this informal pyramid, but simply that the lieutenants play the role of intermediaries, conveying the leader's thinking to the men and theirs to him. Homans believes that as a general rule the leader should respect this channel and transmit his orders through the lieutenants. If he does otherwise, he undermines the standing of the lieutenants and disturbs the whole social organization of the group. The same point applies to formal leaders. There are times when not using the established channels can be justified, but few people would argue that it is acceptable conduct for the supervisor as a common practice to bypass his assistants and deal directly with their subordinates. In both formal and informal organizations, this would not only be unfair to the assistant chiefs but also cause confusion.

Sixth, *the leader will not thrust himself upon his followers on social occasions*. Homans does not mean that the leader should spurn all social contact with the followers. He should be present at parties and other functions, but he should not behave like someone in a position of authority on such occasions. In human groups, those of equal social rank tend to interact with great frequency, as was brought out in Chapter 7. If a leader has greater contact with one of the rank-and-file than with his own lieutenants, he thereby lowers his own social rank and invites the possibility that the person with whom he becomes so familiar will not obey his orders. Homans makes clear that he is not recommending a caste system. He writes: "Even if all members of the armed forces attended the same clubs and used the same recreational facilities—and we believe they should—certain persons would tend to eat together, drink together, and play games together, and these persons would tend to be social and organizational equals."[37] Such persons gravitate together, without an outside directing force. This may be an undemocratic aspect of human life, but it serves the important function of maintaining authority relationships.

Seventh, *the leader should neither blame nor, in general, praise a member of the group before the other members*. The leader who criticizes someone in public not only humiliates the individual but raises doubts in the minds of the others as to his fairness. They may not feel that the rebuked person's behavior merits such treatment. If it is one of his lieutenants that he scolds with others present, he lowers the lieutenant's status in the group and thus weakens the whole system of authority. The objection to praise in public is that the rest of the men may not be ready to accept the leader's high opinion of the person lauded. Furthermore, the individual himself may feel embarrassed at being singled out for praise before the other members of the group.

Eighth, *the leader will take into consideration the total situation*. Homans' basic point here is that the leader must fully understand the nature of the organizations as social systems with numerous interrelated elements. Americans, he believes, have developed "admirable technical processes," but generally do not adequately understand the "relations between technology, organization, and the other aspects of

[37] *Ibid.*, p. 431.

a social system," i.e., they still do not fully comprehend the relationships between the informal and the formal organization. "Consideration of the total situation" is not possible without "explicit, conscious, intellectual understanding" of these relationships.

Ninth, *in maintaining discipline, the leader should be less concerned with inflicting punishment than with creating the conditions in which the group will discipline itself*. The controls maintained by the group over its members were mentioned in Chapter 7. What the leader should do is to establish the kind of relationship with the group that encourages it to apply the pressures of social discipline on members who violate its code. Homans does not say that the leader should never inflict punishment. If the offense is clearly in violation of the group code, the group and even the guilty party may expect the leader to punish. When the group accepts the leader's decisions, it can be expected to do a better job of overseeing their execution than he could.

Tenth, *the leader will listen*. Homans refers here to the difficulties in upward communication, referred to in Chapter 9 of this text. The leader, he stresses, must make positive efforts to get his subordinates to talk to him "about *anything* that is on their minds." Listening, says Homans, is work. The leader is tempted to do the talking and to cut off the follower. In listening, the leader should make it clear that "he wants to hear *everything*." He should do nothing which leads the subordinate to believe that it would be better to tell only part of the story. The leader should accept what is told him, without indicating approval or disapproval. Otherwise, the subordinate will take his cue and tell him only what it seems he wants to hear. Homans makes the sage observation that "communication feeds on communication." By listening, the leader really is not as passive as might be thought. He is really playing a positive role by opening the door for constructive relations between superior and subordinate.

Finally, *the leader must know himself*. "Self-knowledge," states Homans, "is the first step in self-control." The leader, after all, is only human. He must be aware of those "passions in him that, unchecked, will destroy him as a leader. . ." His responsibilities are greater than those of anyone else in the group. The requirement for "self-knowledge," then, is greatest in his case. Many people understand intellectually the first ten points made, yet they all too frequently fail to observe them, because they do not practice self-control. To the degree that they keep themselves under constant scrutiny and check, they will do a better job of leading.

Reviewing Homans' points, we find that all except the second are as applicable to formal as to informal leaders. The second point is not fully applicable, because the formal leader cannot be expected to live up to the groups' norms if it means working against the management. The ideal situation, of course, would be one in which the desires of the informal groups are all perfectly reasonable and could easily be satisfied by the management. As one example, work restriction can hardly be accepted as a management norm. Yet, as the Hawthorne experiments brought out, it is when the management is oblivious of the thinking of the workers, that it embarks upon programs which can result in work restriction and other forms of employee resistance. Knowing how the employees think and feel, without necessarily accepting all their values, will give the formal supervisor the perspective he needs.

It will be noted that this chapter on leadership has necessarily led us from the discussion of one management topic to another: decision-making; authority relationships; delegation; communications; and control. It also caused us to probe into the profound subject of human motivation: how to stimulate the worker to put forth his best efforts is the most important of all leadership requirements. This brings us to Part IV of this book, Personnel Administration. Effective leadership and good personnel administration go hand in hand.

BIBLIOGRAPHY

Argyris, Chris., *Personality Fundamentals for Administrators*, New Haven, Conn.: Labor and Management Center, Yale, 1953.

Argyris, Chris., *Personality and Organization*, New York: Harper and Row, 1957.

Argyris, Chris., "The Individual and Organization: Some Problems of Mutual Adjustment," *Administrative Science Quarterly*, **II,** No. 1 (June, 1957).

Bavelas, Alex, "Leadership: Man and Function," *Administrative Science Quarterly*, **IV**, No. 4 (March, 1960).

Bennis, Warren G., "Leadership Theory and Administrative Behavior: The Problem of Authority," *Administrative Science Quarterly*, **IV**, No. 3 (December, 1959).

Cartwright, Dorwin, and Zander, Alvin (eds.), *Group Dynamics, Research and Theory*, New York: Harper and Row, 1960. Part Five.

Evans, Richard I., "Prejudice: A Threat to the Leadership Role," *Personnel Administration*, **XXV**, No. 1 (January–February, 1962).

Ginzberg, Eli, "Perspectives on Worker Motivation," *Personnel*, **XXXI**, No. 1 (July, 1954).

Golembiewski, Robert T., "Three Styles of Leadership and Their Uses," *Personnel*, **XXXVIII**, No. 4 (July–August, 1961).

Halpin, Andrew W., *The Leadership Behavior of School Superintendents*, Columbus, Ohio: College of Education, The Ohio State Univ., 1956.

McMurry, Robert N., "The Case for Benevolent Autocracy," *Harvard Business Review*, **XXXVI**, No. 1 (January–February, 1958).

Patchen, Martin, "Supervisory Methods and Group Performance Norms," *Administrative Science Quarterly*, **VII**, No. 3 (December, 1962).

Petrullo, Luigi, and Bass, Bernard M. (eds.), *Leadership and Interpersonal Behavior*, New York: Holt, Rinehart and Winston, 1961.

Presthus, Robert, "Authority in Organizations," *Public Administration Review*, **XX**, No. 2 (Spring, 1960).

Selznick, Philip, *Leadership in Administration*, New York: Harper and Row, 1957.

Stanton, Erwin S., "Which Approach to Management—Democratic, Authoritarian or . . .?" *Personnel Administration*, **XXV**, No. 2 (March–April, 1962).

Tannenbaum, Arnold S., "Control in Organizations: Individual Adjustment and Organizational Performance," *Administrative Science Quarterly*, **VII**, No. 2 (September, 1962).

PART IV

PERSONNEL ADMINISTRATION

CHAPTER 13

Evolution of Public Personnel Administration in the United States

Quite often those studying problems thought to be primarily organizational in character become convinced that the more important consideration is that of attracting and retaining high-calibre personnel; witness the following statement by Senator Henry M. Jackson of Washington, Chairman of a Senate subcommittee which recently made a thorough study of the machinery for formulating and carrying out national security policy:

> This study had something of a surprise ending: we concluded that the heart problem of Government is not machinery but men. Good national policies require both good organization and good people. But people are the critical factor. Wise, experienced, hard-working, incisive Government officials may win out over poor organization. But poor people will defeat the best organization. Moreover, reforms in machinery cannot cure troubles which are really not due to defects of machinery. Organizational gimmickry is no substitute for practical measures to improve the competence and the performance of Government officials.[1]

The relationship between good administration and high-quality personnel is by no means a discovery of the modern age. Indeed, it

[1] Henry M. Jackson, "Environment of Excellence," *Civil Service Journal,* II, No. 4 (April–June, 1962), 8.

was recognized in the earliest civilizations. In Plato's *Republic*, there occurs this interesting bit of dialogue between the narrator, Socrates, and Glaucon, one of the auditors:

> Do you know, I said, that governments vary as the dispositions of men vary, and that there must be as many of the one as there are of the other? For we cannot suppose that States are made of "oak and rock," and not out of the human natures which are in them, and which in a figure turn the scale and draw other things after them?
>
> Yes, he said, the States are as the men are; they grow out of human characters.[2]

Governments can be no better than the people who create them and the officials who run them. Since "they grow out of human characters," the quality of that human element is of decisive importance. John M. Gaus is reported to have said that *The Republic* is really a treatise on personnel administration, concerned as Plato is with a comprehensive plan for selecting and training the philosopher-kings. Of course, Plato's specific program is impractical for the modern age, but that the "states are as the men are" is just as true today as it was in his times. In fact, centuries later, the American philosopher, John Dewey, said "the state is as its officials are." Dewey believed, just as did Plato, that public officials could not be "mean, obstinate, proud, and stupid, and yet the nature of the state which they serve remain essentially unimpaired."[3] Here is the great challenge of personnel administration; it deals with the key human element, and how to make it equal to the greatly increasing public-service needs of the people.

In the United States, public personnel administration as it exists today is the product of a long evolution. Let us briefly examine this background with the intention simply of identifying the main strands which have gone into the public personnel movement.[4]

[2] Plato, *The Republic* (trans. Benjamin Jowett), New York: Vintage Books, Random House, p. 293.

[3] John Dewey, *The Public and its Problems*, New York: Holt, Rinehart and Winston, 1927, pp. 68–69.

[4] The following historical account is from Paul P. Van Riper, *History of the United States Civil Service*, New York: Harper and Row, 1958.

RECORD OF FIRST SIX PRESIDENTS

The first six Presidents have frequently been praised for maintaining good standards in the selection of federal employees. Paul P. Van Riper, the leading authority on the history of the federal civil service, recounts that, in the main, these first Presidents did give a good deal of weight to merit principles in making their appointments. He stresses, however, that they also took political factors into account to some extent. Washington, for example, emphasized job fitness, but in choosing from among the candidates, he was careful to select individuals who were friendly to the Federalist cause, and Jefferson made no bones about removing men from posts for political reasons. It should be made clear, however, that both under the Federalists and the Jeffersonians most of the government jobs were filled by persons with an upper middle-class background. Under Jefferson, there was no program of replacing such persons with embodiments of the common man. Comments Van Riper: "American government in the early years of the nineteenth century was still the prerogative of those with considerable means."[5]

THE SPOILS SYSTEM, 1829 TO 1883

The class composition of federal employees changes drastically, however, with the advent of Andrew Jackson to the Presidency, for he strongly felt that no one social class should have a monopoly of the public service. Such a monopoly was not only undemocratic, it was also unnecessary in terms of governmental efficiency. In his opening message to Congress in December, 1829, he said: "The duties of all public officers are, or at least admit of being made, so plain and simple that men of intelligence may readily qualify themselves for their performance; and I can not but believe that more is lost by the long continuance of men in office than is generally to be gained by their experience."[6] For these reasons, Jackson believed that rotation in office was highly desirable. Under such a policy,

[5] *Ibid.*, p. 24.
[6] *Ibid.*, p. 36.

holdovers from previous Administrations are swept out, and, acting accordingly, Jackson made numerous removals. Van Riper and others have stressed that Jackson had good intentions about the public service and did not want to damage it. He was not the machine politician who is intent on building personal power and indifferent to the harmful effects on the government. Nevertheless, with his new policies, he did open the gates for the spoils politicians at the national level.

Beginning approximately with the year 1800, the spoils system had begun to take hold in state and local governments. Under the spoils system, the party winning the election reasons that to the victor belongs the spoils, so it makes gifts of government jobs to party workers. By 1829, this policy was strongly entrenched in many states, particularly in New York and Pennsylvania. Political parties were just then emerging, replacing the former mere factional groupings. The professional politician was being born, and it was not long before he discovered that gifts of government jobs could be used to lubricate the party machinery. Such men were motivated, not by the egalitarian ideals of Jacksonian democracy, but rather by considerations of the raw struggle for political power. Historians differ about who was personally responsible for bringing the unadulterated spoils system to Washington. Some blame it on Martin Van Buren, the clever New York politician whom Jackson made his first Secretary of State, but Van Buren's biographers dispute this.[7] In any case, the unmitigated spoils system had started in other parts of the country, and it naturally spread to Washington and the federal service when Jackson adopted the new policy of rotation in office. Under the Presidents who followed Jackson, political removals were made on a more extensive basis, and, by 1860, the original opening provided by Jackson had produced a spoils systems with an "adhesive . . . grip upon the political machinery of the United States."[8] Van Riper describes in specific terms what was involved in terms of obligations and rewards:

That politics was often a touchstone to success in private enterprise via land grants, franchises, and government contracts only heightened interest

[7] See Felix A. Nigro, "The Van Buren Confirmation before the Senate," *Western Political Quarterly*, XIV, No. 1 (March, 1961), 148–159.

[8] Van Riper, *op. cit.*, p. 42.

in public office. In return, however, public servants were expected to contribute their votes and a portion, often substantial, of their time, energy, and income to the political party to which they were indebted for their employment. All this was not a matter of contract, though such might be implied. Rather, it was usually a recognition of a sort of partnership, often entered into with considerable enthusiasm by all concerned. Loyalty to one's political party was as appropriate, and just about as frequently assumed, as loyalty to the nation, a church, or an individual state. Most frequently the penalty for both administrative and political failure was removal. In addition, however, one might be cut off from any access to other types of political favors, both those directly at the command of the party, such as nominations, and those available only through governmental channels, such as contracts. On the whole, the motivations and methods of private enterprise were those of the spoils system.[9]

Under Lincoln, the "spoils system reached new heights." In order to develop support in the North for carrying on the war with the Confederacy, Lincoln was forced to make numerous appointments for political reasons. In fact, he made the "most complete sweep of the offices" of any president up to that time. From a personal standpoint, however, Lincoln found the spoils system distasteful. One day, observing a crowd of office-seekers in his outer office, he remarked that "the spoils system might in the course of time become far more dangerous to the Republic than the rebellion itself."[10] To the man in the street, however, there was nothing wrong with the spoils system. In Lincoln's time and during the immediate post-Civil War period, most Americans still agreed with the Jacksonian view that the duties of public office were so simple that they could be entrusted to almost anyone.

THE CIVIL SERVICE REFORM MOVEMENT

However, important changes were taking place in American society, and the role of government was being expanded as the country became increasingly industrialized. Government jobs no longer were as simple as they used to be, so some people became concerned that the government could not discharge its responsibilities effectively with personnel chosen for political reasons and not for merit. Not

[9] *Ibid.*, p. 46.
[10] *Ibid.*, pp. 43–44.

enough people were concerned about governmental efficiency, however, for this to become the primary moving force for civil service reform. It was the evidence of widespread corruption in the federal service, tied in with the spoils system, that gave civil service reform its real impetus. The scandals in the Grant administration, involving some members of the Cabinet, aroused a public now increasingly aware of the connection between the spoils system and graft. Those who obtained appointments as a reward for political service were willing allies of predatory outside interests in different kinds of frauds perpetrated against the government, such as the awarding of contracts. The moral argument for civil service reform soon caught hold in an America which, at that time, thought largely in moral terms. The spoils system was an evil which had to be extirpated from American society if standards of decency were to be maintained, and this became the battle cry of a small group of dedicated individuals, known to history as the "civil service reformers." These men were mostly from the eastern part of the country, representing the "top strata of politics, law, business, journalism, and education,"[11] and they had the personal means to devote their time to developing public interest in civil service reform. Their crusade had proved so successful by 1872 that both the Republican and Democratic parties picked up civil service reform as an issue in the election campaigns for the Congress. One year previously, in March, 1871, Congress had actually voted authorization for President Grant to establish a merit system. This came in the form of a last-minute rider to an appropriation bill, the motivation being the Republican-controlled Congress' desire to improve its position with the electorate after losses suffered by the Republicans in the mid-term elections of 1870. Grant established a Civil Service Commission which developed a set of civil service rules and administered competitive examinations in some federal departments. In 1873, Congress failed to vote any further funds for this Commission, and it was forced to suspend its operations.

The Pendleton Act

When a disappointed job-seeker assassinated President Garfield in 1881, many Americans previously not moved by the pleas of the civil service reformers now could see that "spoils equalled murder."

[11] *Ibid.*, p. 80.

Van Riper believes that Congress would have acted to adopt a civil service system even if this tragedy had not occurred. The Republicans suffered a disastrous defeat in the mid-term election of 1882. They feared that the next President would be a Democrat, and that he would turn out all the Republican office-holders. Although in December, 1880, Senator George H. Pendleton of Ohio introduced a bill providing for adoption of a civil service system, which he later replaced with one sponsored by the New York Civil Service Reform Association, no action was taken in the Senate until Garfield's assassination and the Republican reverses in the 1882 elections. Faced by the possibility that the Democrats would win in the 1884 presidential elections, the Republicans now decided to support Pendleton's bill. It was passed by Congress in December, 1882, and signed by the President on January 16, 1883. Van Riper writes, "As a later observer cynically put it in 1888, 'the devil was sick, and the devil a monk would be.' "[12]

The civil service reformers and Pendleton were much influenced by the example of the English civil service system. Dorman B. Eaton, one of the leading figures in the reform movement, had been commissioned by President Hayes to visit England and make a study of the English system. Eaton served as the second Chairman of the Grant Commission and later became the first Chairman of the United States Civil Service Commission created by the Pendleton Act. The British had had their spoils system, no less venal than the American, but, by 1870, the merit system was beginning to function in England and attracted the attention of Americans like Eaton, anxious to prove to the American people that the spoils system was not a necessary evil.

It was Eaton who persuaded Pendleton to introduce his second bill, so it is not surprising that the Pendleton Act incorporated certain features of the English civil service system. Three basic elements were borrowed: (1) the use of competitive examinations for entrance into the public service; (2) relative security of tenure, with removals for political reasons forbidden; and (3) the guarantee of the political neutrality of the civil servant by providing that he cannot be coerced to make political assessments and to contribute his services to political campaigns. All three principles represented important changes from existing practices in the federal service. It took some years to

[12] *Ibid.*, p. 94.

make the ban on political removals and assessments effective, but the legislative intent in the matter was clear enough.

There is, however, another feature of the British system which was originally included in the Pendleton bill but which was rejected by Congress: the principle of the closed career service. In England, recruitment to the public service is articulated with the educational system. In accordance with a definite plan, the best products of the latter are tapped for the entrance jobs in each line of work. In general, the principle of initial recruitment to the bottom rungs of certain career ladders is followed. To be eligible for appointment to a beginning position in one of these career progressions, the individual must have completed a certain level of education. For example, candidates for the administrative class, a relatively small group for whom the top administrative policymaking positions are reserved, must be university graduates, no younger in age than twenty and a half or older than twenty-four. In the British system, what is known as "lateral entry" is kept to a minimum. Very few opportunities are available for entering one of the career ladders at one of the intermediate steps or at the top rung *after* having had outside work experience. This is what lateral entry means, namely, permitting persons who have already had other employment to be brought in from outside the government service to fill openings in jobs above the entry level. The British career system is a closed one, because it discourages free movement of individuals, no matter what their age and education, from private to public employment.[13]

In his bill, Pendleton proposed that entrance into the public service be permitted only "at the lowest grade." This provision met with a decidedly adverse reaction on the part of most of his colleagues in the Senate. They found it contrary to one of the most treasured values of American society: the right of anyone, no matter what his formal schooling, age, or past work history, to demonstrate his ability in any walk of life. Eliminating the spoils system was one thing; making federal employment the virtual monopoly of persons with a certain educational background was another. The United States

[13] For the basic principles of the British system of recruitment, see "The Northcote-Trevelyan Report," reprint of report submitted to both Houses of Parliament by command of Her Majesty in February, 1854. (Paper 1713). *Public Administration*, XXXII (Spring, 1954), 1–16.

was a democracy, an open society with no class distinctions like those in Britain. The "efficient" features of the British system should be borrowed, but not those which seemed undemocratic. This is why Van Riper calls the Pendleton Act an "Americanization of a foreign invention." The opposition was so strong to this provision in his bill that Pendleton himself made a motion to eliminate it. The motion was overwhelmingly adopted, and as a result, "from 1883 to this day, one may enter the American public service at almost any level and at almost any age."[14] As we shall see in the next chapter, strong efforts are being made to make government service a highly desired career for young persons, but the feeling remains as strong against any closed system. Open career systems, with plenty of lateral entry, are the goal, and it is one consonant with American values.

As it was passed, the Pendleton Act created a three-member commission, the members to be appointed by the President subject to Senate confirmation. Of these three members, not more than two may be adherents of the same political party. By not placing the new agency directly under the President and by including this requirement for bipartisanship, Congress clearly indicated its desire to keep the civil service system free from partisan presidential control. On the other hand, Congress just as certainly did not intend the Civil Service Commission to be completely independent of the President. James Watson, formerly Executive Director of the National Civil Service League, states that the debates in committee and on the floor of Congress clearly show that "Congress did not intend the Commission to be so independent as to prohibit executive responsibility for administering the civil service."[15]

With respect to coverage, the Act provided for immediately placing under the competitive service only about 10.5 percent of all federal jobs. Furthermore, these were mainly clerical positions in Washington and in post offices and customs houses in the field service. To obtain approval of any civil service measure at that time, it was

[14] Paul P. Van Riper, "Adapting a British Political Invention to American Needs," *Public Administration*, **XXXI** (Winter, 1953), 321–322. See also his "The Tap Roots of American Personnel Management," *Personnel Administration*, XXV, No. 2 (March–April, 1962), 12–16, 32.

[15] *Administration of the Civil Service System*, Senate Committee on Post Office and Civil Service, Washington, D.C.: Government Printing Office, 1957, p. 44.

necessary to go slow. Despite public pressures, there was still considerable opposition in Congress to adopting the merit system. Actually, the Civil Service Commission was not equipped anyway to administer examinations for any large proportion of federal positions. It needed time to get started. Within the limitations of its modest budget, it found it difficult enough to develop a satisfactory program even for the small proportion of employees originally placed under its jurisdiction. Total employment in the federal service averaged about 140,000 in the 1880s.

Extension of the Civil Service System, 1883–1964

The Pendleton Act, however, gave the President the authority by executive order to bring additional positions under civil service as he saw fit. Without this provision, the civil service reformers would not have won much of a victory. Once the Pendleton Act was passed, they could and did renew pressure on the Chief Executive to make the civil service system more inclusive. Presidents still found it necessary to retain a certain number of spoils positions to use as a means of persuading recalcitrant Congressmen to accept their legislative leadership. On the other hand, it was now good politics to demonstrate to the electorate positive support of the civil service principle by covering in large numbers of additional positions.

Political self-interest marched hand in hand with civil service idealism. When a President of one party was leaving the White House to turn over direction of the government to a successor elected by the opposing party, he found it convenient, as one of his last acts, to bring large numbers of additional jobs under civil service. These jobs had been filled with individuals friendly to his Administration, so the departing Chief Executive both protected the position of his party and advanced the cause of civil service. This process is known as "blanketing in." To qualify to retain their jobs, all the incumbent had to do was pass a noncompetitive examination, consisting of a review by the Civil Service Commission of his service record on the job. Practically everybody could pass this kind of examination, since they already had some experience in the jobs.

Lest a cynical view be formed of Presidents like Cleveland, T. R. Roosevelt, and F. D. Roosevelt who "blanketed in" thousands of additional jobs, it should be made clear that at heart they did not relish using the "club" of spoils positions. Carl Russell Fish, the historian, came to the conclusion that throughout the nineteenth century the President's patronage proved an indispensable weapon for overcoming the obstacles to presidential leadership inherent in a system of separation of powers.[16] In the twentieth century, however, the picture had changed. Congress itself in 1940 took positive action to encourage President F. D. Roosevelt to bring under civil service by far the greater number of positions still outside the merit system. When the New Deal first appeared, the Democrats, out of power for twelve long years, were hungry for patronage. Positions in the flock of new agencies created in the effort to fight the depression were usually exempted from civil service. By 1940, the situation was different. No longer harried by the same pressures, F.D.R. gladly issued the executive orders, the net effect of which was to clinch the victory for the merit system in the federal service. Specifically, F.D.R. "covered in" some 200,000 positions formerly exempted by law. By 1943, approximately 85 percent of all federal personnel were within the permanent civil service. Since approximately the same percentage is covered today, for some twenty years now civil service has covered the great bulk of federal jobs.

Interestingly enough, the Pendleton Act as it still stands makes it possible for the President to remove positions from civil service as well as to place them under it. That no recent President has sought to capitalize on this authority and remove large numbers of positions is testimony to the strength that the civil service principle now has at the national level. Presidents still have some patronage jobs to dispense, such as those of federal district attorneys and marshalls, but the argument that the national government could not be satisfactorily administered without large numbers of spoils jobs to give out is now accepted by very few people, inside and outside Congress. As a simple reading of the newspapers shows, a much more effective control over Congressmen is to threaten them with curtailing expenditures for new post offices and other federal projects in their home constituencies. The "patronage" available today is largely of this character.

[16] See Carl Russell Fish, *The Civil Service and the Patronage*, Cambridge, Mass.: Harvard Univ. Press, 1904.

Civil Service in the States and Cities, 1883–1964

Progress in obtaining civil service in the state governments has not been nearly as great. Thirty of the 50 states have adopted comprehensive merit systems, meaning that a large proportion of the positions in the state service is covered.[17] New York (1883) and Massachusetts (1884) were the first to follow the federal example. As late as 1958, only 23 states had comprehensive merit systems. In the last few years, the picture has brightened considerably, with seven additional states joining this group. The outlook is even better, however, because a merit system functions in all state agencies administering federally aided programs for public assistance, child-health and welfare services, and public-health and employment security programs. Amendments made by Congress in 1940 to the Social Security Act provide that states desiring grants-in-aid under the Act must establish and maintain an effective merit system. Similar requirements were extended to the different public-health programs by regulations under the Public Health Act and were included in 1946 in the Hospital and Survey Construction Act, as well as in 1950 in new assistance programs for the permanently and totally disabled. Thus, there is no state in the Union in which the merit system does not function in some part of the executive branch. Furthermore, some states have placed certain agencies under merit systems of their own, in addition to what is required under the Social Security Act.

In the nation's counties, civil service coverage is still quite small. Only about 200 of the nation's more than 3050 counties have civil service laws or are covered by the state law. In the cities, coverage is much higher. The latest information available shows that of an estimated 1,071,000 full-time city employees (excluding teachers), possibly 800,000 are under civil service. All cities of more than 500,000 population, all but one between 250,000 and 500,000 (Kansas City, Missouri), most cities between 100,000 and 250,000, and many smaller ones have civil service systems.[18]

[17] See *Good Government*, LXXVII, No. 3 (March, 1960), which contains a map showing the Civil Service States. Since then, the states of Washington, Kentucky, Alaska, West Virginia, and New Mexico have joined this group.

[18] H. Eliot Kaplan, *The Law of Civil Service*, Albany, N.Y.: Matthew Bender, 1958, pp. 27–28.

Reviewing the entire picture in state and local governments, it can hardly be said that the spoils system is dead. In many state and local jurisdictions, it obviously still thrives. Local politicians argue that the political machine needs the patronage to survive. Getting merit systems approved in these jurisdictions constitutes some of the toughest unfinished business on the personnel front. The battle is just as hard in many places as it was for the original civil service reformers.[19]

THE MODERN CONCEPT OF PERSONNEL ADMINISTRATION

The modern thinking about the role of personnel administration is very different, however, from what it was in the days of these crusaders. It was stated earlier in this chapter that they emphasized moral arguments, not the goal of efficiency. Their objective was to remove a social evil, the spoils system, not to develop more efficient public administration as such. Of course, eliminating the spoils system would mean an end to the employment of many incompetents hired only because of their political connections. But it would not guarantee the appointment of the most fit persons available. This could only be accomplished through adoption of a genuine merit system, based on the principle of efficiency.

For many years after the passage of the Pendleton Act, not only in the federal government but also in the state and local jurisdictions that followed suit by adopting civil service laws, success was measured by the degree to which political influence was kept out of appointments and promotions. This was the significant consideration, not whether the persons appointed or promoted were of high quality. The essential requirement was to give competitive tests to candidates who presented themselves and to refuse to relax the standards to suit the politicians. It is unfair to judge the personnel procedures then in use on the basis of the more sophisticated techniques we have today, but the basic point remains that it was a limited, negative type of program that these first civil service agencies conducted. Apart from giving examinations and maintaining records, they did little else. Efforts were not made to search out the best available candidates.

[19] For a more sanguine view, see Frank J. Sorauf, "The Silent Revolution in Patronage," *Public Administration Review*, XX, No. 1 (Winter, 1960), 28–34.

Clerks, rather than trained personnel technicians, held most of the jobs in these agencies. Comprehensive personnel programs as we know them today did not exist.

Such limited programs were understandable in the first years after the adoption of civil service. Appropriations were generally very small, and much time had to be devoted to staving off the attempts of the politicians to undermine the merit system. Even today personnel administrators in places which have had civil service for many years do not assume that a reincidence of the spoils system is impossible. Realistically, they recognize that some attention must be given to the "protective function," that is, standing ready to fight any spoils threats. The trouble is that too many of the early civil service agencies continued to spend much of their time on the protective function long after the merit system had become firmly established in these jurisdictions. Their programs were not updated to meet a new situation, one in which the test of success is the ability to staff the public service with the high-quality personnel needed to carry out government activities of an increasingly complex character. The Jacksonian concept of the essentially simple nature of government jobs clearly did not square with the realities of the twentieth century. Increasingly, leaders in the personnel field began to urge their brethren to adopt a broader view and to develop truly "modern" personnel programs. By a modern program, they meant one which was positively oriented toward the goal of recruiting and retaining efficient public employees. They wished the creation of personnel offices staffed with professionally trained individuals rather than clerks. Their objective was the development of a broad-gauged personnel program, not one limited just to giving examinations and keeping records.

Some jurisdictions began to broaden their programs, but in general the following gives the picture of public personnel administration in the country as a whole in the late 1930s:

1. A preponderance of the daily working hours devoted to the routine aspects of appointments, records, and classification.
2. Centralization of most important personnel decisions in the civil service commission or board, and normal delays of several weeks in placing someone on the departmental payroll.
3. Very little in-service training activity.

4. Only scattered evidence of interest in improved personnel practices being developed in private industry, despite the obvious importance of some of these techniques and the possibility of using them in the government.
5. Very little career planning in the line departments, despite the rush of college graduates, attracted by the New Deal, to Washington.
6. Very few personnel directors with any real voice in the management policies of their agencies.
7. Almost a complete neglect of the importance of good supervision and of the personnel responsibilities of line officials in general.
8. Little attention to employee welfare and health, apart from some low-priced cafeterias, emergency rooms, bowling leagues, and softball.[20]

In 1938, F.D.R. issued an executive order requiring all major departments and agencies to establish bona fide, professionally staffed personnel offices. Previously, personnel functions had mainly been entrusted to high- and low-ranking clerks. They kept records and maintained liaison with the Civil Service Commission on appointments and other personnel actions requiring Commission approval. Issuance of the executive order ushered in a new era in federal personnel management, marked by emphasis on developing a true merit system. Progress was not spectacular, but it was steady. Procedures were speeded up, and college-trained persons replaced the clerks. Important delegations of authority were made by the Commission to the operating departments, inaugurating a decentralization movement which led in a relatively few years to giving the departments the responsibility for making the great bulk of the appointments without any requirement of prior Commission approval.

The instrumentality used is the agency Board of United States Civil Service Examiners. It consists of agency officials approved by the Commission as its agents for conducting all phases of the examination program, from issuing notices of the examinations, grading them, preparing eligible registers, and certifying the names of eligibles to appointing officers. These boards are found both in the departmental service in Washington and at agency field locations. The Civil Service Commission periodically reviews their operations to be sure that they are observing legal provisions and conforming to its regu-

[20] Felix A. Nigro, "Public Personnel: Agenda for the Sixties," *Public Administration Review*, XXI, No. 4 (Autumn, 1961), 191–192.

lations. In other words, only a post-review is conducted. Furthermore, in addition to appointments, other phases of the personnel program, such as promotions, classification of positions, and administration of service rating systems, have been decentralized on the same basis.

The unimaginative and restricted recruiting programs of the past have been replaced with intensive efforts to attract good candidates. Liaison with educational institutions has been improved, and, after experimenting with several approaches, the Commission developed the highly successful Federal Service Entrance Examination to attract college students. The FSEE, as it is known, will be mentioned again in the next chapter. Training programs, too, received a great stimulus with passage by the Congress of the Government Employees Training Act of 1958. This legislation extended authority for the first time to *all* federal agencies to expend funds on the training of their employees, both by sending them to outside facilities, such as universities, and by organizing programs using the agency's own personnel and facilities. Since passage of this legislation, federal training activity has greatly increased.

Early in 1962, President Kennedy issued an executive order providing a new basis for employee-management relations in the federal service. As a result, the whole role of public-employee unions is being expanded, opening an entire new chapter in the history of personnel administration in the government. In October, 1962, Congress passed new pay legislation designed to make federal salaries more competitive with private industry rates than they have been in the past. All these developments are treated in some detail in the chapters that follow.

Whereas for many years after passage of the Pendleton Act the Civil Service Commission functioned in relative isolation from the President, it now has a closer relationship with the White House. The present Chairman, John W. Macy, Jr., is an influential advisor to the President. He is not on the White House staff as such, but he works closely with the President in obtaining the Chief Executive's support for improvements in federal personnel policies. This closer relationship with the Chief Executive reflects present-day thinking about the necessary equipment of chief executives, namely that they should be in control of staff services such as budgeting, planning, and personnel. The industry executive is frequently held up as an example, for he has these staff services directly under him. Congress, however, has never been willing to approve placing the personnel function in the President's Executive Office, which is what should be done if the industry model were followed. Congress has feared that making such a change would give the President undue power and possibly endanger the merit system. So the Commission still remains legally largely independent of the President, but in practice works closely with him.

State and local governments also have substantially improved their personnel programs. In fact, in some areas the states and cities moved ahead of the federal government in introducing more enlightened practices. Paid advertising was used by quite a few state and local governments long before the United States Commission announced in late 1957 that in the future federal agencies would be permitted to use such advertising in recruiting for scientists and engineers. Formal programs and machinery for dealing with management-employee union relationships had already been developed and were functioning in cities like Philadelphia, New York, and Cincinnati before President Kennedy issued his executive order. Before passage of the new federal pay legislation, California, Georgia, Illinois, Michigan, New York, Ohio, and Pennsylvania had all established higher top career salaries than those paid in the federal service. The same was true of Los Angeles City and County, Denver, Detroit, St. Louis, San Francisco, and Philadelphia.

In other areas, state and local governments have lagged behind. Training as a personnel activity of real importance has been developed in relatively few state and local jurisdictions. In most such jurisdictions nothing comparable to the Federal Service Entrance Examination has been developed. Recruiting methods are unimaginative, and the personnel program is still of an essentially negative character in many state and local jurisdictions.

In general, however, for the country as a whole public personnel administration today bears little resemblance to what it was prior to World War II. The whole concept of the role of the personnel function has changed. Today there is far more recognition of the vital role that personnel management can play in accomplishing agency objectives. It is no longer considered just an adjunct to the agency's program. On the contrary, it is now accepted by many as an indispensable part of the management equipment for carrying out the agency program successfully. Far from being a high-ranking clerk, indistinguishable from those in charge of routine administrative services, the personnel director is increasingly considered a member of the agency-management team.

The *content* of personnel programs has also been greatly influenced by the human-relations approach mentioned in Chapter 1 of this book. If there is any phase of public administration where application of this approach is clear and direct, it is personnel administration. Protecting the merit system still remains a necessity; efficient procedures will always be necessary. Understanding the employees as human beings and stimulating them to do their best work is the real challenge. As previous chapters of this book have indicated, we still do not know enough about human motivation. Personnel research needs to be expanded greatly in the years that lie ahead. As we shall see in the chapters that immediately follow, much remains to be accomplished besides the gains already noted above. These gains have been substantial, but as Cecil E. Goode said when he was Interim Director of the National Civil Service League: "We have made some progress in governmental personnel administration since 1883 but more progress lies ahead than behind."[21]

BIBLIOGRAPHY

"A Basic Bibliography in Public Personnel Administration," *Public Personnel Review*, **XXII**, No. 4 (October, 1961).

Beckett, Paul L., "Operation Self-Help: Washington State's New Merit System Law," *Public Personnel Review*, **XXIV**, No. 1 (January, 1963).

Bode, Carl, "The Professor and Form 57," *AAUP Bulletin*, **XLVI**, No. 4 (Winter, 1960).

Buchanan, Paul C., and Mahler, Walter R., "The Personnel Executive as

[21] "Message from the Executive Director," *Good Government*, **LXXVI**, No. 6 (November–December, 1959).

a Specialist," *Personnel Administration,* **XXIV,** No. 5 (September–October, 1961).

Chapman, Brian, *The Profession of Government,* London: G. Allen, 1959.

Fish, Carl Russell, *The Civil Service and the Patronage,* Cambridge, Mass.: Harvard, 1904.

Goode, Cecil E., *Personnel Research Frontiers,* Chicago, Ill.: Public Personnel Association, 1958.

Hoogenboom, Ari, *Outlawing the Spoils: A History of the Civil Service Reform Movement, 1865–1883,* Champaign–Urbana, Ill.: Univ. of Illinois Press, 1961.

Nigro, Felix A., "Public Personnel: Agenda for the Sixties," *Public Administration Review,* **XXI,** No. 4 (Autumn, 1961).

Page, Thomas (ed.), *"The Public Personnel Agency and the Chief Executive—A Symposium,* Chicago, Ill.: Public Personnel Association, 1960.

Sayre, Wallace S., and Mosher, Frederick C., *An Agenda for Research in Public Personnel Administration,* Washington, D.C.: National Planning Association, 1959.

Sorauf, Frank J., "Patronage and Party," *Midwest Journal of Political Science,* **III,** No. 2 (May, 1959).

Sorauf, Frank J., "The Silent Revolution in Patronage," *Public Administration Review,* **XX,** No. 1 (Winter, 1960).

Van Riper, Paul P., *History of the United States Civil Service,* New York: Harper and Row, 1958.

Van Riper, Paul P., "The Tap Roots of American Public Personnel Management," *Personnel Administration,* **XXV,** No. 2 (March–April, 1962).

Waldby, H. O., *The Patronage System in Oklahoma,* Norman, Oklahoma: Transcript Company, 1950.

CHAPTER 14

Recruitment and Selection

Several years ago an editorial appeared in the journal of one of the public-employee unions under the heading, "Bargain Days are Over." This editorial quoted a public official who, in an address to a group of civil servants, had said, "You people were bought at a bargain because of the great depression. The state will never again be able to purchase such high quality personnel for such low money."[1] The recruitment picture was very different during the depression days from what it now is. Plenty of job applicants were available because of the great scarcity of jobs in industry. It is true that examining techniques were not as good as they are today and that frequently the lesser- rather than the better-qualified candidates were appointed. Nonetheless, there were numerous candidates and consequently no serious problem of competition with industry. Furthermore, at that time fringe benefits, meaning benefits in addition to salary such as pension rights and paid vacations, were generally superior in the public service to those offered by most private companies. This was before passage of the Social Security Act of 1935 and before the great growth in the strength of the unions. Public service as a career by no means enjoyed great prestige, but, with employment prospects in private business so slim, government jobs definitely had their attractions.

[1] See "Message from Executive Director," *Good Government*, LXXVI, No. 3 (May–June, 1959).

There was never any justification for simply waiting for applicants to present themselves, but, with the labor market as loose as it then was, it is understandable why so many civil service agencies decided that this was all that was necessary. They were under no pressure to improve their recruiting techniques. The jobs might not be filled with as good a quality of person as might be obtained, but still they would be filled.

That these "bargain days" are over is clearly seen when we look at the present labor market. Despite the persistence of some unemployment and the constant threat of layoffs, as in the defense industry, for most Americans job security is far from the problem that it was during the depression. A whole generation of young Americans never even experienced the depression. Jobs have been plentiful in industry, and they now pay much better. Furthermore, private companies have greatly improved fringe benefits, to the point that there is now general agreement that these benefits are at least as good as in government. Naturally, this varies with the company, but most of them offer far better pension, leave, and other rights than used to be the case. To cap it all, defense contractors now offer challenging jobs in many professional fields. Government has rarely been able to capitalize on the vital and interesting nature of its work as a recruitment incentive, and now it must compete for talent with the defense industry it supports with multimillion dollar contracts. When to all this is added the inflexibility of government salaries in periods of rapidly rising living costs, it can be appreciated how handicapped public agencies have been in competing with private employers in the postwar period.

LOW PUBLIC SERVICE PRESTIGE

The salary situation will be discussed shortly, but first let us examine the question of low public service prestige. This problem is fundamental, because the public will not support higher salaries and other measures to make government service more effective if it continues to hold public employees in low esteem.

Studies of public service prestige have not been numerous, but a sufficient number has been made in the past few decades to enable certain conclusions to be formed. Leonard D. White pioneered with this kind of study in the 1920s, and in later years others made similar investigations to see whether the picture had changed.[2] Basically, they found the same conditions as those described by White: a distinctly more favorable opinion of private than of public employment on the part of the general public. Some of the more recent studies have concentrated on the attitudes of college students towards public-service careers, and they have revealed that the majority of them place a higher rating on private employment. In one survey, the opinions were sought of 147 political-science professors in 57 schools in all parts of the country, with enrollments ranging from less than 1,000 to more than 10,000. The professors reported that their junior and senior students generally had negative attitudes towards public service. They estimated that sixty percent of them were "unfavorable, vague, apathetic, or skeptical," and that only six percent were "very favorable."[3]

Recently a Municipal Manpower Commission was established by the Ford Foundation to make a detailed analysis of the needs of urban governments for administrative, technical, and professional personnel. One of its major findings was that *"low prestige of government employment adversely affects the quality of local government personnel."*[4] The American Society for Public Administration (ASPA) and the Public Personnel Association (PPA) both helped the Manpower Commission to obtain data on this question of prestige. After canvassing the opinions of some of its local chapters located in urban areas, the ASPA concluded that "the low prestige of urban governmental employment is the greatest obstacle in staffing urban governments."[5] The PPA reported that nearly half of the local offiicals responding to its questionnaires said that low prestige made it especially difficult to fill key positions in local governments.[6]

[2] Leonard D. White, *The Prestige Value of Public Employment in Chicago*, Chicago: Univ. of Chicago Press, 1929.

[3] "Young Collegians and Civil Service Careers," *Good Government*, **LXXVI**, No. 4 (July–August, 1959), 35. For a comprehensive recent study, see Franklin P. Kilpatrick, Milton C. Cummings, Jr., and M. Kent Jennings, *The Image of the Federal Service*, Washington, D.C.: Brookings Institution, 1964.

[4] Municipal Manpower Commission, *Governmental Manpower for Tomorrow's Cities*, New York: McGraw-Hill, 1962, pp. 44–45.

[5] *Public Administration News*, **XI**, No. 3 (Summer, 1961), Chicago: American Society for Public Administration, 1.

[6] Municipal Manpower Commission, *op. cit.*, p. 46.

Reasons for Low Prestige

Why is it that Americans do not hold more favorable opinions of public employment? We saw in Chapter 2 that ours is a business civilization and that young people are reared in an environment in which the accomplishments of the businessman are much admired. In Chapter 3 we saw how the reverse situation exists in some other countries of the world where government service is a high-prestige occupation. Clearly our history and traditions are such that it would be surprising if most young people preferred public to private employment. No one suggests that young Americans as a group should shun private employment and believe that the only good job is one in government. What is a legitimate source of worry, however, is that so many people in the community, young and old, have such mistaken ideas about the nature of government employment. Far too many people are discouraged from seeking government employment because of the persistence of these erroneous notions.

One widely held belief is that government agencies are very inefficient and that public employees put out very little work. "Parasites" and "tax-eaters" are favorite epithets that some sections of the press hurl at the government worker. Young persons grow up in homes and communities where the truth of these statements is taken for granted. Undoubtedly, many people make the public employee the scapegoat. They resent the extension of government services into so many new areas. This means more government control and higher taxes. At bottom, they know that these new services are necessary in present-day society, but someone has to be blamed, and the easiest scapegoat is the government worker; somehow or other, he must be responsible. Of course, if he administers an unpopular program like tax collections, he easily becomes a special object of scorn.

Nor is this kind of reaction unique to this country. In England, public employees are also frequently severely criticized. As one group of prominent Englishmen stated in a report made some years ago to the Chancellor of the Exchequer: "The urge to 'shoot the man at the piano' often arises not so much from the demerits of his performance as from dislike of the tune."[7] The "tune" in many countries today is

[7] Report of the Committee on the Training of Civil Servants, reproduced in Felix A. Nigro (ed.), *Public Administration: Readings and Documents*, New York: Holt, Rinehart, and Winston, 1951, p. 255.

too much government. In the United States, with its strong tradition of suspicion of the executive power, this tune is all the more irritating.

In Defense of Government Service

Quite a few businessmen themselves have tried to correct some of the erroneous opinions about government employees. These company executives have served in the government themselves. In some cases, they entered the government fully expecting to find evidences of widespread inefficiency and to be surrounded by more than a sprinkling of incompetents. Instead they were pleasantly surprised to find that the career public servants were both industrious and efficient. Witness this statement by Marion B. Folsom, a director of the Eastman Kodak Company who served from 1955 to 1958 as Secretary of Health, Education, and Welfare:

> I found in my experience here that there are very able people in the government, civil service executives who do a fine and understanding job and who put in long hours of work. And I can testify from first-hand experience in both government and a large business organization that the top ranks of civil service constitute a high level of skill, competence, and loyalty capable of holding their own with those in equivalent ranks in the business world. I do not think that the country as a whole appreciates the work our civil service people are doing.[8]

Men like Folsom have been more than willing to cooperate with government spokesmen in the intensified efforts now being made to dispel these myths about public employees and to create more favorable attitudes towards government service. In recent years, public relations activities of personnel agencies have been greatly expanded. Through press releases, television and radio programs, dissemination of attractive brochures, and closer links with citizen groups, people in the local community are now becoming much better informed about the government service. Naturally, there is still much to be ac-

[8] Marion B. Folsom, "The Most Effective Way to Improve Government Administration," *Good Government*, LXXIX, No. 6 (June, 1962), 27. See also W. Lloyd Warner *et al.*, "A New Look at the Career Civil Service Executive," *Public Administration Review*, XXII, No. 4 (December, 1962), 188–194.

complished along these lines, but the indisputable fact is that intensive public relations activity is now an accepted part of the "modern" personnel program. Not too long ago, public relations activities of most public personnel agencies were of a decidedly skimpy nature.

THE SALARY PROBLEM

Returning to the question of inadequate salaries, this has been a particularly serious problem in the postwar period. A chief difficulty has been the rigidity of government pay rates. Private companies are able to raise salaries and wages just as fast as the management takes to make up its mind. It is true that in the past few years the government has urged the unions not to seek inflationary wage agreements and the companies not to increase prices too much. The fact still remains, however, that in peacetime there are no laws which prevent private firms from adjusting compensation rates upwards as fast as they see fit. The situation is different in government because, for the great majority of public employees, changes in pay scales are not possible until the legislative body of the jurisdiction decides to act. This means delay, sometimes of a prolonged character. In the postwar period, legislatures have raised the salaries of government workers, but not nearly as fast as those of private companies have been raised. It takes time for the legislature to meet and deliberate. Furthermore, because this is the political environment, points of view generally not found in the realm of private management are manifested. Many rural members of state legislatures and of the national Congress cling to the suspicion that government employees are already paid too much. They are unconcerned that industry pays much more, because to them the executive branch is at best a necessary evil. Furthermore, there is the understandable reluctance to authorize top salaries which exceed those paid the legislators themselves. The discrepancy between salaries of top executives in government at all levels and those received in industry for comparable work has been enormous. The legislators usually are much more generous with the employees in the lower ranks. They sympathize more with these "little people," particularly since there are so many more of them, and they can exert great pressure on the legislature.

Blue- vs. White-Collar Workers

Until passage of the Federal Salary Reform Act of 1962, briefly mentioned in the preceding chapter, federal compensation policy was more inflexible than that of some state and local governments. In recent years, salary increases received by public employees at all levels of government have not only been less frequent but also less substantial than those obtained by workers in industry. Quite a few state and local jurisdictions have, however, made annual or biennial adjustments in rates in accordance with the principle of trying to pay salaries equal to those paid for comparable positions by private employers.

Until Congress acted in 1962, the national government was not pledged to paying the industry prevailing rates. There was one important exception to this, namely blue-collar workers numbering some 660,000 out of the total of two-and-a-half million federal employees. These blue-collar workers are employed in trades and crafts jobs, most of which are found in the Defense Department. For many years now, their wages have been set by local boards which continuously study industry rates in the particular areas and make changes in federal pay to keep it on a par with what private firms are currently paying. Changes in pay rates authorized by these local boards do not require prior approval of Congress. As a result, federal pay for blue-collar workers has been competitive with industry rates for such jobs.

In the case of white-collar workers, Congress alone could raise rates of pay, and it chose to do this generally every few years. There was no fixed policy, as in many local jurisdictions, of reviewing the adequacy of the rates each year at budget time. A few state governments had even acted to delegate to the executive branch the authority to fix the salary scales and to make changes in them, without any need for prior approval by the legislature. In such cases, the only participation in setting salaries by the lawmakers is to provide the appropriations required to finance any increases. No one suggests that the legislature should abandon its control of the purse, but delegating to the executive branch the authority to set the salary scales and to make changes in them in accordance with the movement of industry rates provides very desirable flexibility. The first Hoover Commission strongly recommended that Congress adopt a similar policy.

It proposed that Congress "limit its participation to establishing the minimum and maximum rates of payment within which all general adjustments in federal compensation"[9] would be made. Congress would set the salary floor and ceiling, and subject to approval by the President, the Civil Service Commission would fix the individual pay scales within this framework, making annual adjustments as necessary.

The Federal Salary Reform Act of 1962

In the legislation it approved in October, 1962, the Congress does not go this far. No delegation is made to the executive branch to fix and to change the pay scales as circumstances warrant. On the other hand, for the first time Congress accepts the principle of paying prevailing industry rates for all kinds of federal jobs. The law states this in no uncertain terms: "Federal salary rates shall be comparable with private enterprise salary rates for the same levels of work."[10] The President is directed to report annually to Congress on the relationship between private and federal pay and to recommend the changes in the federal scales needed to keep them on a par with those in industry. The recommended adjustments in federal rates will be based on the annual survey now made by the Bureau of Labor Statistics of professional, administrative, and technical salaries in industry. It is the national average of the private rates that will be followed, not the pay in each locality. Uniform pay scales for federal white-collar workers on a nationwide basis will still be the rule, but these scales will be periodically adjusted to keep up with the national average of the rates paid by industry for comparable positions.

Experience since 1923 had clearly shown that equal pay for equal work could not be guaranteed unless the prevailing-rate principle was also enacted into law. It has been small solace for federal employees to receive equally *inadequate* salaries for the same work. Unfortunately, this is what equal pay for equal work used to mean in practice. Positions of approximately the same difficulty and re-

[9] Commission on Organization of the Executive Branch of the Government, *Personnel Management*, Washington, D.C.: Government Printing Office, 1949, pp. 27–28.

[10] Federal Salary Reform Act of 1962, Public Law 87–793, 87th Congress.

sponsibility were placed in the same pay grades. The incumbents did receive the same pay, but often got a lot less than persons holding similar jobs in industry.

Top Officials' Salary Limitations

When he recommended the prevailing-wage principle to Congress, President Kennedy also strongly urged it to give special attention to raising the rates for those in the top Classification Act grades. In a message to Congress, he stressed that "the federal employee's top salary, if he stays to reach it, will be less than half that of his private enterprise counterpart."[11] However, although the President recommended a top salary of $26,000 by January 1964,[12] Congress would not go higher than $20,000.

In its report on the pay bill, the Senate Committee on Post Office and Civil Service did urge the President to recommend "for consideration at the next session of the Congress appropriate increases in federal executive salaries at all levels." The Committee stated very plainly that it considered these salaries inadequate, but it believed that before Congress acted on this phase of salary reform, it should receive specific recommendations from the President on pay rates for all federal executives, including those not compensated under the Classification Act.[13] The President had told Congress that he knew that the increases he was recommending for those in the very top Classification Act grades would make their pay higher than that of Cabinet and sub-Cabinet officials. As to the delicate question of the relationship to Congressional salaries, he said that it was neither "customary nor appropriate" to "specify congressional increases in a Presidential message." Congressional pay in 1962 was $22,500, well below the salaries recommended by the President for the top civil service employees. The President said the executive branch stood

[11] *Message from the President of the United States*, House of Representatives, Document No. 344, 87th Congress, 2nd Session, Washington, D.C.: Government Printing Office, February 20, 1962, p. 2.

[12] *Summary Analysis of the President's Proposal for Reform of Federal Statutory Salary Systems*, House Committee on Post Office and Civil Service, Washington, D.C.: Government Printing Office, March, 1962, p. 17.

[13] *Postal Service and Federal Employees Salary*, Senate Committee on Post Office and Civil Service, 87th Congress, 2nd Session, Washington, D.C.: Government Printing Office, September, 1962, p. 10.

ready to "cooperate with the Congress in determining what executive and congressional pay scales would be appropriate following the terms of the present incumbents."[14] The Senate Committee, in effect, was giving the President the "go" signal to offer this "cooperation" during the next session of the Congress. 1962 was an election year, and Congressmen are sensitive about public criticisms that they may be feathering their own nests. Some people have been just as unreasonable about Congressional salaries, as they have been about those of the executive branch.

In his budget message for fiscal 1964, the President included a section on salary reform. He applauded the Congress for having accepted the principle of comparability with private pay, but he reminded the lawmakers that "salaries of upper-level career personnel are still too low when measured by the compensation provided outside of Government." He continued:

> Having taken a major step toward establishment of a proper system of compensation for career employees, we must wait no longer to initiate a review of the salaries of department and agency heads and their deputies. . . . When the Congress enacted the Federal Salary Reform Act of 1962, it requested that recommendations be submitted to the next session for appropriate increases in Federal executive salaries at all levels. Accordingly, I intend to establish an advisory panel, made up of distinguished private citizens, to examine the present compensation for top positions in the executive, legislative and judicial branches, and to suggest appropriate adjustment in the pay for these positions. After the panel concludes its study, I will make recommendations to the Congress.[15]

The panel was appointed and made its report in August, 1963. It recommended that the pay of Congressmen be increased to $35,000 (with $5,000 of this tax deductible), that the $25,000 salary of Cabinet members be doubled, and the compensation of Supreme Court justices raised from $35,000 to $60,000. Early in 1964, an administration supported bill providing $32,500 for Congressmen, $35,000 for Cabinet officers, and $45,000 for Supreme Court justices was defeated in the House of Representatives. The bill seemed certain of passage, but economy-conscious rural members insisted on a roll call vote. This stratagem worked because, although they found their sala-

[14] *Message from the President of the United States, op. cit.*, p. 6.
[15] *New York Times,* Western Edition, January 18, 1963.

ries very inadequate, some representatives were unwilling to risk voting themselves substantial raises in an election year. Finally, however, new legislation was approved in August, 1964, which provides for pay increases for employees in the executive, legislative, and judicial branches. The pay for senators and representatives was increased to $30,000 a year; cabinet members are to receive $35,000. The new salary schedule provides $40,000 for the chief justice of the Supreme Court and $39,500 for associate justices. In addition to increases averaging 4.3 percent for civil service workers and 5.6 percent for postal workers, the bill provides four new pay categories for high-level executives. Pay raises of up to $7,000 boost scales to a level of $26,000 to $30,000 for 367 sub-cabinet posts.

DIFFICULTIES IN ATTRACTING POLITICAL POLICYMAKING OFFICIALS

This action to provide pay increases for top political policy-making officials, as well as for career personnel, was essential. A Task Force of the second Hoover Commission identified these political policy-making officials as the men through whom the "President directs and controls the administration." The Task Force said:

> In them the public sees itself represented in the administration of national affairs. They are the necessary expendables who give flexibility to the machinery of Government and who make it possible for the Chief Executive to adapt his management team to changing circumstances—profiting from the success of certain members and compensating for the failure of others. Constantly criticized, frequently attacked, and seldom praised, they are an essential element of responsible government in an age of big administration.

Specifically, the Task Force said there were three main groups of political executives: (1) heads of agencies and their deputies; (2) assistant agency heads; and (3) aides, assistants, heads of policy staff offices, general managers of boards and commissions, and similar positions.[16] Many of these jobs are filled by the President with the

[16] Commission on Organization of the Executive Branch of the Government, *Task Force Report on Personnel and Civil Service*, Washington, D.C.: Government Printing Office, 1955, p. 39. For a brief summary of comprehensive recent research on this class of executives, see W. Lloyd Warner, *et al.*, "Federal Political Executives—A New View," *Good Government*, LXXX, No. 1 (January, 1963).

confirmation of the Senate. Some are filled by the Chief Executive on his own authority; others are named by the department heads. In all cases, the positions are filled through political channels. They are not civil service jobs, and their compensation is set by statute. Many political policymaking positions of this same type are found in state governments and the larger municipalities and counties. These jurisdictions have the same trouble in not being able to offer sufficiently high salaries, so this is by no means a unique problem of the federal government.

The principal source of recruitment for these positions has been private industry. In its ranks are men with tested ability to direct large-scale operations. Businessmen as a social group are not preferred as such; it is rather a question of the experience that they have. Universities and colleges, private foundations, labor unions, farm organizations, and quasi-public agencies have also been tapped. While many able persons have been recruited from these sources, it usually has taken a good deal of persuading to secure and retain their services.

Why has this been so? As we have just seen, the inadequate salaries have been a major deterrent, but there are other reasons. It would be unrealistic to assume that all that needs to be done to attract high-grade executives is to offer better pay. Some companies frown on their men "getting into politics," which is what some senior company executives think is entailed if they let a junior official accept a policy-making position in government. "Keep out of the government mess" is what they often advise the younger man. The Task Force of the second Hoover Commission made an impassioned plea for the leaders of the business world to encourage their best young men to accept government assignments.[17] More recently, the Senate Subcommittee on National Policy Machinery investigated this same problem intensively and made a number of important recommendations.

The Conflict of Interest Problem

A hindrance of significant proportions in attracting industry personnel has been the conflict-of-interest statutes. (These will be discussed in greater detail in Part VI of this book, "Administrative

[17] *Ibid.*, p. 46.

Responsibility.") Congress acted in October, 1962, to bring these anachronistic statutes up to date. The new legislation retains essential protections for the government against possible abuses of their public trust by industry officials on government assignments.[18] It also eliminates certain "absurdities," as they were called by the Senate Subcommittee.

One example will demonstrate this. Before the statutes were revised, part-time consultants employed by the government were subject to the same restrictions as those placed on regular employees. This meant, for one thing, that they could not assist private parties for pay in transactions involving the government. Consequently, many people refused to accept such consulting assignments. As the Subcommittee said: "A consultant working for the Government a week or two a year can scarcely sever his economic ties with his regular business or profession."[19] The new law makes a distinction between regular and "special" employees who serve not more than 130 days in a year's time. As a special employee, the part-time consultant is not subject to the prohibitions on outside compensation. A lawyer who is a part-time consultant can represent private parties in such routine matters as income tax appeals. Under the statutes as they stood previously, he could not do so. In all, there is good reason to think that the conflict-of-interest laws will no longer be the deterrent to federal service that they used to constitute.

Other Deterrents

Even if they were offered better salaries and conflict-of-interest complications were removed, many businessmen would still hesitate to accept government assignments. The executive in mid-career is risking a good deal when he leaves his company even for a couple of years. During his absence, he may lose out on chances for promotion. Vacancies which develop in higher ranks while he is on government leave must be filled notwithstanding. The company can protect his pension rights and similar privileges, but it cannot agree to hold up

[18] Public Law 87–849, 87th Congress.

[19] *Organizing for National Security, The Private Citizen and the National Service*, Senate Subcommittee on National Policy Machinery, 87th Congress, 1st Session, Washington, D.C.: Government Printing Office, 1961, p. 3.

all promotions until he returns.[20] Certainly an executive on the rise cannot be blamed if he is unwilling to leave his firm at this critical stage in his career. Yet, as the Senate Subcommittee stressed: "The person in midcareer is in many ways the private citizen whose services the Government needs the most. He may be in his late thirties or forties. He is at the very height of his vigor and powers. He is bold and innovative." The Subcommittee concluded that "any improvement of this situation depends primarily upon employers—not the Government." They should contribute to the best interests of the nation by "releasing some of their best personnel for national service, and welcoming them back."[21] The best way of welcoming them back, of course, would be to reward them with more responsible posts, in recognition of their enhanced value to the company.

If too gloomy a picture of the possibilities of attracting high-grade industry executives seems to have been presented, it should be remembered that quite a few of them have made a personal decision to take government jobs anyway. Despite the lower pay, the irksome restrictions, and the uncertainty as to what awaits them when they return to private industry, they have been attracted by the challenges and great responsibilities of government work. The task ahead is to attract more of them and create the conditions which make them want to return to the government for future assignments. High on the personnel agenda for the rest of this decade and for future ones is a well-conceived plan for obtaining the services of more high quality executives in political policymaking jobs.

IMPROVEMENTS IN RECRUITMENT

In the previous chapter, mention was briefly made of the improvements being made in government recruitment procedures. Let us now give additional examples, because some public agencies now conduct much more aggressive recruiting campaigns as the competition with private industry for the available manpower becomes increasingly

[20] See *Organizing for National Security, Mobilizing Talent for Government Service*, Hearings before Senate Subcommittee on National Policy Machinery, 86th Congress, 2nd Session, Washington, D.C.: Government Printing Office, May, 1960, p. 480.

[21] *Organizing for National Security, The Private Citizen and the National Service*, *op. cit.*, pp. 6–7.

keen. Positive recruiting, which means going out and finding good candidates instead of waiting for them to apply, is now very much emphasized by leaders in the public personnel field.

College Recruitment

Techniques used successfully in industry are being borrowed. Private firms pioneered with college recruitment. For many years now, they have regularly sent representatives to college campuses to interview the best of the graduating students. In the past few years, this has now become the established practice of federal agencies and of progressive state and local jurisdictions.

Contacts are made with students well before the time of their graduation. The United States Commission regularly schedules "career days" on college campuses, sometimes sponsored jointly with state and local agencies and held on the particular campus on the same day, so that the students can speak to recruiters from all levels of government. On these occasions, the government representatives answer the students' questions about career opportunities in the public service. They distribute brochures and other materials describing these opportunities and the procedure to follow in making application. Meetings, both of a formal and informal nature, are held with faculty members to enlist their support in making information about government jobs available to the students. That much still remains to be done in programs to attract college graduates is seen, however, in another of the findings of the Municipal Manpower Commission. It refers to the "poor effectiveness of local government recruiting at the campus level" and states that, even in the larger governments, "visits to campuses are sporadic; examinations are seldom keyed to the school year; firm job offers are slow in coming."[22]

Rapid Recruitment

Private companies have had the advantage of being able to make job offers very quickly, not only to graduating college students but to all job applicants. Because they are administering a merit system in which everyone who meets the minimum qualifications is guaranteed the right to show whether he can do the job, civil service agencies

[22] Municipal Manpower Commission, *op. cit.*, p. 81.

must follow certain procedures. The candidates' qualifications must be measured, by written tests or otherwise, in such a way as to give assurance that only the best are offered positions. All the same, this does not mean that government cannot greatly speed up its recruitment procedures; and this is what some agencies are doing, with increasing success. Examinations are in some cases given in the schools themselves, for example when recruiting typists and stenographers from secretarial schools, high schools, and junior colleges. Sometimes the civil service agency even grades the examinations on the spot and makes immediate job offers to those who score the highest.

"Rapid recruitment," as it is sometimes called, has numerous forms. Candidates can visit the civil service agency, fill out applications, take tests, and receive offers, all in the course of one visit to the agency's premises. New York City's Personnel Department has such a program for stenographers, junior civil engineers, and other jobs of a "hard to fill" nature. In some jurisdictions, application forms have been shortened and made much easier to complete. Written examinations are graded much more quickly than used to be the case, and the interval between date of receipt of the candidates' applications and the preparation of the civil service registers has been greatly reduced. Some state and local personnel agencies also now recruit on a nationwide basis. They send out recruiting representatives who travel from city to city to be able to examine applicants all over the country. Sometimes they are also authorized to make on-the-spot offers, as in the case of the Los Angeles County Civil Service Commission.

For certain positions, including some at the entrance level, written examinations are not required. The examination takes the form of an evaluation of the candidates' background of training and experience, with an oral interview sometimes also included. The different kinds of tests used in public-service recruitment will be discussed later in this chapter. The purpose here is to show how the recruitment process is being accelerated in some jurisdictions. Speed is essential in meeting industry competition. Merit safeguards cannot be swept away, but cumbersome procedures certainly can be eliminated. Many of industry's supposed "inherent" advantages in recruitment have been found to be perfectly transferable to the government.

It would be wrong to give the impression that all or most public personnel agencies have highly developed programs of positive recruitment. Many lag far behind, others are just beginning to make progress. As we saw in Chapter 1, no government agency will ever function exactly like a private company. There is no reason to think, however, that civil service recruitment cannot be fast, efficient, and truly competitive with industry.

THE GOAL OF CAREER SERVICE

A paramount objective is to create a true career service, as against simply recruiting to fill individual jobs. In such a career service, the recruits, whether fresh from college or already possessing some work experience, would be guaranteed the opportunity to move up the line as they demonstrate their capacity. Ultimately, the best of them would fill the highest-ranking positions. They would have every inducement to continue in the government service, instead of leaving after a few years because of the lack of any planned system of career development for them. In the past, for many people in the United States government service has tended to be a mere episode which precedes or follows private employment. Movement in and out of the service has been too great. As we saw in the preceding chapter, lateral entry is desirable, but not if it means that people are constantly shuttling in and out of the government. Furthermore, the individual should not be expected to have to do all the career planning for himself in the government. This, again, is unfortunately what has happened too often in the past. Promising young persons have entered the government service and decided that they wanted to make a life work of it; but they had been recruited for individual jobs, not for careers. The responsibility pretty much devolved on them of locating promotional opportunities and preparing themselves for posts of higher responsibility. Typically, this meant making "contacts" and shopping around for better jobs. Many of them did make careers for themselves, but in spite of the personnel system, not because of it.

Success of the FSEE

Today many government agencies are recruiting people for careers, instead of individual jobs. In the previous chapter, mention was made of the Federal Service Entrance Examination (FSEE). It represents one important phase of career-service planning at the federal level.

It provides the entrance gate for college students, a broad one because it is open to all college majors with only a few exceptions. Separate entrance examinations are now given only for engineers, physicists, chemists, accountants, and a few other technicians.

The existence of this main entrance gate clearly shows the college student how to get started on a federal career. He need not enroll in a special collegiate program of study to be able to qualify. All he has to do is pursue his major. In fact, he can even take the examination in his junior year in which case, if he passes it, he will become eligible for a temporary appointment during the summer between his junior and senior years. Most students take the examination during their senior year. It is offered several times during the period from October to May. First given in 1955, the FSEE has now become an institution. It is given such widespread publicity that it is hard to see how any college student can claim that he does not know about it. The successful candidates are appointed not only to staff jobs, such as in personnel and budget work, but also to positions in program administration, such as in housing management, food and drug inspection, transportation, business analysis and regulation, social security administration, and agriculture and the natural sciences. This is significant, because it means that careers are opened up not only in the staff jobs but also in the administration of the many different substantive fields in which the government now functions. In previous years, those interested in careers in administrative work were mostly restricted to the "housekeeping" kind of job. The FSEE makes it possible for persons with broad collegiate training to qualify for careers in program administration. In the past, most administrative jobs of this kind have been filled by persons trained in technical specialties like engineering, medicine, and law. Some of them have performed capably in such assignments, but many have proved far too narrow in their approach. The FSEE seeks to develop in the lowest ranks of the federal service a corps of generalist trainees who, it is hoped, will eventually fill many of the program administration posts.

Making Good on the "Career Contract"

The FSEE, like any examination, constitutes only one part of career planning. It is the beginning. The rest consists of training and promotion programs which make it possible for the recruit to climb up the ladder as he proves his ability. Such programs are now being developed through the joint efforts of the Civil Service Commission and the line agencies. Training and promotion are discussed in the next chapter, but they are mentioned here as an essential part of what Henry Reining, Jr. calls the "career contract,"[23] which entails assuming responsibility for the recruit's development after he passes the entrance examination. It is not fair from the college student's standpoint if he is given an entrance job but then required to shift for himself. It is clear that some federal agencies are delivering on the career contract, and consequently their recruits are staying with them. Much remains to be accomplished before a true career service comes into being throughout the entire federal executive branch, but definite progress is being made in that direction.[24]

Only a few state and local governments give an examination which is in any way comparable to the FSEE. As we saw, training programs are not highly developed in many state and local jurisdictions. There are some exceptions, but the Municipal Manpower Commission found no general evidence in urban governments of a real career service based on selection, training, and promotion of individuals on a merit basis. It said:

> There is an urgent need for able men and women who want to devote their lives to progressive growth and achievement in each branch of local government. But such men and women will not be attracted or held by a system that endows the incapable and slothful with a right to permanence in a job, that gears advance for the efficient and inefficient alike to years of service, and that awards a pension after a career of time-serving.[25]

THE SELECTION PROCESS

The selection process will be best understood if it is decribed in step-by-step sequence. The first step is for the candidate to file his application. Before he does this, he should carefully study the examination announcement to see whether he possesses the minimum qualifications; these are the experience, training, and other requirements

[23] Henry Reining, Jr., "The FSEE: The University Point of View," *Public Administration Review*, **XVI**, No. 1 (Winter, 1956), 11–14.

[24] See the stimulating article by Frederick C. Mosher, "Careers and Career Services in the Public Service," *Public Personnel Review*, **XXIV**, No. 1 (January, 1963), 46–51.

[25] Municipal Manpower Commission, *op. cit.*, p. 116.

that the individual must meet if his application is to be accepted. There is no point in his applying if he does not have these qualifications. The civil service agency cannot be expected to incur the expense of having to examine any and all candidates. Usually it sets the minimum qualifications low enough and words them sufficiently flexibly to permit all candidates who stand a reasonable chance of passing the examination to take it. This is a convenient point at which to mention that many jurisdictions now make use of open, continuous examinations, that is, examinations with no closing date for filing applications. Under this system, it is possible to accept the applications of individuals at any time, just as private companies do. Someone entering the labor market for the first time is not told that it is too late for him to apply. Formerly, most jurisdictions exclusively gave the closed-type examination, with arbitrary cutoff dates for accepting applications. This was understandable during the depression when thousands of persons applied to take civil service examinations. In the tight labor market that now exists, a general policy of insisting on closed examinations would be self-defeating.

Assuming that his application is accepted, the next step is for the candidate to take the examination. This usually consists of several different tests, the scores on which are weighted to produce the individual's final grade. Usually no single test has sufficient validity, in other words, accuracy in measuring ability to perform well in the kind of position for which the individual is examined, to justify using it alone. The reason for this will become clear as the different kinds of tests are discussed in turn. In most cases, the candidate is required to take a written test. This is administered by the personnel agency at a location where the candidates assemble to take the examination. For this reason, this is known as an assembled examination. State and local jurisdictions have always made great use of assembled examinations. In the past, the federal government has sometimes given many more unassembled than assembled exams. In the unassembled type, candidates mail in their applications, together with supplemental sheets in which they describe their work background in detail. It is these applications which are scored and given a numerical grade, just like a written test. The examination load in the federal government is so heavy that it sometimes has not been able to give assembled examinations. Furthermore, written tests of acceptable validity have been lacking in testing for some high level professional and administrative posts. More recently, however, the United States Civil Service Commission has mostly been giving assembled examinations, with the unassembled kind usually reserved for higher level positions.

Kinds of Written Tests

What kinds of written tests are given? From the standpoint of content, there are two principal types: achievement and aptitude tests. The first kind measures the candidate's ability to perform the duties of the position immediately upon appointment, without the need for extended training. Traditionally, this has been the preferred kind of test in the United States as far as community opinion is concerned. Civil service laws and regulations commonly require that "practical tests" be given. A "practical test" in effect means one which measures what the candidate already knows about the duties and responsibilities of the job. By contrast, aptitude tests measure the applicant's potentialities, not his immediate ability to do the job. In recruiting for career service, aptitude is what really counts: the individual's evidence of ability to master the duties of jobs of increasing difficulty, not his immediate equipment to fill just one job. In practice, both achievement and aptitude tests are frequently combined in the same written examination. This is a good compromise solution, because, while personnel agencies usually would like to make more extensive use of tests of general ability than public opinion permits, some use of the aptitude kind of question is better than none at all.

Most civil service tests are of the multiple-choice variety. Essay tests are given on occasion, but, besides requiring much more time to grade, they can, of course, only include a limited number of questions. Multiple-choice tests, consisting as they frequently do of dozens of items, permit a much wider sampling of the candidates' knowledges and aptitudes. True-false questions are sometimes given, but they are generally avoided because of the high guessing factor. Furthermore, experience has shown that it is very difficult to frame questions which are completely true or false.

The Evaluation of Training and Experience

If the position is one which requires experience, another part of the examination will consist of an *evaluation of training and experience.* The examination announcement states the weight to be assigned to it in comparison with other parts of the examination. Those possessing the minimum qualifications automatically receive the minimum passing score on the evaluation of training and experience. They are given additional points, based on the examiners' appraisal of the quantity and quality of their experience and training.

There has been much criticism of this part of the examination, but few persons question that it is needed for positions requiring experience. Basing everything on the written test would mean placing 100 percent faith in its validity. Experience shows that this is too much to expect of any written test. The evaluation of training and experience entails many subjective judgments, but in practice it has served as a desirable supplement to the written. It is the unassembled examination which has been criticized the most, since the individual's final grade is based entirely on the evaluation of training and experience unless an oral examination is also given.

The Oral Examination

The oral as a weighted part of the examination is usually required only for positions above the entrance level, although in some cases it is also included in competition for jobs not requiring previous experience. State and local jurisdictions have made much greater use of the oral as a weighted part of the examination than has the federal government. The much heavier examining load at the federal level has made it impossible to include the oral as a matter of course in the competition for all higher level posts. Where time and funds permit, however, it is given, and in recent years the Civil Service Commission has been using it more often than used to be the case.

Usually the purpose of the oral is to evaluate the individual's personality characteristics. Sometimes it is used, however, to evaluate the candidate's training and experience, as well as his personal traits. In the past, there used to be a good deal of suspicion about the oral for fear that bias and hasty judgments by the members of the interviewing panels would lead to breaking down the merit system. With all their shortcomings, it was argued, written tests can be scored objectively. Answers to multiple-choice questions are either right or wrong. The machine that scores these answers can have no favorites. Undoubtedly, the oral has many subjective elements. For that matter, all tests are subjective. Multiple-choice questions can be graded objectively, but that does not mean that there will be perfect agreement that the answers in the scoring key are really the most correct. Preparation of the scoring key is itself a subjective process, to some extent at least. The essential point is that, particularly for higher-level positions and those requiring frequent contacts with the public, evaluation of a candidate's personal qualities is necessary. The oral cannot be eliminated as part of the examination process simply because it has subjective elements. Although criticisms of the oral continue, as they should until this examining device is further improved, there is increasing awareness that the government cannot, as one congressional subcommittee put it, "buy a pig in a poke."[26] Many people fail on the job, not because they lack technical knowledge and skills, but because they do not get along well with the persons with whom they must deal, inside and outside the government. Very few employees in modern, complex organizations function in relative isolation from other persons. Usually, they must work together closely, and it is a rare worker who has nothing to do with the public.

In recent years, public personnel agencies have made significant improvements in the oral. Greater care has been exercised in selecting the interviewers, and they are given intensive training. Interview rating forms have been developed which define more precisely the meaning of the characteristics on which candidates are to be evaluated.

An innovation which has aroused considerable interest is the group oral. In this kind of oral, the candidates do not appear singly before an interview panel. Instead they are assembled in small groups and assigned a topic for discussion. To the side, seated at a distance of some five to ten feet from the candidates, are several representatives of the oral examining staff of the personnel agency. They do not ask the candidates any questions. Instead they observe intently what goes on during the discussion. After the participants have withdrawn, the examiners then jointly agree on the final rating to be given each candidate. The principal advantage of the group oral is that it gives the examiners an opportunity to judge how the candidates might conduct themselves in a group situation. The word "might" needs to be em-

[26] *Personnel Recruitment and Employment Practices in the Federal Government*, Senate Subcommittee on Federal Manpower Policies, 83rd Congress, 1st Session, Senate Document No. 37, Washington, D.C.: Government Printing Office, 1953, pp. 37–38.

phasized, because, like any interview, the group oral represents an artificial situation. The participants might interact differently in a real work situation. All the same, the examiners do see the candidates perform with others present. In the traditional-type interview, the candidate simply *says* how he would react in a group situation. He is unable to provide the panel with a sample of his behavior, even if synthetic. On the other hand, in a group oral the individual may fail to impress simply because he has the bad luck of being assigned to a truly outstanding group. Conversely, he looks much better than he really is when the others happen to be mediocre. Both kinds of orals have their advantages, so some personnel agencies have the candidates submit to both a panel interview and a group oral. Their feeling is that the individual's composite rating on both kinds of orals will tell more about his personality than his score on just one of them alone.[27]

The Reference Check

Although it is not a weighted part of the examination, a reference check is also a standard part of the selection procedure. Sometimes it consists of a routine mail inquiry sent to previous employers and to personal references listed by the applicant. This may be supplemented by telephone inquiries and, in some cases, by visits by trained investigators who ask detailed questions about the candidates. Sending out investigators to previous employers is highly desirable because they can ferret out significant information about the candidate's personal qualities, as well as the kind of work experience he has had. What former employers say about the way the candidate works with others is often much more reliable than the impressions he gives during an interview. Unfortunately, in the past funds have been too limited for personnel agencies to make intensive investigations of this kind except for a relatively few top positions.

The question will logically be asked, "How good are civil service tests anyway?" Some observers believe that the selection process is better in government than in industry. Even within business circles, the opinion has been voiced that too much emphasis is given to train-

[27] See Milton M. Mandell, *Employment Interviewing*, Washington, D.C.: U.S. Civil Service Commission, 1956, Personnel Methods Series No. 5, pp. 1–103.

ing by comparison with selection. If so, this is unfortunate, because the quality of the participants has a good deal to do with the success of any training program. For that reason, it is sometimes said that "an ounce of selection is worth a pound of administrative cure." The government appears to be doing a commendable job in the selection of workers for lower-level positions and also of professional and administrative personnel in the entrance and middle-level ranks. The greatest weakness seems to be in the selection of individuals to fill the very top positions, just below those of the political policymaking officials.[28] The principal reason for this is that not enough is yet known about the qualities which make for executive success and how to test for them. This is why it is so important to expand personnel research, for it is the key to developing improved selection techniques.

Preparation of Examination Registers

The successful candidates are ranked in the order of their final scores on the examination as a whole. Most jurisdictions follow the "rule of three" in making appointments. This means that, when it receives a request for the names of eligibles to fill a vacancy in one of the departments, the central personnel agency "certifies" the names of the three persons at the top of the register. "Certification" simply means including these names on a document, technically known as a "certificate," which is sent to the operating department. The civil service law or rules specify the number of names to be certified. For many years, the United States Civil Service Commission elected to use the rule of three. The Pendleton Act did not require it, but the rule of three was later made a matter of law, and it is now binding on the Commission.

In recent years, a few jurisdictions have liberalized the certification procedures. There is widespread feeling among the personnel experts themselves that the appointing officer should have more leeway. Frequently, eligibles are bunched so closely together on the civil service registers that they are separated by only a point or two,

[28] See Albert H. Aronson, "A Look at Selection Methods," in the *Federal Career Service*, Washington, D.C.: Society for Personnel Administration, 1954, Pamphlet No. 8, p. 42.

perhaps by only a fraction of a point. The tests used do not possess sufficient validity to justify the conviction that such small differences in scores really indicate significant differences in the capacities of the eligibles. On the other hand, fear is expressed that, if the appointing officer is given too wide latitude, he may pass over the best qualified persons and appoint some favorite or other person whose abilities he overrates. The jurisdictions which have liberalized the certification procedures use different systems. In some, the rule of five or six is followed. In others, a variable number of names is certified, depending on the difference in points which separate the top eligible on the list from the remaining ones. For example, the Minnesota Civil Service Department certifies the top three names plus those of any others whose scores are within three points of the top-ranking eligible on the list at the time. The California League of Municipalities recommends that, in medium and small size cities, the appointing officer be allowed to make his selection from *all* the persons on the register.[29] Some small cities are following the practice of certifying the entire list. Such a procedure would, of course, be difficult to administer in large jurisdictions which have very long eligible lists. The appointing officer would have to interview far too many people.

Some people believe that the greatest need is to improve the tests and thus the calibre of the candidates on the eligible lists. They argue that if the eligibles really were of high quality the appointing officers would be satisfied with the rule of three. Somewhat more leeway for the appointing officer and better tests pretty well summarize what many persons feel is necessary.

The Probationary Period

The final stage in the selection process is the probationary period. Since tests are not perfect, and since in any case there is no assurance that individuals will work up to their abilities, this trial period is necessary. Unfortunately, in most jurisdictions the probationary period is not taken very seriously. Only a tiny percentage of appointees is dropped, even though in most places all the appointing officer has to do is file a report that the probationer's services are not satisfactory.

[29] *A Suggested Personnel System*, League of California Cities, Hotel Claremont Building, Berkeley, 5, 1958, pp. 3–4.

As nonpermanent employees, the probationers usually do not have the same appeal rights as those who have permanency. Greater efforts should certainly be made to persuade supervisors to make real use of the probationary period, but in private industry as well the human tendency not to want to dismiss anyone has been noted.

The duration of the probationary period varies according to the jurisdiction. In the federal government, it is one year. In some state and local governments it is the same, though others require only six months. In recent years, some jurisdictions have authorized the central personnel agency to use a working test period of variable length, depending on the nature of the position, in the interests of flexibility. In the State of Wisconsin, the Director of the Bureau of Personnel now has the authority to establish a probationary period of up to two years for some positions over a certain salary level.[30] The rationale is that it takes longer to judge the effectiveness of persons in responsible jobs than it does for those with routine duties.

In closing this chapter, it should be stressed that good selection is the key to good personnel administration. If the recruits are of high quality, promotion, training, and other programs stand a much better chance of being successful than when the new appointees are of poor calibre. With good people coming into the service, prospects are excellent for developing a really efficient public service.

BIBLIOGRAPHY

Chapman, Brian, *The Profession of Government*, London: G. Allen, 1959. Chap. 2.

Corson, John J., "Comparable Pay for Comparable Work?" *Public Administration Review*, **XXI,** No. 4 (Autumn, 1961).

Davy, Thomas J., "Competing for Administrative Brainpower," *Public Administration Review*, **XIX,** No. 4 (Autumn, 1959).

[30] *Personnel News*, Public Personnel Association, Chicago, Ill., **XXVIII,** No. 2 (February, 1962), 10.

Gould, Stephen, *Your Future in the Federal Government*, New York: Richards Rosen Press, 1962.

Gould, Stephen, "A Case Study in Effective Recruitment," *Personnel Administration*, **XXV**, No. 6 (November–December, 1962).

Lehman, William P., "Federal Pay Reform: Some Facets of Comparability," *Public Personnel Review*, **XXIII**, No. 3 (July, 1962).

Mandell, Milton M., "Some Hypotheses on Administrative Selection," *Public Administration Review*, **XIX**, No. 1 (Winter, 1959).

Mosher, Frederick C., "Careers and Career Services in the Public Service," *Public Personnel Review*, **XXIV**, No. 1 (January, 1963).

Municipal Manpower Commission, *Governmental Manpower for Tomorrow's Cities*, New York: McGraw-Hill, 1962.

Otten, Dorothy W., "How to Take a Civil Service Examination," *Public Personnel Review*, **XVI**, No. 2 (April, 1955).

"Recruitment for the Public Service," *Public Personnel Review*, **XXII**, No. 1 (January, 1961). Bibliography prepared by Library of U.S. Civil Service Commission.

Rose, Bertram M., "The Man that Got Away," *Personnel Administration*, **XXV**, No. 2 (March–April, 1962).

Senate Subcommittee on National Policy Machinery, 86th Congress, 2d Session, *Organizing for National Security, Mobilizing Talent for Government Service*, Washington, D.C.: Government Printing Office, 1960.

CHAPTER 15

The In-Service Personnel Program

In many ways, the real challenge in personnel administration begins after the selection process has been completed and the appointments of new employees have been made. The formidable task then facing the jurisdiction is to provide the incentives which will induce these new appointees to make a career of public service. Specifically, this requires the development of training, promotion, and other programs which meet the needs of the employees at the various stages during their employment. The new recruit represents a valuable resource, an investment which will yield dividends only if careful attention is given to his development. The time and money spent on the search for high-quality recruits will be wasted if the in-service personnel program—that is, actions taken after the initial appointment—is uninspired.

IN-SERVICE TRAINING

In Chapter 13 it was noted that, as late as the end of the 1930s, in-service training was a weak activity in most government agencies. The atmosphere simply was not one in which persons desirous of improving their capabilities could count on much help from the government as employer. Legislative bodies, and the public generally, considered that the employee should meet the costs of any after-hours instruction, such as in the evening programs of local educational institutions. If the employee felt that after-hours instruction was not enough and that he should enroll as a full-time day student in a local or other institution, it was expected that he would request a leave of absence *without* pay. Naturally, very few people could afford to do this; furthermore it was far from certain that their request for leave would be approved. Many supervisors were skeptical about the value of further formal instruction for either themselves or their subordinates, and there was no policy which required them to view the matter any differently.

In the federal government, rulings of the General Accounting Office (GAO) severely limited the kinds and amount of in-service training activity which could safely be attempted without incurring the risk of later exceptions by the GAO. When the GAO made such exceptions in its audits, the agency certifying officers were required to make restitution to the government of the sums expended, just as in the case of any other expenditures found illegal by the GAO. The Comptroller-General made it very clear that payments of the salaries and other expenses for employees' training at nonfederal facilities would be disallowed unless Congress had specifically granted legal authority to the agency to make such expenditures. The appropriations acts of the Defense and State Departments, and of a few other agencies, regularly carried such authorization, but for all other federal establishments *external training*, as it is called, was prohibited. This meant that if the agency could not itself—using its own buildings, personnel, and other facilities—provide the needed training, the employee and the agency were simply out of luck. This was a serious limitation, because in many kinds of work, the skilled instructors and the necessary equipment for proper training do not exist in the government.

Even when the agency did organize internal training programs—those using its own facilities—it had to proceed with great caution: GAO rulings stated that any training given, such as in classes, discussion sessions, and work shops, had to be directly related to the *present* official duties of the participating employee. If the instruction was of a broad character—intended to develop the general potential of the individual, but not directly tied in with the current duties of his job—it clearly did not meet this criterion. Furthermore, the GAO cautioned that only a "reasonable amount" of internal training would be regarded as legal in any case. While only nominal sums might have been spent on supplies, materials, travel, and other items, the salary payments of the participants covering the hours during which they were away from their jobs ran into substantial sums which the GAO could rule had been illegally expended. With this possibility always existing whenever internal training programs of any real scope or duration were proposed, it is no wonder that agency heads reluctantly decided to cancel the programs and take no chances with the GAO.[1]

The situation was generally the same in state and local governments. Training activity of either the external or internal variety was very scanty, the principal exception being training for policemen and firemen. At all levels of government, training in supervision and in the development of administrative skills was very inadequately developed.

The Current Situation

The picture is much improved today. At the federal level, the Government Employees Training Act, passed in July, 1958, has wrought a vast change, and represents a substantial mental revolution, because it not only authorizes, but also *requires* the heads of all the agencies to provide for the training of their employees, using both governmental and nongovernmental facilities. In the few years since passage of this legislation, training activity in the federal government has greatly expanded, and most agencies now have well-developed programs of internal training. Under the leadership of the Civil Service Commission's new Office of Career Development, much training is now offered on an interagency basis, meaning that the different agencies specialize in programs in which they have developed valuable experience, and which they throw open, not only to their own employees, but also to those of other agencies. Naturally, funds are not unlimited for training programs, anymore than they are for other government functions, but elimination of the legal obstacles has resulted in an initial burst of training activity of sizeable dimensions. Unquestionably, in-service training in the federal government now has considerable momentum behind it. Cooperation with educational institutions and other outside organizations in meeting the

[1] See Arthur D. Kallen, "Training in the Federal Service—170 Years to Accept," *Public Administration Review*, XIX, No. 1 (Winter, 1959), 36–46.

training needs of federal employees is now possible in a way in which it was not before passage of the Government Employees Training Act. Up to now, most of the external training which has taken place under this legislation has been in the form of after-hours instruction in local educational institutions. Federal agencies can now reimburse the employee for his tuition and related expenses. Such instruction is less expensive and more convenient than sending the employee to a training facility on a leave of absence with pay, but the latter kind of program is now legal and is used when the employee's training needs cannot be met in any other way. Specifically, the new legislation authorizes payment of salary, travel, subsistence, tuition, and other expenses of employees granted training leaves. In future years, such leaves may well become common; what has happened up to now is clearly only a beginning.

The picture in state and local governments is not so rosy. A few states, counties, cities, and other local government units have developed excellent programs of internal training, but most have not. Gladys M. Kammerer points out that "most state departments are not 'training minded' if they have not been recipients of federal funds" and that "few state personnel agencies have promoted training to the extent that it is actually needed."[2] The Municipal Manpower Commission reported that "this country's local governments are doing little to develop the persons who must bear vital responsibilities." It found that "less than one-third of local governments carry on any training for key administrative, professional, and technical people in their employ."[3] Most of the existing training is for police, firemen, and office workers. Yet there are some ferments of activity. One evidence of this is the increasing tendency of local government units to pay tuition and related expenses for the further education of their employees in colleges, universities, and other outside facilities, a development which reflects the spirit of the public personnel administration of the postwar days.[4]

[2] Gladys M. Kammerer, "Opportunities Missed: The 'Little Hoover Commission' Reports," *Public Personnel Review*, XXI, No. 4 (October, 1960), 239.

[3] Municipal Manpower Commission, *Governmental Manpower for Tomorrow's Cities*, New York: McGraw-Hill, 1962, p. 73.

[4] See Beatrice Dinerman and Eugene P. Dvorin, "Formal Education Programs for Local Government Employees," *Public Personnel Review*, XX, No. 1 (January, 1959), 33–37.

Kinds of Training Programs

The various kinds of training activities have been described so far only in very general terms. Let us now turn to a description of some of the programs currently carried on in "training-conscious" agencies.

Orientation programs of one sort or another are now very common. It is recognized that the employee needs some help in adjusting to his new job and work environment. Too often in the past new appointees were ushered to their desks, given some hasty instructions and told to start. This frequently led the newcomer to become lonely and unhappy during his first day of work, at least. He was in the dark as to the concrete objectives of the agency program and his intended role in it. He might even have been left to find out for himself who the principal officials in the agency were. No information was given him in convenient form about his vacation, sick leave, and other privileges. Today, however, public agencies realize that it is a wise investment to help the new employee get oriented. Instead of requiring him to go to work immediately, a period of a week or two or at least of some days can profitably be devoted to telling him about the agency and its work. Orientation programs in government now typically include such activities as special classes and discussion groups, films depicting the work of the agency, tours of work locations, and distribution of employee manuals describing the worker's privileges and responsibilities. For some kinds of new employees, such as those recruited for overseas service, the orientation often is of longer duration, and the recruit undergoes intensive preparation before he is given his first assignment.

On-the-job training, that is, instruction the individual receives while he carries out his regularly assigned duties, is, in many cases, the most important kind of help that can be given to the worker. There is nothing new about on-the-job training, for it has been traditional for many years in such vocations as the skilled trades where apprentices receive instruction from the journeymen. The supervisor, as the experienced worker, observes the performance of the beginner and shows him how to correct his mistakes. On-the-job training, or "coaching," as it is sometimes called, has also been practiced in white-collar and professional positions.

In recent years, increased attention has also been given to training the supervisors themselves in supervisory skills. This is sometimes referred to as "training the trainers," that is, instructing supervisors in how to teach the subordinates to do the job. Much emphasis is given to training the supervisors in human-relations skills, that is, how to treat the employee and to motivate him to improve his work performance. Formerly it was all too often assumed that the most skilled individual worker in the group should be named the supervisor, but now it is recognized that the ability required of a supervisor is usually only partly technical and that the key to his success in his new role will be his ability to deal effectively with the subordinates.

A shortage of administrative talent has led to a considerable sprouting of executive-development programs. Here much use is made of external facilities, such as educational institutions, foundations, and the management institutes of professional associations. This parallels industry experience where, for quite a few years now, "executive development" has been a familiar type of training activity. The objective of these programs is to broaden the individual's perspective and to improve his understanding of such problems as planning, coordination, communications, decisionmaking, delegation, headquarters-field relationships, and public relations. Executive-development programs are needed in government, because the majority of administrative posts at all levels of government have in the past gone to persons with technical backgrounds, such as engineers, lawyers, and medical doctors. The results of a recent survey made by the United States Civil Service Commission of the academic preparation of federal service executives showed that only 12 percent had majored in government and public administration, whereas "much larger numbers" had majored in "business and commerce, economics, law, engineering, and the physical sciences." The Commission commented: "Therefore, while career executives need acute perceptions of the broad role of the Federal Government as a major institution in society, few have had an opportunity to gain such perceptions through academic work or in previous assignments."[5]

The internship is another important kind of training activity. For the young person just completing his academic training, it is the

[5] *University-Federal Agency Conference on Career Development*, held May 4–5, 1962, at Berkeley, California, Washington, D.C.: U.S. Civil Service Commission, 1962, pp. 8a, 9a.

bridge between theoretical and "live" work. By "live work" is meant actual exposure to practical situations on the job where the intern can gain valuable experience. The essence of the internship is that the beginner is given the opportunity to learn the particular job or function with the help of experienced workers who counsel him. The intern is more than an observer, for he is given actual work assignments. He is getting started on the work phase of his career, and he receives the benefit of the advice of those with long work experience.

In recent years, the administrative internship has appeared on the scene. Its purpose is to start the individual on a career in administration, as opposed to a subject-matter specialty. In the absence of an administrative class as such in the American public service, the administrative internship meets a very important need. In 1934 a private organization, the National Institute of Public Affairs (NIPA), introduced the first program of this kind in the federal service. The NIPA selected outstanding college graduates and gave them financial assistance to meet their living expenses while assigned as interns in federal agencies. These internships lasted nine months and principally consisted of on-the-job training in the particular agency. This was supplemented by after-hours university courses, counselling by the educational director of the program, and weekly discussion meetings with authorities in the field of government. In 1944, the Civil Service Commission initiated a program of its own, which is carried out by the participating federal agencies, but under the leadership of the Commission. It is not limited to beginners, being open to qualified individuals with some previous federal work experience.[6] In addition, quite a few of the agencies have their own intern training programs for new recruits, such as those named from the Federal Service Entrance Examination registers.

The NIPA program was terminated in 1949, after having accomplished its objective in getting administrative apprenticeships launched in the federal government, but it is now being revived in a new form. Specifically, the NIPA has received a substantial grant from the Ford Foundation to be used for a program of career education for promis-

[6] See Charles A. Uhlmann and Walter F. Bayen, *Management Intern Programs—A Tool for Developing Better Managers*, Washington, D.C.: U.S. Civil Service Commission, 1957, Personnel Management Series, No. 11. Also William H. Cape, "Undergraduate Internships in Personnel Administration," *Public Personnel Review*, XXIII, No. 4 (October, 1962), 257–260.

ing young administrators at all levels of government. Initially, the participants will mainly be federal employees with some four to six years of governmental experience. At a later date, much larger numbers of state and local government employees will be admitted to the program. Those selected will receive on-the-job training in their agencies designed to meet their particular developmental needs. They will then receive leave from the agency to study for a year as graduate students in selected educational institutions from all over the country which offer broad training in public administration and government. Costs of tuition and other expenses will be met from the Ford grant. It is expected that up to 500 persons will participate in this program in the next eight to ten years.[7] The educational phase is of special significance, for, as indicated, up to now only small numbers of federal employees have been released full time to attend university courses under the new training legislation. Furthermore, those who have received educational leaves generally have enrolled in programs of study in the physical sciences. Thus, the new NIPA program will not only produce a substantial increase in the numbers of employees receiving educational leaves, but it will also provide much wider opportunities for training in public administration and government.

A few state and local jurisdictions have for some years now had administrative intern programs. When the NIPA educational grants are made in larger numbers to employees of state and local governments, this will mean that more jurisdictions will be able to have administrative internships. Some of these jurisdictions may then decide to develop permanent programs of their own.

Another kind of training program—that for foreign nationals—is now offered not only by the federal government, but also by many state and local jurisdictions.[8] A brief description of this kind of program will illustrate the variety of instructional techniques used in training efforts. Since the developing countries lack trained personnel in the different fields required to support programs of economic development, they have sent many of their nationals to the developed

[7] *Personnel News*, Public Personnel Association, Chicago, Ill.: XXVIII, No. 9 (September, 1962), 47.

[8] See Albert Lepawsky (ed.), *Agenda for International Training*, Vancouver, Canada: Publications Centre, Univ. of British Columbia, 1962.

countries to obtain the required training. National governments, international organizations like the United Nations and its specialized agencies, private foundations, and individual corporations have for many years been providing special training for these foreign nationals. They have also helped the governments of the developing countries establish and operate training facilities of their own, thus obviating the need for sending some of their nationals abroad for training. Up to now, most of the training needs of the developing countries have had to be satisfied by sending trainees abroad, but real progress is being made in the development of indigenous training facilities.

Training for foreign nationals takes various forms. Some of it is provided by their admittance as degree undergraduate and graduate students in the programs of academic institutions. Frequently, it consists principally of observation training, supplemented by evening courses at educational institutions in the host countries. Observation training simply means that the foreign official is escorted on guided tours of work installations during which he has the opportunity to observe in detail how certain programs are conducted. He listens to explanations of these programs by the officials in charge of them, asks questions, digests reading materials, and generally learns from the opportunity to make these first-hand observations. In other cases, the foreign national is assigned to work under supervision for a period of time in public or private agencies in the host country.

Brief as this review of current in-service training programs has been, it describes a picture of vastly expanded activities, all of which have developed in a relatively few years. Furthermore, the indications are that this activity will be multiplied many times over in the years to come.

Evaluation of Training Programs

As training programs have been expanded, increasing concern has been expressed over the difficulty of measuring the benefits in tangible terms. In such areas as typing, taking dictation, and other activities where performance prior to and after the training can be measured concretely, the evaluation process presents no great difficulties. But objective units of measurement, such as typing speed, are lacking in most kinds of government work. This is illustrated in supervisory and executive training programs, because strong doubts have been expressed that the participants really profit from such programs. It is standard procedure to request the executive trainees, upon completion of the program, to fill out questionnaires giving their opinions as to the effectiveness of the training. These comments are of limited value, however, because no matter how favorable the individual's reaction, there is no certainty that he will actually practice what he has learned. Furthermore, the participants themselves often disagree widely as to the value of the different training courses and sessions. An added limitation is that there is a definite tendency on the part of some of them to praise the program simply for reasons of courtesy even though they are not required to sign their names to the questionnaires. A method generally felt to be more reliable is to obtain some measure of the individual's work performance sometime after he returns to his agency. Yet, since this is done by checking with his superiors, his colleagues, and even his subordinates, here again the method remains subjective, so the results of the evaluation can be regarded with some skepticism. Nonetheless, in the past too little evaluation of any kind was made of training programs, and subjective as these evaluations may be, they are better than none at all.

PROMOTIONS

If a true career service is to be created, staffing patterns should be developed showing the succession of progressively responsible posts to which the new recruit can in time be promoted depending on his performance. The employee should know exactly what he has to do in order to earn promotion to each of these higher ranks. Furthermore, only the best qualified of the candidates should receive promotion, just as in original recruitment only those ranking highest on the entrance lists receive appointments. These requirements are easy to state. In practice, as past experience clearly indicates, they are very difficult to achieve.

One of the biggest stumbling blocks has been undue emphasis on seniority. Pressure for the seniority principle is generally strong in all kinds of organizations, private or public. There is a strong suspicion that if promotions are decided on the basis of merit, too many subjective judgments will be introduced which would probably lead to decisions based on favoritism. Older workers also reason that long service must indicate the development of a more mature viewpoint and of greater skill on the job. There is no question about the objectivity of the seniority rule. All that has to be done is add up the years of service. An English scholar clearly expresses what is wrong with this principle notwithstanding:

> The trouble with the seniority system is that it is so objective that it fails to take any account of personal merit. As a system it is fair to every official except the best ones; an official has nothing to win or lose provided he does not actually become so inefficient that disciplinary action has to be taken against him. Thus, although it is fair after a fashion to the officials themselves, it is a heavy burden on the public and a great strain on the efficient handling of public business.[9]

The question then arises: "How is it possible in *merit* systems for undue weight to be given to seniority in making promotions?" A description of past and present practices in the American public service will make this clear.

The New Federal Promotion Policy

In most agencies of the federal service there was no formal system of competition for filling promotional jobs until very recently. The supervisory officer simply selected one of his subordinates, and, if this person met the Civil Service Commission's *minimum* qualification standards for the kind of job in question, the promotion was approved by the agency personnel office. There was no requirement for making the decision on the basis of a comparison of the attributes of all those who possessed the minimum qualifications. Enjoying this great discretion, appointing officers tended to follow the time-honored practice of seniority and to promote the man with the longest service. As a result, too often it was the mediocre employee who was promoted. In the long run, most employees could be expected to move up the line, because basically all they had to do was to wait patiently until their turn came.

Since 1959, however, the Civil Service Commission has required federal agencies to establish formal promotion systems. Under this

[9] Brian Chapman, *The Profession of Government*, London: G. Allen, 1959, p. 164.

new policy, promotions must be made on the basis of merit from among the best-qualified candidates. Use of written tests is not mandatory, but the candidates must be rated as objectively as possible on the basis of evaluation methods which are reasonable, valid, and fair. This guarantees true competition and makes it impossible to base the decision on the sole question of seniority, no matter what the other attributes of the candidates. Furthermore, agencies must open the competition as widely as possible; they must not limit it narrowly, such as by following the general rule of only accepting applications from persons holding positions in the organization unit in which the vacancy occurs. If the field of choice is restricted in this way, as it frequently was in the past, the quality of the promotees will probably not be very high. It is again a question of emphasizing seniority, because the employee is in effect rewarded for having remained within the same organization unit. It is not enough just to have a promotion system. It should be one which brings to the top only the best-qualified people. The new federal policy points very clearly in that direction and, when it has been in effect long enough, it should have had the effect of improving substantially the quality of the promotees throughout the executive branch.

Practices in State and Local Jurisdictions

In state and local merit systems, competitive procedures have long been used in filling promotional positions. Written examinations are given and eligible registers prepared, just as in the case of the competition for original entrance. The practice is sometimes followed, however, of augmenting the candidates' scores with additional points for length of service. Furthermore, competition is often narrowly limited, giving the advantage to persons holding jobs in the same department or even smaller organizational unit where the vacancy is being filled. Despite the existence of formal competition, in practice seniority may, therefore, be a decisive factor. An encouraging development is the recent action of some jurisdictions to broaden the area of competition greatly. For example, the Denver, Colorado, Career Service Authority now permits any employee in the city service who meets the minimum requirements to apply for a promotional examination.[10]

[10] *Personnel News,* Public Personnel Association, Chicago, Ill., XXVIII, No. 10 (October, 1962), 52.

Promotion from Within or Without

The problem may be raised whether individuals not in the government should be allowed to compete for vacancies in the higher jobs, along with existing public employees. The law and the regulations of the federal service do not prohibit this. The individual agency can frame its promotion policy in such a way as to permit making judicious use of appointments of outsiders. This, of course, is the lateral entry referred to earlier as an essential element of the American tradition. Mobility between private and public employment is considered highly desirable. Furthermore, prevailing opinion is that such mobility should apply not only to jobs filled through political channels but also to career positions. Flexibility also exists in state and local merit systems, because the central personnel agency is often given the discretion to open the competition to outsiders. The Municipal Manpower Commission found, however, that most urban governments are rarely willing to fill middle and top positions with outsiders.[11]

What should be done is to strike the proper balance between promotion-from-within and promotion-from-without. Too much promotion-from-within leads to inbreeding and the stagnation which this produces. Some promotion-from-without is desirable to provide the stimulation of new ideas and to counteract any tendency towards excessive "conformism." On the other hand, too free a policy of filling the higher posts with outsiders can damage the morale of those passed over for promotion despite their being well qualified for the jobs in question.

Many people support the principle that no one should be appointed from outside the government, or from outside the particular agency, unless he has qualifications clearly superior to those of the best-qualified aspirant for the promotion within the agency. This is both fair and logical, but as a guiding principle it falls down in practice at the point of measuring the qualifications of the individuals concerned. Whether the outsider is better qualified or not can be and frequently is a matter for dispute.

[11] Municipal Manpower Commission, *op. cit.*, pp. 76–78.

Comparison with Industry

Imperfect as government promotion procedures have been in the past, disillusionment over practices in industry has been far greater. Articles and research findings recently published paint a picture of favoritism, chance, scheming, and other extraneous factors as the decisive ones in obtaining promotions. The senior executive often prefers to advance the man who most resembles him in his work habits and personal characteristics. The junior executive who is the "carbon copy" of his boss gets the promotion. Of course, this is not true in all companies, but it does appear to be widespread.[12] Foreign governments have also wrestled with the problem and come up with some solutions, which, however desirable in their environments, would probably be rejected by most Americans. In Europe, some countries establish a quota of higher jobs to be filled on the basis of seniority alone, and another quota of the same jobs to be awarded on the basis of merit. For example, in Italy the "posts of *primo segretario* in the *carriere di concetto* (executive class) are filled for a quarter by competitive examinations amongst those in the class below, and for three-quarters by *ideoneitá*: that is, promotion from seniority amongst those who have satisfactorily passed a test of competence."[13] There is no precedent for establishing such a quota system in the American public service. Nevertheless, study of foreign experience and other research in the area of promotional systems should be highly desirable. Existing American practices have been used too long without the kind of critical examination which recently produced the new federal promotion policy.

SERVICE RATINGS

From the employees' standpoint, it is essential that they know whether they are doing their work satisfactorily and how they can improve their performance. Naturally, they also want appropriate

[12] See Charles H. Coates and Roland F. Pellegrin, "Executives and Supervisors: Informal Factors in Differential Bureaucratic Promotion," *Administrative Science Quarterly*, II, No. 2 (September, 1957), 209–215. Also Robert N. McMurry, "The Executive Neurosis," *Harvard Business Review*, XXX, No. 6 (November–December, 1952), 33–47.

[13] Chapman, *op. cit.*, p. 170.

recognition for the quality of the services they render. As to the management, it wants to help the employees achieve the highest levels of performance possible. It is glad to reward superior performance and to treat the employees fairly, in accordance with an accurate evaluation of their respective value to the organization. Again, what should be done is easy to state in terms of broad principles. Achieving the result is in this case more difficult than in many other areas of personnel administration. The reason is that this "accurate evaluation" of the employees' services is exceedingly difficult to make: a quick resume of the experience to date with service ratings will show the reason.

Public Rewards or Penalties

The outstanding characteristic of service rating plans in government has been what the first Hoover Commission termed the system of mandatory *public rewards or penalties*.[14] The employees are given adjective ratings by their supervisors, such as "Excellent," "Very Good," "Good," "Fair," and "Unsatisfactory." These ratings have controlled the individual's work destinies, favorably or unfavorably. One of the best examples of this is eligibility for a within-grade increase. This is not the same as a promotion: a promotion is a movement from a position in one class to another ranked higher in the salary plan; the within-grade increase means a raise from a lower to a higher rate in the salary scale for the *same* class of positions. The scales typically consist of several intermediate rates besides the minimum and maximum. The supervisor knows that, unless he gives the employee the minimum rating required by law, he will be depriving him of his next "increase." Similarly, the last service rating frequently has at least something to do with the individual's ranking on reduction-in-force and reemployment registers. It is sometimes even weighted in promotional examinations and, if the rating is low enough, immediate dismissal action against the employee may be required.

There is nothing wrong with rewarding good employees and

[14] Commission on Organization of the Executive Branch of the Government, *Task Force Report on Federal Personnel*, Washington, D.C.: Government Printing Office, 1949, pp. 60–62, 71–72.

penalizing poor ones. The trouble is that the mandatory system of public rewards or penalties has by no means produced this result, since the supervisor hesitates to give ratings which will adversely affect the employee. The situation has sometimes been complicated by the innumerable appeal rights granted to the employees. Rather than have to be tied up in time-consuming hearings, the supervisor simply decides to give the subordinate an acceptable rating. Furthermore, many employees regard any rating of less than Excellent or Very Good as reflecting on their performance. The net result is that the ratings tend to be far too high. In some cases, as many as 50 percent and even more of the employees have been rated "Excellent." The Performance Rating Act of 1950, still in effect in the federal government, provides for three levels of rating: Outstanding, Satisfactory, and Unsatisfactory. In recent years, 98 to 99 percent of the employees have received ratings of "Satisfactory." The only reason why so very few employees are now rated Outstanding is that the law allows such a rating only when the individual is outstanding in *all* aspects of his job performance.

Recommendations of the Hoover Commissions

Both Hoover Commissions recommended that the system of *public rewards or penalties* be ended, and that instead supervisors should be required to make periodic reports of a confidential nature on the performance of their subordinates and their growth potential. These reports would be used within the agency as the basis for granting or denying within-grade increases and taking any other actions. Employees would be continuously evaluated, but summary adjective ratings would not be given. The supervisor would call the employee in for frequent confidential chats during which he would give his reactions to his work performance.

Why would such a procedure be better? Would not the employee who is denied his "increase" or otherwise treated adversely resent the rating? Very likely he would, but no service rating system can be expected to eliminate hard feelings. The important thing is to create a situation in which the supervisor is encouraged to take the job of evaluating his subordinates seriously. The confidential talks, it is hoped, will produce such an atmosphere. Furthermore, with the final adjective ratings eliminated, the employees would not be constantly making the invidious comparisons which poison the atmosphere.

In making this recommendation, both Hoover Commissions were influenced by the example of private companies which have achieved good results without summary ratings and other characteristics of the system of public rewards or penalties. The Civil Service Commission has supported these recommendations, but up to now no such change has been made in the Performance Rating Act of 1950. However, the Federal Salary Reform Act of 1962 definitely severs the connection between the last service rating and the within-grade increases. It provides that, after a specified period of time at his existing salary rate, the employee will be eligible for an increase if "his work is of an acceptable level of competence as determined by the head of the department."[15] There is no requirement that this determination by the head of the department must be based on the last service rating. Previously, within-grade increases had to be granted to all employees who got a service rating of "Satisfactory." Since practically everybody received such a rating, this made the increases virtually automatic. In practice, however, this new provision of law does not seem to have made for any real change. Department heads have been reluctant to state that the employee's services are not acceptable. This would raise the question of why the employee was not dismissed. As we shall see in the next chapter, appointing officers are reluctant to bring dismissal actions for fear that they will be reversed when the employee appeals.

For some years now, several state and local governments have disassociated within-grade increases and other personnel actions from the ratings. An example is the State of California which made this change in April, 1961. Under the new procedures established by the State Personnel Board, the supervisor must evaluate the subordinate's performance at least once a year. These evaluations, however, are no longer the basis for granting or denying salary increases or determining order of layoff. Increases are now given on the basis of length of service, plus certification by the employee's supervisor that he has met the standards of efficiency required for his position. The employee's performance appraisal has nothing to do with order of layoff, and it is given no weight in promotional examinations.

[15] Section 701 (a) (B), Public Law 87–793, 87th Congress.

Summary adjective ratings are still given, but the system of *public rewards or penalties* based on them has been ended.[16]

Trait-Rating Plans

The rating process itself is very difficult no matter what kind of evaluation system is used. The most common kind of plan used in the past in both government and industry is known as "trait rating." There are several variations of this plan, but essentially it consists of rating the individual on aspects of his personality, such as industry, initiative, intelligence, dependability, courtesy, cooperation, and tact. If the graphic trait scale is employed, the employee is rated according to the degree to which he possesses certain qualities.

This kind of plan is simple to administer, because large numbers of employees can be rated rapidly simply by making the appropriate marks in the indicated spaces. It is, however, highly subjective for two important reasons. First, there is no common agreement on what the traits in question mean. What does a characteristic like "cooperativeness" really mean? Sometimes brief definitions of each trait are given on the rating form, but usually they consist of descriptive phrases and adjectives which again do not have the same meaning to all raters. Secondly, the best intentioned of raters will disagree, sometimes sharply, as to whether an employee possesses a given trait, and to what degree. How do we know when an employee is "very cooperative" rather than just "cooperative"?

Performance Standards

In an effort to reduce this subjectivity, some public agencies have developed rating systems based on performance standards. Under this kind of system, the employee is rated not on his personality traits but on his performance in carrying out the different tasks in his job. This creates the necessity, however, of breaking the job down into its essential components and of rating the employee's performance on each. It is undoubtedly an educational process for superior and subordinate to identify the job components and to agree on the performance standard. The performance standard is the minimum acceptable level of performance by the employee on each

[16] *Personnel News*, Public Personnel Association, Chicago, Ill. XXVII, No. 3 (March, 1961), 16.

task, measured in terms of both quantity and quality of work. Still it is a laborious undertaking to list the tasks, and determine the performance standards for each and every task, in hundreds and thousands of positions. When every employee has to be rated on how he performs each task in his job, this is a time-consuming process except in very small organizations.

Some agencies do not require the preparation of written performance standards, but they do instruct the supervisors to base their evaluations on the employee's work performance, rather than vague personality traits. The supervisor is urged to make entirely clear to the subordinate what his job is and what work results are expected of him. If the supervisor believes that the subordinate's performance is not up to the desired standards, he is expected to show him in specific terms why this is so. When the emphasis is on performance, the supervisor can set work improvement targets for the subordinate to try to meet by the time of the next evaluation conference. This gives the conferences themselves a constructive character and presents the worker with a challenge. He sees the superior as someone personally interested in his development, not as a judge on high who gives him no real help but is quick to lecture him on his deficiencies. When this kind of evaluation system is employed, it is immaterial whether a rating form as such is used or whether the superior simply prepares a memorandum or other report for the official records in which he gives his latest observations on the subordinate's performance. The essential element is that the evaluation is based on a careful definition of the employee's responsibilities and of his progress in meeting the work goals mutually agreed upon between him and his superior. Quite a few private companies have in recent years switched from trait rating to performance evaluation conducted on this basis and are better satisfied with the results.[17] In government, there has also been a noticeable attempt to shift the emphasis to rating specific work performance, rather than personality characteristics.

Need to Train Supervisors in Rating

No matter how good the service rating system, it will fail if the supervisors do not understand it. For this reason it is unfortunate that

[17] See Robert K. Stolz, "Can Appraisal Interviews be Made Effective," *Personnel*, XXXVIII, No. 2 (March–April 1961), 32–37.

such inadequate attention has in the past been given to training supervisors in rating. Very few jurisdictions schedule enough supervisory training conferences for this purpose. What happens too often is that the rating time arrives, and the supervisor is ill-prepared to do his job as rater of so many subordinates. Sometimes, because of the pressure of other duties, he leaves this chore for the last minute. The night before the ratings are due, he puts the forms in his briefcase and does the job at home that night.[18] Ratings prepared so hurriedly naturally could be greatly improved if the supervisors devoted more time to this important task. It is the agency's responsibility to explain the system to the supervisors and to stimulate them to do the best job possible of rating.

Both in industry and government, there is marked dissatisfaction with the results obtained with service rating systems to date. The need to improve ratings has definitely emerged as a high-priority objective, as the too meagre accomplishments of past years are viewed in retrospect. In the case of government, it now seems clear that really good service-rating systems will not be developed unless legislative bodies and the public come to recognize that much more money is going to have to be invested in this part of the personnel function than at present. As with tests, evaluation of employee performance requires a great deal of study and experimentation, which costs money. If this had been recognized a long time ago, much better results would undoubtedly have been achieved in this area.

BIBLIOGRAPHY

Batson, Robert J., *Employee Evaluation: A Review of Current Methods and a Suggested New Approach,* Chicago, Ill.: Public Personnel Association, 1957.

[18] *Performance Rating Plans in the Federal Government,* House Subcommittee on the Federal Civil Service, 83rd Congress, 2nd Session, Washington, D.C.: Government Printing Office, 1954, pp. 11–12.

Chapman, Brian, *The Profession of Government*, London: G. Allen, Ltd., 1959. Chaps. 3 and 8.

Corson, John J., "Equipping Men for Career Growth in the Public Service," *Public Administration Review*, **XXIII,** No. 1 (March, 1963).

DeLisser, Herbert, "Have Performance Standards Been Oversold?" *Personnel Administration*, **XXIII,** No. 6 (November–December, 1960).

Dinerman, Beatrice, Dvorin, Eugene P., and Staniford, Edward F., "Furthering Employee Education in State and Federal Governments," *Personnel Administration*, **XXIII,** No. 1 (January–February, 1960).

"Educating Executives: Social Science, Self-Study, or Socrates," *Public Administration Review*, **XVIII,** No. 4 (Autumn, 1958). Symposium of five articles analyzing different educational programs for executives.

Guetzkow, H., Forehand, G. A., and James, B. F., "An Evaluation of Educational Influence on Administrative Judgment," *Administrative Science Quarterly*, **VI,** No. 4 (March, 1962).

Kallen, Arthur D., "Training in the Federal Service—170 years to Accept," *Public Administration Review*, **XIX,** No. 1 (Winter, 1959).

Miner, John B., "Management Development and Attitude Change," *Personnel Administration*, **XXIV,** No. 3 (May–June, 1961).

Nolting, Orin F., *Post-Entry Training in the Public Service in Western Europe*. Chicago, Ill.: International City Managers' Association, 1962.

Tickner, Fred J., *Modern Staff Training*, London: Univ. of London Press, 1952.

Warner, W. Lloyd, *et al.*, "New Light on Lateral Entry," *Personnel Administration*, **XXVI,** No. 3 (May–June, 1963).

CHAPTER 16

Employee Relations

The term "employee relations" is broadly used to refer in general to the relationships between employees and management. Since these relationships are so numerous, practically everything in personnel administration could be considered a part of employee relations. In this chapter, we will concentrate on a number of areas which pose important policy questions about the government's role as employer. How should the government treat its employees? Which rights should it guarantee and which should it deny them? What responsibilities should it assume in relation to them, and what obligations should it impose upon them?

THE ROLE OF EMPLOYEE ORGANIZATIONS

A first question is whether public employees should not only be permitted but also *encouraged* to join unions. Permission to do so has been federal service policy ever since passage of the Lloyd-LaFollette Act of 1912. It is significant, however, that this legislation was passed only after a history of open opposition by department heads such as the Postmaster-General to employee unions.

Indeed, one reason why the Lloyd-LaFollette Act was passed was to legislate out of existence an executive order issued in 1906 by President Theodore Roosevelt which came to be known as the "gag rule." This executive order forbade federal employees to make direct contact with members of Congress about pay increases or other legislative proposals in their interest. The Lloyd-LaFollette Act expressly guaranteed the right of federal employees to "petition" Congress, and it provided that membership in an employee union not affiliated with an outside organization imposing a duty to engage in or assist in any strike against the government could not be made the grounds for reduction in rank or removal. It gave the employee a vital protection which he had not had before, but essentially it was only a negative piece of legislation because it did not express any government policy of encouraging unions.

The New Federal Policy

All this was changed with the issuance by President Kennedy on January 17, 1962, of Executive Order 10988.[1] This Executive Order makes clear in its preamble that it is in the government's interest to develop "orderly and constructive relationships" between "employee organizations and management officials." It requires the head of each agency to advise employees of their rights to organize and to see to it that "no interference, restraint, coercion, or discrimination is practiced within such agency to encourage or discourage membership in any employee organization." Just as the Wagner Act of 1935 greatly strengthened labor's position in the private sector, so does this Executive Order usher in a new era for public-employee unions. In the years since the passage of the Lloyd-LaFollette Act, government unions had gained strength, but, with few exceptions, they had not reached the point of being formally recognized and guaranteed the right to be consulted before agency personnel policies were adopted. The new Executive Order provides for such recognition and definitely ends the era of consultation with the unions only at the pleasure of the agency head.

Kinds of Recognition Extended

Specifically, the Executive Order provides for three kinds of recognition of employee organizations: (1) informal, (2) formal, and (3) exclusive. When an employee organization receives informal recognition, it is given the right to present its views to the management on

[1] The Executive Order is reproduced as Appendix B in *Unions Are Here to Stay*, Washington, D.C.: Society for Personnel Administration, February, 1962, Pamphlet No. 17.

matters of concern to its members. In extending such recognition, however, the management does not obligate itself to advance consultation with representatives of the organization before making decisions on personnel policies. The rights of organizations recognized on this basis are limited, because they do not have a sufficient number of members within "a unit as defined by the agency" to qualify for formal or exclusive recognition. Nevertheless, informal recognition does commit the management to allowing the employees to deal with it through representatives of their own choosing. Previously, the federal employee had numerous rights to present grievances and petitions individually, but, in many agencies, any efforts on his part to do this through representatives of his union were resisted.

Formal recognition must be granted to an employee organization which, although it is not qualified for exclusive recognition, has a membership of at least ten percent of the workers in the unit. The difference between informal and formal recognition is that the latter binds the management to consult regularly with the employee organization on the "formulation and implementation of personnel policies and practices." The plain implication of the Executive Order is that agency managements should give careful consideration to the views expressed by the union representatives at these meetings.

Exclusive recognition is given when the employee organization has been designated by a majority of the workers in the unit as their representative. An organization accorded exclusive recognition is entitled to negotiate agreements with the management covering *all* employees in the unit, duplicating the practice in industry under the National Labor Relations Act for unions representing the majority of workers in the bargaining unit. The Executive Order states that the bargaining unit "may be established on any plant or installation, craft, functional or other basis which will ensure a clear and identifiable community of interest among the employees concerned." It is the responsibility of each agency first to define the bargaining unit and, second, to determine whether any employee organization has the majority of employees necessary for exclusive recognition. Upon the request of the agency, or of any employee organization which has already been granted formal recognition, the Secretary of Labor may nominate arbitrators to be employed by the agency for help in making either or both of these determinations. These arbitrators are selected from the National Panel of Arbitrators maintained by the Federal Mediation and Conciliation Service. Except in special circumstances, no organization will be given exclusive recognition if it includes in its membership any "managerial executive." The same prohibition applies if it has any members performing federal personnel work in "other than a purely clerical capacity." It also applies if the membership of the organization includes "both supervisors who officially evaluate the performance of employees and the employees whom they supervise." Finally, exclusive recognition will not be given to organizations with both professional and nonprofessional employees unless a majority of the professional workers vote to be included in such a union.

The Permissible Area of Negotiation

The Executive Order allows "grievances, personnel policies and practices, or other matters affecting general working conditions of employees in the unit" to be covered in the agreements signed by the government and employee organizations. It makes clear that agreements can only be made "subject to law and policy requirements." If the matter is not one within the agency's discretion because of the existing laws, regulations, and administrative policies, it cannot negotiate with the unions on such questions. The Executive Order closely follows the recommendations of the President's Task Force on Employee-Management Relations, a group of Cabinet and other high federal officials appointed to prepare a report on this problem. The Task Force stressed in its report that there is an important difference between employee-management relations in industry and in the federal government. In the latter case, neither party is "free to bargain in the ordinary sense."[2] The employees cannot legally strike, and since the pay, hours, and fringe benefits of most federal employees are prescribed by law, the agency management cannot negotiate with the unions on such issues. So long, for example, as Congress sets pay rates for white-collar workers by statute, agency managements have no authority to negotiate such rates with the unions. On the other hand, since the departments are authorized to set blue-collar wages in accordance with the local prevailing rates, the unions have the right

[2] *Report of the President's Task Force on Employee-Management Relations in the Federal Service*, Washington, D.C.: U.S. Civil Service Commission, November 30, 1961, p. 32.

under the new Executive Order to bargain with the agencies as to these prevailing rates.

The Task Force specified the following as areas in which agencies can negotiate with employee organizations: "working conditions, promotion standards, grievance procedures, safety, transfers, demotions, reductions in force, and other matters, consistent with merit system principles."[3] Actually, this covers a good deal, because under the Civil Service Commission's decentralization policy the agencies have considerable autonomy in these areas. The Civil Service Commission's new promotion policy, already described, is a good example. The departments are authorized to adopt employee promotion plans, following the Commission's guide lines. Prior approval of the plan by the Commission is not required. It checks up on promotion practices in its regular program of inspection of agency personnel programs as a whole. This decentralization policy opens a wide field in which the agency can develop its promotion policies in consultation with employee organizations. Determining the area of competition, the standards to be used in measuring qualifications for promotion, and similar matters may be negotiated with the unions. So, while the typical federal agency is not free to negotiate in the same way as in industry, it is by no means restricted to a very narrow field in its dealings with employee organizations.

Collective Bargaining

The Executive Order does not employ this term, collective bargaining, very probably to avoid giving the impression that industry practices are fully applicable in the federal service. Yet, so long as the agency recognizes a union and agrees to consult with it before reaching decisions on personnel policies, this is collective bargaining, even if wages and hours of work cannot be negotiated as in industry. Of course, from a legal standpoint, collective bargaining in government cannot be the same as in industry, because every agreement negotiated is subject to the "overriding power of the government."[4] Private-company officials are not restricted by laws or government regulations as to what matters they can negotiate with the unions.

Yet, while all of this is true, some observers feel that public offi-

[3] *Ibid.*, p. 33.

[4] Sterling D. Spero, "Collective Bargaining in Public Employment: Form and Scope," *Public Administration Review*, XXII, No. 1 (Winter, 1962), 2.

cials have too often used the excuse that they cannot really bargain collectively with employee unions. In the opinion of these critics, the emphasis upon the legal distinctions inherent in the government's sovereign powers has served to obscure the real issue. That real issue is whether government officials can recognize employee unions and sit down at the conference table to negotiate binding agreements in some important areas of personnel policy at least. Since they have this discretion, why not call it collective bargaining? This seems to be a realistic approach, and in fact many local jurisdictions have passed legislation and issued official statements of policy in which they grant "collective bargaining rights" to the employees. Cincinnati is a case in point.[5] In April, 1960, its City Council passed an ordinance stating that it would be its policy, acting through the City Manager, to "bargain collectively with city employees, their unions, or other authorized representatives" on wages and working conditions. Yet the same ordinance makes clear that the City Council will regard as advisory only the agreements which the City Manager and the unions refer to it. The Council reserves the right to reject, accept, or make changes in these proposals. Subsequently, the City Manager and other officials representing the "management" signed an agreement with the district council of the American Federation of State, County, and Municipal Employees (AFSCME), recognizing it as the exclusive bargaining agent for most of the city's employees. Yet in this agreement it is carefully stated that "wages, fringe benefits, and working conditions" must be in accordance with the "ordinances from time to time passed by the City Council." These ordinances are made a part of the agreement itself, a very clear way of saying that the City Council will make the final decision and by no means function simply as a routine ratifying agent. Nonetheless, the Council is pledged to guarantee the unions the opportunity to work out an agreement with the City Manager which will then be referred to it for action. City employees can use the power and pressures of their exclusive bargaining agent in an effort to be as forceful as possible with the City Manager and the Council. Legally, this is still not equivalent to the

[5] See W. D. Heisel and J. P. Santa-Emma, "Unions in City Government: the Cincinnati Story," *Public Personnel Review*, XXII, No. 1 (January, 1961), 35–38. Quotations are directly from the city ordinance and the agreement with the AFSCME.

kind of collective bargaining permitted in industry, but in practice it can bring much the same results for the employees.

Affiliation and the Right to Strike

The right to organize and to affiliate with the outside labor movement is recognized in most state and local governments, as well as in the federal government.[6] Evidence of the strength of the unions in state and local governments is seen in the fact that more than 400 of them, as well as "scores of school and special districts," have signed collective agreements with their employees.[7] A few states and local governments, however, do not permit public employees in general or specified groups of them to form unions or to affiliate. Policemen sometimes are not allowed to join unions, or else their unions are not allowed to affiliate.

Affiliation is a great help to the public-employee union because it gives it the support of powerful unions operating in the private sector. The AFSCME is affiliated with the AFL-CIO. This means that it can count on the latter's help in bringing pressure upon legislative bodies to increase salaries and pass other legislation favorable to the employees. The record clearly shows that much legislation, beneficial not only to the employees but also to the governmental jurisdictions concerned, has been passed as the result of the backing given public employee locals by the strong national labor organizations. In its most recent policy statement on employee organizations, the National Civil Service League recommends that affiliation be permitted "unless the public interest would thereby be jeopardized or public confidence impaired." The League states unequivocally that affiliation should not be allowed with any "outside union the leadership of which has a record of subversive activities or of using illegal methods."[8] It further believes that policemen and firemen should not be permitted to affiliate with organizations which claim the right to strike. As to strikes by public employees of any kind, it rejects any notion that this is a

[6] For a good, brief discussion of legal status of public-employee unions, see *Public Employee Labor Relations*, Springfield, Ill.: Illinois Legislative Council, November, 1958.

[7] Spero, *op. cit.*, 1.

[8] "Employee Organizations in Government," *Good Government*, LXXVII, No. 11 (November, 1960), 1.

"conscionable weapon in the best interests of the public service." It does not recommend specific legislation prohibiting such strikes, because most public-employee organizations have expressly renounced use of the strike weapon.

As previously noted, in the federal service, the Lloyd-LaFollette Act banned affiliation with any organization claiming the right to strike. The Taft-Hartley Act of 1947 went further and made it illegal for any federal worker to go on strike. Stiff penalties are provided: Any employee who strikes must be discharged immediately; if he has civil service status, he forfeits it, and, in any case, he is not eligible to be reemployed in any federal agency until three years after his dismissal. President Kennedy's Executive Order excludes from its coverage any employee organization which asserts the right to strike or which advocates forceful overthrow of the government. As a matter of fact, it also excludes organizations practicing any form of discrimination "because of race, color, creed, or national origin."

In most states there is no law prohibiting strikes, but the courts have ruled that "strikes against governmental bodies are contrary to public policy and illegal at least in a general sense."[9] Eleven states have passed legislation outlawing such strikes, but even in these states strikes do take place. As Sterling D. Spero, a long-standing authority on public-employee unions, has pointed out: "The history of strikes in the American civil services indicates that where employees believe they have a grievance sufficient to warrant the risks they will strike regardless of legal prohibitions."[10] This was very clearly demonstrated in the spring of 1962 when more than 20,000 New York City public-school teachers dared strike despite the severe penalties to which they exposed themselves. At the time of this strike, the state's Condon-Wadlin Act provided for automatic discharge of any public employee who went out on strike and for his reemployment only with loss of tenure and no pay increases for several years. Both Governor Rockefeller and Mayor Wagner agreed that these penalties should not be invoked. The New York state legislature amended this law in 1963, but only to the point of reducing the waiting period for be-

[9] *Public Employee Labor Relations, op. cit.*, p. i.

[10] Sterling D. Spero, "The New York Teachers' Strike," *Good Government*, LXXIX, No. 9 (September, 1962), 2.

coming eligible for salary increases and regaining tenure upon re-employment.

Spero indicates that the strike itself was understandable, because of the "authoritarian spirit" of the New York school system, an attitude which extended "from the administration through the principals to the teachers down to the children."[11] Like some other observers, he finds it inconsistent to allow telephone operators, milk-truck drivers, and other private-company workers supplying the community with vital services to strike but to prohibit government workers from doing so. Some public services are far less important to the public than others provided by private companies. Spero does not advocate that government workers use the strike, but he makes clear that "the strike is not a significant weapon in the American public service,"[12] since public employees have resorted to it only infrequently, and because other means have been found of settling the disputes. The positive approach is to correct the conditions which might lead public employees to use the strike as a last resort. As Rollin B. Posey has observed: "A strike against the government is a breakdown in its employee relations, for workers do not lightly undertake to strike. A strike can injure them as much as it can injure the employer. A strike is a result, not a cause. The control of strikes lies with preventing the cause of strikes."[13]

The Closed and Union Shops

How about the closed shop? Is this desirable in the public service? President Kennedy's Task Force emphatically said that it was not. The closed shop means that, to be eligible to obtain a job in the agency, the individual would have to be a member of the union. Anyone on a civil service list who was not a member of the union could not be appointed. If the union refused to admit someone as a member, he would be barred from public service no matter what his qualifications. Because it so obviously conflicts with the principle of merit, there does not seem to be much support for the closed shop in the public service.

[11] *Ibid.*, 1.

[12] Spero, *Collective Bargaining in Public Employment, op. cit.*, 4.

[13] Rollin B. Posey, "Employee Organization in the United States Public Service," *Public Personnel Review*, XVII, No. 4 (October, 1956), 244.

Kennedy's Task Force also found the union shop "contrary to the civil service concept upon which Federal employment is based."[14] Under the union shop, as practiced in industry, the employer agrees to keep only union members on the payroll but he may hire non-members provided that they join the union within a designated time period, usually 30 days. If, after appointment, someone refuses to join the union, he must be dropped, no matter how good his performance. This again would conflict with the merit principle, but some public-employee unions are pressing for the union shop anyway. The assumption presumably is that the civil service employee will want to join the union. In the trades and labor fields which, incidentally, account for a large proportion of the total number of public employees who are union members, this is a reasonable expectation. The AFSCME claims to have 88 contracts negotiated by its locals "containing this strongest form of union security provision."[15]

The case of Philadelphia is interesting because in March, 1961, its City Council passed an ordinance authorizing the Mayor to enter into modified union-shop agreements. Such an accord was then signed by the Mayor and by representatives of the District Council of the AFSCME. Specifically, it covers some 12,000 of the city's total of 18,000 employees, including both blue- and white-collar workers. Those not union members when the agreement was signed were not compelled to join. Those already members were required to continue their membership, but they were permitted to resign from the union during an annual 15-day "escape period." New employees were required to join the union before completion of the six-month probationary period. Once they joined, they were obligated to stay in but had the same privilege of being able to drop out during the "escape period."[16]

This is not the complete union shop as it functions in industry, but the point remains that new employees must join the union and remain members at least for a time. The Philadelphia agreement does

[14] *Report of the President's Task Force, op. cit.*, p. 50.

[15] Arnold S. Zander, "A Union View of Collective Bargaining in the Public Service," *Public Administration Review*, **XXII**, No. 1 (Winter, 1962), 8.

[16] *Good Government*, **LXXVIII**, No. 5 (May, 1961), 4. See also Foster B. Roser, "Collective Bargaining in Philadelphia," in Kenneth O. Warner (ed), *Management Relations with Organized Public Employees*, Chicago, Ill.: Public Personnel Association, 1963, pp. 103–115.

demonstrate that some white-collar workers will accept the modified union shop. Whether any large numbers of cities will follow the Philadelphia example is, however, by no means certain. Prevailing sentiment among most government workers to date has been that, while the union shop may be essential in industry, it is not in the public service. Spero is of the opinion that "although the union shop seems to be winning increasing acceptance in local governments and exists for practical purposes, without formal recognition, in some federal agencies, it is not an essential element of collective bargaining in the public service."[17] It should be explained that for many years now the older organized trades have in effect maintained the union and even the closed shop in some federal agencies, even though in theory official government policy prohibits it.

Check-off of Union Dues

Another question is whether public agencies should accept responsibility for collecting union dues. Check-off of dues, as it is known, is common practice in industry. Some people feel strongly that no governmental unit should act as a collection agency for any union or other organization. Their reasoning is that this is a private matter and that the government should do nothing to create the impression that union membership is compulsory. This was the viewpoint of the majority of the members of the National Civil Service League's Special Committee on Employee Organizations. Other members of the same Committee disagreed. They argued that there could be no objection to the check-off if the following conditions were met: (1) the employee gave his written authorization; (2) he was allowed to withdraw this authorization at any time; and (3) the administrative costs were borne by the union.[18]

President Kennedy's Task Force could see nothing wrong with the check-off if these same conditions were met. It did think, however, that legislation by Congress was needed to establish clearly the legality of the check-off in the federal service. Accordingly, it recommended to the President that he propose such legislation to Congress.[19] The Comptroller-General later ruled that the necessary

[17] Spero, *Collective Bargaining in Public Employment, op. cit.*, 3.
[18] "Employee Organizations In Government," *op. cit.*, 2.
[19] *Report of the President's Task Force, op. cit.*, pp. 40–41.

legal authority did exist. Accordingly, the President directed the Civil Service Commission to develop a voluntary check-off system to be placed into effect by the federal agencies by January 1, 1964. In state and local governments, the check-off is fairly widespread. The Task Force noted that, by statute, ten states had authorized it for state employees and that in 38 states it was permitted by law for state and/or local governments.

Reviewing recent developments at all levels of government, Spero's statement is justified that "labor management relations in the public service are moving towards the patterns prevailing in private employment."[20] There are some important differences, as we have noted above, but the era of collective negotiations is clearly under way. As the result of President Kennedy's Executive Order, membership in unions of federal employees will probably increase substantially. The President's Task Force stated that some 762,000 persons representing approximately one-third of all federal employees were union members. By far the greatest number of these, some 489,224, were in the Post Office Department. Most of the rest were craftsmen and other blue-collar workers in Defense Department and other installations. Relatively few white-collar workers were members, but many more are apt to become members in the years to come. In May, 1964, the Department of Labor reported that, as the result of Kennedy's Executive Order, union membership in the federal government rose by 155,000 between 1960 and 1962. Outside the federal service, the AFSCME alone has a membership of 220,000. Accurate figures on total union membership in all state and local governments are not available.

The Grievance Procedure

Another important aspect of employee relations is the grievance procedure. In industry, one of the advantages of joining the union is that it helps the worker to obtain redress of his grievances. The details of the grievance procedure are an important subject for discussion in the collective-bargaining negotiations. In public agencies, the workers have usually been well protected from the standpoint of their

[20] Spero, *Collective Bargaining in Public Employment, op. cit.*, 1.

rights as individuals to present complaints and appeal adverse personnel actions. Employee organizations, however, have very frequently been left out of the grievance procedure. They have not been consulted in its development nor have they been encouraged or, in some cases, even been allowed to give the individual employee help in presenting his grievance.

President Kennedy's Executive Order provides that the details of the grievance procedure may be included in the negotiations between the agency managements and the employee organizations. Agreements reached must conform with Civil Service Commission standards governing agency grievance systems, but the plain intent is that the agencies work out the details with the employee organizations. The President's Task Force stated that in the past some federal agencies had taken the stand that grievances were purely personal problems of the employees with which the unions did not need to concern themselves. The Task Force termed this "a form of paternalism" which prevented "development of a mature relationship between employee organizations and the management."[21] A recent survey of practices in state and local jurisdictions shows that the employee unions generally do not have a strong role in the grievance procedure, particularly in the state governments.[22]

DISMISSALS

The dismissal procedure is naturally one of the most sensitive areas in management-employee relations. The workers justifiably want to be protected against arbitrary action by the supervisors. In turn, the latter understandably do not want unreasonable obstacles placed in the way of their discharging clearly unfit subordinates. As to the public, it wants "deadwood" eliminated and is concerned about the often heard statement that "you can't fire anyone" in government. Two policies with respect to dismissals have been followed in the public service. They are known as the "open back door" and the "closed back door."

[21] *Report of the President's Task Force, op. cit.*, p. 43.

[22] Eleanor R. Batson, "A Survey of Current Practice," in *Management Relations with Organized Public Employees, op. cit.*, pp. 147–148.

The "Open Back Door"

Under the first policy, the decision of the appointing officer in discharging an employee for reasons of inefficiency cannot be cancelled by the central personnel agency. Any employee who has completed his probationary period has the right to appeal to the Civil Service Commission, just as he has the right to appeal the dismissal first within his own agency. All the Civil Service Commission can do, however, is to recommend to the appointing officer that he reinstate the dismissed employee. If the appointing officer still feels that he is right, he does not have to follow this recommendation. The law sometimes permits the Commission to place the employee's name on the reemployment list for the class of positions involved, but that is as far as it can go. It should be made clear that under the "open back door" the employee is protected against dismissal for political, religious, or racial reasons. If the Commission is convinced that the action was taken for such a reason, it can order the reinstatement of the employee.

The "Closed Back Door"

Under the policy of the "closed back door," the central personnel agency can order the appointing officer to restore the employee to his position. In state and local jurisdictions, the "closed back door" policy is more common than the "open back door." In the federal service, the Pendleton Act as originally passed provided for the "open back door." It is interesting that, anxious as they were to eliminate the spoils system, the civil service reformers still did not want to make it hard to get rid of the incompetents. The Veterans Preference Act of 1944, however, made an important change. It provided for special treatment of veterans in dismissal cases and gave them the protection of the "closed back door." Specifically, they were allowed to appeal a dismissal action to the Civil Service Commission, and the latter was given the power to reverse it. Nonveteran employees, as before, could not appeal to the Commission unless they could show that the action was taken for political, religious, or racial reasons, or that the appointing officer, in making the dismissal, had failed to comply with the procedural steps required by law and the

Commission's regulations. In the same Executive Order in which he provided for recognition of the unions, President Kennedy extended to nonveterans the same appeal rights given the veterans under the 1944 act. The "closed back door" now applies to all federal employees under civil service. The President's purpose was to make the policy uniform, without favored treatment for any group of employees.

The Pros and Cons of Each Policy

Those who favor the "closed back door" argue that it is always possible that an appointing officer may be prejudiced against an employee and want to fire him simply because he does not like him. Accordingly, protection against dismissal for political, religious, or racial reasons is not enough. Since past experience suggests that a few supervisors, at least, can be expected to abuse their authority, there must be a court of higher appeal to which the employee can take his case. True, the central personnel agency, after conducting its hearing and weighing the evidence for and against the employee, may err and order the reinstatement of someone whose dismissal was fully justified. This is unfortunate, but it is better than making it possible for unjust supervisors to dismiss perfectly good employees. All the appointing officer is being asked to do is justify the dismissal. If he cannot do this to the central personnel agency's satisfaction, then he probably was wrong.

Advocates of the "open back door" argue that the appointing officer is in a much better position than the central personnel agency to make a judgment as to the efficiency of the employee. The management of the agency in which the employee has been working has direct knowledge of his work performance and conduct. For the central personnel agency to disagree with the supervisor and tell him that the employee must be taken back creates an impossible situation. The supervisor is responsible for the work of his unit. If he is to be forced to keep someone he is convinced is incompetent, he is denied the support that he deserves. Of course, the reinstated employee can be assigned to a different supervisor. The point still remains, however, that an outside group, in no way responsible for the work of the agency, is interfering with its management determinations. The authority of the agency management before the other employees can only suffer when they see the vindicated worker return to the agency. Furthermore, what control can the agency exercise over the reinstated employee? Is he not apt to feel that he is now free to behave as he pleases? It is also argued that the record clearly shows that central personnel agencies let the employees play upon their sympathies and all too easily come to the conclusion that the supervisor was too tough in resorting to dismissal action. The civil service commissioners who hear the employee's defense can afford to be more lenient than the supervisor. Once they decide the case, their contacts with the employee are ended. This is not so in the case of the supervisor if the employee's reinstatement is ordered. He and the agency management must still deal with the employee for every minute of the working day. Under the "open back door," a few employees may be dismissed without adequate justification, but a much larger number of incompetents will be gotten rid of than under the "closed back door." No system can be expected to guarantee perfect justice to all employees. The "open back door" is better because appointing officers are much more likely to take action against unsatisfactory employees. The probability of a time-consuming hearing before the central personnel agency, with the possibility always present of being overruled, discourages many a supervisor from initiating dismissal proceedings against even the most patently incompetent employees.

The public-employee unions generally support the "closed back door." Professional organizations like the National Civil Service League and the American Municipal Association strongly recommend the "open back door."[23] The second Hoover Commission was very critical of the provision of the Veterans Preference Act of 1944 which gave the veterans special appeal rights. It said that appeals by veterans in dismissal cases heard by the Civil Service Commission resembled a "judicial-criminal proceeding," with the appointing officer as much on trial as the employee. For the first time in the history of civil service, "Civil Service Commission control of the power of a department head to discipline his staff" had been introduced.[24]

[23] See the *Model State Civil Service Law*, revised edition, 1953, prepared jointly by these two organizations.

[24] *Task Force Report on Personnel and Civil Service*, Commission on Organization of the Executive Branch of the Government, Washington, D.C.: Government Printing Office, 1955, pp. 95–96.

The Hoover Commission recommended that the special appeals rights of veterans be limited to the first five years after the date of honorable discharge. Congress did not accept this recommendation, and, as mentioned above, President Kennedy's solution was to extend the same appeals rights to nonveterans. In the absence of action by Congress to restore the "open back door" for all employees, the President elected to make the procedure uniform on the basis of the "closed back door."

Appeals Procedures

Whether or not an appeal is allowed to the central personnel agency, at least one appeal and formal hearing should be permitted within the agency in which the employee has been working. To allow the employee no right of appeal whatsoever would be indefensible. On the same day he issued the Executive Order dealing with employee organizations, President Kennedy released another one establishing uniform policies to govern agency systems for appeals from adverse actions. Besides guaranteeing ordinarily at least one level of appeal and one hearing, this second Executive Order states that the employee organizations must be consulted in the development and operation of the appeals procedures. Furthermore, the employee is guaranteed the right to be represented by someone of "his own choosing in presenting his appeal." He also must be given "a reasonable amount of official time to present his appeal." The appeal itself must be "resolved expeditiously."[25]

Prior to issuance of this Executive Order, appeals procedures varied greatly in the federal service. Some agencies permitted endless hearings and appeals, whereas others did not adequately safeguard the rights of the employees. Furthermore, it is intended that the appeals procedures in the agencies be integrated into their grievance systems. Adverse personnel actions do not cause all the grievances ("adverse personnel action" refers to any decision by the management which is not favorable to the employee). The employee may have a grievance even if no adverse action is taken against him. His grievance may have to do with working conditions, indeed with any problem relating to his work which bothers him. If he is unable

[25] Executive Order 10987, reproduced as Appendix A in *Unions are Here to Stay, op. cit.*

to work the problem out with his supervisor, he may want to appeal to a higher authority. The objective is to develop one integrated appeals procedure in each agency covering all kinds of grievances, not just those arising from adverse personnel actions.

THE PROBLEM OF POLITICAL ACTIVITIES

Turning to a different kind of problem, to what extent should public employees be allowed to participate in political activities? Civil service laws usually place severe restrictions on such activity, and similar prohibitions are frequently placed on noncivil service employees as well.

The Hatch Acts

The federal government is a good case in point. The two Hatch Acts, one passed in 1939 and the other in 1940, make it illegal for federal employees to be active in any real sense in political affairs. They may become members of political clubs and attend meetings and rallies, but they cannot hold office in any political organization. They may not solicit or handle political contributions, and they cannot even write for publication any letter or article, signed or unsigned, in favor of or against any political party or candidate. They cannot become candidates for nomination or election to any office, federal, state, county, or municipal, which is filled through a partisan election. These restrictions apply not only to civil service but also to all noncivil service employees except those in top policymaking posts. They also apply to employees of state and local governments whose principal employment is in connection with programs supported in whole or part by federal grants or loans. The prohibitions on political activity are so sweeping that Civil Service Commission posters have warned federal employees that it is illegal to assume "political leadership" or become "prominently identified with any political movement, party, or faction, or with the success or failure of any candidate for election to public office in a partisan political campaign."

The Hatch Acts carry strong enforcement provisions. Prior to 1950, the Civil Service Commission was required to order the removal of federal employees guilty of violations. An amendment passed in August, 1950, makes it possible for the Commission to assign a lesser penalty if it believes the facts so warrant, but in no case of less than 90 days' suspension without pay. All disbursing and auditing officers are required to withhold payments to employees found guilty by the Commission of violating the antipolitical-activity rules. In the case of state and local employees in federally aided programs, the Commission is expected to order the removal of the offending individual. If the state or local government in question refuses to do so, the federal government can withhold from its aid funds to it a sum equal to two years' salary of the official.

What is the purpose behind these restrictions? The two Hatch Acts were passed at least partly as a reaction to political use of patronage employees by the New Deal agencies. These employees were being required to engage in partisan political activity in support of the New Deal Administration. One possible solution would have been to allow voluntary political activity but to prohibit any coercion of employees by their superiors in political matters. Congress rejected this approach as unworkable, because of the obvious difficulty in distinguishing between voluntary and coerced political activity. It decided that the only sure way of preventing use of government employees for political purposes was to prohibit them from taking any active part in partisan activity.[26]

The Argument for Political Freedom

More than two decades of experience with the Hatch Acts and similar legislation in many state and local jurisdictions has led to serious doubts about the desirability of such rigid curbs on public employees. Is it sound policy in a democracy to make virtual "political eunuchs" of millions of citizens simply because they happen to work for the government? Is it fair to exact as the price for holding a government job a commitment on the part of the individual not to become "prominently identified" with political movements? Does not the state injure itself when it requires its employees to stifle the de-

[26] See Leon D. Epstein, "Political Sterilization of Civil Servants: the United States and Great Britain," *Public Administration Review*, X, No. 4 (Autumn, 1950), 281–290.

sires some of them may have to exercise a role of leadership in political affairs? So long as the employee does not engage in political activities on government premises or otherwise abuse his official position for partisan purposes, why should he not be given the same privileges as any other citizen in political affairs? The argument is compelling, resting as it does on the plea for political freedom for the public employee. There is, however, another freedom, that from "the abuses of party machines."[27] Fear of such abuse explains why up to now Congress has refused to relax the prohibitions contained in the Hatch Acts. A House Committee recommended in 1958 that state and local employees no longer be covered, but Congress has not acted to make this change.[28]

In some state and local jurisdictions, proposals are being actively considered to loosen the tight restrictions on political activities. One argument is that public employees should not be banned from an active role in *any and all* political campaigns. For example, in the case of the employee of a city government, it may be justifiable to prohibit him from taking an active part in municipal political campaigns. What justification is there, however, for barring him from such a role in county, state, and federal political campaigns? The assumption here is that the danger of the employee being used as a tool by the party machine exists mostly in the jurisdiction where he is employed.

Basically, the issue comes down to which alternative is better: relaxing the prohibitions and inevitably opening the way for some abuses, or maintaining them unchanged in order to take no chances? If the first alternative is chosen, the political freedoms of American public employees will undoubtedly be increased. The gains to the nation in terms of greater citizen participation in politics may well outweigh by far any abuses of the political machines. It is, after all, possible that restrictive legislation along the lines of the Hatch Acts is outmoded and represents a vestige from the era of great concern over the spoils system. The point of view can be defended that the dangers today are not so great. At the moment of writing, the answer

[27] *Ibid.*, 283.

[28] See *Report of the Special Committee to Investigate and Study the Operation and Enforcement of the Hatch Political Activities Act*, Committee on House Administration, 85th Congress, 2nd Session, Washington, D.C.: Government Printing Office, 1959.

to this problem is still inconclusive. Perhaps after some jurisdictions have experimented with liberalized political-activity rules, it will be possible to come to more definite conclusions.

BIBLIOGRAPHY

Chapman, Brian, *The Profession of Government*, London: G. Allen, 1959. Chaps. 14 and 15.

Epstein, Leon D., "Political Sterilization of Civil Servants: The United States and Great Britain," *Political Science Review*, **X,** No. 4 (Autumn, 1950).

Friedland, Louis L., "Fair Employment Practices in the Public Service," *Public Personnel Review*, **XXIII,** No. 2 (April, 1962).

Godine, Morton R., *The Labor Problem in the Public Service*, Cambridge, Mass.: Harvard, 1951.

Hart, Wilson R., *Collective Bargaining in the Federal Service*, New York: Harper and Row, 1961.

Heisel, W. D., and Santa-Emma, J. P., "Unions in City Government: The Cincinnati Story," *Public Personnel Review*, **XXII,** No. 1 (January, 1961).

Kaplan, H. Eliot, *The Law of Civil Service*, Albany, N.Y.: Matthew Bender and Company, 1958.

Noble, George W., "Labour Relations in Canadian Municipalities," *Public Personnel Review*, **XXII,** No. 4 (October, 1961).

Personnel Administration, **XXVI,** No. 1 (January–February, 1963). Entire issue devoted to union–management relations.

Smith, Oscar S., "Are Public Service Strikes Necessary?" *Public Personnel Review*, **XXI,** No. 3 (July, 1960).

Spero, Sterling D., *Government as Employer*, New York: Remsen Press, 1948.

Warner, Kenneth O. (ed.), *Management Relations with Organized Public Employees,* Chicago, Ill.: Public Personnel Association, 1962.

PART V

FINANCIAL ADMINISTRATION

CHAPTER 17

Organization for Financial Administration

In Chapter 2 we saw how many demands are made on government to expand services to the citizens in the present age. Financial administration is of special importance today for the simple reason that, while there seems to be no limit to what we may ask of government, there is always a limit to the funds available. There is rarely enough money available to carry out all the functions which ideally ought to be performed. The significance of the budget process is that it is here where the decisions are made as to which new programs to launch and which old ones to expand, contract, or eliminate. These are decisions as to spending priorities, within the limits of estimated future income, and as such they represent important determinations of public policy.

Financial administration is not simply a matter of keeping books and records. The budgets, accounts, and detailed reports are essential, but only as tools for planning and carrying out the substantive programs of government in such a way as to make the wisest and most efficient use of resources available. Financial administration is an inextricable part of management responsibility, not a mere appendage to it. Every executive's budget is a plan of operation and reflects the executive's best thinking as to the work which should be undertaken and how it should be executed. The chief executive's financial plan for the entire jurisdiction represents his judgment as to the services that should be provided and how they should be financed. The legislative body makes the final determinations as to the expenditures and revenue measures to authorize, and it regards this, not as a routine matter, but rather as one of its most important responsibilities.

Specifically, in addition to budgeting, the components of financial administration are accounting, auditing, purchase and supply management, tax administration, and treasury management. The last two are specialized fields of administration which are not appropriate for detailed treatment in an introductory textbook. Broadly speaking, financial administration also includes fiscal policy and government's role in regard to economic stabilization. Since courses in public finance take up these problems, they are not covered in this book. We will concentrate on financial administration as part of management planning.

The problem of organization for financial administration has been a serious one, because there has been a history of scattering of finance functions with consequent duplication and lack of coordination. A strong belief in "checks and balances" led many state and municipal governments to assign parts of the finance responsibility to a number of different elective officials, each independent of one another and none subject to effective control by the chief executive of the jurisdiction. The theory was that these officials would watch one another, to the resultant benefit of the public. In practice, however, "they were able to detect only the gross violations of fiscal provisions, so crude were their methods and records in most cases."[1] With reference to the cities, the International City Managers' Association concludes that "in fact, there was no financial administration in those days."[2] The same could be said of most state governments.

THE INTEGRATED FINANCE DEPARTMENT

Beginning around 1913, some city and state governments acted to concentrate responsibility for financial administration in an integrated department of finance, placed under the direct control of the chief executive. It was during this period that the concept of financial administration as part of management planning began to emerge.

[1] *Municipal Finance Administration*, Chicago, Ill.: International City Managers' Association, 1962, p. 21.

[2] *Ibid.*, p. 20.

Budget offices were created for the first time. Today most governmental experts recommend the creation of such integrated departments and in recent years there has been a definite trend to establish them in the states and cities. Some scattering of finance functions, however, still exists in many jurisdictions.

Figure 10 shows the form of financial organization recommended by the National Municipal League in its *Model City Charter*.[3] This document is often consulted by charter-review and other groups charged with making proposals for changes in existing municipal governments or for establishing new ones. Reviewing the essential elements of this plan, we see that it clearly establishes the responsibility of the city manager as the chief executive for finance matters. In mayor-council cities, the same principle would be followed, with the department of finance under the mayor. The department is broken down into five divisions: accounts, budget, assessments, purchasing, and treasury. The department head is appointed by the manager and serves at his pleasure. Division chiefs are selected by the department head. In smaller cities, some of the functions, such as accounting and budgeting, would probably be combined.

Some cities prefer to place the budget staff directly in the chief executive's office. It is argued that this is necessary to ensure that the chief executive maintains as close control as possible over the budget function. In other cities, effective working relationships have been established between the chief executive and the budget staff in the Department of Finance. In other words, either plan for location of the budget function may work satisfactorily, depending on the circumstances in the particular jurisdiction.

In its draft of a *Model State Constitution*, the Committee on State Government of the National Municipal League also recommended an integrated finance department for state governments. Explaining Article VII of this Constitution, A. E. Buck states that what is contemplated is a finance department having the following bureaus or divisions: (1) budget; (2) accounting; (3) treasury; and (4) purchasing. In smaller states, the department might also include a division of taxation to administer the state tax system. In the larger states, a separate tax department would be required. Buck points out that, while several states have located the budget function directly

[3] *Model City Charter*, New York: National Municipal League, 1941. pp. 36–45 deal with the Department of Finance.

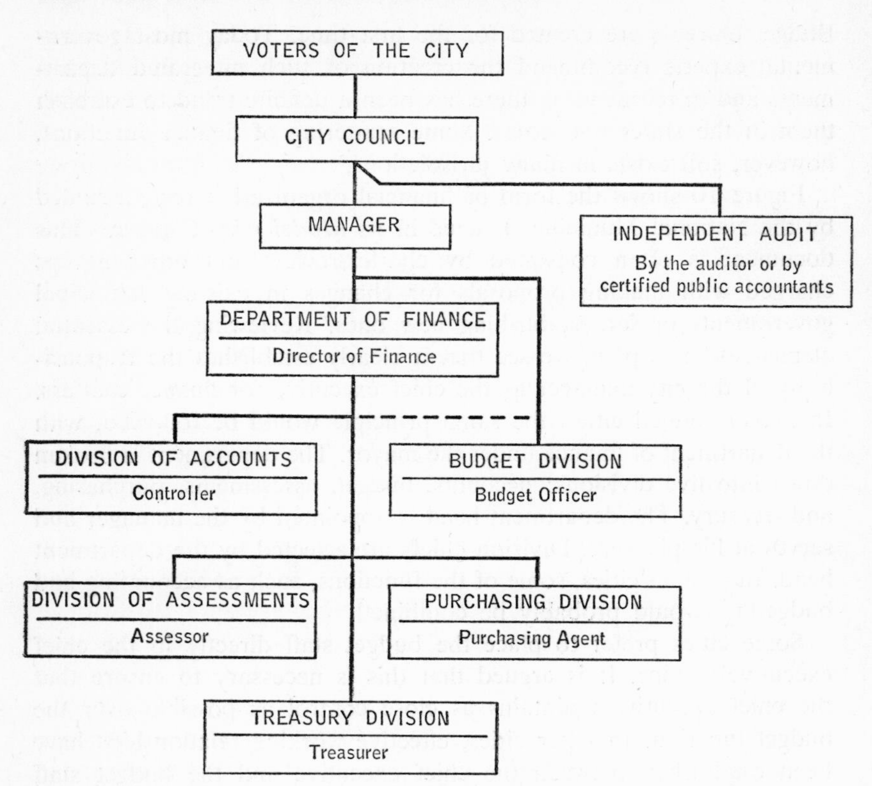

Fig. 10. Organization chart, Department of Finance. Based on Model City Charter Plan (Large City). From *Municipal Finance Administration*, Chicago: International City Managers Association, 1962, p. 23.

in the governor's office, this is usually the case when no integrated finance department exists. When one is established, the budget staff is usually transferred to it.[4]

ORGANIZATION ARRANGEMENTS AT THE NATIONAL LEVEL

In the national government, there is no one department in which the principal finance functions are placed. Since 1939, the Bureau of the Budget has been a part of the Executive Office of the President.

[4] *Model State Constitution*, New York: National Municipal League, 1948, pp. 40–44.

When originally established in 1921, it was placed in the Treasury Department. Franklin D. Roosevelt's Committee on Administrative Management recommended that the budget function be placed directly under the President, so that it could be coordinated with other staff services to the Chief Executive. Since 1939, there has been no strong movement to return the Budget Bureau to the Treasury, although this was recommended by a Task Force of the first Hoover Commission. This Task Force wanted the Treasury Department to "be so reorganized that it would be a real department of finance."[5] All nonfiscal units, such as the Coast Guard, the Bureau of Narcotics, and the Secret Service were to be transferred to other departments. The reorganized Treasury Department would be responsible only for genuine finance functions, on an integrated basis. In addition to budgeting, it would have control over the administrative accounting system of the government. This would have meant removing this function from the General Accounting Office (GAO), a change which has never been made and could only be accomplished by amending the Budget and Accounting Act of 1921, which legislation established both the Budget Bureau and the GAO. The Treasury Department would retain its responsibility for collection of taxes, custody and disbursement of funds, operation of the Mint and the Bureau of Engraving and Printing, and management of the debt. These recommendations were accepted by neither the Hoover Commission nor Congress. The Treasury Department still retains the above-mentioned nonfiscal functions; it has neither gained nor lost any finance functions.

Purchasing and supply in the federal government originally was also a responsibility of the Treasury Department, but it is now one of the functions of the General Services Administration (GSA), which was established in 1949, largely as the result of a recommendation of the first Hoover Commission. It is responsible for providing a variety of general administrative services to the other agencies. We will be concerned with its purchase and supply operations in some detail in Chapter 20. Among its other responsibilities are those for the national archives, records administration, public buildings, and transportation and communications services. The GSA is

[5] Commission on Organization of the Executive Branch of the Government, *Task Force Report on Fiscal, Budgeting, and Accounting Activities*, Washington, D.C.: Government Printing Office, 1949, p. 2.

not a part of the Executive Office of the President. It is one of numerous independent offices and establishments, the heads of which report directly to the President. Proposals have been made to place it in the Executive Office, where it could be integrated with other staff services, but there seems to be no immediate prospect that such action will be taken. It has clearly been established, however, that the President has overall responsibility within the executive branch for financial planning and administration. Better arrangements for the financial functions under him may be made in the future, but the basic problems of finance in the federal government today are not questions of internal assignment of responsibilities within the executive branch. The fundamental need is for improvements in the financial-planning process itself, a subject dealt with in the succeeding chapters.

BIBLIOGRAPHY

Commission on Organization of the Executive Branch of the Government, *Task Force Report on Fiscal, Budgeting, and Accounting Activities,* Washington, D.C.: Government Printing Office, 1949.

International City Managers' Association, *Municipal Finance Administration,* Chicago, Ill., 1962. Chap. 2.

Lepawsky, Albert (ed.), *Administration, the Art and Science of Organization and Management,* New York: Knopf, 1949. Chap. 15.

National Municipal League, *Model City Charter,* New York, 1941.

National Municipal League, *Model State Constitution,* New York, 1948.

Nigro, Felix A. (ed.), *Public Administration, Readings and Documents,* New York: Holt, Rinehart and Winston, 1951. Chap. V.

President's Committee on Administrative Management, *Report with Special Studies,* Washington, D.C.: Government Printing Office, 1937.

CHAPTER 18

The Executive Budget System

It was stated in the previous chapter that financial administration is an inextricable part of the management responsibility, yet not too long ago chief executives at all levels of government did not control the budget. In the case of the national government before 1921, there was no real budget, in the modern sense of a carefully conceived plan for making expenditures in terms of essential needs and within the limits of available financial resources. The procedure followed was for the departments and agencies to prepare estimates of proposed expenditures for the future budget period and send them to the Treasury Department. The Treasury did not make any changes in these estimates; it simply transmitted them to Congress. The President was not consulted. All he could do was make his views on financial problems known to Cabinet members and other department heads. Congress was anxious to retain for itself complete control over the government's finances. Originally, it was the Treasury Department's own decision that it should make no changes in the estimates. Later, Congress gave it no discretion at all by passing legislation prohibiting the Secretary of the Treasury from making any changes. This action evidenced Congress' clear desire to play the role of financial manager for the government.

Within Congress, for the first 75 years (1789–1864), both expenditure and revenue measures were acted upon by the House Ways and Means Committee. It was not until after the Civil War that the

House created a Committee on Appropriations. From 1865 to 1885, this new Committee was charged with consideration of expenditure bills, while the Ways and Means Committee continued to work on tax measures. In 1885, a new procedure was adopted, requiring the referral of appropriation bills to a half dozen or more committees instead of the Committee on Appropriations. The committees considering expenditures did not coordinate their activities, with resulting confusion. A department's request for funds might be refused by one committee, but upon application to another, be approved. The Senate also established this same "multiple committee system." Expenditure requests were not examined with proper care, money was wasted on unjustified projects, and overspending, leading to deficiency appropriations, was very common.

This haphazard and inefficient procedure was tolerated basically because, in this period of American history, the Treasury was full. Indeed, the protective tariff brought in so much revenue that surpluses at the end of the fiscal year were typical. In December, 1887, President Cleveland sent a message to Congress in which he said:

> You are confronted at the threshold of your legislative duties with a condition of the national finances which imperatively demands immediate and careful consideration. The amount of money annually exacted, through the operation of present laws, from the industries and necessities of the people largely exceeds the sum necessary to meet the expenses of the government.

To Cleveland, "this wrong inflicted upon those who bear the burden of national taxation" multiplied "a brood of evil consequences." It made of the Treasury "a hoarding-place for money needlessly withdrawn from trade and the people's use, thus crippling our national energies . . . and inviting schemes of public plunder."[1]

With revenues so ample, there was no sustained pressure for economies. This situation was soon to change, however. By the turn of the century, federal outlays had increased greatly due to the expansion of governmental functions required to meet the demands of a more complex society, as well as to meet the costs of the Spanish–American War. Whereas federal expenditures ran between $300 and $400 million in the 1890s, by 1909 they were nearly $700

[1] Jesse Burkhead, *Government Budgeting*, New York, Wiley, 1956, pp. 11–12.

million. Deficits were recorded from 1894 through 1899, after many years of sizeable surpluses. No longer could a surplus confidently be expected at the end of each fiscal year. The financial situation became increasingly tight, to the extent that during the first year that Taft was President, a deficit of $89 million out of a total budget of $694 million was incurred.[2]

THE MOVEMENT FOR THE EXECUTIVE BUDGET

Meanwhile important developments were taking place in some of the states and cities. In 1906, the New York Bureau of Municipal Research was established. It immediately became active in urging governmental reform and the use of more efficient financial practices. As a result of its efforts, New York City adopted a budget system for its health activities, the budget-reform movement spread to other cities, and "by the mid-20's most American cities had undergone a more or less thorough reform in municipal financial practices and had established some sort of a budget system."[3] The process was hastened by the financial pinch resulting from increased expenditures for schools, paved roads, and other required services, accompanied by loss of revenue from the sale of alcoholic beverages after the passage of the 18th Amendment. Businessmen now began to give strong support to budgetary reform. They were interested in economy and in keeping taxes down. More efficient financial administration was to them a first step in that direction. They were joined by others in the community who also believed that more systematic finance procedures would eliminate much of the corruption in municipal governments in the awarding of contracts and in other financial transactions.

There was the same movement in the states as in the cities to introduce budget reform as a means of realizing economies and also to eliminate dishonest practices. In 1910, the first state law authorizing the governor to prepare a budget for submission to the legislature was passed. Other states followed suit, and by 1920, 44 states had taken action to improve their budget procedures.[4]

Leaders in the budget-reform movement in the states and the

[2] *Ibid.*, pp. 15–17.
[3] *Ibid.*, p. 14.
[4] *Ibid.*, pp. 21–25.

cities naturally also directed their attention to the situation in the national government. Concerned by the lack of an efficient system of financial planning, President Taft in 1909 asked Congress to provide funds for a thoroughgoing study of the administrative organization and the financial and other management practices of the federal government. When, in the following year, Congress voted the funds, the President named a Commission on Economy and Efficiency to make the necessary studies. Significantly, he appointed Frederick A. Cleveland, who at the time was also Director of the New York Bureau of Municipal Research, to be chairman of this Commission.

Report of Taft's Commission on Economy and Efficiency

In June, 1912, Taft transmitted to Congress the Commission's historic report on "The Need for a National Budget," which strongly recommended making the President responsible for preparation of the budget. The Commission made clear that it did not consider that the United States had a real budget system. According to its own definition, a budget was a "proposal to be prepared by the administration and submitted to the legislature." Under the procedure then followed, Congress received the estimates directly from officials in the spending departments acting as "agents of the legislature." This procedure should be reversed so as to make effective the President's leadership as the head of the administrative branch. The proper relationship was for the executive branch to "submit a statement to the Legislature which would be its account of stewardship as well as its proposals for the future." Congress could most effectively exert control at the point of reviewing the budget proposed by the President and deciding whether or not to vote the requested appropriations. In other words, an "executive" rather than a "legislative" budget would far better serve the interests of the nation.[5]

Congress, however, was in no mood to approve an executive budget. When it learned that Taft was planning to submit to it a sample budget for the fiscal year 1914, it promptly passed legislation requiring that persons charged with the duty of preparing estimates were to do so only in the form and at the time stipulated by existing

[5] See Dwight Waldo (ed.), *Ideas and Issues in Public Administration*, New York: McGraw-Hill, 1953, p. 293.

law. Taft's position was that he had the constitutional power to prepare estimates and send them to Congress, but the latter body quickly made clear that it would not accept presidential leadership in budget matters. Taft went ahead anyway and submitted the sample budget, which had been prepared by his Commission on Economy and Efficiency. At the same time, however, he instructed the department heads to make their usual submission of estimates to Congress. The President's budget was referred to the House Committee on Appropriations which gave it no consideration.

While Taft failed in his effort to obtain Congressional acceptance of an executive budget, he and his Commission on Economy and Efficiency clearly laid the groundwork for later approval of this essential reform. The public was educated in the need for better financial practices, and various influential professional and business groups continued the campaign to persuade the Congress to act. The financial strains of World War I finally brought victory for the advocates of a national budget system. The debt had climbed so high as to cause great concern, and the tax burden had been greatly increased.

Passage of Budget and Accounting Act of 1921

Public pressure finally led Congress to pass in June, 1921, the Budget and Accounting Act.[6] It provided for an executive budget and created the Bureau of the Budget as the President's staff arm for preparing and executing the budget. From a world standpoint, the legislation came late; before its passage the United States had been the only major country which did not operate under a national budget system.

The modern period of financial administration in the federal government thus begins with the enactment of the Budget and Accounting Act in 1921. Initiation of the executive budget was naturally no panacea; the problem remains of developing detailed procedures and practices which make the executive budget system a success in

[6] For the text of this Act and important financial legislation later passed by Congress, see *Financial Management in the Federal Government*, 87th Congress, 1st Session, Senate Document No. 11, Washington, D.C.: Government Printing Office, 1961, Part VIII: "Appendixes," pp. 275–369.

practice. Obtaining the executive budget was, however, the essential starting point. Today, it also exists in most state and municipal governments. In numerous county and rural governments, however, the legislative budget is still in force. For example, in many counties, the board of supervisors appoints a committee from its members to prepare the budget. This committee receives the expenditure estimates directly from the county department heads. The county treasurer supplies it with the revenue estimates. In these jurisdictions, there is no one administrative officer responsible for preparation and execution of the budget; execution of the budget once approved is left to the spending departments, and "under these circumstances the absence of executive authority with responsibility for either review or financial planning, or for execution, makes of budgeting little more than a bookkeeping operation."[7]

ESSENTIALS OF AN EXECUTIVE BUDGET SYSTEM

An Adequate Budget Staff

A first necessity for the executive budget system to be a success is the existence of an adequate budget staff to assist the chief executive. The work of carefully reviewing the expenditure estimates is time consuming and cannot be performed well if the chief executive and his budget officer do not have adequate help. In some governments where executive budgets exist, results are unsatisfactory because the budget staff is so undermanned that it is unable to make a critical review of proposed expenditures. Several years ago the Governor of Missouri frankly told the legislature that, unless it authorized funds for additional members of his budget staff, he could not assure it that his expenditure proposals could be justified. There simply was no opportunity with the limited staff available to make a careful review of the spending requests of the administrative agencies. The legislature acceded to the Governor's request, the budget staff was expanded, and Missouri now has a much more effective executive budget system.

Until 1939, when the recommendations of Franklin D. Roosevelt's

[7] Burkhead, *op. cit.*, p. 86.

Committee on Administrative Management substantially increased the staff, the national Bureau of the Budget employed less than 50 persons. With such a tiny staff in the years from 1921 to 1939, it naturally could not do a really effective job of expenditure review. Understaffing, however, was not the only problem. In the early years of its history, the Bureau had limited impact largely because of its own narrow conception of its role. As we have seen, the partisans of economy had joined ranks with the professional students of government in urging adoption of the executive budget. The political scientists viewed budget reform as essential, not only to eliminate waste, but also as a means of making government more effective with its services to the community. Economy *per se* was not their objective, but a strong, efficient government, with high levels of expenditures if public needs so required. It was the economy point of view, however, that dominated the Bureau's thinking during these first years. With the emphasis on economies, use of the budget as an instrument of advance planning of government programs did not develop. Parsimony too often was the watchword, not program planning through the budget.

The Management Approach to Budgeting

A second essential requirement is adoption of the management approach to budgeting. Not only was the Budget Bureau's staff increased after 1939, but its whole approach to the budget job was changed. Roosevelt's Committee on Administrative Management conceived of the Bureau as a managerial agency of the President which should be responsible for the formulation and execution of the budget as a national fiscal plan.[8] Since 1939, the Bureau has reflected what Frank P. Sherwood and others call the "management approach" to budgeting.[9] Instead of viewing the budget as a collection of figures and thus a subsidiary of the accounting system, it is thought of basically as a plan of operations for the jurisdiction.

This "management approach" is now increasingly taking hold both

[8] See *Financial Management in the Federal Government, op. cit.*, pp. 13–17, for summary of the Committee's finance and other recommendations.

[9] Frank P. Sherwood, *The Management Approach to Budgeting*, Brussels: International Institute of Administrative Sciences, 1954, pp. 10–12.

in business and government, and is applicable to all aspects of financial administration, not just budgeting. Joseph Pois, in a 1962 review of the role of the financial manager, stresses that it was not until the latter "broke the relatively narrow confine of his responsibilities" that he became an effective member of the management team:

> As long as financial management permitted its perspective to be narrowly defined or circumscribed by the technical accounting field, the separation and aloofness of financial management was that much more resistant to any corrective or remedial action. In fact, there is a definite incompatibility between the ostensible precision, unbending attitude, indiscriminate concern with minutia and exaggerated impersonality too frequently attributed—and not entirely without justification—to the accountant and the dynamic, creative, and flexible approach that is implicit in effective management.[10]

It should be made clear that there are still many enterprises, both public and private, in which financial managers do not yet have this broad conception of their responsibilities. Furthermore, adopting the "management approach" as a guiding principle does not solve all problems. It is necessary to develop techniques and methods which make that approach effective in practice. The transition from the "old" and the "new" in financial administration is also very difficult. As we shall see shortly, legislators, for example, resist changes in the long-established ways of preparing budgets and presenting financial data. Intellectually, they can see the advantages of the changes; emotionally, they cling to the traditional practices. Concerned with maintaining control, they are afraid that the "management approach," no matter how much more efficient, may have the effect of lessening their authority.

Applying the Management Approach to Budget Preparation

Thus, the third necessity is to develop the budget in such a way as to make it of maximum use as a tool of management. This is the problem with which budget agencies have been concerned for many years. As we shall see, notable improvements have been made, but

[10] Joseph Pois, "Evolutionary Role of the Financial Manager," *The Federal Accountant*, XI, No. 3 (March, 1962), 38–39.

much still remains to be accomplished. If governmental agencies were small and their programs limited, the problem would be much easier. What makes it so very difficult is that governmental activities and budgets have grown so greatly. Developing refined budgetary techniques for so huge a volume of operations represents a monumental task.

Deficiencies of Object-of-Expenditure Budgeting

For many years, budgets of public agencies in the United States were presented on an object-of-expenditure basis. The "object" is what the money is used for, such as personal services, supplies and materials, equipment, travel, printing and binding, and rental of buildings. A typical budget consisted of a detailed listing of the positions to be filled, followed by the recommended amounts to be spent on each object of nonpersonal services. Three columns of figures frequently were shown: first, the actual expenditures for each object in the last complete fiscal year; second, the estimated amounts to be expended on them during the current fiscal year; and, third, the sums desired for each object for the future fiscal year. A budget of this type could quickly be put together without the need for careful planning of future work programs. All that was necessary was to obtain a list of the existing positions, make the usual request for some additional ones and for certain salary increases, and then make some quick and usually quite liberal guesses as to what would be needed for such objects as travel, supplies, and equipment. The head of the agency and his principal lieutenants could quickly hammer out a budget in this way. Particularly in the relationships with the central budget staff for the jurisdiction, this became more a bargaining than a planning process. Estimates were frequently padded in anticipation of the cuts of the "hatchet boys" in the budget bureau. The process was highly unscientific, to say the least.

Object-of-expenditure budgeting in practice becomes rule-of-thumb budgeting. A division head who is asked to present his estimates in terms of what he needs to spend for individual positions, telephone service, and the like does not have to develop detailed plans. Previous years' expenditures as recorded in the accounts provide him with the basis for his estimates for the future fiscal period. This is why the traditional approach to budgeting tended to make it a subsidiary of the accounting system. The emphasis was on figures, supported by past cost data, but without any real indication of how effectively the agency was conducting its programs.

Fundamentally, budgets prepared on this basis left unanswered the really important question: exactly what work was proposed and what accomplishments were anticipated, compared with those realized in the past? This is the central consideration, because the real "object" of government is to provide necessary and useful services to the public in the most effective way possible. Certainly, what is spent on travel, telephone service, and the other traditional objects of expenditures is important, and extravagant expenditures on these items should not be tolerated. However, the detailed estimates of such expenses belong in the supporting schedules of the budget estimates, preceded by a clear statement of exactly what work is to be performed. It is not easy to develop work units or other objective measures of the work, but usually some concrete indication can be given of the purpose for which the money is to be used. What security is there in increasing or decreasing travel and other expenses if there is no way of knowing what impact such increases or decreases will have on the work programs of the agency? Legislators tend to feel that object-of-expenditure budgeting provides them with detailed control which is essential. Actually, it may give them very little control over what should be of most concern: the overall effectiveness of the agency program.

Performance Budgeting

The deficiencies of object-of-expenditure budgeting have been recognized for some time. As early as 1913, the Borough of Richmond in New York City developed budget estimates for public works activities in terms of physical work units like miles of streets flushed. Under the leadership of its first budget officer, William A. Jump, the United States Department of Agriculture had placed by the mid 1930s its budgeting on a functional basis, with the estimates shown by clearly defined projects under each appropriation.[11] Most other federal agencies, however, continued to budget principally on an

[11] See Ralph S. Roberts, "USDA's Pioneering Performance Budget," in a symposium, "Performance Budgeting: Has the Theory Worked?" *Public Administration Review*, XX, No. 2 (Spring, 1960), 74–75.

object-of-expenditure basis until after World War II and the publication of the reports of the first Hoover Commission.

The latter group severely criticized federal budgetary practices. "The Federal budget," it said, "is an inadequate document, poorly organized and improperly designed to serve its major purpose, which is to present an understandable and workable financial plan for the expenditures of the Government. The document has grown larger and larger each year as the Government's requirements have increased, but its general framework and method of presentation have not changed."[12] The Commission noted that the budget for 1949–1950 contained 1,625 closely printed pages, with about 1,500,000 words. Exactly what all this detail meant in terms of work proposed and accomplished was far from clear. Accordingly, the Commission recommended that "the whole budgetary concept of the Federal Government should be refashioned by the adoption of a budget based upon functions, activities, and projects."[13] It designated this the "performance budget." The term "program budget" has also come to be used by many people to mean the same thing.

In the vigorous efforts made to obtain Congressional approval of the first Hoover Commission's recommendations, the concept of the performance budget was given much publicity. In 1949, Congress approved an amendment to the National Security Act providing for performance budgeting in the Defense Department.[14] In January, 1950, President Truman sent to Congress the first budget for the entire federal executive branch prepared on a performance basis. Quite a few jurisdictions have adopted the principle of the performance budget. It has been used in large cities, such as Los Angeles, San Diego, Detroit, Denver, and Cleveland, as well as in smaller municipalities. It is also being adopted in a growing number of state governments. For the country as a whole, though, performance budgeting has by no means replaced the traditional methods. Even in a state so progressively administered as California, in late 1962 its Legislative Assembly Interim Committee on Ways and

[12] Commission on Organization of the Executive Branch of the Government, *Budgeting and Accounting*, Washington, D.C.: Government Printing Office, 1949, pp. 7–8.

[13] *Ibid.*, p. 8.

[14] See *Financial Management in the Federal Government, op. cit.*, pp. 332–333.

Means found it necessary to recommend that "the emphasis in budget planning and presentation should be shifted *from* itemized detail of people to be hired and things to be bought *to* programs to be accomplished and data about what it costs to get the desired results, with established work standards."[15] In early 1964, however, steps were being taken in California to shift to performance budgeting.

DIFFICULTIES IN IDENTIFYING UNITS OF WORK. Even in the jurisdictions using the performance approach important problems remain to be solved. The changeover from budgeting on an object-of-expenditure basis to making the budget a real work plan is far from easy. In some governmental activities, units of work can be readily identified. Examples are tons of garbage collected, miles of new roads paved, acres of land reclaimed, and numbers of trees planted. In most government programs, however, the work is of such a nature that work units like these cannot be developed. Unfortunately, in the early enthusiasm for performance budgeting, it was erroneously assumed by some people that production units could be identified in all or most government programs. On the other hand, the fact that such measurements are unavailable does not mean that the programs in question cannot be budgeted for on a performance basis. So long as the estimates are made in terms of work activities, and the program is broken down into its constituent parts, this is performance budgeting, even if quantitative measures of the work cannot be developed. As Jesse Burkhead stresses, "for many programs the work process or the activity must serve as the performance unit."

The personnel office is a convenient example. Its responsibility is to motivate the employees to put forth their best effort for the jurisdiction. The results it achieves are largely intangible; it produces no "end products which will effectively measure" its accomplishments. Some of its activities, like the number of applications processed and tests given, can be measured quantitatively, but the resulting statistics tell nothing conclusive about the effectiveness of the personnel program. Yet the budget for the personnel office can be prepared on a performance basis by breaking down its program into its constituent parts and showing the estimates separately for each major component.

[15] Assembly Interim Committee on Ways and Means, *Long Range Program and Budget Planning*, Sacramento, Calif.; September, 1962, p. 3.

Burkhead suggests that the breakdown into activities might be as follows: general administration; recruitment and examination; reclassification; training; maintenance of records; employee relations; research in classification; and administration of welfare programs. Each such activity can be described concretely in the budget, and the anticipated changes in work load indicated.

The advantage of budget presentation on this basis is that it shows "what government is doing." This is exactly what budgeting by object-of-expenditure does not show. The comparison to make is with the traditional methods, not with the areas of government where physical work units can be used. Every effort possible should be made to prepare the budget on the basis of objective measurements of the work, but performance budgeting should not be abandoned in frustration simply because it is difficult to develop such measurements.

INCONCLUSIVE NATURE OF SOME WORK MEASUREMENTS. As a matter of fact, data based on quantitative work units are not necessarily conclusive. A reforestation service cannot make comparisons of accomplishments simply on the basis of the number of trees planted during different periods. In one year, most of the trees may be planted in valleys; in another, they may have to be planted on hillsides, a much more difficult operation. The work is not as comparable as the work unit makes it seem. Similarly, figures on the number of miles of new road paved need to be interpreted with the same care. The terrain may make it much more difficult to build certain stretches of road than others. The completed product will also vary in quality. Some trees and some sections of road will be of superior quality, others will only meet minimum standards. Accomplishment is not equal, even though the number of work units produced is the same.[16]

The same reservation about the validity of some of the work units being used is made by Marion L. Henry and Willie Proctor in an article on performance budgeting in the New York State Health Department. They point out that the "work unit, X-ray Examination, does not differentiate between routine chest X-rays and a time-consuming planigrafic series which requires a number of exposures."[17]

[16] Burkhead, *op. cit.*, pp. 143–144.

[17] Marion L. Henry and Willie Proctor, "New York State's Performance Budget Experiment," in "Performance Budgeting: Has the Theory Worked?", *op. cit.*, 73.

When they wrote this article, all laboratory examinations were grouped in the budget under the heading of Laboratory Tests. Illustrating the difficulty in developing performance units which are not misleading, the classification Major Operations was being used for surgery requiring from one to six hours. To make the problem even more complex, sometimes a large number of a particular work unit indicates failure rather than success. The number of purchasing orders, for example, may be considered an invalid work unit for the central purchasing office, because the latter was created precisely in order to combine requisitions and keep purchasing orders down.[18] Of course, this is no argument against developing the work units. It is rather an explanation of the need to select valid ones and to make careful judgments in interpreting the work data based on them.

Besides the difficulty in identifying objective measures of the work, performance budgeting, particularly in large organizations, sometimes suffers from what one federal official has termed "ponderosity," meaning the paper work required in developing activity breakdowns and recording the corresponding work-load data:

> Eternal vigilance is necessary to prevent the sheer weight of paper work from overshadowing the value of the system. Once the performance budget concept was adopted throughout the executive branch and formally implemented in the 1951 budget, there was a natural tendency to refine and extend the classification of budget activities wherever possible. This resulted to some extent in development of functional classifications to assemble detail beyond what budget making or efficient management demanded.[19]

This is not offered as an argument against performance budgeting, but rather to point to one of the important lessons learned from experience with performance budgeting, namely, that there is this tendency to go into excessive detail. Most budget experts are convinced that the extra effort required in budgeting on a performance, rather than object-of-expenditure, basis is clearly justified.

Long-Range Budgeting

Traditional practice has been to prepare budgets for a one-year period. However, if the budget is to be a tool of management, it

[18] Vernon E. Koch, "Cincinnati's Budget Developments," *Ibid.*, 83.
[19] Roberts, *op. cit.*, 78.

should also function as an instrument of long-range planning. For some years now, progressive private companies have planned their spending and investment programs years ahead. In 1959, a group of business leaders recommended that estimates of both revenues and expenditures in the federal government be prepared for as much as four and five years ahead. In the closing days of the Eisenhower Administration, its Budget Director issued an official projection of the budget for a ten-year period, from 1960–1970.

It was not until the estimates were prepared for the fiscal year 1963, however, that the agencies were requested by the Budget Bureau to develop their estimates for more than one year ahead. Specifically, they were asked to prepare them for a five-year period. Elmer B. Staats, Deputy Director of the Budget Bureau, explains:

> If we are to make sensible decisions about the Federal budget—expenditures and revenues alike—we must think in terms, not of annual budgets only, but of the budget outlook for a span of years. It should be clear that many decisions which we make today will affect Federal expenditures and our domestic and international posture for years to come. When we start on a Polaris submarine program or adopt a commitment for the manned exploration of the moon within a decade, we are in fact committing future resources. The same applies to other programs of the Federal government, for example, atomic energy, economic assistance to foreign governments, public highways, education, research, and aids to business and to agriculture.[20]

It should be made clear that expenditures continue to be requested by the President and approved by Congress for a one-year period only. The new feature is that decisions for the fiscal year immediately ahead are made as part of a tentative program of operations for a five-year period. As conditions change with each new fiscal year, the five-year projection can be modified accordingly. Thus, budgeting for a longer time span does not make for rigidity, rather it makes possible flexible planning.

The example set by the federal government in budgeting on a long-range basis may well influence many state and local jurisdictions to adopt a similar policy. A California Assembly Interim Committee recently recommended that each year's budget estimates in that state

[20] Elmer P. Staats, "Relationship of Budget Planning to Long-Range Planning," *The Federal Accountant*, XI, No. 3 (March, 1962), 29–30.

contain a five-year projection of both revenue and expenditures,[21] and also the Governor of Missouri requested the heads of all state agencies to submit their budget estimates in the future on a ten-year basis. Revenue estimating in Missouri was also placed on the same basis. The federal Bureau of the Budget considered using ten-year projections, but finally decided that there were too many uncertainties in the national picture to make it wise to go beyond five-year planning. In state and local governments, where the programs are more stable and the future somewhat easier to predict, ten-year plans may prove feasible. At this stage, no one can be absolutely sure what the time period should be. A growing number of persons, however, is convinced that one-year estimates are unsatisfactory. Long-range budgeting is really a logical culmination of performance budgeting. Once the emphasis is placed on the work to be accomplished, it becomes necessary to take a longer look than one year into the future.

There is ample precedent for long-range budgeting in the experience of many state and local jurisdictions with capital-improvement planning, that is, the planning of dams, roads, schools, streets and roads, water and sewerage systems, and any similar physical structures. These capital outlays have long life, and are to be distinguished from the current expenditures' category which is for goods consumed and services used during the period of the annual budget. These states and cities have for years kept up-to-date capital-improvement plans listing the projects to be undertaken over a future time period. For example, in some cities a six-year plan is prepared and then integrated each year into the municipality's budget. This is accomplished by making the first year's listing of improvement projects serve as the capital outlay part of the city's annual budget. Another year is then added to the plan so that it remains a six-year projection. To illustrate this, City A, which has a capital-improvement plan for the years 1965–1971, is considering its annual budget for 1966–1967. It examines the list of projects scheduled for this period, makes any changes it considers necessary in the light of changed conditions, and then incorporates the desired projects as the capital budget for 1966–1967. Another year is then added to the capital-improvements plan, so that it now covers the period 1966–1972. It should be

[21] Assembly Interim Committee on Ways and Means, *op. cit.*, pp. 13–16.

stressed that budget time each year provides opportunity for reviewing the plan as a whole, not just the projects scheduled for the fiscal year in question. The decision may be made to make changes in the projects scheduled for any one of the future years.

The problems are naturally not the same in planning physical-growth facilities as they are in making projections for other kinds of governmental activities. A longer look ahead can usually be taken in the case of physical improvements, but even these are subject to many uncertainties. The point is that some long-range budgeting is desirable and feasible for nonphysical growth as well.

Capital vs. Current Expenditures

Whether or not a jurisdiction adopts long-range budgeting, it should show the estimates for capital and current expenditures separately in the budget. If the estimates make no distinction between the two, some misleading impressions will be created and the budget will not function effectively as a management tool. For example, a capital improvement, such as a dam, has a life expectancy of a hundred years or more; "to charge the entire cost of a dam against a single year's operation would give a completely distorted picture of financial operations for that period. The actual fact is that a pre-payment is being made for 100 years of service; and the capital outlay cost should be pro-rated over that period of time."[22] Segregating the capital outlays from current expenditures also makes it possible to analyze the wisdom of proposed capital expenditures for one budget period in terms of the commitments they create for the future. The first year's cost frequently is only one installment, because large additional expenditures will be needed before the entire project can be completed. The legislature and the public will not be aware of these future commitments if they have no way of knowing which part of the budget is for capital outlays and which for current expenditures.

The first Hoover Commission recommended that the "budget estimates of all operating departments and agencies of the Government should be divided into two primary categories—current operating expenditures and capital outlays."[23] Since then, quite a few bills

[22] Sherwood, *op. cit.*, p. 47.

[23] Commission on Organization of the Executive Branch of the Government, *op. cit.*, p. 16.

have been introduced in Congress to make such segregation mandatory but, to date, none have been passed. Since 1931, however, the Bureau of the Budget has included in the budget document a special analysis which divides the expenditures into two categories: (1) those yielding benefits primarily in the current year, and (2) those yielding benefits primarily beyond the year in which they are made. However, the annual estimates for each department do not as yet show a breakdown between capital and operating expenditures.

In 1959, the Joint Economic Committee recommended adoption of a capital budget by the federal government. It said:

> We should also realize that a considerable amount of our national expenditures in any given year is for direct and indirect capital investments. In the Federal Government, unlike the sound accounting practices of private business, these are charged to operating expenses. Apparent deficits are, therefore, frequently not deficits at all. The adoption of sound budget principles which would separate capital outlays from operating charges is badly needed.[24]

THE QUESTION OF VALUE PREFERENCES

In closing this chapter, it must be stressed that adoption of the executive budget alone will not solve the fundamental question of *how to justify spending on one activity rather than another.* Should a community spend more money on schools than on highways? Should the military's request for additional funds be denied and programs such as federal aid for education and for improving local mass-transportation facilities be authorized instead? Desirable as it is, performance budgeting cannot solve this problem. All performance budgeting can do is to make clear the purposes of proposed expenditures and indicate the work results anticipated. It shows how many schools or roads would be built if certain proposed expenditures were approved by the legislature. The presentation of the estimates on a performance basis comes *after* the basic policy decisions on these matters have been made within the executive branch. The performance budget is a tool for implementing the policy decisions, not for making them.

[24] *Financial Management in the Federal Government, op. cit.,* pp. 250–251.

Competing requests for funds should, of course, be weighed very carefully. Funds should not be appropriated for projects of minor importance and denied for those urgently needed by the community. While this may be granted, it must still be realized that there is no exact science which can tell a jurisdiction how much to spend on one purpose and how much on another. The reason for this is clearly stated by Aaron Wildavsky:

> The budget is the life-blood of the government, the financial reflection of what the government does or intends to do. A theory which contains criteria for determining what ought to be in the budget is nothing less than a theory stating what the government ought to do. If we substitute the words "what the government ought to do" for the words "ought to be in the budget," it becomes clear that a normative theory of budgeting would be a comprehensive and specific political theory detailing what the government's activities ought to be at a particular time. A normative theory of budgeting, therefore, is utopian in the fullest sense of that word; its accomplishment and acceptance would mean the end of conflict over the government's role in society.[25]

One interesting proposal is to prepare the budget estimates in terms of alternatives. Instead of proposing one kind of activity or one level of expenditures, alternatives would be shown. Verne B. Lewis has outlined a plan under which officials would prepare a basic estimate, supplemented, however, by "skeleton plans for alternative amounts." In addition to stating the specific services to be provided if the basic budget were approved, the official would also "indicate the recommended revisions in the plan of service for each of the alternative amounts and the benefits or sacrifices which would result."[26] Lewis uses the analogy of architectural services in explaining the advantages of such a procedure: "The architect's advice as to whether I should spend eight, twelve, or sixteen thousand dollars for a house is not very helpful. On the other hand, the architect can be very helpful in advising me as to how I can get the most of what I want in a house for any given sum I choose to spend."[27] That the value

[25] Aaron Wildavsky, "Political Implications of Budgetary Reform," *Public Administration Review*, XXI, No. 4 (Autumn, 1961), 184.

[26] Verne B. Lewis, "Toward a Theory of Budgeting," *Public Administration Review*, XII, No. 1 (Winter, 1952), 49.

[27] *Ibid.*, 50.

of alternative estimates is recognized is seen in the fact that the Bureau of the Budget compiled a set of alternative forward projections for use by the President in establishing guidelines for the 1963 federal budget.[28] It is impossible to predict to what degree the alternative budget idea will be accepted in the future, but it does seem promising as a means of making budget determinations more meaningful.

BIBLIOGRAPHY

Appleby, Paul, "The Role of the Budget Division," *Public Administration Review*, **XVII,** No. 3 (Summer, 1957).

Burkhead, Jesse, *Government Budgeting*, New York: Wiley, 1956. Part II.

Caulcott, T. H., "The Control of Public Expenditure," *Public Administration*, **LV** (Autumn, 1962). Lucid account of differences in British and American systems of expenditure control.

Collins, E. A., "The Price of Financial Control," *Public Administration*, **LV** (Autumn, 1962).

Lawton, Frederick J., "Legislative–Executive Relationships in Budgeting as Viewed by the Executive," *Public Administration Review*, **XIII,** No. 3 (Summer, 1953).

Lewis, Verne B., "Toward a Theory of Budgeting," *Public Administration Review*, **XII,** No. 1 (Winter, 1952).

Massey, Robert J., "Program Packages and the Program Budget in the Department of Defense," *Public Administration Review*, **XXIII, No. 1,** (March, 1963).

Moak, Lennox L., and Bowman, Emma L., "A Long-Range Operating Program," *Public Administration Review*, **XX,** No. 1 (Winter, 1960).

Mosher, Frederick C., *Program Budgeting: Theory and Practice*, Chicago, Ill.: Public Administration Service, 1954.

Patterson, Kenneth D., "Legislative Budget Review: An Economist's Viewpoint," *Public Administration Review*, **XXIV,** No. 1 (March, 1964).

[28] *Organizing for National Security, The Bureau of the Budget and the Budgetary Process*, Senate Subcommittee on National Policy Machinery, 87th Congress, 1st Session, Washington, D.C.: Government Printing Office, 1961, p. 5.

"Performance Budgeting: Has the Theory Worked?" *Public Administration Review*, **XX,** No. 2 (Spring, 1960). Symposium of articles reporting experiences in public agencies using performance budgeting.

Shadoan, Arlene Theuer, "Developments in State Budget Administration," *Public Administration Review*, **XXIII,** No. 4 (December, 1963).

Sherwood, Frank P., *The Management Approach to Budgeting*, Brussels: International Institute of Administrative Sciences, 1954.

Waldo, Dwight (ed.), *Ideas and Issues in Public Administration*, New York: McGraw-Hill, 1953. Part IV.

CHAPTER 19

Steps in the Budget Process

PREPARATION AND APPROVAL OF BUDGET

The procedure for the preparation and approval of the budget varies greatly depending on the place. We will use two jurisdictions as examples: the City of San Diego and the federal government.

City of San Diego

In San Diego, usually around late October of each year, the City Manager schedules what are known as preliminary-budget conferences with the department and division heads. For example, on October 30, 1962, he sent a memorandum to department heads advising them of the schedule for such conferences as a basis for the 1963–1964 municipal budget. (In San Diego—as in the federal government—the fiscal year is from July 1 to June 30.) This schedule showed the day and time the particular department or division head was to meet with the City Manager and the City Budget Officer. Each conference lasted about an hour or less. The first one took place on December 5 and the last on December 21. The significance of these conferences is that the department and division heads were instructed to come prepared to discuss their future work plans. At this stage, they were not asked to present financial estimates, but rather to give their ideas as to the work which should be undertaken in 1963–1964. Specifically, they were told to be ready to discuss the following:

1. The status of the department or division's work program; its progress on recently added or expanded activities; and the areas in which it had been possible to make significant cost reductions.
2. Its recommendations as to new or expanded programs needed by the community, with supporting justifications.
3. Its proposals as to how existing levels of service could be expanded without increasing costs.
4. Its recommendations as to which existing programs to reduce or eliminate.
5. Its ideas as to the organization changes that might be made to increase efficiency.

Since San Diego uses a performance budget, these are logically the kinds of questions to put to department and division heads. In performance budgeting, as we have seen, the emphasis is on work planning, and money figures are not discussed during these preliminary conferences in order to avoid the temptation to request funds without a prior searching analysis of real needs and the possibility of economies. Shortly after announcement of the schedule for these conferences, the budget-estimate forms are sent to the departments on a staggered basis, and the departments are given different deadline dates for returning them to the Office of Administrative Management in which the San Diego budget staff is located.

By February, the completed estimate forms normally will have been returned from the individual departments, and members of the city's budget staff begin their detailed examination of them. They visit the offices of the departments and divisions concerned, ask for additional supporting data as needed, and, in general, seek an agreement with the initiating officials as to the amounts which should be requested. Disagreements which the analysts are unable to resolve are referred to the Budget Officer who, in turn, may decide to take the matter up with the City Manager. The department and division heads have the same privilege. As we saw in Chapter 4, as the chief line officer of the municipality, the Manager makes the final decisions as to the funds to request for each department. The City Manager has usually made up his mind by late April on the budget he will present to the San Diego City Council.

Beginning in February, the Budget Officer provides the Manager with forecasts of revenue for the following fiscal year. Since the future revenue picture is not clear at this early date, the Budget Officer also supplies the Manager with later estimates. When the budget goes to the City Council in the first part of May, the Manager has been able to make his determinations on the basis of the latest revenue estimates available.

The City Council considers the budget as a Committee of the Whole. The estimates are not sent to a finance committee, as in some other cities. Because the information on assessed valuations of property is not available until the third week in August, the Council passes a preliminary ordinance at its first meeting in July. The final ordinance is then approved on or before the fourth Tuesday in August, as required by the City Charter.

The ordinance is of an omnibus character, providing for all expenditures of the city government. Another ordinance fixes the tax rate and levies taxes for the fiscal year in question. In some jurisdictions, several different appropriation and tax ordinances are passed, which is why this point is noted. In San Diego, expenditures are authorized on a lump-sum, rather than a line-item, basis. This means that the funds are appropriated for general categories of expense, such as personal services, rather than for individual items such as one employee's salary or one piece of equipment. In a lump-sum budget, savings from unfilled positions can be used to fill other ones. In line-item budgeting—once used in many jurisdictions but now largely abandoned as too restrictive—the money could only be spent for the item shown on the particular line in the budget. Individual positions, pieces of equipment, and other details were all listed separately.

The Federal Government

The Expenditure Budget

In the federal government, the starting point is the departmental estimates of expenditures. Usually in April—and in some departments even earlier[1]—the budget officer, after conferring with the agency head, requests the division heads and other directors to make their estimates of expenditures for the next fiscal year. This is known as the "call for estimates"; it consists of budget request forms together with a statement of the policy assumptions upon which the estimates are to be based.In May and June, the director of the Bureau of the Budget initiates discussions with the department heads about the budget. The purpose of these conferences is to form some idea of each department's anticipated spending requirements. At the same time, the Bureau receives preliminary estimates of anticipated revenues from the Treasury Department. After consultation with the President, in late June or early July, the Bureau sends its call for estimates to the departments, together with an explanation of the Chief Executive's policy decisions as to permissible levels of spending.

Until very recently, the major departments were advised at this time of their spending "ceiling," as fixed by the President and the Director of the Budget. The purpose behind setting these "ceilings" was to try to bring together the estimates of both expenditures and revenues at an early stage in the budget process. As we shall see, the expenditure and the revenue sides of the federal budget have never really been coordinated. The "ceiling" device was one effort in that direction, but it was abandoned by the Kennedy Administration. As explained by Deputy Director of the Budget Staats, the Kennedy Administration preferred to use "planning guides which may be adjusted by the agency without violating Holy Writ."[2] Apparently it was convinced that the "ceilings" do not improve financial planning and may create undesirable rigidity.

The next step is for the departments to revise their internal budgets and to prepare their final estimates in accordance with the President's policy directives; this usually takes place in July and August. The departmental budget officer schedules meetings with the division

[1] The description of the federal procedure which follows is from two principal sources: budget officers' conference training material prepared by the Bureau of the Budget, and Jesse Burkhead, *Government Budgeting*, New York: Wiley, 1956, pp. 88–100. Dates for the various steps in the procedure are approximate because they vary from year to year.

[2] Elmer P. Staats, "Relationship of Budget Planning to Long-Range Planning," *The Federal Accountant*, XI, No. 3 (March, 1962), 34.

heads, and the final details of the departmental estimates are determined. The Budget Bureau usually requires the departments to submit their estimates by the middle or end of September. Some agencies send them in earlier, thus making it possible for the Bureau to get an early start on reviewing them. The Bureau has teams of budget examiners that specialize in reviewing the estimates of particular departments. These work groups first critically examine the estimates to determine the points which need to be clarified. They next hold hearings at which the agency officials are interrogated. The head of the examining group serves as chairman for these meetings, with the departmental budget officer helping the officials of the particular agency to defend their estimates. After making its decisions, the examining unit sends its recommendations to the Director of the Bureau of the Budget, and then what is known as the "director's review" is conducted. A committee, made up of division heads and other top officials of the Bureau, holds a meeting at which the examining team is asked to defend its recommendations. Representatives of the department concerned are invited to attend these meetings and given an opportunity to appeal the examining unit's recommendations. After this review is completed, the Director of the Bureau decides on the funds he will recommend that the President approve for the department in question. By the end of November, the hearings in the Budget Bureau and the director's review will normally have been concluded for all the agencies. About this time, the Budget Bureau receives the final estimates of revenues from the Treasury Department. With the expenditure and revenue information now ready, the next step is for the Bureau to put the budget document together. Usually, in the third week in January, the President sends his budget message and the accompanying estimates to Congress.

The budget goes first to the House Appropriations Committee. Article 1, Section 7, of the Constitution requires that all revenue measures be initiated in the House, but it does not so require in the case of appropriations. The practice has been traditional, however, for spending bills also to originate in the House. Although there is one budget, Congress takes action by approving a number of different appropriation bills—in recent years totaling about 15. Except for the military functions of the Defense Department which are covered in a single measure, these bills authorize expenditures for groups of agencies. After the President's budget is received, House Appropriations Committee subcommittees begin detailed consideration of the estimates for the agencies included in the appropriation bill or bills in which the subcommittee specializes.

The subcommittees hold hearings at which the departments concerned have another opportunity to be heard. Representatives of the Bureau of the Budget usually do not testify at these hearings. The task of defending the estimates is left to the departmental budget officer and other top officials of the department. Witnesses are almost always "official," that is, they represent government agencies, not the general public. When these hearings are over, the subcommittee meets in a closed session to agree on its recommendations to the Appropriations Committee. It then meets with the latter and explains its recommendations. Usually the Appropriations Committee will register no serious objections; it is recognized that the subcommittee members have made a detailed study of the estimates, whereas the full Committee has not. After the full Committee acts on the draft appropriation bill, it is reported for consideration on the floor of the House where it is treated like any other piece of legislation. The subcommittee chairman leads the debate, but he usually asks other subcommittee members to assume responsibility for defending certain parts of the bill. The House of Representatives itself usually makes few important changes in the Appropriations Committee's recommendations, and thus, the opinions and attitudes of the subcommittee and committee chairman are important.

After House action is completed, the appropriation bill is sent to the Senate where it is referred to that body's Appropriations Committee. The same procedure of referral to the appropriate subcommittee is followed. The subcommittee may go over the same ground as did its House counterpart by holding full-scale hearings. In recent years, the Senate has, however, sometimes followed what is known as the "protest" procedure. Under this arrangement, the departments concerned advise the Senate Appropriations Committee whether or not the House-approved version of the bill is satisfactory. If it is, no hearings are held on the Senate side. If it is not, the Senate appropriations subcommittee holds hearings, but with the emphasis placed on the features in the House bill to which objection is made. In such cases, the Senate serves as a court of appeal from the House. As any reader of newspapers knows, the Senate has, in recent years, often incurred the wrath of the House by restoring substantial portions of the cuts made in the lower chamber.

Almost always the House and Senate versions of the appropriation bill will not coincide. This makes a conference committee necessary, which is made up of representatives from the House and Senate Appropriations Committees designated by their respective chairmen. During the 87th Congress, the chairmen of these two committees became involved in a bitter dispute. The House Committee objected to the custom which had developed over the years of having a member of the Senate invariably preside over the conference-committee sessions. The Senate Committee offered to let a House member preside on occasion if the House would agree to let the Senate initiate some appropriations measures. The House, in turn, charged that this would be unconstitutional. The Senate passed a resolution on October 13, 1962, asserting its right to originate spending measures. It declared "its willingness to submit either for declaratory judgment by an appropriate appellate court of the United States or to an appropriate commission of outstanding educators specializing in the study of the English language to be chosen in equal numbers by the President of the Senate and the Speaker of the House."[3] House resentment over the Senate's habit of restoring cuts was clearly manifested during this dispute.

After the conference committee makes its report to both Houses, each House decides whether it wants to accept or reject. Either house may reject the report and request that the bill be sent back to conference for further consideration, but this seldom happens. By this time, the old fiscal year is just about to conclude, and there is great pressure to get the appropriation bill for the next fiscal year approved.

After action by both Houses on the conference-committee recommendations, the bill is sent to the President. Under the Constitution, he must reject or approve the bill as a whole. He does not have the item veto, which means that he cannot eliminate individual items in the bill; thus, Presidents almost never veto appropriation bills, since to do so would mean leaving the agencies altogether without funds when the new fiscal year begins. Time is not available to start the machinery of legislative consideration of the appropriation bill all over again. In signing, though, Presidents do not hesitate to indicate

[3] *Congressional Record*, October 13, 1962: 22191.

their disapproval of any expenditures they believe unwise. The budget authorizations, it should be added, are enacted on a lump-sum basis. It is not unusual, however, for Congress to restrict the amounts which can be spent for certain purposes, such as for administrative expenses or for certain categories of expenditures like printing and binding.

The Revenue Budget

For many years the President's budget message did not even deal with tax policy. It is only since 1954 that it has contained "more than a passing reference to taxation, and even recently this falls short of an extensive analysis."[4] Traditionally, Congress itself has exercised the predominant role in developing revenue policy, its instrumentalities being the all-powerful House Ways and Means Committee and the Senate Finance Committee. Presidents frequently have strong recommendations to make to these Committees on tax measures, but it is usually not until February or March that the Treasury Department submits the Administration's tax program to Congress. As Burkhead so aptly remarks, "as a result of this organizational and time-sequence separation, the budget of the United States is primarily an expenditure document."[5] President Kennedy's budget message to the Congress for the fiscal-year 1963–1964 did place great emphasis on tax policy; in fact, he dealt with the revenue side of the budget in the opening paragraphs and then followed with his expenditure recommendations. The explanation is that he was making the need for tax reductions and reforms one of the "must" measures in his legislation program for the first session of the 88th Congress.

Within Congress, consideration of expenditure and tax measures is not coordinated:

> The committees which pass on tax legislation have no lively sense of responsibility for bringing in tax proposals to meet proposed expenditures and to implement a consistent fiscal policy; similarly the Appropriations Committees are under no compulsion to keep expenditures within revenues. This separation has become so fixed in this country that when we speak of the federal budget we refer only to proposed expenditures; the revenue program is not regarded as a part of the budget.[6]

[4] Burkhead, *op. cit.*, p. 94.
[5] *Ibid.*
[6] Joseph P. Harris, "Needed Reforms in the Federal Budget System," *Public Administration Review*, XII, No. 4 (Autumn, 1952), 244.

Proposals to Improve Federal Budgetary Procedure

A number of proposals have been made to improve federal budgetary procedures. One suggestion is to shorten the period between initiation of the estimates and the beginning of the fiscal year in question. A Task Force of the second Hoover Commission reported that in the military services, preparation of the estimates began as much as 18 months before the opening of the fiscal year. In the Navy Department, the estimating process for fiscal 1954 started on February 14, 1952. In this case, Congress did not approve the appropriation until August 1, 1953, one month after the beginning of fiscal 1954. Thus, the complete budgetary cycle was 522 days. The Task Force was of the opinion that too much time was being spent trying to make detailed estimates of expenditures for the future fiscal year. With so long a budget cycle, "detailed estimates so laboriously compiled" often had to be "modified drastically or scrapped." In the Defense Department as a whole, "approximately 90 percent of the detailed estimates for materiel procurement were rendered practically useless as a result of last-minute basic policy changes."[7]

The solution was to start the estimating process at a later date and to reduce the amount of time required to prepare the estimates. Specifically, the Task Force recommended that "the period of budget preparation in the executive branch and consideration by the Congress should be shortened so that it is confined to 1 year immediately prior to the beginning of the fiscal period to which it relates." The estimating process within the agencies could be completed much faster if the agency budgets were prepared in more "simplified and concise form." Elimination of much of the detail in the estimates would also make it possible for Congress to spend less time reviewing the spending proposals. The difficulty is that Congress wants the estimates prepared in detail. Up to now, it has been unwilling to take action on the basis of "simplified" estimates. So long as it insists on detailed presentations, it will be very difficult to reduce the budget cycle materially.

Many people feel that expenditures could be better controlled, or

[7] Commission on Organization of the Executive Branch of the Government, *Task Force Report on Budget and Accounting*, Washington, D.C.: Government Printing Office, 1955, pp. 21–25.

their implications more clearly grasped at the time of authorization, if such coordination were achieved. Congress sought to deal with this problem with Section 138 of the Legislative Reorganization Act of 1946.[8] Section 138 provides that the House Ways and Means and Appropriation Committees, and the Senate Appropriations and Finance Committees shall annually meet jointly and, by February 15, report to their respective houses a "legislative budget for the ensuing fiscal year, including the estimated overall Federal receipts and expenditures for such year." Specifically, they are to recommend the "maximum amount to be appropriated for expenditure in such year." If the estimated receipts exceed the estimated expenditures, their report must contain a "recommendation for a reduction in the public debt." The report is to be accompanied by a resolution providing for its adoption by Congress. If the proposed expenditures exceed the estimated revenues, the resolution must include the following language: "That it is the sense of the Congress that the public debt shall be increased in an amount equal to the amount by which the estimated expenditures for the ensuing fiscal year exceed the estimated receipts, such amount being $---------."[9]

The maximum amount approved by Congress in this concurrent resolution was to guide the Appropriations Committees of both Houses in acting on the appropriation bills. Section 138 has not been repealed, but only on one occasion has Congress approved a legislative budget. This was for the fiscal year 1949, but even then Congress failed to keep within the ceiling amount, exceeding it by $6 billion. Congress found the legislative budget unworkable because it requires setting a limit on total expenditures very early in the session, long before a detailed review of the spending proposals of the executive agencies has been finished. As one Congressman said, "We can no more expect success, Mr. Speaker, with this well-meant but hopeless proposal than we can expect a verdict from the jury before it has heard the evidence."[10] It was further objected that it was unrealistic to put a ceiling on expenditures in view of the many unpredictable circumstances which may create the need for Congress to vote addi-

[8] For the details on the legislative budget, see *Financial Management in the Federal Government*, 87th Congress, 1st Session, Senate Document No. 11, Washington, D.C.: Government Printing Office, 1961, pp. 29–32.

[9] *Ibid.*, p. 30.

[10] *Ibid.*

tional funds later in the session. The time allowed for preparation of the legislative budget is short, and the joint committee, an unwieldy group of more than 100 members, was not adequately staffed to do its job.

Since the failure of the legislative budget, strong efforts have been made to obtain the creation of a Joint Committee on the Budget.[11] Senator McClellan of Arkansas, Chairman of the Senate Committee on Government Operations, introduced a bill for this purpose which was passed by the Senate in 1957 but not approved by the House. McClellan's bill would have created a Joint Committee on the Budget composed of 14 members, with the House and Senate Appropriations Committees each having seven representatives. Of these, four would have been from the majority party and three from the minority, as designated by the respective committees.

The basic purpose behind the creation of such a Joint Committee was to provide Congress with more adequate staff for reviewing the spending proposals of the executive branch. In general, it was hoped that such a committee would function in much the same manner as the Joint Committee on Internal Revenue Taxation, which is made up of members of the House Ways and Means and Senate Finance Committees, and which has a permanent professional staff that studies revenue proposals and gives the committee members expert advice. This professional staff has provided a valuable service, and it is felt that Congress could use similar help on the expenditures' side. McClellan's bill assigned functions to the proposed Joint Committee on the Budget which could only have been carried out effectively with the help of such a staff. Specifically, the proposed Joint Committee was to study the budget estimates in detail and make recommendations thereon to the Appropriations Committees. Similarly, it was to analyze the available information relating to the revenue side of the budget and propose a fiscal program to the Joint Committee which would meet essential spending requirements within the anticipated income. Not only was the Joint Committee to provide the Appropriations Committees with these analyses, but it was also to lend them the services of members of its staff during the periods when appropriation bills were being considered. In all, the Joint Committee, utilizing its expert staff, was to do everything possible to help the Ap-

[11] *Ibid.*, pp. 195–218.

propriations Committees and individual members of Congress in their review of the executive branch's spending proposals.

The Appropriations Committees do have some professional staff of their own, which is one reason the House Appropriations Committee objected to the McClellan bill. Its argument was that the Appropriations Committees of both Houses already had the authority to employ any additional staff needed. Some members of the House also feared that the Senate-approved McClellan bill might be an effort by the second chamber to have a say in introducing appropriations measures.

Still another proposal is that for an omnibus appropriation bill. Under the procedure of approving a number of different spending bills, neither the Appropriations Committees nor the members of each House know what the full tab for expenditures will be at the end of the session. The advantage of the omnibus bill is that it would make this total bill clear, even if it proved impossible to keep expenditures down to the level some Congressmen want. Legislation has been introduced in recent years to provide for an omnibus appropriations bill, but, although this proposal was twice approved in the Senate, it was not passed by the House. The House Appropriations Committee did decide to try the single package bill on a voluntary basis when considering the budget requests for the 1951 fiscal year. On March 21, 1950, it reported a single bill to the House which approved it on May 10, 1950. The Senate Appropriations Committee reported the bill to the Senate on July 8, 1950. It was approved with amendments by the Senate on August 4, sent to conference committee where it was considered for three weeks, and finally signed by the President on September 6, 1950. Late as this date is, it is true that the last appropriation bill for fiscal year 1950 was not passed until October 29, 1949.

Although its Chairman favored using the omnibus approach again in 1951, the House Appropriations Committee decided to drop it. For one thing, it was argued that Congressmen were in a much better position to vote against individual appropriation bills than to defeat a single measure containing such an enormous number of items. It was also objected that excessive delay was inevitably associated with an omnibus bill, because neither House could take any action on expenditures until its Appropriations Committee had finally completed consideration of the mammoth measure. Individual members of Congress were asked late in the session to vote on a single appropriation bill which they had no real time to study. Under the existing procedure of considering several different bills separately, the Congressman has time to study the reports of the Appropriations Committees on each bill and inform himself better on the issues.

These and other arguments were made against continuing the omnibus bill, but many Congressmen were of the opposite opinion. They felt that the experiment had been successful and should be continued. The objectives of the Legislative Reorganization Act of 1946 had been achieved, because Congress had known the total amount of the expenditures it was approving. The delay was not excessive, the individual Congressmen had had adequate opportunity to study the proposals in the omnibus bill, and the appropriation committees had done a careful job of reviewing the estimates. Whether or not the experiment was successful thus remains a matter of opinion, but the reality is that the omnibus bill idea will not be approved unless the House Appropriations Committee changes its mind.[12] Still, that the omnibus bill proposal is not dead is demonstrated by the fact that no sooner did the first session of the 88th Congress convene in January, 1963, than Senator Byrd, Chairman of the Finance Committee, introduced a resolution providing for the single package bill. Long an arch exponent of economy, he said that this was the only way to achieve effective control of federal spending.

Another objection to the omnibus bill is that it puts the President in the position of having to approve or disapprove *all* expenditure requests for the fiscal year in question. The President does not have the item veto, that is, the power to delete items from expenditure bills. As Article 1, Section 7, of the Constitution is worded, he must approve or reject the bill *in toto*. By contrast, in 42 of the 50 states, the governor now possesses the item veto. Consequently, the legislatures in these states tend to follow the governor's expenditure proposals much more closely than the national Congress does the President's. They know that the governor can delete any items they add to his budget of which he does not approve.

Numerous proposals have been made in Congress to give the President the item veto. Some of these have sought to accomplish the ob-

[12] *Ibid.*, pp. 229–236.

jective through the ordinary route of passing a new law. Others have been made in the form of a proposed amendment to the Constitution on the assumption that this was necessary. Quite a few Presidents, including Franklin D. Roosevelt, Truman, and Eisenhower, have urged that the Chief Executive be given this power. There has been much discussion of the matter in recent years, and the issue is still very much alive. Those in favor argue that, if he could eliminate or reduce items in appropriation bills, the President could save the taxpayers much money. They have in mind "log-rolling," the practice whereby Congressmen mutually help one another to obtain approval of spending projects desired by local constituents. Those opposed claim that the item veto would give the President too much power. Congressional control over the purse would be weakened, to the detriment of the nation. The Chief Executive might even use the item veto to intimidate Congressmen by threatening them with disallowing expenditures in their home districts unless they supported his policies.[13] Obviously, the item veto would strengthen the Presidency. Since this is the case, it is understandable why many Congressmen are reluctant to give the Chief Executive this power.

EXECUTION OF THE BUDGET

Once the appropriation bill or bills are passed by the legislative body, the budget must be executed. In some foreign governments, the legislative authorizations are not made directly to the administrative agencies but to the ministry of finance or budget office. The latter then controls the release of funds to the agencies and may reserve portions of the appropriations whenever it considers this necessary in the light of changing conditions affecting the nation's finances.[14] In the United States, with few exceptions, the funds are voted directly to the administrative agencies.

Control over expenditures, however, is exercised by the central budget office or staff through the system of apportionments. The United States Bureau of the Budget, exercising powers granted to it by law, requires the departments to submit requests for apportionments

[13] *Ibid.*, pp. 236–249.

[14] *Government Accounting and Budget Execution*, New York: United Nations, 1952, p. 14.

before any of the funds voted by Congress for the next fiscal year can be used. Legal provisions in the states and cities also typically provide for an apportionment system. In the federal service, the apportionments are usually made for a quarterly period; in some states and cities, they are made on a monthly basis. The purpose of the apportionments is to control the rate of spending so as to make deficiency appropriations unnecessary. Without such control, an agency might exhaust its funds before the end of the fiscal year. As previously noted, before passage of the Budget and Accounting Act of 1921, deficiency appropriations were quite common. Another reason for having an apportionment system is that it makes it possible to time expenditures with collection of taxes and receipt of other income. In this way, spending can be kept within income throughout the entire fiscal year, and there is no need to seek short-term loans in anticipation of later revenue.

If an agency does not spend all of its apportionment for a particular period, it is usually allowed to carry over the unused portion for expenditure in future periods. The Model City Charter authorizes the City Manager to revise the apportionments at any time during the budget year if he finds that the available income, plus balances from previous years, will be less than the total appropriations.[15] Similarly, the Model State Constitution gives the governor the power to reduce expenditures "whenever actual revenues fall below the revenue estimates upon which the appropriations were based, or when other changed circumstances warrant economies."[16]

The Controversy Over Impounding Funds

In the federal government, the Bureau of the Budget has from time to time impounded funds, that is, placed them in reserve, not for reasons of insufficient income but because the President does not believe it wise to make the particular expenditures. The justification given for impounding funds is that an appropriation is an authorization, rather than a mandate, to spend for a particular purpose.[17]

[15] *Model City Charter*, New York: National Municipal League, 1941, p. 39.

[16] *Model State Constitution*, New York: National Municipal League, 1948, p. 14.

[17] See Robert Ash Wallace, *Congressional Control of Federal Spending*, Detroit, Mich.: Wayne Univ. Press, 1960, pp. 144–146.

Although it has impounded funds on relatively few occasions, in recent years the Budget Bureau has done so in an area very sensitive to many Congressmen: defense appropriations and, in particular, weapons systems.

This issue came to a head in 1962 with the controversy over the desirability of putting more money into the development of the RS-70, the 2000-mile-an-hour bomber believed essential by the Air Force and its supporters in Congress. The position of President Kennedy and of Defense Secretary McNamara was that more money should not be spent on this project, because, by the time the RS-70 was operational, it would be obsolete because of expected further developments in missile warfare. Representative Carl Vinson, Chairman of the House Armed Services Committee, disagreed and also charged that when it impounded funds, the executive branch was exceeding its powers. Accordingly, he proposed that the House insert a provision in the appropriation bill ordering the Secretary of the Air Force to spend the sum Congress considered necessary on this project. A compromise agreement was later reached whereby Vinson dropped his request for such appropriation language, but the President also agreed to restudy the RS-70 question. Congress then voted funds for development of a number of RS-70 prototypes, but some Congressmen continued to be suspicious that the Defense Secretary and the President were determined to kill the RS-70 project.

This and similar controversies, such as that arising from the Administration's later decision to cancel the Skybolt missile-carrying plane project, have raised important constitutional questions: Does Congress' control of the purse give it the right to decide which weapons systems should be developed? Was the President exceeding his powers when he refused to use funds voted for such projects as the RS-70 and Skybolt? Vinson complained that the House Armed Services Committee was being restricted "to the passive role of supine acquiescence in programs handed to it by the Department of Defense." But others argued that if Congress, and not the President, makes the decisions on weapons systems, how can the Chief Executive function effectively as Commander-in-Chief of the armed forces? If his opinions on such matters are not followed, how can he be held responsible for the nation's security? Many observers felt that Vinson was taking an extreme position, but, basically, the issue really is academic. There is no way of forcing the President and the executive agencies to spend funds appropriated by Congress if they do not choose to do so. As Lippmann has said, "Congress cannot go to court."[18] Realistically, Congress can only try to put enough pressure on the Administration to get it to change its mind.

BIBLIOGRAPHY

Brundage, Percival F., "A Critical Look at the 'Budget Process'," *Public Administration Review*, **XIV**, No. 4 (Autumn, 1954).

Burkhead, Jesse, *Government Budgeting*, New York: Wiley, 1956. Part III.

Burkhead, Jesse, "Federal Budgetary Developments: 1947–8," *Public Administration Review*, **VIII**, No. 4 (Autumn, 1948).

Financial Management in the Federal Government, 87th Congress, 1st Session, Document No. 11, Washington, D.C.: Government Printing Office, 1961.

Gibson, Frank, "A Bloody Tenet Washed and Made White," *Midwest Journal of Political Science*, **IV**, No. 1 (February, 1960).

Government Accounting and Budget Execution, New York: United Nations, 1952.

Harris, Joseph P., "Needed Reforms in the Federal Budget System," *Public Administration Review*, **XII**, No. 4 (Autumn, 1952).

Nelson, Dalmas H., "The Omnibus Appropriation Act of 1950," *Journal of Politics*, **XV**, No. 2 (May, 1953).

Smithies, Arthur, *The Budgetary Process in the United States*, New York: McGraw-Hill, 1955.

Wallace, Robert Ash, "Congressional Control of the Budget," *Midwest Journal of Political Science*, **III**, No. 2 (May, 1959).

[18] *St. Louis Post-Dispatch*, March 14, 1962, editorial page.

CHAPTER 20

Accounting, Auditing, and Purchasing

Governmental financial systems should be so devised as both to facilitate program planning and to safeguard the use of the public's funds. This brings us to three important aspects of fiscal management: (1) accounting, (2) auditing, and (3) purchasing and supply.

ACCOUNTING AND AUDITING

Accounting has been defined as the "art of recording, classifying, and summarizing transactions, wholly or in part of a financial nature, in terms of money, and interpreting the results thereof."[1] Accounting is intimately related to budgeting because it is the accounting system which provides current information on expenditures and permits adherence to the budget. Periodic financial reports based on accounting data make it possible to compare actual with estimated costs of operations. Budgets could not be prepared and controlled on a performance basis if the accounting system did not show costs by specific work activities. Thus, it is frequently stated that accounting, like budgeting, is a management tool. Without a good accounting system, those responsible for both the long-range planning and the day-by-day administration of any enterprise could not be expected to achieve the desired results.

[1] *Puerto Rico and Its Public Administration Program*, Rio Piedras, Puerto Rico: Univ. of Puerto Rico, 1945.

Auditing is an analysis of proposed or past expenditures with respect not only to their legality but also to their desirability. Accounting data provides much of the information upon which audits are made. Auditors examine expenditure vouchers and other documents showing proposed or past financial transactions. If the audit takes place prior to payment of an obligation, it is known as the *pre-audit*. Usually the pre-audit is conducted within the executive branch. This is logical because the purpose is for those in government administration to exercise a control on the use of funds by subordinate officials. If an external group, such as auditors responsible directly to the legislature, were responsible for the pre-audit, the managers of the executive branch would not be making the decisions as to how best to use the available funds. In effect, the external auditors would be the managers of the executive branch.

The *post-audit* takes place after payment, in fact sometimes many months afterwards. There are numerous past financial transactions to review, so the auditors frequently have a big backlog of work. The purpose of the post-audit is to check upon the judgments made by the responsible officials in the executive branch. Perhaps in some cases they erred or authorized illegal expenditures. The legal provisions governing the use of funds are numerous, complicated, and sometimes subject to several different interpretations. Did the agency concerned respect the intent of the law? Legislators are naturally very much concerned about this; they want the funds spent as they intended. They also want to be sure that efficient use was made of the funds. Money can be spent legally but foolishly, and thus, the post-audit should be broad enough to encompass the question of efficiency. A few years ago, the post-audit was very narrowly conceived in the federal government and in many other jurisdictions: it was limited to catching financial irregularities, frequently in the expenditure of very small sums.

Since the post-audit is a check on the administrative branch, it should be performed by persons outside that branch. The logical arrangement is for the auditors to be responsible to the legislature and to report their findings directly to it. The objectivity of post-auditing could not be trusted if it were carried out by representatives of the same branch which authorized the expenditures in the first place. It follows that it is illogical to put the same official in charge of both pre-auditing and post-auditing. If someone approves an expenditure in the pre-audit, he naturally will not be inclined to question his own judgment when he makes the post-audit. Indeed, such a combination of functions is apt to put temptation in the way of any weak character who functions in both roles. He could, as one example, accept bribes from vendors, approve overpayments to them, and later certify the transaction as having met legal requirements. A few years ago the State of Illinois voted to separate the responsibilities for pre- and post-auditing, after an official responsible for both functions was found to have embezzled millions of dollars from the state. Post-auditing in that state is now the responsibility of an Auditor-General appointed by the legislature, who submits audit reports to a Legislative Audit Commission whose function it is to review them for the legislature.

The Case of the Federal Government

It was noted in Chapter 17 that the Budget and Accounting Act of 1921, besides establishing the Bureau of the Budget, also created the GAO, the head of which—whose title is the Comptroller-General—is appointed by the President, subject to Senate confirmation, for a period of 15 years. He may not be removed by the President for *any* reason. Only Congress can remove him, either for cause as stated in a joint resolution or through impeachment proceedings. The Budget and Accounting Act makes clear that the GAO is to be independent of the executive branch. The reader will recall that the GAO is one of the few agencies which report directly to Congress.

The Budget and Accounting Act, however, does not limit the GAO to post-auditing; it also gives it the power to "prescribe the forms, systems, and procedure for administrative appropriation and fund accounting in the several departments and establishments, and for the administrative examination of fiscal officers' accounts and claims against the United States."[2] This meant that control of agency accounting systems and the pre-audit were also the responsibility of the GAO.

[2] See *Financial Management in the Federal Government*, 87th Congress, 1st Session, Senate Document No. 11, Washington, D.C.: Government Printing Office, 1961, pp. 275–289, for text of the Budget and Accounting Act of 1921.

Views of the President's Committee on Administrative Management

This is the reason Franklin D. Roosevelt's Committee on Administrative Management was so critical of the GAO when it made its 1937 report. In its opinion, the GAO was exercising management functions which belonged to the executive branch. Accounting systems should be prescribed by the administrative branch, since accounting was a tool of management. Any body which it did not control could not be expected to perform this function satisfactorily. Only the responsible administrative officials could devise the systems of accounts which best suited their needs. As to the pre-audit, it should be carried out within the administrative agencies as part of their systems of internal control. They should be able to go ahead and make expenditures about whose legality and wisdom they were convinced. The GAO could catch irregularities in the post-audit. Pre-audit by the GAO meant interfering with the management judgments of the agency heads.

As to the actual accomplishments of the GAO since its creation in 1921, Roosevelt's Committee believed that it had fulfilled neither its legislative mandate to develop an administrative accounting system nor its responsibility to provide Congress and the public with an independent post-audit. It was spending most of its time on the detailed checking of expenditure vouchers and supporting documents for each and every financial transaction consummated in the administrative agencies. This was not a genuine post-audit, because no attempt was made to evaluate the efficiency of individual agency operations. The emphasis rather was on checking each transaction, no matter how small, to be sure that all legal requirements had been observed. Accordingly, the Committee recommended that the GAO's accounting functions be transferred to the Treasury Department, along with the authority to settle claims for or against the government. The GAO could then concentrate exclusively on a real post-audit, with the title of the Comptroller-General changed to Auditor-General. In making these proposals, the Committee stated that it was only repeating recommendations previously made to Congress by President Hoover in December, 1932, and also put forth in 1934 by a special committee of the United States Chamber of Commerce.[3]

Roosevelt accepted these recommendations, but Congress refused

[3] *Ibid.*, pp. 13–18.

to approve them. After a decade and a half of regarding the GAO as its special ward, Congress would not agree to any diminution of its powers. To make the recommended changes would mean increasing executive strength at the expense of Congress. This was the interpretation many Congressmen placed on Roosevelt's recommendations, and it is an attitude Congress still holds to strongly. As we shall see shortly, the GAO today functions very differently from the way it did when Roosevelt's Committee made its studies. Its powers, however, remain basically the same. It retains all the authority given it under the Budget and Accounting Act of 1921.

The Joint Program for Improving Accounting

In the years immediately following defeat of the Roosevelt plan, the government continued without a satisfactory system of administrative accounts. The GAO, the Treasury Department, and the Bureau of the Budget all had important finance responsibilities, but there was no formal arrangement for coordinating their activities.

In October, 1948, the Joint Program for Improving Accounting in the Federal Government was initiated. The participants were these same three agencies. The purpose was to unite their efforts in a systematic attempt to develop an integrated pattern of accounting and financial reporting for the government as a whole. The GAO's desire to assume a constructive role in its relations with the administrative agencies may be seen in this statement by the Comptroller-General announcing the new program:

> I wish to deal with the concept of my responsibility in the prescribing of accounting systems. I believe this function should be exercised so as to provide all possible encouragement to the agencies to exercise their own initiative and responsibility in the solution of their accounting function. In line with this, it will be my objective as the program progresses to prescribe requirements largely in terms of standards, principles, and basic forms, procedures, and terminology.[4]

Recommendations of First Hoover Commission

The Joint Program had just been put into action when the first Hoover Commission began its studies. Neither the Task Force on

[4] Commission on Organization of the Executive Branch of the Government, *Budgeting and Accounting*, Washington, D.C.: Government Printing Office, 1949, p. 38.

Fiscal, Budgeting, and Accounting Activities nor the full Commission felt that a voluntary arrangement of this kind was adequate. The Task Force essentially made the same recommendations as Roosevelt's Committee on Administrative Management. The only difference was that it proposed that the responsibility for accounting be that of a new unit to be located in the Executive Office of the President, not the Treasury Department. This new unit was to be headed by an Accountant-General appointed by the President with the confirmation of the Senate. The Task Force was convinced that appointment of such a "chief accounting officer, with undivided responsibility for accounting activities and with final authority in all accounting matters" was necessary "to fill the void that lack of provision for an integrated accounting system makes in the Government's fiscal structure."[5]

The full Commission agreed with the Task Force that the then existing arrangements were not satisfactory. What was needed was to designate one "responsible official with authority to give continuous motive force to reform in accounting." Unlike the Task Force, however, it did not want to see the GAO removed completely from the field of accounting. In effect, what it proposed was a compromise. An Accountant-General would be established in the Treasury Department "with authority to prescribe general accounting methods and enforce accounting procedures." Approval of the Comptroller-General, however, would be required before these "methods and procedures" could go into effect.

Would such a "compromise" arrangement really work? The majority of the Commission saw "no inherent conflict between the present position of the Comptroller General and our recommendation to create the position of Accountant General."[6] Two members of the Commission, John L. McClellan and Carter Manasco, disagreed with the majority, because they thought that adoption of the compromise inevitably would lead to legislation removing the GAO from

[5] Commission on Organization of the Executive Branch of the Government, *Task Force Report on Fiscal, Budgeting, and Accounting Activities*, Washington, D.C.: Government Printing Office, 1949, p. 94. See also Felix A. Nigro (ed.), *Public Administration, Readings and Documents*, New York: Holt, Rinehart and Winston, 1951, pp. 353–370.

[6] Commission on Organization of the Executive Branch of the Government, *Budgeting and Accounting, op. cit.*, pp. 38–41.

the accounting field entirely. Their dissent is significant, because it reflected the views of many members of Congress when a bill was later introduced to establish the Accountant-General position. McClellan and Manasco believed that a new effort was being made "to have the Congress shirk its constitutional duty and relinquish its authority over public expenditures to the executive branch of the Government by transferring accounting functions from its *own* agency to an office in the executive branch." (Italics ours.)[7] These two commissioners simply did not accept the argument that accounting was a management tool and thus the responsibility of the executive branch. Another commissioner, James H. Rowe, Jr., disagreed with the majority for exactly the opposite reason. In his opinion, the Task Force had been right. He did not see how the President could effectively discharge his responsibilities as Chief Executive without control over the accounting system. In business, the management controls the accounting system, and he saw no reason why this should not also be so in the government.[8]

Congress did not pass the bill to establish the position of Accountant-General. The Senate and House Committees on Government Operations unanimously rejected it. The Senate Committee stated in its report on the bill that the GAO's power to prescribe accounting requirements for the executive agencies was "essential to legislative control of appropriations and expenditures in the executive branch" and had to be held "inviolate."[9] In view of Congress' flat rejection of even this compromise solution, it seems highly unlikely that it will consent to any real alteration in the GAO's formal powers. However, what the GAO agrees to delegate to the administrative agencies is its own business; so long as it retains its ultimate control over the administrative accounts, most Congressmen will apparently be satisfied.

Other accounting recommendations of the first Hoover Commission fared much better. The Commission recommended that the GAO discontinue the practice of requiring the administrative agencies to submit the supporting documents for every financial transaction approved within the agencies. It emphasized that freight carloads of vouchers from all over the country were being hauled to Washington

[7] *Ibid.*, pp. 47–54.
[8] *Ibid.*, pp. 55–63.
[9] *Financial Management in the Federal Government, op. cit.*, p. 67.

for individual examination in the GAO. Half of the GAO's budget, it estimated, was being devoted to the central examination of individual expenditure vouchers and documents.

The way to conduct the post-audit was on a sampling basis at the work locations where the transactions had taken place. This was the accepted practice in industry. Detailed checking of vouchers was a responsibility of the agencies when they made their pre-audits and should not be repeated by those making the post-audit. The sampling technique would make it possible to detect cases of possible fraud or of gross negligence, in which event the GAO auditors could then make a more intensive examination of the financial practices of the agency in question. The Comptroller-General accepted this recommendation, and the GAO now conducts its audits on a sampling basis at the site of agency operations. Furthermore, the GAO now explores the question of efficiency of operations, as well as legality of expenditures. It makes what are known as "comprehensive audits," which are really evaluations of the adequacy of the systems of accounting and of the internal controls maintained by the agencies. GAO audit reports today are basically critical reviews of the management decisions of the responsible officials in the executive branch. As such, they provide Congress with a basis for evaluating the efficiency of agency operations. When the post-audit consisted mainly of detailed voucher checking, it gave Congress little to go on in appraising the performance of the agencies as a whole.

The first Hoover Commission also recommended that the government adopt the *accrual* basis of accounting for both expenditures and revenues. When the accounts are on an accrual basis, revenues are posted when they are earned, rather than waiting until the money is collected. Similarly, expenditures are recorded when the commitments are entered into, rather than delayed until the payments are made to those supplying the goods or services.

Under the cash system of accounting, entries are not made in the accounts until money is actually paid out or received. Cash accounting is misleading, because the available balances cannot be trusted. Since commitments to spend are not reflected, the actual amount of money available for obligation may be far less than the cash balance shown. Conversely, if revenues already earned are not shown, the balance may imply a financial stringency which really does not exist.

Furthermore, with the accrual accounting system the cost of materials and supplies is charged to expense in the period when they are consumed, rather than charging the whole cost at the time when the entire shipment of the commodity is received. Using the illustration of the Task Force: "If several months' supply of coal is purchased and received during one fiscal year, but will not completely be consumed until the next fiscal year, it would be improper to charge all of the cost of the coal as expense of the year in which it is purchased and received."[10] Similarly, in the case of fixed assets like plant and equipment, which have a useful life beyond the current budget period, the cost is spread over all the periods benefited.

Accrual accounting is essential for what is known as "cost-based budgeting." Under such budgeting, the estimates show exactly what costs will be incurred during the fiscal year in question. It is not enough simply to show the requests for new authorizations to spend money during the budget period. Supplies, materials, and equipment already on hand will be used, as well as resources which become available during the budget period from orders placed during prior years. The true cost of operations for a given period is not accurately measured by the estimates for new obligations to be entered into during that period. Cash accounting cannot provide the data needed for cost-based budgeting. Congress should know when reviewing the budget proposals exactly what the costs will be for the budget year in question. Otherwise it is not really exercising effective budgetary control.

The Budget and Accounting Procedures Act of 1950

In 1956, Congress passed legislation requiring the heads of each agency to maintain their accounts on an accrual basis, in accordance with principles and standards prescribed by the Comptroller-General.[11] The GAO has in recent years been helping the agencies make the transition from cash to accrual accounting. Earlier, in the Budget and Accounting Procedures Act of 1950, Congress had adopted a

[10] Nigro, *op. cit.*, p. 368.

[11] *Comptroller General of the United States, Annual Report*, Washington, D.C.: Government Printing Office, 1961, p. 69. See Donald C. Rowat (ed.), *Basic Issues in Public Administration*, New York: Macmillan, 1961, pp. 301–312.

statement of policy on accounting and auditing in line with the first Hoover Commission's views on how these functions should be performed. According to this Act, it is the policy of the Congress that:

(a) The accounting of the Government provide full disclosure of the results of financial operations, adequate financial information needed in the management of operations and the formulation and execution of the budget and effective control over income, expenditures, funds, property, and other assets.

(b) Full consideration be given to the needs and responsibilities of both the legislative and executive branches in the establishment of accounting and reporting systems and requirements.

(c) The maintenance of accounting systems and the producing of financial reports with respect to the operation of executive agencies, including central facilities for bringing together and disclosing information on the results of the financial operations of the Government as a whole, be the responsibility of the executive branch.

(d) The auditing for the Government, conducted by the Comptroller General of the United States as an agent of the Congress be directed at determining the extent to which accounting and related financial reporting fulfill the purposes specified, financial transactions have been consummated in accordance with laws, regulations, or other legal requirements, and adequate internal financial control over operations is exercised, and afford an effective basis for the settlement of accounts of accountable officers.

(e) Emphasis be placed on effecting orderly improvements resulting in simplified and more effective accounting, financial reporting, budgeting, and auditing requirements and procedures and on the elimination of those which involve duplication or which do not serve a purpose commensurate with the costs involved.

(f) The Comptroller General of the United States, the Secretary of the Treasury, and the Director of the Bureau of the Budget conduct a continuous program for the improvement of accounting and financial reporting in the Government.[12]

This is generally considered the most important finance legislation since the 1921 Budget and Accounting Act. Its significance is that it requires the adoption of modern accounting practices to replace the antiquated methods which had persisted for so many years. With the initiation of the Joint Program for Improving Accounting in 1948,

[12] Commission on Organization of the Executive Branch of the Government, *Task Force Report on Budget and Accounting*, Washington, D.C.: Government Printing Office, 1955, p. 51.

the GAO had already indicated its desire to see more up-to-date practices adopted. The 1950 Act gave its sanction to the Joint Program and made the principles voluntarily followed by the three participating agencies a matter of law.

Recommendations of Second Hoover Commission

When the second Hoover Commission made its studies in 1955, it had words of praise for the accounting reforms introduced by the GAO. It believed, however, that what was still lacking was "the stimulus of central accounting direction in the executive branch itself."[13] To meet this need, it proposed that there be established in the Bureau of the Budget a new Staff Office of Accounting, to be responsible for developing an "overall plan for accounting and reporting, consistent with broad policies and standards prescribed by the Comptroller General."[14] The proposed new Office was to expedite the "introduction of modern accounting methods in the executive agencies consistent with the over-all plan."[15] It was to "stimulate the building of competent accounting and auditing organizations"[16] in the agencies and help them find and train competent personnel. Finally, it was to set time schedules for performance and to report at least annually to the Budget Director on accounting progress in each of the agencies.

The proposed Office has never been established. The Budget Bureau continues to cooperate in the Joint Program which, incidentally, has been renamed the "Joint Program for the Improvement of Financial Management in the Federal Government." The change in title reflects the belief that, if full benefits are to be obtained from accounting reforms, they must be accompanied by improvements in budgeting, reporting, and related procedures. With many concrete accomplishments to its credit, the broadened Joint Program appears to be meeting satisfactorily the injunctions laid down in the Act of 1950.[17]

[13] Commission on Organization of the Executive Branch of the Government, *Budget and Accounting*, Washington, D.C.: Government Printing Office, 1955, p. 30.

[14] *Ibid.*, p. 31.

[15] *Ibid.*, p. 32.

[16] *Ibid.*

[17] See L. N. Teitelbaum, "How to Improve the Financial Management Improvement Program," *The Federal Accountant*, XI, No. 3 (March, 1962), 80–90.

Although there is general satisfaction with the broadened scope of the GAO audits, the criticism is made that Congress is not properly organized to give the reports the careful study they deserve. No committees have been created in the Congress to receive the reports and hold hearings on them, with representatives of both the GAO and the agencies concerned present. The reports are simply sent to Congress for the information of its individual members. That some Congressmen study them carefully is clear, but the fact remains that there is no organized machinery in Congress to give them systematic attention. The first Hoover Commission's Task Force proposed the establishment of a Congressional joint committee to review the reports. Its plan was that a GAO representative would sit with the Committee when it was in session and explain the audit findings to them. The finance officials of the agencies dealt with in the reports would also be present to make their defense.[18] This recommendation was strongly supported by one of the members of the Commission, James K. Pollock. He said, "Audit findings do not automatically achieve reforms. They must be supported by the Congress, and frequently be implemented by legislation to become effective instruments of congressional control."[19] Pollock suggested creation of a committee on the model of the Public Accounts Committee in England. In that country, the annual audit findings of the Comptroller and the Auditor-General are sent to this Committee which holds hearings on them. Some observers are of the opinion that the Public Accounts Committee has contributed to making parliamentary control of expenditures more effective. Congress has not created such a committee, but it is possible that this proposal will be revived in future plans to reorganize Congress.

Human Relations and the Auditors

One should not leave this discussion without mentioning a source of much of the difficulty: friction between the internal auditors and the officials responsible for directing program activities. Auditors

[18] Commission on Organization of the Executive Branch of the Government, *Task Force Report on Fiscal, Budgeting, and Accounting Activities, op. cit.*, pp. 83–84.

[19] Commission on Organization of the Executive Branch of the Government, *Budgeting and Accounting, op. cit.*, p. 66.

can make very narrow interpretations of the law which virtually handcuff the operating officials. In making the pre-audit, there usually are a host of regulations to interpret. If the agency finance officer is unduly timorous, he will hesitate to approve proposed expenditures even when the possibility of later objections by those who make the post-audit is extremely remote. To resolve every doubt by automatically saying "no" is an unfortunate characteristic of some finance officers. Some also overstep their bounds and object to expenditures, not because there is any doubt about their legality, but because they personally do not think the money should be spent for the particular purpose. It is easy to develop doubts about the legality of expenditures with which one is not in sympathy.

It is not necessary to give other examples. Some finance officers can be unreasonable. It is also true that their critics can be grossly unfair. The agency head should appoint and retain in finance positions only those individuals who combine professional competence and integrity with a real desire to be of help to operating officials. As we saw in Chapter 4, there are many sensitive points in staff-line relationships. The better the quality of the finance personnel, the more likely it is that unnecessary conflicts will be avoided. As the second Hoover Commission's Task Force said: "The most perfectly conceived accounting system in incompetent hands is not as useful as an imperfect system in competent and experienced hands. *The personal and inspirational qualities of accounting leadership are all important.*"[20]

PURCHASING AND SUPPLY

Purchasing and supply management is important because the required materials, supplies, and equipment must be on hand if the agency's programs are to be carried out successfully. The public is naturally concerned about waste in government purchasing operations, particularly when it hears the claim that millions and even billions of dollars could be saved annually with more efficient procedures. We will be concerned later with the details of these criticisms; it is first advisable to describe briefly the essential elements of an efficient

[20] Commission on Organization of the Executive Branch of the Government, *Task Force Report on Budget and Accounting, op. cit.*, p. 62. Italics ours.

system of purchase and supply management. Just as there has been a budget reform movement, so has there been a purchase reform movement. The same forces which impelled public jurisdictions to adopt the executive budget have led many of them to modernize their purchasing and supply operations.

Essentials of Efficient Purchase and Supply Management

The first essential is the establishment of a central purchasing agency, headed by a technically trained purchasing agent. If the government is to obtain full value for the commodities it buys, expertise on the part of those who make the purchases is indispensable, just as it is in private companies. When operating officials in each department contact the vendors directly and make their own purchases, the result is usually inefficiency and waste. There is no attempt to standardize quality and to consolidate requisitions in order to obtain the lower unit prices available when bulk purchases are made. The central purchasing office should itself make the purchases for all using departments, subject to whatever delegations of authority to the departments it believes appropriate. For example, it may be advisable to have the public hospitals purchase perishable commodities directly. In state and local governments, there usually should be few exceptions to the rule of centralized purchasing. In fact, in many cases it is advantageous for local governments to enter into joint purchasing programs for various articles of supply. Dozens of such cooperative agreements have been in force for years. Because of its great size, decentralization of purchase authority must be practiced on a much wider scale in the federal government. The special case of the federal government will be discussed later.

Specifically, what are the expert services provided by the central purchasing agency? One of the most important is the preparation of commodity specifications. Just as the class specification in personnel administration defines the kind of job and the qualifications needed to fill it, so does the commodity specification describe in detail the characteristics of the article which is to be purchased. The magnitude of this task will be appreciated when it is remembered how many thousands of items of different kinds are procured by public agencies. Fortunately, by this time many sets of specifications have been published which can be consulted. State and local governments, for example, can adapt specifications available from the Federal Supply Service in the General Services Administration. Another important source is the National Bureau of Standards. Leaders in the purchasing movement have stressed that preparing the specifications should be a cooperative enterprise of the central purchasing office and representatives of the using agencies.[21] The help of chemists, engineers, and other technicians in the line departments is valuable in developing specifications for materials and equipment to be used on construction and other projects.

Stimulation of real competition among the bidders is another important responsibility of the central purchasing agency; indeed, it is of anyone who is authorized to make the purchases. The usual procedure is to require the vendors to submit sealed bids and for the order to be placed with the lowest bidder. Usually the legal provisions are worded flexibly, however, so as to make it possible to reject a bid even though it is the lowest one. Based on past experience, the purchasing office may not have confidence in the integrity of the vendor or in the quality of his merchandise. Further, when commodities are available from only one vendor, the formality of bids is unnecessary.

There have been cases where an unscrupulous individual in the position of purchasing officer has dispensed with competition so as to favor certain vendors. He may do this in open violation of the law or because there are loopholes in it. For purchasing agents who violate the law, criminal penalties are usually provided in the statutes. Civil action can also be instituted to recover money lost by the jurisdiction because of irregularities. Several years ago the purchasing agent of one state government resigned after publication of a series of articles in a leading newspaper charging that he had accepted gifts from vendors and had otherwise violated the law.[22] Such cases are exceptional, but they do serve as a constant reminder of the indispensable requirement of high integrity on the part of those in purchasing operations.

Inspection and testing of goods when received from the vendors is

[21] See Russell Forbes, *Purchasing for Small Cities*, Chicago, Ill.: Public Administration Service, 1951, p. 5.

[22] *St. Louis Post-Dispatch*, November 29, 1959.

another essential element of good purchasing procedure. Some vendors will ship inferior merchandise if they know that it will not be checked carefully upon delivery. Goods may be damaged in transit, or errors made by the vendors' shipping clerks in counting the items shipped. They may even send the wrong goods. Just as any shopper should open and check deliveries from the local stores as soon as they are received, so should public agencies.

When deliveries are made by the vendors directly to the using department, the usual procedure is to require someone to open the packages, check the materials, and advise the central purchasing office of any discrepancies or deficiencies in the goods received. If the deliveries are made to warehouses and other supply centers maintained by the central purchasing agency, the shipments are inspected there. To relieve the pressure on storage facilities, agreements are often made with the vendors for them to make partial shipments at designated periods of time. A commitment is made to buy from them large quantities of certain commodities so as to obtain lower unit prices. The vendor, however, does not ship all the goods immediately, but stipulated quantities at the times agreed until finally the entire order is filled. In this way, the government gets the vendor to supply the storage facilities. Certain kinds of commodities should undergo careful testing upon receipt. Mere counting and inspection for damage is not enough. In such cases, the purchasing office arranges for the use of existing testing facilities in the laboratories of the governmental jurisdiction or it contracts with private companies to perform this work. Without a central purchasing office to see to it that this testing takes place, a jurisdiction may, without knowing it, accept costly shipments of goods which really do not meet the standards.

An efficient system of warehousing and of supply management is also essential. Stock levels should be sufficient to meet needs, but not so high as to make it necessary later to declare much material surplus. The inventory records should accurately show the quantity of the stocks on hand of each item stored. If they are inaccurate, materials may have been over or under ordered. Furthermore, all government property should be protected against theft, fire, or other loss or damage. Finally, there should be an orderly procedure for declaring property surplus and disposing of it on the best terms available to the government. The same kind of material which is being purchased by one agency should not be disposed of as surplus by another. So small a return is received on sales of surplus property that it is gross waste to dispose of items at only a tiny fraction of their cost when exactly the same article is needed by another agency.

Purchasing Functions of the GSA

As stated in Chapter 17, the General Services Administration (GSA) was established largely as the result of the recommendations of the first Hoover Commission. One of the latter's Task Forces stated that "the problem of supply is treated all too casually by the United States Government."[23] It believed that the Bureau of Federal Supply in the Treasury Department did not have adequate powers. Greater centralization of responsibility for purchasing and supply management in the federal government was needed. What should be done was to create a new Bureau of Federal Supply in an Office of General Services.[24] When the GSA was created in 1949, it not only took over from the Treasury the functions of the Bureau of Federal Supply, but it was also given responsibility for other general management services such as public buildings, the national archives, and records administration.

The legislation establishing the GSA gave it general servicewide responsibility for purchasing and supply management. Its Federal Supply Service functions more effectively than did the Bureau of Federal Supply which it replaced. The GSA does not, however, attempt to do all the purchasing for the federal government. Under the law it delegates purchasing authority to the administrative agencies, and, because of the great size of many of them, it has made many such delegations. The original legislation also provided that, depending on the discretion of the department head or of the President, some agencies like the Veterans Administration and the Defense Depart-

[23] Commission on Organization of the Executive Branch of the Government, *Task Force Report on the Federal Supply System*, Washington, D.C.: Government Printing Office, 1949, p. 1.

[24] See Commission on Organization of the Executive Branch of the Government, *Office of General Services*, Washington, D.C.: Government Printing Office, 1949.

ment could elect to remain outside the GSA's jurisdiction or to come under it only partly.

Recent Criticisms of Federal Supply Operations

When the second Hoover Commission made its studies, it had some strong criticisms of government supply operations, particularly in the Defense Department. "The Government," it said, "has mountainous accumulations of property which it would not have bought if it had a good inventory system. It is estimated that with proper inventory control and more realistic stock levels from $10 billion to $25 billion of supplies now in Government warehouses could be eliminated."[25] Fantastic examples of overbuying and waste were cited. In some military depots, supply items easily obtainable from the manufacturers were being stocked in quantities sufficient to meet needs for 20, 30, and, in one case, even 128 years. Inventory records in some cases were grossly inaccurate. Spot checks at one depot showed that the stock actually on hand of certain items exceeded the inventory records by ratios ranging from 1 to 367 percent. In other cases, the stock in storage was short of the totals shown in the inventory records by proportions ranging from 2 to 100 percent.[26] In many cases, property was declared surplus by one branch of the military when the same items were being purchased in the open market by other branches. Since property sold as surplus produced a return of only 5 to 7 percent of its original cost, millions of dollars were being squandered. For that matter, property procedures throughout the government were inefficient. Civilian agencies were also buying and selling the same items as surplus at the same time. However, since the Defense Department accounted for almost 98 percent of all goods bought and stocked by the government, it came in for the strongest criticisms.

The second Hoover Commission made a number of specific proposals for tightening up supply operations. More realistic stock levels should be maintained. Better procedures for circularizing lists of property excess to the needs of individual agencies should be developed. No

[25] Commission on Organization of the Executive Branch of the Government, *Surplus Property*, Washington, D.C.: Government Printing Office, 1955, p. xii.

[26] *Ibid.*, pp. 6–7.

property should be declared surplus when another federal agency needed it. Cost-conscious civilians should replace military officers in Defense Department supply operations. The Commission tactfully said that "it is not an indictment of their abilities to say that the psychology of professional military officers does not normally follow patterns of thought commonly found among civilians engaged in business."[27] The powers of the GSA over disposition of surplus property should be strengthened. Unfortunately, evidence of great waste in military supply operations still continues. In one of its recent audit reports, the GAO stated that the services were still wasting millions of dollars by buying the same items they were selling as surplus at cut-rate prices. The GAO made a spot check of a certain number of items in a total of $1,100,000,000 worth of new unused property declared surplus to military needs in the year ending June 30, 1961. The items covered in the spot check were valued at $52,000,000. No less than $3,100,000 worth of them was found to consist of items actually needed by the military services. The GAO declared that this situation would continue unless the Defense Department improved its procedures for screening surplus property. The Defense Department promised to do so, but improvements of this kind cannot be developed overnight in an agency with such an enormous supply operation.[28]

Incidentally, this kind of report exemplifies the constructive role of the GAO in its new, broader type audits. Individual members of Congress use the GAO findings to bring whatever pressure they can on the President and the department heads to end this waste. Senator Douglas of Illinois is one of those who have been very vocal in his protests about loose spending in the Defense Department. He has claimed that two to three billion dollars could be saved each year by squeezing "scandalous and appalling" military waste out of the Pentagon.[29]

Recent Improvements

The impression should not be given that waste exists only in the military services. GAO reports have criticized operations in many

[27] *Ibid.*, p. 14.
[28] *St. Louis Post-Dispatch*, September 9, 1962.
[29] *Ibid.*, April 18, 1961.

of the civilian agencies. A constructive development is the recent creation by Secretary of Defense McNamara of the Defense Supply Agency (DSA). This new agency is in charge of purchasing and supply operations for the Defense Department as a whole. It represents a centralization of authority within the Department, because it carries out functions formerly exercised by the individual service commands. McNamara estimated that, as a result of the DSA's creation, the cost of logistical operations would be reduced by at least $3 billion a year.[30] The Defense Department also recently arranged to turn over to the GSA the responsibility for buying all its nonmilitary supply items. This should also lead to significant economies, since the GSA purchases the same items for the other agencies. In April, 1963, Senator Douglas, in an address in the Senate, complimented Mr. McNamara for Defense Department savings of almost $2 billion in fiscal 1963 and anticipated savings of $3.5 billion a year by the end of fiscal 1965.[31]

Just as the spoils system became intolerable when the functions of government became more complex, so too is the "casual" approach to purchasing outmoded. Where faithfully applied, the principles of the purchasing movement have clearly proved their value. Wider application of these principles constitutes one of the areas of unfinished business for public administration in the years ahead.

BIBLIOGRAPHY

Bordner, H. W., "The Development of Army Accounting," *Public Administration Review*, **IX**, No. 2 (Spring, 1949).

Commission on Organization of the Executive Branch of the Government (First Hoover Commission), Washington, D.C.: Government Printing Office, 1949.

Task Force Report on Fiscal, Budgeting and Accounting Activities.
Budgeting and Accounting.

[30] *Ibid.*, April 17, 1962.
[31] *Ibid.*, April 26, 1963.

Commission on Organization of the Executive Branch of the Government (Second Hoover Commission), Washington, D.C.: Government Printing Office, 1955.
Task Force Report on Budget and Accounting.
Budget and Accounting.
Surplus Property.

Financial Management in the Federal Government, 87th Congress, 1st Session, Senate Document No. 11, Washington, D.C.: Government Printing Office, 1961.

Government Accounting and Budget Execution, New York: Department of Economic Affairs, United Nations, 1952.

Mansfield, Harvey C., and Marx, Fritz Morstein, "Fiscal Accountability," in Marx, Fritz Morstein (ed.), *Elements of Public Administration*, Englewood Cliffs, N.J.: Prentice-Hall, 1959.

Report of the President's Committee on Administrative Management, Part II, "Financial Control and Accountability," Washington, D.C.: Government Printing Office, 1937.

Shakdher, S. L., "The Comptroller and Auditor-General in India and the United Kingdom," *Public Administration*, **XXXVII** (Spring, 1959).

PART VI

ADMINISTRATIVE RESPONSIBILITY

CHAPTER 21

The Problem of Administrative Power

Public officials must act responsibly. Even if their power and discretion were small, in a democracy the acts of public officials could not in all cases be absolutely final. Although there is some exaggeration of abuses of power, the great discretion now exercised by government agencies makes this a serious problem. All criticisms of the "bureaucrats" cannot simply be dismissed as propaganda by people opposed to the governmental programs concerned. Some men will misuse their authority; this is true in any kind of organization, public or private. One is reminded here of James Madison's remark in one of the Federalist papers: "If men were angels, no government would be necessary. If angels were to govern men, neither external nor internal controls on government would be necessary."[1] It is with these external and internal controls on administrative officials that we will deal in this part of the book. In this chapter, the possible abuses will be described, and the next chapter will deal with the available means of control.

POSSIBLE ABUSES

Criticisms of public officials are sometimes made in general, even sweeping, terms, without any specific indication of the wrongs which have been committed. From such statements, it is difficult to define

[1] Alexander Hamilton, James Madison, and John Jay, *The Federalist*, Cambridge, Mass.: Harvard Univ. Press, 1961, p. 356.

the real problem, so we will present a number of examples as a factual basis for the discussion in the next chapter of control measures. In this identification of areas of possible abuse, some illustrations will be given which are already familiar to anybody who reads the newspapers and follows current events to some extent at least. Other illustrations will deal with possible misuses of authority which are less well known to the average citizen and may even be of no particular concern to him as an individual, yet they are sources of deep preoccupation to economic and other groups in their relations with the government, as well as to legislators and others interested in preventing the abuses in question.

Dishonesty

First, and most obvious, some public employees may be dishonest. They may steal from the government, as when a bridge toll collector pockets some of the money he receives and then falsifies the records of receipts. Many different employees receive, or otherwise have control over, government funds. Embezzlement may be in small or large amounts, perpetrated by low- or high-ranking officials. It is, however, only one of many different kinds of fraud that can be practiced in government programs.

The employee may accept bribes for either minor or major favors. Traffic-ticket "fixing" belongs in the first category; steering a multimillion dollar contract to a particular firm for a consideration falls in the latter one. Sometimes the bribe is conveniently described as a "gift." Several years ago a House subcommittee investigating frauds in the federal-state highway program found that it was common practice in some state governments for highway department officials to accept cash and other "gifts" from the contractors building the roads. Some officials regularly received $25 weekly cash payments which they admitted they assumed came from the contractors. In other cases, the handout took another form, such as $500 "loans" and even gifts of hunting licenses, lumber, and other things of value. State and federal inspectors testified that all these were inducements to sway the state road officials to accept substandard construction work by the contractors.[2] Another kind of conspiracy takes the form of ex-

[2] *The New York Times*, December 11, 1960.

changing favors, all at the government's expense. In the same federal-state highway program, it was discovered that state-hired appraisers had placed inflated values on land which had to be acquired from private parties. In return for these overappraisals, the sellers of the property reciprocated by giving business to companies in which these appraisers had a financial interest.[3]

Unethical Behavior

Second, officials may keep within the letter of the law and do nothing for which they could be criminally prosecuted, yet their behavior is such as to raise a serious question about their ethics. Sometimes there are convenient loopholes in the law which make it possible for someone lacking integrity to engage in practices which defeat the intent of the legislation. This is like the thief who finds the front gate firmly secured but is able to slip in through a hole in the wire fence. As Ralph Eisenberg has said: "The area of concern today is the oft-cited 'gray zone'—that lying between behavior that is 'clean as a hound's tooth' and behavior obviously improper and illegal, involving such things as bribery, embezzlement, and theft."[4]

The whole field of conflict of interest illustrates this very well. In general terms, a conflict of interest exists when a "public official is placed in a position where, for some advantage to be gained for himself, he finds it difficult or impossible to devote himself with complete energy and loyalty to the public interest."[5] With some conflict-of-interest situations, the law can deal in no uncertain terms. It can, for example, make illegal the acceptance of any payment in cash or in services from contractors with whom the government does business. But this is only one kind of conflict of interest, for the official may accept no money but make decisions which favor personal friends or political allies. The purchasing agent may decide that the lowest

[3] *St. Louis Post-Dispatch*, February 22, 1962, and January 19, 1963. See *Relationship Between Road Contractors and State Personnel in Florida*, House Subcommittee on the Federal Aid Highway Program, 87th Congress, 1st Session, Washington, D.C.: Government Printing Office, 1961.

[4] Ralph Eisenberg, "Conflicts of Interest Situations and Remedies," *Rutgers Law Review*, XIII, No. 4 (Summer, 1959), 666.

[5] *Report Submitted by the Legislative Research Council Relative to Conflict of Interest*, Boston: Commonwealth of Massachusetts, May 1961, p. 15.

"best" bid is the one submitted by an old friend. Those awarding government contracts may prefer firms which have made substantial contributions to the political party in power. Some years ago the head of the General Services Administration justified making insurance brokerage awards on a political basis, because to him "practical politics" required that the business should not go to firms which "did not help this administration get into office."[6] He resigned because of adverse public reaction to his views on this matter, but the point remains that legislation cannot be framed which eliminates all such possibilities of favoritism.

Overriding the Law

Third, although personally honest, some officials may act without legal authority, or otherwise violate the law. Here the official seeks no bribe or other personal gain. Perhaps he is very strong minded and has decided that he is going to take certain action no matter what doubts may later be raised about its legality. A Senate Subcommittee which investigated ethical standards in government some years ago made this observation:

> Heads of agencies commonly turn to legal officers whom they appoint for rulings as to whether or not they can proceed in a given manner. The resulting opinions are not unbiased. They commonly tell the administrators what they want to hear. Undoubtedly they are leading to an undue expansion of administrative power under which administrators are changing or creating law, and hence usurping legislative functions.[7]

Sometimes an official may think he is proceeding legally, but he may inadvertently omit some procedural step required by the law or the regulations issued under it. In other cases, whether he acted legally or not will depend upon the interpretation which is to be given to the facts. Was there "probable cause" for arrest? Was the arrested person really given a "prompt" preliminary hearing or arraignment? Were the civil rights demonstrators creating a public disturbance? The courts to which such cases are appealed examine the facts, be-

[6] *St. Louis Post-Dispatch*, March 15, 1960.

[7] *Ethical Standards in Government*, Senate Subcommittee on Labor and Public Welfare, 82nd Congress, 1st Session, Washington, D.C.: Government Printing Office, 1951, p. 32.

cause this is the only way of determining whether or not the action taken by local enforcement authorities was proper under the laws and the relevant constitutional principles. In some cases, the official may be strongly biased and have taken action on the assumption that it would not be possible to prove in court or otherwise that his interpretation of the "facts" was prejudiced.

Unfair Treatment of Employees

Fourth, some agency decisions may violate principles of fair play in relations with their own employees. Someone may be dismissed allegedly for inefficiency, but the true motivation for the action is otherwise. Perhaps he was too outspoken in his criticisms of his superiors; perhaps he is a holdover from a previous Administration which blanketed him in under civil service. The new regime would like to replace him with someone whose name is on the civil service lists but of whose political and personal loyalty it can be sure. There is nothing about government which insures that all its decisions affecting its employees will be justifiable; the management can act arbitrarily, just as in private companies.

The loyalty program illustrates how government employees may be dealt with summarily. There is no question about the right of the government to dismiss individuals who are guilty of subversive activities. The difficulty is in making defensible decisions as to who should be fired as a security risk. According to one point of view, frankly stated on occasion by high-ranking federal officials, if there is any doubt at all about the employee's loyalty he should be dismissed. Furthermore, he should not be given the opportunity to confront his accusers and cross-examine them, for allowing him to do so would jeopardize the government's chances in the future of being able to persuade individuals to serve as informers. It would also give important clues to other subversives as to how the government goes about finding out who they are. During the first years of the loyalty program instituted in the federal government after World War II, quite a few employees were summarily dismissed or suspended, without even knowing the nature of the charges against them. The Supreme Court, however, ruled in 1956 that the loyalty procedures being used could only be applied in the case of "sensitive positions," namely those in which the individual has access to security information.[8] This greatly reduced the scope of the loyalty program, because it previously had been extended to cover all employees, whether or not in sensitive positions. The Supreme Court has not handed down any decision which guarantees a federal employee in a sensitive position the right to confront and cross-examine his accusers. In 1959, it did declare illegal the summary dismissal of an executive employed by a company doing defense work for the government. This executive was dismissed by the firm when the Defense Department, without giving him an opportunity to confront his accusers, revoked his security clearance. The Supreme Court ruled that the executive should not have been deprived of his security clearance, without the safeguards of confrontation and cross-examination, because neither Congress nor the President had authorized such a procedure.[9]

Violations of Procedural Due Process

Fifth, some agency decisions violate principles of procedural due process in relationships with outside parties. In general terms, procedural due process, based on the Fifth and Fourteenth Amendments to the Constitution, means that public officials at all levels of government must be fair in their dealings with private citizens and groups. In specific terms, it means that certain procedural safeguards must be observed. The right of confrontation, just referred to above, illustrates procedural due process as it relates to proceedings against an individual. In this fifth point, however, we have primarily in mind the relationships of government regulatory agencies with business and other groups.

Congress and individual states have sought to deal with this problem by passing what are known as Administrative Procedure Acts.[10] Congress passed such a law in 1946, and there has been considerable discussion and much disagreement about its adequacy ever since. Much of the controversy revolves around technical points which are most appropriately dealt with in the courses in administrative law. For our purposes, it should suffice to say that legislation of this kind

[8] Cole *v.* Young, 351 U.S. 536 (1956).

[9] Greene *v.* McElroy *et al.*, 360 U.S. No. 3, pp. 474–524 (1959).

[10] See Ferrel Heady, "The New Reform Movement in Regulatory Administration," *Public Administration Review*, XIX, No. 2 (Spring, 1959), 89–100.

seeks to establish fair procedures to govern both administrative rule-making and the quasi-judicial decisions made by administrative agencies when they decide whether or not a private individual or group has violated any of the agency's rules or the provisions of the law itself. The legislation usually requires advance notice of issuance of the rule and that an opportunity be given the interested parties to make their reactions known. As to the quasi-judicial proceedings, it spells out the details of the adjudicatory procedure, covering "such matters as specifying issues and giving adequate notice, admissibility of evidence, opportunities for cross-examination, and the process by which decisions are reached."[11] The federal law deals with the problem of impartiality in deciding such cases by making the Civil Service Commission, not the individual agencies, responsible for the appointment of the hearings examiners. The latter "preside in cases not heard by agency heads" and "issue initial or recommended decisions."[12]

Failure to Respect Legislative Intent

Sixth, public officials may keep within the law and respect procedural due process, yet fail to respect legislative intent or to consider the viewpoints of all the groups in a community affected by their decisions. The administrative agency may fully understand what the legislative intent was and decide not to be guided by it. In Chapter 19 instances were cited where the President and the Secretary of Defense have refused to spend additional funds voted by Congress for certain weapons systems. In such cases, the executive branch disregards the legislative intent, because it is convinced that the law-makers have exceeded their powers.

The recent controversy over stockpiling of strategic materials is a good illustration of the disagreements which can arise as to legislative intent. The quantities of certain materials purchased from private companies for the stockpile were found to be far in excess of the nation's security needs. Some members of Congress charged that the Eisenhower Administration had made these excessive purchases

[11] *Ibid.*, p. 91.

[12] Ferrel Heady and Eleanor Tabor Linenthal, "Congress and Administrative Regulation," *Law and Contemporary Problems*, XXVI, No. 2 (Spring, 1961), 247.

simply to help out the domestic producers of the minerals concerned. In their opinion, this was not what Congress had intended when it passed the legislation authorizing the stockpiling program. Purchases were to be made for national security purposes only, not to subsidize domestic producers. Revelations about the billions of dollars of unneeded materials in the stockpile came shortly after John F. Kennedy became President. The issue became partisan, with defenders of the Eisenhower Administration claiming that its decisions did respect Congressional intent, and its critics holding to the opposite view.[13]

As we saw in Chapter 1, in many areas all the legislature can do is to state broad policies in the law and leave their application in individual cases to the administrative agencies. In so doing, the agency's decisions may infuriate individual legislators. The action taken, the latter charge, was not what Congress intended; or on the other hand, action that the legislation plainly called for was deliberately avoided by the agency.

The Federal Communications Commission (FCC) is a case in point. Its function is to regulate radio and television stations in the "public interest," but there are varying interpretations of what this means. Under one view, the FCC should merely function as an "electronic traffic cop," limiting its responsibilities to assigning radio frequencies and television channels. Under another interpretation, it should construe its function to extend also to assuring that the broadcasters provide balanced programming and that they improve the quality of the programs.[14] For years, the FCC functioned mostly as the "electronic traffic cop." Station licenses were renewed as a matter of course; there was very little critical review of the programming. Kennedy's first Chairman of the FCC, Newton N. Minow, frankly stated that he thought that the television stations and the commercial sponsors had too low an opinion of the public's tastes, and under Minow, the FCC initiated a new policy under which renewal of station licenses was no longer virtually automatic. More careful scrutiny was made of the broadcaster's past programming to determine whether or not it really was in the "public interest." Robert W.

[13] See *Inquiry into the Strategic and Critical Material Stockpiles of the United States*, Senate Subcommittee on National Stockpile and Naval Petroleum Reserves, 87th Congress, 2nd Session, Washington, D.C.: Government Printing Office, 1962 and 1963.

[14] See *Broadcasting and Government Regulation in a Free Society*, Center for the Study of Democratic Institutions, Santa Barbara, Cal.: 1959.

Sarnoff, Chairman of the Board of the National Broadcasting Company, immediately challenged Minow's interpretation of the public interest. He said that the FCC's authority to license stations did not give it the "responsibility of raising viewers' tastes or broadening their interests to conform to its own views on what those tastes and interests should be."[15] Disagreeing with Sarnoff, one editorial writer asked, "What is that public interest, if not in 'raising viewers' tastes' and 'broadening their interests'?"[16]

The regulatory commissions are by no means the only agencies which function under general mandates, making possible the charge that they have disregarded legislative intent. Decisions of the Secretary of the Interior are sometimes criticized as favoring special interests, such as the private power companies, mining concerns, and the livestock grazers. Partisans of public power, the conservation of natural resources, and the improvement of recreation facilities for the general public have allies in Congress who can and do raise the charge of failure to observe legislative intent. As we saw in Chapter 11, there are numerous "publics" which the same administrative agency must serve. Of course, there are some clear-cut cases where, by no stretch of the imagination, can administrative decisions be said to conform with policies specifically stated in the law. Frequently, however, the decisions can be justified by the agency as obeying part of its legislative mandate and being in direct conflict with no other provision of the law.

Gross Inefficiency

Seventh, some public officials or their subordinates may prove grossly incompetent, and, as a result, the public suffers. No matter how good their intentions, if the administrative agencies fail to get their job done properly, they have not met their responsibilities. The legislators and the public should not, and usually do not, expect perfect performance. If millions and even billions of dollars are wasted because of carelessness, this is hardly excusable. Some mistakes and some inefficiency will be tolerated as inevitable; gross inefficiency, however, falls in a different category.

If, through inefficient procedures, the agencies themselves are re-

[15] *St. Louis Post-Dispatch*, February 3, 1962, editorial page.
[16] *Ibid.*

sponsible for their huge backlog of work, this is not responsible administration. In 1960, James M. Landis reported that the national regulatory commissions had many cases pending before them for more than three years; that it was taking the Securities and Exchange Commission two or three times the 20-day statutory period to register new securities; and that it would take the Federal Power Commission 13 years to clear its pending cases with the procedures it was then following.[17] Landis found that the commissioners were trying to decide too many of the cases themselves, so he recommended that they delegate much of this work to panels specially constituted within the commissions and to hearing examiners. Congress has since approved Presidential reorganization plans for several of the commissions, incorporating these recommendations of Landis.

The regulatory commissions are by no means the only agencies which have in the past been bogged down because of inefficient procedures. An official indifferent to the need for efficiency is an irresponsible official, no matter how honest he is. Observing the law means not only respecting the statutes dealing with improper activities, but also those requiring completion of the work within designated time periods. If it is humanly impossible to meet these deadlines, that is another matter. Sometimes the legislature itself is to blame, because it refuses to authorize the money needed to hire all the staff that is required to do the job adequately. It is sometimes very difficult to pinpoint responsibility for administrative failures, as charges and countercharges are made by administrative officials, the legislators, the press, and others. An administrative agency with a proven record of efficient operations in the past is in the best position to come out on top in such disputes.

Covering up Mistakes

Eighth, some officials may try to cover up their mistakes and errors, or refuse to cooperate with the legislative body or the public, as was shown in detail in Chapter 11, Public Relations. As we saw, whether the official has refused to cooperate is often a matter of opinion. The staunchest defenders of the public interest sometimes refuse to accede to certain demands of the legislators. What the in-

[17] James M. Landis, *Report on Regulatory Agencies to the President-Elect*, Senate Subcommittee on Administrative Practice and Procedure, 86th Congress, 2nd Session, Washington, D.C.: Government Printing Office, 1960, p. 6.

furiated legislator brands irresponsible conduct, the press and much of the public may regard as great courage on the part of the official concerned.

Failure to Show Initiative

Ninth, some public officials fail to make positive decisions and to exercise the discretion they have under the law. What we have primary reference to here is the unwillingness of public officials to take action, not because they do not sympathize with the laws they administer, but basically because they lack initiative. A number of examples will make this clear. The official may be afraid of criticism if he takes a certain action even though the circumstances clearly call for it. He decides to play safe by doing nothing, and, in a good many cases, no one will criticize him. Indeed, his superiors may never even know that there was action that he could have taken had he been more courageous. As another possibility, the official may decide it is too much work to find out whether something can be done. He saves himself from this "extra work" by saying "no" to the solicitor. The latter may be another employee asking about some privilege, or a member of the public asking for a certain service. Of course, complaints can be made about officials who evade their responsibilities in this way. Often, however, the solicitor does not have the necessary knowledge to question the validity of the denial of his request. Furthermore, many people are reluctant to complain. Many who do get nowhere with superior officers who treat the complaints perfunctorily and give them small consideration.

This ninth and final point is of particular importance, because too often responsibility is thought of in negative terms only. Unless he commits an overt wrong, the public employee cannot be said to have failed to fulfill his public trust. This is faulty reasoning, because the employee should contribute a maximum, not a minimum, of service.

Charles S. Hyneman writes: "It is possible that government in America fails to accord with the will of the people fully as much because administrative officials fail to rise to these demands for initiative and leadership as because they overextend the authority that is given them."[18] V. O. Key, Jr. says:

[18] Charles S. Hyneman, *Bureaucracy in a Democracy*, New York: Harper and Row, 1950, p. 33.

The danger of the rise of a bureaucracy aggressively grasping for unwarranted power is probably much less than the danger of drifting into a condition in which the bureaucracy is purely a negative force. A seasoned bureaucracy, without heroic measures to the contrary, tends to become attached to the time-honored ways of doing things, hostile toward innovation, lacking in initiative, and timid. These qualities are admirable at the right time and place, but the next few decades in the United States will hardly be the time and place for pleasant habituation to the customary.[19]

BIBLIOGRAPHY

"Ethics in the Public Service," An Annotated Bibliography, *Public Personnel Review*, **XXIII,** No. 4 (October, 1962).

Heady, Ferrel, "The New Reform Movement in Regulatory Administration," *Public Administration Review*, **XIX,** No. 2 (Spring, 1959).

Hyneman, Charles S., *Bureaucracy in a Democracy*, New York: Harper and Row, 1950.

Long, Norton E., "Power and Administration," *Public Administration Review*, **IX,** No. 4 (Autumn, 1949).

Redford, Emmette S., *Administration of National Economic Control*, New York: Macmillan, 1952.

Schwartz, Bernard, *The Professor and the Commissions*, New York: Knopf, 1959.

Senate Subcommittee on Administrative Practice and Procedure of the Committee on the Judiciary, 86th Congress, 2nd Session, *Report on Regulatory Agencies to the President-Elect*, Washington, D.C.: Government Printing Office, 1959.

Special Subcommittee on Legislative Oversight of the House Committee on Interstate and Foreign Commerce, 85th Congress, 2nd Session, *Independent Regulatory Commissions*, Washington, D.C.: Government Printing Office, 1959.

[19] V. O. Key, Jr., *Politics, Parties, and Pressure Groups*, 4th ed., New York: Crowell, 1958, pp. 763–764.

CHAPTER 22

Enforcing Administrative Responsibility

In describing the possible abuses of administrative power, some of the methods of administrative control were mentioned in the previous chapter. What now follows is a more complete discussion of these controls, as well as a critical examination of their effectiveness.

LAWS AGAINST FRAUDULENT ACTS

As to embezzlement, accepting bribes, and similar acts of dishonesty, the control problem is relatively simple as far as punishment is concerned. As one example, federal law makes it a crime for anyone who "corruptly gives, offers, or promises anything of value to any public official or person who has been selected to be a public official . . . with intent to influence any official act; or to influence such public official or person who has been selected to be a public official, to commit or aid in committing, or collude in, or allow, any fraud, or make opportunity for the commission of any fraud, on the United States. . . ."[1] The employee who accepts the "thing of value" is also guilty of fraud under the law. All the states have laws against bribery and graft.[2] Thus, the public employee who is tried in court

[1] Section 201, Public Law 87–849, 87th Congress.

[2] *Report Submitted by the Legislative Research Council Relative to Conflict of Interest,* Boston: Commonwealth of Massachusetts, May, 1961, p. 28.

and found guilty of fraud will be given a jail term, like any other criminal. Naturally, not all acts of fraud are detected in government, anymore than they are in industry. It sometimes also happens that, while the evidence of malfeasance is clear enough, it is not sufficient to obtain a conviction in court. In such cases, however, the employee concerned can be dismissed.

CLOSING THE LOOPHOLES IN CONFLICT-OF-INTEREST STATUTES

But sometimes the laws have loopholes; they may even require punishment of lesser offenses but permit no action to be taken against those guilty of major ones. For many years, this was true of the federal conflict-of-interest statutes. Before these laws were changed recently, a former federal official was barred for a period of two years after his separation from the service from handling any claim which was pending anywhere in the government when it employed him. The courts interpreted the word *claim* to mean demands for money only. Actually, much of the influence peddling, by present or former employees, has to do with applications for federal licenses and contracts which run into millions of dollars. A former government lawyer could not help a client with a claim for an income tax refund, but he could use his contacts in the government to influence the awarding of contracts involving very large sums of money. As President Kennedy said in a special message to Congress in April, 1961: "The fundamental defect of these statutes as presently written is that on the one hand, they permit an astonishing range of private interests and activities by public officials which are wholly incompatible with the duties of public office; on the other hand, they create wholly unnecessary obstacles to recruiting qualified people for Government Service."[3] The new federal conflict-of-interest statute corrects this lamentable omission by covering not only claims but any application or matter before the government.

Another kind of loophole exists when certain categories of officials are exempted from the law. In Chapter 1, it was stated that public administration also includes the work of the legislators. The new federal statute excludes them from its coverage. This is frequently

[3] *St. Louis Post-Dispatch*, April 28, 1961.

referred to as the *double standard*, even by some legislators themselves. Senator Keating of New York has said:

> It is slightly hypocritical for us to sit there and question nominees for the executive branch, and set rigid standards for them, and not insist on such standards for ourselves. . . . We question the nominee for Secretary of the Treasury and ask him if he has any oil stock, because he may have to make a decision regarding the depletion allowance. But the ones doing the questioning may themselves own stock in oil companies.[4]

James Reston has written:

> As the government gets deeper into the national economy, with a 50-billion-dollar defense budget alone, the scramble for defense contracts becomes increasingly savage, and the pressure of Congressmen to help get contracts—which, in turn, often produce campaign contributions—add to the perplexities about how to vote and even how to act. Meanwhile, the Congress, which is so alert to conflicts of interest and the need for modernization in the executive branch of the government, is more riddled with conflicts of interest, more dominated by individual power and whim, and more out of date than any branch in Washington.[5]

Another exempt group is the military. Many high-ranking military men have retired and accepted jobs with defense contractors as lobbyists. Charges have been made that, in making decisions or letting contracts, Defense Department officials favor the companies which hire their former colleagues. Senator Russell of Georgia, Chairman of the Armed Services Committee, in expressing disappointment over the exclusion of this group, said, "while I am not impugning anyone's motives, this situation is certainly susceptible to more abuse than any other conflict of interest area in the Government."[6]

State governors urging passage of conflict-of-interest laws sometimes find a singular lack of interest on the part of the legislators. The latter fear that the legislation will be so drafted as to include them along with officials of the administrative branch. Much of the practice of lawyer members of state legislatures consists of representation of private individuals before state licensing and other agencies. One governor who recently urged that a comprehensive

[4] *New York Times*, February 19, 1961.
[5] *St. Louis Post-Dispatch*, July 25, 1962, editorial section.
[6] *Ibid.*, October 10, 1962.

conflict-of-interest law be passed in his state had this to say: "I certainly do not believe the argument that lawyer members of the legislature will lose large parts of their law practice has any cogency, because I believe that if a large part of their law practice is of a nature to be affected by this action, they have the practice not because they are lawyers but because they are legislators."[7]

PREVENTING UNETHICAL CONDUCT

Those drafting conflict-of-interest statutes realize that they cannot be so worded as to identify and proscribe every kind of possible influence peddling. The opening section in the statute passed in 1960 in Kentucky reads: "The purpose of this Act is to prescribe standards to guide public officers and employees in the conduct of their offices or employment, and to proscribe improper conduct *to the extent which such conduct may be sufficiently described to enable statutory prohibitions against it to be properly enforced.*"[8] As previously indicated, the dilemma is that, if the conflict-of-interest statutes are too tightly drawn, they may have the effect of deterring perfectly honest persons from accepting government jobs.

Conflict-of-interest situations, however, are not the only ones in which public employees may be guilty of unethical conduct. Favoring one of the agency's "publics" over the others does not exemplify high integrity. Other illustrations could be given, but suffice it to say that a faulty sense of ethics accounts for much of the censurable behavior by public employees.

Codes of Ethics

This brings us to the consideration of codes of ethics. Eisenberg writes:

> A code of ethics is best defined as a statement of acceptable standards of behavior for government officials and employees. The code may be embraced in a statute or merely in departmental regulations or in a legislative resolution. It serves the purpose of clearly stating to public

[7] *Ibid.*, March 30, 1962.

[8] *Report Submitted by the Legislative Research Council Relative to Conflict of Interest, op. cit.*, p. 37. Italics ours.

officials and to the public what is acceptable behavior. A code too may carry with it sanctions—although the sanctions are seldom criminal. Dismissal from office is a common sanction associated with codes of ethics. Implicit in the promulgation of a code of ethics, however, is the notion that each situation in the future will be evaluated on its particular merits.[9]

A number of state and municipal governments have passed legislation providing for codes of ethics. New York State has a Public Officers Law which, in addition to a section on conflicts of interest, includes a code of ethics. The code prescribes standards of conduct, some fairly specific and others very general. As an illustration of a general standard, it is stated that the public employee "should endeavor to pursue a course of conduct which will not raise suspicion among the public that he is likely to be engaged in acts that are in violation of his trust."[10] This makes clear one of the limitations of codes of ethics. Descriptions of the desired conduct are couched in such general terms that the employee can easily justify his behavior as proper. Nonetheless, many people are strong partisans of the codes, and they are increasingly being adopted, sometimes through the voluntary action of professional organizations of public employees, sometimes in the form of departmental regulations. In his message on conflicts of interest, President Kennedy announced that he was instructing "each Cabinet member and agency head to issue regulations designed to maintain high moral and ethical standards within his own department."[11] He also said that he was asking each agency to establish an ad hoc committee "to serve in an advisory capacity on ethical problems as they arise."[12] Finally, in order "to insure that all employees are held to the same general standards of conduct," he planned to designate a member of his Executive Office staff, reporting directly to him, to be in charge of "coordinating ethics administration" throughout the government. The idea of agency codes, however, was nothing new. Even prior to the President's directives, they had been adopted in several of the agencies.

[9] Ralph Eisenberg, "Conflicts of Interest Situations and Remedies," *Rutgers Law Review*, **XIII**, No. 4 (Summer, 1959), 672.

[10] *Report Submitted by the Legislative Research Council Relative to Conflict of Interest, op. cit.*, p. 43.

[11] *St. Louis Post-Dispatch*, April 28, 1961.

[12] *Ibid.*

"Legislating Morality"

An oft-repeated argument against the codes is that you cannot "legislate morality." If people do not have it in their hearts to adhere to high ethical standards, no code of ethics will reform them. The counterargument is that organized society has always legislated morality:

> A defensive view that "You can't legislate the Ten Commandments" overlooks the fact that wherever the Ten Commandments are held in high regard, legislative bodies have found it necessary to elaborate and enforce their basic principles. It is the function of a considerable part of the penal code to deal in more detail with matters which are specifically prohibited by the Ten Commandments. Every civilized people supplements its moral code with an extensive criminal code and with a vast body of civil law.[13]

Another objection is that you cannot expect the ethics of public officials to be any higher than those of the public as a whole. The Senate Subcommittee just quoted acknowledged that "the clever man who makes a 'fast buck' gets a certain amount of acclaim, provided he makes enough of them. The political trickster frequently can claim his rewards—if he wins. There is a tolerance in American life for unscrupulous methods which bring immediate rewards, even though those methods, if they should become universal, would destroy the very society in which they are tolerated."[14] The Subcommittee pointed out, however, that there is a two-way relationship between standards of conduct in public affairs and those prevailing in the country generally. If the people are not too much concerned about ethical considerations, this will be reflected in the behavior of many public officials. Conversely, if the latter go about setting an example of high integrity, this should raise the standards of the public. Those in positions of public leadership can inspire the citizen to follow certain principles—provided they themselves practice them.[15]

After all, the codes can do no harm, and their potentialities for doing good may be great. If they were totally ineffective, it is hard to

[13] *Ethical Standards in Government*, Senate Subcommittee on Labor and Public Welfare, 82nd Congress, 1st Session, Washington, D.C.: Government Printing Office, 1951, p. 14.

[14] *Ibid.*, p. 9.

[15] *Ibid.*, p. 7.

see why for so long doctors, lawyers, engineers, businessmen, and many others have placed such great reliance on them. While it is true that individual members of these groups have been guilty of unethical conduct, it can hardly be claimed that for the professions as a whole the codes are dead letters. In the main, they serve the very important function of reminding the individual of his professional obligations.

The Inner Check

Some people place great emphasis on what they call the *inner check*. By this, they mean the individual's own sense of responsibility to the public. As John M. Gaus has written: "There is the possibility of influencing directly and personally, in part, as it were, from within, the attitude of the official toward his job. Professional standards and ethics may seem external; yet they operate on the thought and feeling of the individual, opening new vistas of action and objective, creating a warmth of personal association in a corporate enterprise."[16] Other writers are frankly skeptical of the inner check. Human nature being what it is, they are convinced that the main reliance must be placed on external controls over the employee. The disagreement is basically a question of emphasis. Those who emphasize the inner check fully appreciate that external controls are also needed. They feel, however, that every effort should be made to influence the employee "from within."

The official's sense of responsibility is, of course, the product of his entire previous history. This is why discriminating practices in the original selection of personnel are so essential. No code of ethics will make much of an impact on someone who for long has been convinced that the smart man does not let his conscience bother him about the methods he uses in attaining his ends.

CONTROLLING OFFICIALS WHO EXCEED THEIR POWERS

Concerning officials who are personally honest but exceed their legal authority, several kinds of controls are available. If it is a clear case of an *ultra vires* act, that is, one not within the official's powers

[16] John M. Gaus, *Reflections on Public Administration*, University: Univ. of Alabama Press, 1947, pp. 115–116.

as defined in the law, the injured party can appeal to the courts and get the action rescinded. If the official has jurisdiction but uses his authority in such a way as to violate the constitutional rights of the citizen, recourse can also be had to the courts. The example was given of police officers who arrest demonstrators for "disturbing the peace." This action is within the scope of their powers, and they may be sustained in the local courts. When such cases reach them on appeal, the federal courts will, however, set aside the convictions as a violation of freedom of speech and assembly when they are convinced that the demonstrators were behaving peaceably.

PREVENTING INJUSTICE TO THE EMPLOYEE

With respect to unfair treatment by the agency of its own employees, this may, in part, be avoided or corrected by control agencies within the executive branch. An employee who is dismissed allegedly for inefficiency, but actually because he is not liked because of his political views, can appeal to the Civil Service Commission. If it decides that the removal was really made for political reasons, it will order the employee restored to his position. Furthermore, punitive action may be taken against the official responsible for the dismissal. The Model State Civil Service Law provides for a punishment of forfeiture of position and of ineligibility for reappointment in the state service for a one-year period.[17]

Perhaps the situation is different. The case might be one of a federal employee who has lost his job as the result of a reduction in force. He claims the agency did not correctly interpret the law and the relevant regulations when it terminated his services. Let us assume that he appeals to the Civil Service Commission, but the latter decides in favor of the agency. The employee can still take his case to the courts which may decide in his favor. The legal provisions governing reduction in force and many other personnel actions are complicated and susceptible of different interpretations. Palpable injustices are seldom committed by the agency managements, and they are almost always rescinded by the central personnel agency. When appeals do go to the courts, they will not hesitate to uphold the

[17] See Felix A. Nigro, *Public Personnel Administration*, New York: Holt, Rinehart and Winston, 1959, Appendix A, p. 460.

employee if they are convinced that the action taken against him was arbitrary, capricious, and without foundation in law.[18]

INSURING OBSERVANCE OF PROCEDURAL DUE PROCESS

As to failure to observe procedural due process in relations with business and other groups, the injured party can appeal the agency's action to the courts. There would be no purpose in passing administrative procedure acts if the regulatory agencies were not required to observe the detailed requirements spelled out in such legislation. These are questions of law, and the courts will go into them thoroughly. Such appeals from actions of the national regulatory commissions are heard by the United States Circuit Courts of Appeal. They will set aside the commission's decisions if they find any violations of procedural due process. Furthermore, they will also do so if they believe the decisions to be "unsupported by competent, material, and substantial evidence in view of the entire record as submitted."[19] This means that the courts will examine questions of fact as well as of law, and administrative rulings may be nullified on both grounds.

Since judicial remedies have already been mentioned several times in this chapter, it is appropriate at this juncture to stress their limitations in practice. As Gaus comments: "Control by the courts is likely to be control after the event, and preventive largely in the sense of a warning to administrators of 'Don't do it again that way,' and 'Go back in this particular case and start over again,' or 'Do it as we here suggest.' "[20] Don K. Price explains these limitations in more detail:

> The problem of judicial review has been magnified out of all importance, for in numerous types of cases that are handled by administrative agencies the citizen would get little or no tangible protection from appealing to the courts. Many administrative agencies, in matters of adjudication, deal with questions that have to be answered immediately in order to prevent hardship, or that individually do not justify the cost of legal proceedings.

[18] See *Civil Service Journal*, III, No. 3 (January–March, 1963), 26.

[19] Ferrel Heady, "The New Reform Movement in Regulatory Administration," *Public Administration Review*, XIX, No. 2 (Spring, 1959), 91.

[20] Gaus, *op. cit.*, p. 110.

Thus an unsuccessful claimant for a small social security benefit will usually not hire a lawyer to contest a doubtful case, simply because the odds are not worth the cost. A grower will not take to court a decision by an examiner of the United States Department of Agriculture condemning a carload of perishable commodities, for his goods will decay before they could be introduced as evidence. A securities broker will find little satisfaction in appealing from an adverse decision of the Securities and Exchange Commission on the listing of a security, for the opportunity to sell it profitably may have gone.

To depend mainly on judicial review in these cases would be futile. The chief problem is how to organize on a fair basis the system of rendering the original decision. The volume of administrative decisions alone would make it unwise to rely too extensively on review by the courts. . . . What the courts can do, however, is to protect the fundamental rights of citizens to fair treatment in the hearing of their cases, and to maintain the basic political and constitutional relationship between the administrative agency and other branches of government. . . .[21]

PROTECTING THE INTERESTS OF THE WHOLE PUBLIC

Responsible administration takes place only if all groups in the community with a legitimate interest in the agency's program are given the opportunity to make their views known. The provisions in the administrative-procedure acts requiring public notice of intention to issue rules and giving interested parties the opportunity to offer objections are useful in this connection, but they are no guarantee that the agency will give appropriate weight to all the points of view expressed. Furthermore, many decisions, such as in letting contracts, making loans, and deciding which programs within a multipurpose agency to emphasize, are not, and should not, be covered in administrative-procedures legislation.

Use of Advisory Committees

One technique used a good deal is the creation of advisory committees on which the different interest groups are represented. Sometimes the legislation requires establishment of such committees; in

[21] Don K. Price, "The Judicial Test," in Fritz Morstein Marx (ed.), *Elements of Public Administration*, Englewood Cliffs, N.J.: Prentice-Hall, 1959, pp. 488–489.

other cases, the head of the agency decides that he needs outside advice and voluntarily sets up the committee. The advantage of the advisory committee is that it can make known to the administrator points of view of which he otherwise might not be aware. Policies proposed by the agency's expert staffs may overlook practical difficulties which might arise in putting them into effect. The members of the advisory committee can save the agency some mistakes by warning of these difficulties.

If, as Maass and Radway suggest, one of the criteria for judging administrative responsibility should be the extent to which the agency succeeds in "winning group consent," proper use of advisory committees can contribute greatly to that objective. At the same time, another of their criteria is that the agency should equalize "opportunities to safeguard interests" and give "equitable treatment" to each of the major interests affected by its program.[22] It is here that in practice advisory committees often fail to function as they should, for the more powerful groups represented on them may dominate their deliberations. In such case the committee will "provide the administration with a distorted view of interest opinion and provide a focus through which the strong and strategically-located interests may exert a disproportionate amount of influence."[23]

Actually there is no foolproof way of assuring that administrators equalize "opportunities to safeguard interests." It is frequently a matter of opinion whether or not an agency is pursuing policies which benefit one interest group as against another. Individual legislators themselves often exert pressure on the agency heads on behalf of *one* particular group. Each legislator represents the voters in his constituency, not the entire public. Administrators, it can be argued, are in a better position to consider the needs and desires of the whole public. In any event, in some cases it will be clear that the agency is not giving "equitable treatment" to a certain group or groups. The legislators can investigate and put pressure on the Chief Executive to correct such situations, or the latter may take the initiative in the matter and even remove the agency head if he believes this necessary.

[22] Arthur A. Maass and Lawrence I. Radway, "Gauging Administrative Responsibility," in Dwight Waldo (ed.), *Ideas and Issues in Public Administration*, New York: McGraw-Hill, 1953, p. 445.

[23] Emmette S. Redford, *Administration of National Economic Control*, New York: Macmillan, 1952, p. 262.

In many instances, however, conclusive proof will be lacking that the agency failed to act in accordance with the "public interest," and the offended groups will achieve no success with their protests.

ELIMINATING GROSS INCOMPETENCE

The most effective control mechanism to prevent gross incompetence on the part of public employees is a good personnel program. The personnel offices in the line departments and the central personnel agency should exert positive leadership to raise levels of performance. Although the key factor is the quality of the personnel recruited, other staff groups besides the personnel men can make important contributions to efficiency. Administrative analysts, now employed in many agencies, make detailed studies of organization and procedures, with the purpose of eliminating delays, waste, and other inefficiency. Efficiency is, however, more than a question of good organization and procedures; it is also the product of the attitudes and values of the public employees. This is why the discussion of administrative responsibility overlaps at so many points. The inner check can provide the will to be efficient. The best management studies will not result in substantial improvements, if the employees feel no great urge to perform up to their abilities.

As to officials who try to cover up their mistakes, since this subject was dealt with in Chapter 11, Public Relations, it will not be discussed here. Suffice it to say that it is a firmly established principle in American government that administrative officials should be required to justify their actions to the lawmakers. No matter how confident he is that his action was correct, the official must accept the responsibility for explaining "why" to the legislators. If the highest-ranking executive of them all, the President of the United States, can, during his press conferences, patiently answer a barrage of questions, some of them "loaded," it is hard to see why any public official, anywhere in the United States, should have any other attitude.

The employee who lacks initiative and fails to take action is particularly difficult to deal with, because the question then is how to put life into the bureaucracy. The greatest need here is an administrative leadership which encourages and rewards employees who show initiative and creativity. If those in the top positions demonstrate that they really want employees with ideas and energy, then the organizations they direct come alive. This is why legislative bodies err grievously when they put detailed requirements into the laws which narrow the administrative officials' discretion. As Woodrow Wilson so wisely said:

> If to keep his office a man must achieve open and honest success, and if at the same time he feels himself intrusted with large freedom of discretion, the greater his power the less likely is he to abuse it, the more is he nerved and sobered and elevated by it. The less his power, the more safely obscure and unnoticed does he feel his position to be, and the more readily does he relapse into remissness.[24]

EVALUATION OF LEGISLATIVE CONTROLS

Throughout this chapter, reference has been made to some of the methods used by legislatures to control administration. Various control devices used were mentioned, but there was not the opportunity to refer to all of the principal ones. An evaluation was previously made in this chapter of judicial remedies. What are the strengths and weaknesses of the legislative controls?

The principal legislative controls are:

1. passage, amendment, and possible repeal of the enabling legislation under which administrative agencies function;
2. review and approval or disapproval of budgetary requests;
3. investigations by standing or select committees of the conduct of agency programs;
4. direct participation in agency decisionmaking, in line with the doctrine of codirectorship discussed in Chapter 1;
5. performance of *case work* for constituents, also mentioned in Chapter 1;
6. the action taken in confirming or not the appointment of high-ranking officials.

Changing the Enabling Legislation

If Congress is displeased with the policy decisions of executive officials, it can tie their hands by writing certain prohibitions into the law. The President can be directed by law not to make foreign aid available to certain countries; the Federal Communications Act

[24] Waldo, *op. cit.*, p. 73.

can be amended so as to make entirely clear what policies Congress wants the FCC to follow with respect to pay television. It is a post-control, however, and may be criticized also for placing too many shackles on the administrators. In many programs, the administrators must be left with certain discretion, and there is no way of predicting with certainty what kinds of policy decisions they will make. Furthermore, the legislators themselves disagree as to whether the administrators' decisions were correct or not. This greatly reduces the possibilities of passage of amendments to the enabling legislation. Too, it may be that the administrators were right, and that the legislature would be wrong if it amended the law. The press has often criticized legislative decisions which reverse administrative policies and argued that the people should vote such legislators out of office at the next elections.

If the legislature has serious doubts about the agency's program, it can authorize it only for a limited period of time, subject to renewal. This is what Congress has done with foreign aid. Each year it again reviews the whole question of whether or not there should be a foreign-aid program. First, the bill authorizing continuation of the program is considered, and then the amounts to be expended are taken up in a separate appropriations bill. Sometimes the authorizing legislation provides for total expenditures which are reduced drastically in the appropriation bill as finally enacted. V. O. Key, Jr. writes:

> Legislation enacted to be in effect only for one year or some other determinate period assures congressional review of administrative policy and performance when an extension of power is sought. For months preceding the renewal of such an act, its administrators walk warily, perhaps fearing to take steps of urgent importance lest some group in Congress be annoyed. They must wage battle for renewal when the expiration dates of such statutes approach, and the difficulty of obtaining positive action from Congress gives to opponents of a policy based on short-term legislation tactical advantages they would not enjoy if they had to seek outright repeal.[25]

Inability to make long-term commitments may, however, make it difficult or even impossible for a program to be successful. How can

[25] V. O. Key, Jr., "Legislative Control," in Marx, *op. cit.*, pp. 313–314.

foreign aid be effective when the recipient countries are urged to develop long-range economic-development programs but told at the same time that assurances about grant funds can only be made for a twelve-month period? Of course, if the Congressman is not enthusiastic about foreign aid, this argument will fail to convince him. Legislative control means control by the dominant group in the legislature at a particular time. Unfortunately, it cannot always be equated either with correct policies from the standpoint of the national interest or with accurate reflection of what the people of the country really want. This suggests that the people themselves should make more positive efforts to assure that legislative and administrative policies are responsive to their desires.

When the legislature is convinced that an administrative agency no longer serves a useful purpose, it can abolish it outright. Scores of agencies have been abolished, many of the emergency variety. Once created, agencies typically struggle to survive. Franklin D. Roosevelt's Committee on Administrative Management said: "There is among governmental agencies great need for a coroner to pronounce them dead, and for an undertaker to dispose of the remains."[26]

Again, however, there may be a strong difference of opinion as to whether the agency is really dispensable. When Congress finally abolished the National Resources Planning Board in 1943, it decided not to take a chance on the agency rising from the dead. So it specifically provided in the legislation terminating the Board that no similar agency could be created by Executive Order of the President.[27] Many people felt at the time that it was a mistake to abolish this central planning agency, and feel that a similar agency is needed right now. So here again we have an example of how an act of "control" by the legislature is defensible or indefensible, depending on the point of view. In many cases, any threat to abolish the entire agency is out of the question. Perhaps it has existed for decades, and its services must be continued because of the public's demand for them. A much more frequent threat is to reduce the agency's scale

26 *Administrative Management in the Government of the United States*, Washington, D.C.: Government Printing Office, 1937, p. 34.

27 John D. Millett, *The Process and Organization of Government Planning*, New York: Columbia Univ. Press, 1947, p. 150.

of operations or to fail to provide funds for certain of its programs. This brings us to the appropriation process, regarded by many as the most effective weapon in the arsenal of legislative controls.

Control Through Action on Budget Requests

In Chapter 18, it was seen that the form in which the executive branch presents the estimates has much to do with the legislators' understanding of what is being proposed. Efficient budgetary procedures within the executive branch will promote more effective legislative review of proposed expenditures.

Perhaps a Joint Committee on the Budget with its professional staff would help Congressmen make sounder judgments about the justification for the Executive's requests for funds. Yet even if this and other recommended improvements were adopted and proved to have the advantages their proponents claim for them, the task of the legislature in reviewing the budget requests would still remain a difficult one. Governmental programs are now so large and complex that the legislator does not have the time to make a thorough appraisal of all the budget proposals. This, of course, is no argument for their not trying to make the best possible review under the circumstances. It is rather a statement of the practical limitations of legislative budgetary control under present conditions. At the national level, more than half the spending requests are for national defense and related purposes. Although many Congressmen have, on occasion, claimed that defense expenditures could be cut, in practice Congress is generally reluctant to make large reductions in this part of the budget. Many Congressmen feel that they are in no position to substitute their judgment for that of the President and his civilian and military advisors on the security needs of the nation. Thus, the tendency is to try to economize on such programs as foreign aid and to hold the line on expenditures for domestic programs, such as new federal grants to the states.

In desperation, legislators sometimes propose "across-the-board" cuts, i.e., a straight percentage reduction in all programs. They want economies but are not sure where they can be found, so they resolve the problem "equitably" by applying the same percentage reduction to all the agencies. This is frequently referred to as the *meat-ax* approach. The butcher's knife trims the agency programs in a neat, straight line, but in budgeting this means penalizing the efficient programs along with the inefficient ones. Of course, to some legislators, no program is so desirable and so well managed that it should be spared from the meat-ax. Admittedly, the meat-ax may reflect the legislators' conviction that the "empire-builders" in the executive branch habitually submit inflated expenditure requests. The way to protect against this abuse, however, is to identify the agencies which are guilty of such practices, and not to punish the innocent along with the guilty.

Legislators often clamor for economy and demand that the Executive's budget be reduced drastically, yet they will ask for more funds to be spent in their own districts. This is not a characteristic of American legislators alone, because a British financial authority reportedly said: "If you want to raise a certain cheer in the House of Commons, make a general panegyric on economy; if you want to invite a sure defeat, propose a particular saving."[28] Once a spending program is started in a Congressman's district, pressure quickly builds up for him to see to it that it is continued. When he runs for re-election, it is standard practice to remind the constituents of the federal money he has obtained for the district. Members of the state legislatures are also judged largely on the basis of the state funds they get allocated to their home districts. Since this is the role in which the legislator is cast, he cannot be expected to make entirely objective judgments in his votes on spending measures. Yet it can be argued that the legislator's dedication to local interests has its beneficial aspects as well:

> An individual Congressman looks at the budget with concern for the welfare of his region, or district, or state, as well as with concern for national interests. The combined views of many Congressmen will thus reflect an approach to budgeting that is broader geographically but narrower functionally than the approach to budgeting which the President will employ. Both approaches are necessary in a society that is complex and dedicated to pluralistic values. Either one alone could give rise to provincialism or distortion.[29]

[28] Jesse Burkhead, *Governmental Budgeting*, New York: Wiley, 1956, p. 323.
[29] *Ibid.*, p. 321.

Most observers believe that Congress and legislative bodies in general could do a much better job of reviewing spending proposals. Some critics emphasize the need for legislatures to organize themselves more efficiently for purposes of budget review. Others stress the desirability of expanded professional staffs to help the legislators make more thorough analyses of the estimates. Still others express the view that the legislators would be able to exercise more effective control if they stopped trying to go into so much detail, as when they insist on budget presentations on an object-of-expenditure basis. Others see the solution in strengthened party discipline and reorganization of Congress as a whole to make it function more efficiently. Yet, with all its imperfections, legislative budget review does put the administrators on guard. They must be prepared to justify their requests before sharp inquisitors who can ask many embarrassing questions. Few administrative officials are foolish enough to go to legislative budget hearings expecting clear sailing. Most of them do their "homework" well before they make their appearance.

Legislative Investigations

The legislative investigation is a much-used tool of legislative control. Before a single piece of legislation was passed in the 88th Congress, the House and the Senate had authorized or proposed nearly 60 investigations.[30] The purpose of some of these inquiries was to determine new areas in which it might be desirable for Congress to pass legislation. In other cases, the object was to check upon suspected deficiencies in the administration of existing programs. It is safe to say that, whenever allegations are made of serious wrongdoings in the administrative agencies and there seems to be some foundation for the charges, Congress will promptly investigate.

If the purpose of the investigation is simply to dig out the facts and the committee members are not inspired by partisan motives, the inquiry can serve a very useful purpose. A recent example is the investigation made by a Senate subcommittee of the tragedy which occurred in January, 1961, when a radar tower collapsed and sank into the sea during a gale off the Massachusetts coast. Twenty-eight

[30] *New York Times,* Western edition, February 15, 1963.

men died in the disaster. The subcommittee refused to accept the interpretation that the disaster was an act of God. Its conclusion was that all the organizations participating in the construction and operation of Texas Tower No. 4, as it was called, bore a part of the blame. These organizations were: the Navy's Bureau of Yards and Docks, the government's design and construction agency for the project; two private firms, one which was employed to give structural design services and the other to build the tower; and the Air Force, which used the tower. In the opinion of the subcommittee, all four of these groups made mistakes which led to the tragedy.[31] Perhaps the subcommittee erred in at least part of its findings, but our purpose here is only to give an example of a desirable kind of legislative investigations. Not to have made an investigation of a disaster of this kind would be unthinkable. To rely on the government agencies and the contractors concerned to make the investigation would not have been realistic. Self-investigation has never proved itself as an effective corrective of errors or evils of any kind.

Numerous examples could be given of legislative investigations which have spurred the administrative agencies to function more efficiently. On the debit side, some legislators are far more interested in getting publicity for themselves than they are in being impartial fact-finders. The legislator who makes sensational charges can usually count on getting his name in the headlines, so, reasoning that politics is politics, he does not worry about the fairness of his allegations. Recently, Supreme Court Justice William O. Douglas was asked his opinion of Congressional investigations. "Some have rendered outstanding service," he said. "Others have been publicity hounds, men running for office, exposing people for exposure's sake, making a circus of it."[32]

The Chief Executive's enemies in the legislature also often try to use legislative investigations to embarrass him and to gain partisan advantage. They are not interested in an objective analysis of the facts but rather in finding anything which can be used to persuade the electorate that "it is time for a change." Nor is this the tactic of the opposing party only. It is also freely employed by members of the

[31] *St. Louis Post-Dispatch*, April 2, 1962.
[32] *New York Times*, Western edition, Dec. 31, 1962.

Chief Executive's own party who dislike his policies. Pious statements by legislators about the value of a "vigilant" opposition may mask the desire to make it *seem* that the Administration has made a mistake. If enough of the public believe it, then their objective is accomplished. There is evidence, however, that citizens are increasingly aware of the political biases of many of the legislative "investigators." Some of the abuses of investigating committees have become so patent that the supposed beneficiary, the public, is skeptical that it is being served as faithfully as the legislator-sleuths would have it believe.

A leading newspaper makes a balanced statement when it evaluates legislative investigations as follows:

> It goes without saying that some of these investigations will be politically inspired and politically conducted. Some will retrace ground already covered more than once. But whatever their faults and wherever they lead, they cannot be dispensed with. Some may do harm. Others will do good. In either case, and particularly in view of the highly complex problems which confront a 20th century legislator, the power of Congressional investigation is an indispensable instrument of democratic government.[33]

Codirectorship and *casework* were described in Chapter 1 without comment on their desirability as legislative controls over administration, and this will now be considered.

The Pros and Cons of Codirectorship

The principal criticism of *codirectorship* is that it injects Congress into the details of day-by-day administration, a function it is ill-equipped to discharge. Codirectorship is based on the belief that the administrative agencies should be under the direct control of the legislature. While the Constitution permits this interpretation, many people are convinced that the lawmakers exercise more effective control when they accept the principle of "indirect responsibility," namely that "an administrative agency should be responsible to the legislature, but only through the chief executive, and primarily for

[33] *Ibid.*, February 15, 1963.

broad issues of public policy and general administrative performance."[34]

If codirectorship means meddling in details and decisions which competent administrators should be trusted to make, it can justifiably be viewed as interference, rather than desirable collaboration. Questionable acts of administrators can be criticized during the annual budget reviews and in the course of the legislative investigations referred to above. On the other hand, codirectorship may serve the constructive purpose of clarifying legislative intent and preventing erroneous interpretations of the law by the agency heads. If it is true that the bureaucrats sometimes stretch the law, it can be argued that it is desirable to give Congressional committees veto power over certain kinds of proposed administrative action. The difficulty, of course, is in defining which administrative decisions are important enough to fall in this category.

This issue came up in the controversy over the application of the 160-acreage limitation to the federal-state contract for joint construction of California's San Luis water project. Long-standing federal policy, as required by law, is to extend the benefits of irrigation projects only to landowners with tracts of land within this limitation. Basing his decision on a legal opinion given him by the Interior Department's solicitor, Secretary of the Interior Udall approved the San Luis water contract without the acreage limitation. Attorney-General Kennedy offered no objection to this decision, but made the qualifying suggestion that Congress itself should review the matter, since in his opinion there was an area of doubt. Under federal law, such contracts go into effect unless disapproved within a 90-day period by either the Senate or House Interior Committee. Both did approve the contract, despite allegations of Senator Morse of Oregon that suspension of the acreage limitation in effect meant a "giveaway" to the big landowners. Congress can, if it wishes to, of course, change the law and specify what the policy shall be in future cases of this kind.[35] Codirectorship, as revealed in this incident, supplies at least a temporary answer as to legislative intent. So long as the basic legislation cannot cover all contingencies, direct administrative responsi-

[34] Waldo, *op. cit.*, p. 446.
[35] *Los Angeles Times*, April 3 and 4, 1962.

bility to legislative committees can be defended as serving a useful function.

Casework

As to *casework,* it appears to be an indispensable part of the system of administrative responsibility. If administrators were perfect, no constituent would ever have to ask his Congressman for help. On occasion, citizens may not receive the treatment they deserve from administrative officials. Court remedies, as we have seen, are frequently too slow or not even available to correct the particular abuse. Time and time again legislators have intervened to obtain remedial action on justifiable complaints. Of course, many of the complaints are groundless. In such cases, most legislators will be satisfied with the evidence the administrative agency gives them to show that they have acted properly. It also goes without saying that legislative intervention to obtain special favors for constituents is indefensible.

Confirmation of Appointments

Legislative confirmation of appointments to certain high-ranking posts is practiced at all levels of government. In the federal government, positions such as those of department heads, under-secretaries, assistant secretaries, members of regulatory commissions and boards, and ambassadors and ministers are filled by the President, with the advice and consent of the Senate. As explained by Alexander Hamilton in *The Federalist*, the requirement for Senate approval would "tend greatly to prevent the appointment of unfit characters from State prejudice, from family connection, from personal attachment, or from a view to popularity."[36] The President might sometimes slip and make a poor appointment. Presidents sometimes yield to political and personal pressures and nominate persons of mediocre quality. Sometimes they appoint men of undoubted competence but whose past connections make it seem unlikely that they could be counted on to enforce the laws with vigor. An example is Calvin Coolidge's appointment in 1925 of Charles Warren as Attorney-General. Despite

[36] See Felix A. Nigro (ed.), *Public Administration, Readings and Documents*, New York: Holt, Rinehart and Winston, 1951, pp. 443–444.

Coolidge's landslide victory in the elections of 1924, the Senate rejected Warren, not once but twice, when Coolidge resubmitted the nomination. Warren had been connected in various ways with the "Sugar Trust," and opposition Senators did not see how someone with such a background could be trusted to carry out the Attorney-General's responsibility for prosecuting the monopolies.[37]

On the other hand, the Senate sometimes objects to nominees for the opposite reason, namely, because their record indicates that they would press for strong enforcement of the laws. The Senate refused to confirm Truman's reappointment of Leland Olds to the Federal Power Commission (FPC) because of the stand he had taken in favor of FPC regulation of natural gas rates.[38] Hamilton predicted that the Senate would refuse to confirm only for "special and strong reasons," and he assumed that it would carefully scrutinize the nominees' qualifications. In practice, partisan considerations greatly influence the Senators' reaction to a Presidential nomination. If he is of the opposing party, or of a wing in the majority one that does not like the President's policies, he may fight the appointment simply to get at the Chief Executive.[39] Conversely, if he is a loyal follower of the President, he may close his eyes to obvious shortcomings of the appointees.

Legislative confirmation of appointments in practice gives the lawmakers a second opportunity to hold the Chief Executive in check. Even if they do not defeat his legislative proposals, they may be able to cripple their enforcement by rejecting his nominees for key administrative posts. Whether the public has been injured or benefited after the votes have been counted and the nominee accepted or rejected will naturally remain a matter of opinion. Did the people want Charles Warren? Coolidge certainly thought so. But, while the people had elected him, it had also elected the Senate which rejected Warren. Commented the old *New York World*, "if the public elects a Senate which will not confirm the President's nomination, and a

[37] Felix A. Nigro, "The Warren Case," *Western Political Quarterly*, XI, No. 4 (December, 1958), 835–856.

[38] See Joseph P. Harris, "Senatorial Rejection of Leland Olds: A Case Study," *American Political Science Review*, XLV, No. 3 (September, 1951), 677.

[39] Felix A. Nigro, "The Van Buren Confirmation Before the Senate," *Western Political Quarterly*, XIV, No. 1, Part 1 (March, 1961), 148–159.

President who makes a nomination unsatisfactory to the Senate, it must be assumed that the public is getting what it wants."[40]

BIBLIOGRAPHY

Abraham, Henry J., "A People's Watchdog Against Abuse of Power," *Public Administration Review*, **XX,** No. 3 (Summer, 1960).

Chapman, Brian, *The Profession of Government*, London: G. Allen, 1959. Chaps. 9–13.

Gilbert, Charles E., and Kampelman, Max M., "Legislative Control of the Bureaucracy," *Annals of the American Academy of Political and Social Science*, **292** (March, 1954).

Highsaw, Robert B., "The Southern Governor—Challenge to the Strong Executive Theme," *Public Administration Review*, **XIX,** No. 1 (Winter, 1959).

Kammerer, Gladys M., "Legislative Oversight of Administration in Kentucky," *Public Administration Review*, **X,** No. 3 (Summer, 1950).

Key, V. O., "Legislative Control," in Marx, Fritz Morstein (ed.), *Elements of Public Administration*, Englewood Cliffs, N.J.: Prentice-Hall, 1959.

Maass, Arthur A., and Radway, Lawrence I., "Gauging Administrative Responsibility," *Public Administration Review*, **IX,** No. 3 (Summer, 1949).

Nigro, Felix A. (ed.), *Public Administration, Readings and Documents,* New York: Holt, Rinehart and Winston, 1951. Chap. VII.

Waldo, Dwight (ed.), *Ideas and Issues in Public Administration,* New York: McGraw-Hill, 1953. Chaps. 18 and 19.

[40] Nigro, "The Warren Case," *op. cit.*, 854.

PART VII

INTERNATIONAL ADMINISTRATION

CHAPTER 23

International Administration

In this chapter we will be concerned primarily with the problems of administering international organizations. In Chapter 2 reference was made to the social invention of international cooperation in general. In Chapter 3, technical-assistance programs, conducted both by national and international agencies, were discussed in detail. While technical assistance is one of the major activities of international organizations, it is only one part of their work. Because so many new international agencies have been created in recent years, and because they play such an important role in the world of today, this textbook would not be complete without some discussion of this rapidly developing area of administration. Today international affairs loom much larger in the consciousness of the people, both young and old. Many college students show great interest in the possibilities of careers in international agencies or in the foreign services of their own countries. Similarly, quite a few persons who already have substantial work experience are also attracted to overseas employment. They want to do their part to see to it that the "social invention of international cooperation" is perfected to the point that the peoples of the world can live in peace and in general enjoy a happier existence.

THE EXPANDED WORLD COMMUNITY

Multination organizations are by no means new. They are, however, much more numerous today because of a basic change which has taken place in the methods of diplomacy, as explained below:

Traditional diplomacy, with its conventions and accepted practices, assumed that relations between states would normally be carried out on a bilateral basis. Today, account must also be taken of a complex of international and regional machinery, most of it created since World War II. In addition to the United Nations itself, there are many permanent international organizations operating in such specialized fields as agriculture, health, banking, investment, communications, and labor. Beyond these are a variety of regional organizations such as the North Atlantic Treaty Organization, the Southeast Asia Treaty Organization, the Organization of American States, the Intergovernmental Committee for European Migration, and others; and there are countless other multilateral arrangements of one or another type—temporary, *ad hoc*, periodic. Indeed, part of the challenge of diplomacy today lies in the invention of new forms and structures of international relations to meet emerging problems.[1]

The recent great increase in the number of independent nations has affected international administration in several ways. Usually, shortly after the granting of independence to former dependent areas, they are admitted as new members of the United Nations. The result is that the United Nations is now a much bigger organization than it used to be. When it was created in 1945, it had 50 member states; at the moment of writing it has 113 members, many admitted in the past few years. As "colonialism" continues to disappear from the world scene, United Nations membership will continue to grow. The same holds true for the specialized agencies which work closely with the United Nations, such as the World Health Organization, the Food and Agriculture Organization, and the International Telecommunications Union. Furthermore, the greater the number of nation states, the more likely it is that new regional international organizations will be formed and existing ones expanded.

As the world community becomes larger, new voices are heard in the councils of the international organizations and new demands made upon them. The newly independent nations often face a desperate situation as the former "protecting" power withdraws its support. The United Nations and other international organizations must then do what they can to help the new nations survive. As the dra-

[1] *Personnel for the New Diplomacy*, Report of the Committee on Foreign Affairs Personnel, Washington, D.C.: Carnegie Endowment for International Peace, December, 1962, pp. 3–4.

matic example of the Congo illustrates, this may mean having to send an international police force to try to maintain order and to remove the threat to the peace of the world. The evolution of the role of the Secretary-General of the United Nations exemplifies the need for positive action. When the United Nations Charter was signed, it was not contemplated that the Secretary-General would take the initiative and act independently to deal with international crises. The late Dag Hammarskjold developed and put into practice the concept of the *United Nations presence,* namely, that the United Nations should establish itself on the spot in the places where threats to the peace arose. Acting on his own, he himself travelled to these trouble areas, and met his death in an airplane accident on a trip to the Congo. The indications are that his successor, U Thant, takes the same positive view of his responsibilities. We are far from the stage of having an international chief executive in the United Nations Secretary-General, but the strengthening of this post to meet the recurrent crises characteristic of the post-World War II period certainly evidences the greater importance of international administration.

The greater scope of international administration is also evidenced in the innumerable conferences now held between the chiefs of state, foreign ministers, scientists, and other prominent figures of the different nations of the world. Today almost every issue of the daily newspaper contains a report of an international conference of some kind. Domestic matters have become inextricably intertwined with international affairs, with the result that leading officials of national governments must frequently travel abroad. Some officials actually "commute" between their nations' capitals and the sites of conferences abroad, and it is generally appreciated that this is what their jobs require. To the official who has made countless trips to foreign countries, this has become as routine a responsibility as domestic travel. Between July 1, 1961, and June 30, 1962, the United States government sent delegates to a total of 474 international conferences. This represented an average of about two new conferences starting every workday in the year. In these conferences, almost 2800 United States delegates, including private citizens as well as government officials, participated. Some 28 federal agencies employ about 32,000 United States citizens in civilian capacities in some 127 foreign countries, colonies, and dependencies. Most of them are with four agencies: the Department of Defense, the State Department, the Agency for International Development (AID), and the United States Information Agency (USIA). In addition, there are some 95,000 foreign nationals employed by United States agencies abroad.[2]

PROBLEMS OF OVERSEAS PERSONNEL

Many problems of persons serving abroad are much the same, whether they are employed by international organizations or the foreign services of their own countries. Employees of private companies, representatives of missionary groups, and persons working abroad for the numerous voluntary agencies are also exposed to the same problems. This is why the word *overseasmanship* has come into our vocabulary.[3] It means the ability to be effective in relationships with the nationals of the country in which one is stationed. We are not limiting our discussion in this chapter to the problems of staff members of international agencies only. Since people-to-people contacts are so important in international relations today, a general discussion of *overseasmanship* is in order. At the same time, it is recognized that employees of international agencies such as the United Nations do have certain peculiar problems. Working for an international agency, as will be elaborated below, is never completely the same as being an employee of the government of one's own country.

There are a whole host of factors which make the problem of adjustment difficult. Before we discuss some of the most important of them, however, let it be clear that overseas employment has great attractions and is ardently desired by many people. The sense of accomplishment after achieving even limited success in a foreign program is a great sense of satisfaction to persons highly motivated to make a contribution in this kind of work. Furthermore, as we shall see, some of the adjustment problems can be solved, at least in part. The challenge in international service, after all, is that it is difficult and different. If everything were cozy, the challenge, and consequently the interest in the job, would be far less.

[2] *Ibid.*, p. 5.

[3] See Harlan Cleveland and Gerard J. Mangone (eds.), *The Art of Overseasmanship*, Syracuse, N.Y.: Syracuse Univ. Press, 1957.

Social Isolation

A. Loveday, an Englishman who served for 20 years in the secretariat of the League of Nations, mentions first the unhappy circumstance of *social isolation*. No matter how well received he is by the local population, the international civil servant always remains a guest:

> The international official very rarely becomes completely integrated in the local society in which he lives and the international society of which he forms a part never affords full scope for the natural development of the individual personality from its own cultural roots. It is a society based originally on certain tacitly accepted restrictions on self expression and gradually developing from the common experience of its members, a common experience, however, which is in each case divorced from childhood and educational background. The individual, therefore, dumped, as it were, in a community of which he can never form an integral part and limited in self expression, must find either in his work or in some other way an outlet for whatever part of his personality is thus suppressed. If he fails to do so, he gradually shrivels up.[4]

Loveday states that the degree of isolation depends upon the kind of contacts international officials can establish with the local society. Some are more successful than others. The smaller the group, the better are its chances of being integrated into the local community. It is not that the local population has an aversion to the international officials. This may be a contributing factor in the case of some officials who irritate and offend some local residents simply because they are "foreigners." Even in large cosmopolitan settings, such as New York, Paris and Rome, the condition of social isolation exists despite the sophistication of the local society:

> Whatever the country, however, the international official must remain external to the society in which he lives. He is not a working partner; he can play no part in either municipal or national politics. He must accept the social organization for better or worse as he finds it. . . . The international official finds himself therefore with his home, school, and college

[4] A. Loveday, *Reflections on International Administration*, Oxford, England: Clarendon Press, 1956, p. 3.

roots cut and prevented from striking new tap roots. At best he may live as a houseleek lives. He is in consequence forced to join with his colleagues in forming a distinct social group—a quasi-independent and quite artificial community. . . .[5]

Members of national foreign services face the same difficulties as far as integration with local societies is concerned as do international officials. In fact, their situation is worse if they happen to be representative of countries disliked or viewed with distrust by the local population.

Americans are in a somewhat disadvantageous position from this standpoint. In terms of per capita income, the American has an abnormally high standard of living. Desperately poor people are not noted for feelings of friendship towards the extremely wealthy. We are generous in giving foreign aid but this does not make us liked any the more in some countries. In some parts of the world, historical factors also contribute to resentments. Latin America remembers the "big stick diplomacy" of the United States in the early part of the century. No matter how much concrete evidence we have given that we have mended our ways, the stereotypes of "dollar diplomacy" and of Yankee conceptions of superiority still dominate the thinking of millions of Latin Americans.

We are not by any means the only nation plagued by errors and circumstances of the past. The former dependent areas of Africa and Asia have no love for nationals of the powers which once ruled them. Extreme nationalist sentiment in some countries produces animosities towards small neighboring states deeper on occasion than the antipathy towards the United States and other big powers. Of course, the countries which are disliked are also represented in the international organizations. Being a staff member of such organizations does not immunize the official from being the object of prejudice because of his nationality. Nonetheless, there are sometimes distinct advantages in being the representative of a multinational agency, rather than of a foreign government. Those serving in United States technical-assistance programs quickly become aware that in some countries aid from the United Nations is preferred. No nation likes to put itself in any position which can in the slightest be interpreted to mean that

[5] *Ibid.*, p. 4.

it has become the "satellite" of another power. To accept help from an international organization of which the country is a member and to which it contributes financial support is respectable. There are no "strings" attached to aid on a multilateral basis. Accepting help from a government which seems to be making the offer in order to gain "friends" in competition with a rival power offends many countries.

Foreign officials, whether employed by national or international agencies, are forced to live pretty much apart from the local population. Sometimes they do this to the point of forming "national compounds." This is a familiar criticism of the American communities abroad of servicemen, diplomats, and technicians of different kinds, and Mottram Torre has this interesting observation to make:

> This kind of segregation has been criticized by those who believe that American policy is best advanced by maximum personal contact which serves as a bridge for mutual understanding and sympathy. However, compound living has its advantages for Americans who are overwhelmed by a foreign environment and can make only marginal adjustments. Their contacts with the "outside" population are painful and unsuccessful and do not contribute to good public relations. They are much happier when surrounded by fellow-employees and located close to post exchanges, central mess hall, and other American amenities.[6]

This should not be interpreted to mean that Torre favors the idea of compound living. It is a much more satisfactory situation if the Americans can make some cordial contacts with the local residents, rather than sealing themselves off almost completely from them. He points out that the flexible American, even if he lives in a compound, will have many contacts "outside the walls" and can contribute to good public relations.

Climate and Physical Location

A second problem of adjustment has to do with climate and physical location. It is sometimes said that the person who cannot make a satisfactory adjustment to his work and other environment is quick to convince himself that the cause is something outside his control, rather than his own inability to maintain an internal personal equili-

[6] Mottram Torre, "Personality Adjustment in Overseas Service," in *The Art of Overseasmanship, op. cit.*, p. 86.

brium. While this undoubtedly true in some cases, there is ample evidence to show that some of the most balanced personality types find it difficult to maintain their health and vitality in certain climates. For those who have lived all their lives in tropical climates, assignment to such places as United Nations headquarters in New York City may produce health problems, in addition to general discomfort. New York does not pose a health hazard in terms of the sanitation and disease problems found in tropical areas, yet it can prove to be an unhealthy place to live for someone who comes from the tropics. The ability to adapt to the climate depends on previous hot or cold weather experience, as the case may be. Speaking of Americans, Torre writes, "New Englanders, accustomed to seasonal changes in the weather, complain more bitterly about heat and monotony than do employees from southern and southwestern states."[7] His conclusion is that "generally, as compared to stateside conditions, the overseas post imposes greater total demands upon the vitality of the individual."[8] Accordingly, he strongly recommends thorough physical examinations for all candidates for overseas employment. The policy on medical waivers should be tight because examination of the performance records of Americans granted them in the past "shows a direct relationship between past illness and performance." Often persons with such ailments as high blood pressure, diabetes, and heart trouble will perform satisfactorily on job assignments inside the United States, but will suffer recurrence of their health difficulties when stationed abroad.

Inadequate Housing Facilities

Inadequate housing facilities contribute to the health problem, both from the physical and psychological standpoints. Much has been written and said about the luxurious quarters of Americans and some other foreign officials stationed abroad. Americans in some posts do live in houses which they could not afford to rent or buy at home. In many foreign locations, however, the only suitable housing is in the very high price ranges. Since the middle class is usually very small or scarcely existent in the underdeveloped countries, the local

[7] *Ibid.*, p. 84.
[8] *Ibid.*, pp. 84–85.

housing industry is geared to building the kind of large, sometimes fancy, residence that only the wealthy can afford. The mass of the population lives in dwellings which American families in the income groups represented in our missions simply do not occupy in the United States. In such countries, the housing and utility allowances paid by the government in addition to salary may be considered a fortuitous circumstance for the mission member and his family. Yet this contributes to the lack of enthusiasm shown them by representatives of the foreign governments with whom they deal. These men, despite their high positions in their governments, frequently live in much more modest quarters than their foreign advisors.

Yet in many overseas locations, Americans and their families are forced to live in very unsatisfactory quarters. As just one example, a few years ago a United States survey team made up of representatives of military and civilian agencies investigated the housing problem in France. Their findings are reported in testimony given before a House Subcommittee which held hearings abroad on problems of American personnel serving overseas. The Subcommittee was told that the survey team

> . . . found the houses were cold and damp, requiring auxiliary heating in 85 percent of the cases. They lack proper sanitary facilities, including indoor toilets. Proper electrical wiring is not available so that American equipment could be used. Painting and papering are required. The average initial investment of an American family going into a French home required $700 just to make the place habitable, not up to American standards. It is a common practice in France that a landlord will rent you property and permit you to put in the bathroom.[9]

In some locations, the dangers of disease are so great as to create a very serious health problem for foreign personnel. On one occasion, the State Department found it necessary to evacuate fully 70 percent of its employees from one of the new African states. Many Congressmen regard as lavish requests for funds to air-condition offices and living quarters in such locations. Testifying before the House Subcommittee on Foreign Affairs in mid-1962, a State Department rep-

[9] *Personnel Programs and Policies of the Federal Government,* House Subcommittee on Civil Service Commission and Personnel Programs, 84th Congress, 1st Session, Washington, D.C.: Government Printing Office, 1956, pp. 93–94.

resentative explained that these expenditures were necessary if the nation was "to give reasonable care to its foreign service personnel and their families."[10] Air-conditioning and better medical services increased the costs, but they were necessary under the circumstances. Undoubtedly, some of the reductions Congress makes in the requests for such outlays at certain posts are justified. The inability, however, of so many Congressmen to understand how serious the living problems are at some posts does adversely affect the morale of many overseas employees. Economies possible in domestic problems cannot realistically be expected in certain phases of foreign operations.

The Feeling of Insecurity

Insecurity and tensions of various kinds also complicate the adjustment problems of persons serving overseas. Job insecurity is one disturbing factor. Loveday reminds that "there are no good grounds for assuming that any international organization will continue to function indefinitely."[11] There is a casualty list of abolished international agencies, just as in each country there is one of eliminated national agencies. So long as a nation exists, "there will always be some national government. No such certainty exists regarding inter-governmental organizations."[12]

His point is brought home as we look at the United Nations today. To much of mankind it is unthinkable that the United Nations should suffer the same fate as the League of Nations. What the future holds, nobody can be sure, but one thing is certain: Unstable conditions plague the United Nations and will probably continue to do so indefinitely. In truth, by its very nature this is an inherent characteristic of this most important of international organizations. Its deadlocks and financial worries reflect the unresolved issues of world politics. Actually, most of the permanent employees of the United Nations and its specialized agencies are not worried about losing their jobs. Still they feel insecure, because they are in a real sense actors on a

[10] *St. Louis Post-Dispatch*, August 26, 1962. For serious health problems of Americans serving abroad, see also John D. Montgomery, *The Politics of Foreign Aid*, New York: Praeger, 1962, pp. 8–9.

[11] Loveday, *op. cit.*, p. 13.

[12] *Ibid.*

world stage with shaky foundations. As the organization reels under the impact of its crises, so does its staff. The instability of international organizations in a world still groping to make the machinery for international cooperation effective inevitably has an adverse effect on staff morale. As Loveday states: "To the great majority of them the world in which they live is seemingly more unstable and insecure than is the world of, for instance, a farmer or even a business man or a factory hand, and the world—not the state of the weather or of the markets—is what immediately affects their life and work."[13]

Appointment Uncertainties

Most of the United Nations headquarters staff serves under permanent appointments, the only qualification being that these appointments are subject to review every five years. It has been recognized that, unless a goodly percentage of the posts are offered on a permanent basis, it will be impossible to attract persons of high quality. At the same time, the advantages of filling some jobs on a temporary basis have also been appreciated. *Secondment*—that is, giving appointments to officials of the member states for limited periods of time—has the salutary effect of bringing "a certain amount of freshness to the international organization." Attempts have been made to obtain the advantages of both kinds of appointments, with the majority being offered on a permanent or other long-term basis and a substantial minority being filled through secondment.[14]

The above discussion applies to the regular programs of the United Nations and the other international agencies, not to special projects. Under the Expanded Programme of Technical Assistance (EPTA), very few appointments of experts are made for more than a one-year period. Frequently, they are renewed, but there is no guarantee that they will be. EPTA is financed on an annual basis, which explains the inability to offer the experts long-term contracts. Walter R. Sharp has this to say:

> There is general recognition that such a restrictive appointments policy has had two unfortunate effects. On the one hand, it has acted as an

[13] *Ibid.*

[14] Tien-Cheng Young, *International Civil Service: Principles and Problems*, Brussels, Belgium: International Institute of Administrative Services, 1958, pp. 141–150. Quoted words are from p. 145.

obstacle to the attraction and retention of suitably qualified experts in certain subject-matter fields; on the other, it has frequently made it difficult, if not impossible, to plan field projects intelligently . . .

What actually happens in the case of many projects is that the short-term contracts of on-the-job experts are if possible renewed, or new experts have to be engaged, or both. In proportion as new personnel is introduced into a going project, at frequent intervals, lost motion and lack of continuity in project direction may result. To be sure, the infusion of some fresh blood into a project team may be desirable but unless substantial overlap in the membership of a project mission can be assured the chances of successful implementation may be prejudiced or, at best, unduly delayed. The point is relevant to one-man projects as well—all the more because few foreign experts are able to orient themselves effectively in the local, cultural, political, or administrative environment short of several weeks or even months, particularly if they have no previous trans-cultural experience.[15]

If the expert received definite advice about the renewal of his contract well in advance, the situation would be improved. Unfortunately, the matter often remains in doubt until near the end of the contract expiration date. Budgetary uncertainties are not the only reason for this; sometimes the host government is slow in deciding whether or not to retain the services of the expert. Often it is plain "bureaucratic slowness" on the part of both the international agency and the host country which keeps the issue in doubt. Whatever the explanation, it has sometimes happened that, in the absence of a definite word as to their retention, experts have decided to go ahead and wind up their affairs in the particular country. After selling their automobiles and household effects, just when they have everything in order to leave, they suddenly receive an offer of a contract renewal. As Sharp states: "Experienced field experts are lost in the shuffle simply because they cannot arrange at the eleventh hour to stay on—or to return later." He quotes the remark of one experienced mission chief: "the expert is asked to take all the risks while the organization takes none."[16] International-agency headquarters officials are well aware of this problem and its disastrous impact on the morale of the experts. They would like to give these assurances

[15] Walter R. Sharp, *Field Administration in the United Nations System*, New York: Praeger, 1961, pp. 162–163.

[16] *Ibid.*, p. 165.

of contract renewal earlier, indeed, to put more of the appointments on a long-term basis. Unfortunately, up to now this has been impossible for them.

Employment and other uncertainties have also plagued the administration of United States technical-assistance programs. The Agency for International Development (AID), established in November, 1961, is "the latest in a succession of organizations charged with the conduct of United States foreign aid programs over the course of the past two decades."[17] Because of charges of waste and inefficiency, there have been many reorganizations of the foreign-aid program. Nonetheless, there has been some job continuity in this work. The Secretary of State's Committee on Foreign Affairs Personnel found that nearly half of AID's overseas personnel had been with it or its predecessor agencies for five years or more, and that more than one-eighth had ten years or more of such service. Actually, most of AID's professional overseas personnel hold appointments which are made for the duration of its operations. Of course, so long as foreign aid continues under constant attack inside and outside Congress, "duration of operations" can hardly leave the staff member without any doubts at all as to his future employment. Still, this is far better than the one-year contract arrangements under the international agency programs.

A most disturbing element in foreign aid administration has been the frequent changes in top personnel. Since the establishment of the Economic Cooperation Administration in 1948, the "succession of foreign assistance agencies" has had no less than 11 chief administrators or directors. Furthermore, the new director has usually come on the scene determined to make major changes in the internal organization and functioning of the agency. Then, after a relatively short period of service, he has resigned before the changes he instituted had a chance to prove themselves. The new director, under the pressure of Congressional and public clamor for conclusive evidence of good results from the billions spent on foreign assistance, has then proclaimed still another reorganization. Indeed, the foreign aid directorship has come to be considered one of the most difficult jobs in Washington to fill. The problems have been so difficult that up to now no one has been asked to stay in or wanted the job very long.

[17] See *Personnel for the New Diplomacy, op. cit.*, pp. 24–26.

The Secretary of State's Committee stated that "clearly, many of the agencies' weaknesses in personnel and other administrative practices, which have seriously impaired their effectiveness, can be attributed directly to these frequent changes in top leadership." It recommended that "every effort should be made to introduce greater stability at this level than it has had in the past."[18] The Committee also proposed the establishment by statute of a career system for core personnel of AID, similar to that of the State Department's Foreign Service. The AID career group would consist of a cadre of some 1500 persons to "be used in filling positions of mission directors and deputy directors and in providing the core professional staffs of country program offices, administrative, financial, and logistical support sections, and the directing positions in each of the major functional specialties."[19] Similarly, it proposed a career foreign service for the permanent, professional overseas staff of the United States Information Agency, to be known as the Foreign Information Service.[20] Creation of these two new career foreign services would go a long way towards reducing the element of insecurity in overseas jobs. The plan is that they would be associated together with the State Department's Foreign Service to constitute a "family of compatible services governed by uniform statutory provisions regarding personnel management."[21]

Conflicts Between Nationality Groups

The problem of understanding the culture of the country in which an official is stationed was explored in detail in Chapter 3, Administration and Culture. There is no need, therefore, to say much more on this subject, but a few words on the special problems of the staff members of international agencies are in order. These men must adjust during every workday to the points of view and ways of colleagues who represent many different nationalities. In bilateral programs, the cultural problem, difficult as it is, is appreciably less complicated than in an international agency. It takes a high order of leadership to weld the members of these different nationality groups

[18] *Ibid.*, pp. 24–25.
[19] *Ibid.*, pp. 26–27.
[20] *Ibid.*, pp. 22–23.
[21] *Ibid.*, p. 28.

into a real team. The big danger is that the staff will form national blocs, that is, join together with other employees from their own country or part of the world.

There are, however, common interests which do tend to unite the members of the different nationality groups. Loveday points out that in the specialized agencies like the Food and Agriculture Organization, the World Health Organization, the International Civil Aviation Organization, and the World Meteorological Organization, the scientists and other specialists generally work together quite well. In these lines of work, similar professional interests submerge antagonisms based on nationality. The reader will remember that in Chapter 5, mention was made that professional workers representing different levels of government in grant-in-aid programs generally maintain friendly relationships. The same professional bonds unite the employees of some international agencies. However, each of the international agencies given as an example above is restricted to one area of activity. Loveday believes that "where the organization has many facets professional interests tend rather to divide the whole society into separate groups than to unite it."[22] Of course, this is also true in national governments. The more numerous the groups of specialists, the more difficult it usually is to achieve administrative coordination. Where international-agency programs involve value judgments in decisionmaking, and consequently a large area in which national biases can color the thinking of the different staff members, then cooperation is even more difficult to achieve. Social and economic programs of different kinds are a good example. An English meteorologist may find it relatively easy to get along with a Spanish or Latin American meteorologist, yet he may find it difficult to understand the ideas of Spaniards and Latin Americans as to how national civil services should be organized. Furthermore, the more political the implications of the problem under discussion, the more likely it is that national biases will influence the thinking of the participants.

Counteracting these divisive forces is the keen realization of the consequences of failure in the missions of the international agencies. High morale and great enthusiasm can be sensed in meetings of international agency personnel, responding to the appeals of their directors, just as it can be in similar meetings in national agencies.

[22] Loveday, *op. cit.*, p. 5.

Certainly, it would be erroneous to present a picture of the international agency as one paralyzed by the internal bickerings of its staff members. Furthermore, bureaucratic rivalries in national governments sometimes create power blocs which do more damage to total program objectives than the national blocs in international organizations.

The Language Problem

The language barrier is another serious problem; in fact, some persons serving abroad have said that this is their principal problem. The writer recalls one conversation with the deputy head of an American technical-assistance mission who frankly stated that his lack of a real grasp of the language spoken in the host country had greatly limited his effectiveness. AID does much more than its predecessor agencies to give language training to new personnel before sending them out on foreign assignments, yet in Latin America, as one example, only a few United States government representatives are really fluent in the use of the Spanish language. The basic reason is that most adults have great difficulty mastering a foreign language. This is true in any country; it is not a special characteristic of Americans. Absolute command of the language is usually obtained only when it is learned during childhood and then not allowed to lapse completely. The only occasion on which the writer heard any appreciable number of adult Americans speak Spanish perfectly, with all the right intonations and not the slightest trace of an accent, was during a party held in the home of an executive of an American company which has operated in Latin America for many years. These Americans had been reared and largely educated in Latin American countries. Some of the sons had followed their fathers into the service of the company, and the net result was that there was no language difficulty at all. But, of course, it would be impossible for the government to duplicate such conditions. In the great majority of cases those recruited for American overseas posts are born in the United States and have had no such opportunity to gain perfect command of a foreign language. Of course, such perfection is not necessary, except in the case of interpreters and translators. An incorrect accent is inevitable when the language is learned as an adult. Foreign accents jar the national sensibilities of some people in any country, but effective communication can take place even if the foreigner speaks with an accent. What counts is his feeling for the language and the national psychology it represents and his consequent ability to put his ideas across. If they make the necessary effort, and the employing agency gives them encouragement and help, a fair proportion of adults can achieve a very acceptable control of the local language. It goes without saying that previous study of foreign languages during college, high school, and even primary school days should prove very useful.

In some parts of the world, many government officials and the educated groups in general have a good command of English. This, of course, largely eliminates the language barrier. French was thought to be decreasing in importance when suddenly a whole new group of African nations in which that language is spoken became part of the international scene. Suffice it to say that the language problem remains a tough one to solve. In overseas programs, the individual who combines professional competence with language proficiency is rare. Frustration over inability to communicate in the local language is sometimes the chief cause of psychological difficulties of overseas personnel. They find themselves profoundly disliking both themselves and the people of the country concerned. If language deficiency can create such feelings, it is worth careful remedial action, just as in the case of the other major adjustment problems.

Ideally, in international agencies, every staff member should have adequate command of one of the official languages of the organization. Yet, because as many member nations as possible must be represented on the secretariats, some persons must be appointed who do not have a satisfactory knowledge of one of the official languages. They must try to learn it on the job. The services of translators and interpreters are available, but, in the committee meetings where so much of the work of international agencies is conducted, "a perfect command of one of the official languages is of real advantage and those who possess it are likely to advance more rapidly than those who do not."[23] Many United Nations experts have been just as ineffective as Americans in trying to communicate with the local population. The advantage enjoyed by the United Nations, however, is that its experts come from many countries, and thus from cultures or

[23] *Ibid.*, p. 77.

regions in which a particular language fluency or potential can be found, but even the United Nations is frequently desperate in its efforts to find experts with the requisite language ability. On the other hand, to appoint someone with a meagre technical background simply because of his language fluency may be worse than sending a well-qualified person who does not know the language. The fluent, but otherwise poorly qualified, "expert" may do more harm than good, for he may teach the wrong things. Even though his effectiveness is limited by having to communicate through interpreters, the individual who is thoroughly competent in his field may at least get some of the desired aims accomplished.

PROBLEMS OF PERSONNEL POLICY

In the process of describing these adjustment problems of overseas personnel, it was necessary to refer from time to time to questions of personnel policy, such as tenure. The rest of the chapter will be devoted to various other personnel matters which have an important bearing on the morale of persons serving abroad.

Geographical Distribution of Positions

The principle of geographical representation in making appointments to the staffs of the international agencies has already been mentioned. The United Nations and its specialized agencies follow this policy, but it is not new; the precedent already had been firmly established by the League of Nations.

Let us describe in detail how the system of geographical representation is now applied in the United Nations. First, most employees in the lower salary brackets—such as messengers, guards, and clerks —are recruited locally, that is from among nationals of the country where the international agency has its offices. This excludes these positions from geographical representation, the explanation being that "the experiences of every international organization has shown that it is not feasible to go beyond the local area for the recruitment of substantial numbers of staff members in the lower levels."[24] The

[24] International Civil Service Advisory Board, *Report on Recruitment Methods and Standards for the United Nations and the Specialized Agencies,* New York: United Nations, 1950, p. 11.

quoted words are from a report of the International Civil Service Advisory Board, which was created by the United Nations General Assembly in 1946, and advises the United Nations and the specialized agencies on recruitment and other personnel policies. Local recruitment is the more practical policy for lower-level positions, because "financial considerations such as cost of transportation, various allowances, home leave, etc. weigh heavily."[25] In other words, it would be much too expensive to recruit internationally for such jobs. The Board was expressing a generally accepted opinion when it stated that "the value to the organization of geographical distribution in these levels does not outweigh the difficulties."[26] As Tien-Cheng Young comments, it is not necessary to make messenger posts subject to worldwide recruitment in order to give the agency secretariat a "truly international character."[27]

As to positions for which a certain language qualification is indispensable, recruitment must be limited almost entirely to the countries in which that language is the mother tongue. This, therefore, also removes these positions from allocation on a geographical basis. With these exclusions, the number of positions in the United Nations subject to such allocation becomes quite small, compared with the total work force. It consists principally of posts of a professional or administrative character. Since these positions are so few, they are highly coveted, and consequently the pressures from the numerous member states to place as many of their nationals as possible in them are exceedingly intense. On what basis are these positions assigned to the different member governments? Tien-Cheng Young states that in practice the policy is to use as the criterion the size of the member nation's contribution to the regular United Nations budget. The bigger its contribution, the more jobs it gets. This has never been stated as official policy, nor is it rigidly applied, but it is the system used by the United Nations and the specialized agencies. In fact, "not infrequently in the debate of annual budgets delegates bargain for fair inclusion of their compatriots in the Secretariat as a condition of financial contributions to the Organization."[28]

The United Nations employs the concept of a "desirable range" of

[25] *Ibid.*
[26] *Ibid.*
[27] Tien-Cheng Young, *op. cit.*, p. 104.
[28] *Ibid.*, p. 91.

posts for each member country. The ranges are quite broad, and at any one time some countries are either substantially below or above their range. This makes the system flexible, as it must be. Some member states, particularly the newly independent countries, cannot make available technically trained personnel. In a recent report, the Secretary-General said, "in certain cases, Governments have stated specifically that for the time being they are unable to spare people of the type and calibre required."[29] Other governments, below their ranges, are anxious to obtain the additional posts to which they feel they are entitled. The Secretary-General said in the same report cited above that he was giving the "utmost attention to the improvement of geographic distribution, at all levels."[30] Lists of current vacancies were being distributed to the governments which had "disproportionately few or no nationals on the staff," with the request that they propose suitable candidates. Staff members of the Office of Personnel would also make trips to the new member states to "discuss recruitment needs and methods of locating candidates in these countries."[31]

If no consideration at all were given to representing as many of the member states as possible on the secretariat, it would be very difficult to obtain their enthusiastic cooperation in the work of the organization. Each nation retains its sovereignty and does not want to be in the shadow of a few powers which monopolize most of the jobs. Geographical representation would work out splendidly if the different member states could all supply candidates who are well qualified for the posts in question. In practice, many of them cannot do so, yet they must be allocated some jobs anyway. Bluntly stated, this means that sometimes a mediocre or even a poorly qualified individual must be appointed simply because he comes from a certain country.

The Politics of Geographical Appointments

Geographical representation also introduces a political element in the decisions made on appointments by the international agency head. Member governments cannot dictate appointments to him; in theory,

[29] *Geographical Distribution of the Staff of the Secretariat of the United Nations*, Report by the Secretary General, New York: United Nations, General Assembly, October 1, 1959, p. 4.

[30] *Ibid.*, p. 3.

[31] *Ibid.*, pp. 3–4.

he exercises independent judgment. In practice, to win support for his policies and to keep the organization working together, he may have to yield to a member state's pressure to appoint one of its nationals to a high post. This sometimes means passing over for promotion to the vacancy a highly competent employee simply because he comes from a country already above its "desirable range" of posts. Unquestionably, geographical representation adversely affects staff morale. Some observers believe, however, that, even from the efficiency standpoint, the advantages of this policy outweigh its disadvantages. Tien-Chen Young reminds that:

> A person is not *simply* efficient or inefficient. He is efficient or inefficient for a given purpose, and efficiency for one purpose may mean inefficiency for another. For example, in negotiation with the British Foreign Office, an ex-English Foreign Service man may be extremely efficient, but for negotiation with Egyptian authorities he may be terribly inefficient. An international establishment staffed with Frenchmen might be highly efficient in its dealing with the French public, but it would be totally inadequate for functioning effectively on a world-wide scale.[32]

The point is well taken, but nothing is said about the man appointed for geographical reasons who simply lacks the technical qualifications for the job in question. One can agree with the statement that "a slightly incompetent man's nationality may make him more useful than a more expert civil servant of inappropriate nationality."[33] But what if, as sometimes happens, the appointee is more than "slightly incompetent" for the job? Loveday philosophically states that the directors must accept the fact that they will have to "carry a certain proportion of relatively incompetent officials."[34] His suggestion is to assign these misfits to temporary posts, but, of course, the trouble is that their governments may insist on their fair proportion of permanent jobs.

Recommendations of the International Civil Service Advisory Board

The International Civil Service Advisory Board made several suggestions, adoption of which it felt "would go a long way towards at-

[32] Tien-Cheng Young, *op. cit.*, pp. 93–94.
[33] Inis L. Claude, Jr., *Swords into Plowshares*, New York: Random House, 1956, p. 200.
[34] Loveday, *op. cit.*, p. 45.

taining proper balance between competence and geography."[35] One of these was to adopt a "sound career system under which recruitment at the junior level in under-represented countries"[36] would be emphasized. The logic behind this proposal is to recruit young people on the basis of their aptitudes and train them in the skills and knowledges required in the different higher-level posts in the secretariat. The Board was "convinced that while some nations of the world cannot at this time, produce or spare highly trained persons in certain special fields, there is no country in which young persons with all the educational and intellectual qualifications which make for career international civil servants of outstanding quality cannot be found."[37] This, however, is a long-run solution and, in any case, as Loveday points out, "there will be a considerable number of posts requiring practical experience which cannot be filled in this way." Furthermore, "recruits from certain countries where the level of education is low are unlikely to make the grade even when no experience is demanded."[38]

Another of the Board's recommendations was to develop a program of in-service training for new appointees. This, it was hoped, would make "recruiting on a geographical basis much more feasible," by repairing "the inevitable flaws" in such recruitment.[39] In-service training is highly desirable in any organization, but some skepticism can be expressed about the Board's hope that recruitment deficiencies could be remedied in this way. Training programs can reduce the margin of incompetence in some cases and eliminate it in others: that is about all one can expect. In all, it must be concluded that geographical recruitment is a political necessity in international organizations which makes strict adherence to merit principles impossible.

Selection Methods

What methods should be used in selecting persons for overseas service? Taking the international agencies first, the "desirability of selection of international staff by competitive examination" has been

[35] *Report on Recruitment Methods and Standards, op. cit.*, p. 8.
[36] *Ibid.*, p. 10.
[37] *Ibid.*
[38] Loveday, *op. cit.*, p. 45.
[39] *Report on Recruitment Methods and Standards, op. cit.*, p. 10.

recognized since 1921, when a League of Nations report recommended that, with very few exceptions, staff be employed in the future on the basis of "competitive selections." The Preparatory Commission of the United Nations was of the same opinion, and the General Assembly, at its sixth session, recommended selection of staff through competitive examinations wherever possible. Despite these statements of policy, however, the use of competitive examinations in international organizations has been limited principally to positions requiring language ability and to clerical and secretarial jobs. Objection to competitive examinations is largely based on the contention that they could not be administered successfully because of the wide differences in the educational systems of the member states.[40] Yet the International Civil Service Advisory Board must have believed that this difficulty could be surmounted, because it recommended written competitive examinations as "the normal avenue of entry for persons in the professional category." It expressed the opinion

> . . . that all the agencies can and should find within their organization a group of posts which would constitute the commencement to a professional career, and which should be filled by professional examination of young persons with no excessive degree of specialization. Even where specialized study at this level is required, the setting of papers in various fields which must be written only by the candidates seeking employment in those fields should enlarge the usefulness of this type of examination.[41]

By conducting examinations for one country at a time or on a regional basis, the problem of differing educational systems could be solved. "Competitive selection" does not require that written examinations be given in every case. The Board applauded the practice of some agencies like the International Labour Organization of filling posts above the junior professional level through open competition even though written examinations were not considered practicable. Remembering the analysis of selection techniques in Part IV of this book, this would mean unassembled examinations, supplemented by oral interviews and thoroughgoing reference checks and qualifications appraisals.

[40] Tien-Cheng Young, *op. cit.*, p. 100.
[41] *Report on Recruitment Methods and Standards, op. cit.*, pp. 28–29.

The international agencies do, of course, have personnel offices which evaluate the qualifications of the applicants and seek to obtain the employment of only those most qualified. They do not have to follow uniform policies, however, and, in general, it can be stated that the principle of merit is followed only to the extent that the Personnel Office is successful in insisting on it. For this reason, it has been suggested that an International Civil Service Commission be created with jurisdiction over the United Nations and all the specialized international agencies. Tien-Cheng Young favors the establishment of such a Commission, not only because it would enforce common personnel policies but also because he believes it would eliminate political pressures in appointments. The members of such a Commission, he suggests, should be *elected* for fixed terms by the member states.[42] The danger in this proposal is that the politically elected members of such a Commission might engage in logrolling and similar horse-trading. Yet, since so many of its recommendations have not been adopted, the purely advisory character of the International Civil Service Board leaves much to be desired. Prospects of establishing an International Civil Service Commission, however, appear remote. Greatest reliance will have to continue to be placed on the individual international agency to maintain the highest personnel standards it can under present circumstances.

Recommendations of Committee on Foreign Affairs Personnel

Turning to selection of staff for United States government posts abroad, the Secretary of State's Committee on Foreign Affairs Personnel found that the State Department, AID, and USIA were each functioning under different systems for the selection of foreign service personnel. In line with long-established policy, the State Department was recruiting at the junior Foreign Service level on the basis of an examination given each year aimed at attracting young college graduates. In recent years junior-officer appointments have accounted for approximately 80 percent of the Department's foreign-service appointments. By contrast, the AID has mostly recruited persons from inside and outside the government who already have the experience to qualify for positions in the middle and top grades. USIA has fol-

[42] Tien-Cheng Young, *op. cit.*, pp. 59–60.

lowed a policy which "falls in between." It makes more appointments by lateral entry than does State to the middle and top posts, but "it also has a positive junior professional-recruitment program similar to that of the State Department."[43]

The State Department and USIA have in the past given a common written examination, administered on the same day in September at various centers throughout the country. Candidates must indicate in which of the two agencies they want to serve. They cannot apply simultaneously for both agencies by taking this examination. Part of the examination, such as the sections on general ability and English expression, is the same for all candidates. The general-background part is different, with candidates for the State Department answering one set of questions and those for the USIA another set. In 1962, the State Department introduced special options: one in executive management and business, the other in government and public administration. The 1963 examination had three options: history and government and the social sciences; management and business administration; and economics.

The Committee's recommendation was logical: to give a "single written examination, with appropriate options [to] junior officer candidates of all three agencies." A joint Board of Examiners would be created, replacing the State Department's Board of Examiners for the Foreign Service. Each of the three agencies would be represented on the Board, along with the Civil Service Commission. The Board's function would be to develop "standards and precepts to govern the examinations for career appointments in the family of foreign affairs services, including written, oral, and other examinations at all levels of entry."[44] The entrance examination for junior officers would include a "common core of tests that all candidates would take regardless of agency and regardless of major field of study or experience."[45] Besides the options used in the State Department's 1962 examination, others would be offered in "such fields as economics and economic development, behavioral sciences, American civilization, area specialization, agriculture, and labor."[46] The purpose here is to attract

[43] *Personnel for the New Diplomacy, op. cit.*, p. 66.
[44] *Ibid.*, pp. 71–72.
[45] *Ibid.*, p. 72.
[46] *Ibid.*

individuals with backgrounds in such subject-matter areas who otherwise might not realize that there is ample opportunity "to use and develop their talents in a foreign affairs career." The candidates would indicate their agency preference as well as the special field or fields which interested them the most. Where jobs are available in an optional field in more than one of the three agencies, common eligible lists would be established.

The Committee makes several other recommendations which should be mentioned. Since "writing ability is a crucial skill," a "systematic examination" of this kind should be included in the battery of tests. It would be graded only if the applicant passed the short-answer part of the written examination. As to foreign language ability, the Committee was of the opinion that those demonstrating "proficiency in one or more foreign languages, or who obtain a satisfactory score on a test of foreign language aptitude, might properly be given additional credit in the final ranking of successful candidates on appointment registers."[47] The Committee did not recommend eliminating candidates who fail to pass a foreign-language examination. It felt that intensive language study after entry could repair this deficiency. If he did not develop the necessary language ability, however, the recruit would not be eligible for advancement to the next higher class. The wise candidate obviously is the one who starts his foreign-language training early and demonstrates this competence in the entrance examination.

The Committee saw room for improvement in the written examinations being used by the State Department and USIA for junior officers. In its opinion, adequate validity studies of the examination materials were not being made. As to the oral examining process, there was evidence that, "while each panel tends to be self-consistent, there is considerable variation among panels."[48] Better results would be obtained if the interviewers were selected with greater care and trained intensively in interviewing techniques. In addition to the written and oral examinations, candidates would also be rated on the basis of reference letters and related information. The final rating of the candidates and the preparation of the eligible registers would be the responsibility of a professional staff attached to the proposed joint Board of Examiners.

[47] *Ibid.*
[48] *Ibid.*, p. 73.

As to lateral entry, the Committee believed it essential that all three agencies make systematic provision for the appointment of competent persons "to meet specialized needs that are not satisfied through appointments at the bottom levels."[49] The way to do this was for each agency to review its personnel needs at least once a year and decide how many career officers it needed at each level. Naturally the number of persons needed by lateral appointment would depend upon the intake of junior officers, and this would vary from agency to agency and year to year. The Committee estimated that normally lateral appointments in the State Department should not exceed more than 25 percent of the total number of annual career officer appointments. This percentage "would undoubtedly be too low for AID and might be inadequate to meet USIA's needs."

Whatever the number of lateral appointments, the Committee was adamant that mid-career entry standards be "exacting." No one should be appointed who was not highly qualified for the work in question. Instead of the essentially noncompetitive examinations now generally used as the basis for making lateral appointments, "the examining process should be competitive." Besides a "searching" analysis of the candidates' previous backgrounds, a "thorough oral examination" should be used. Furthermore, consideration should be given in some cases to the use of written tests and the "review of other evidence indicating the candidate's ability to apply his knowledge to problem-solving situations, and his ability to write effectively."[50] In other words, the Committee wanted formal, not informal, procedures for evaluating the qualifications of applicants for mid-career appointments.

Salary Problems

Just as it is in domestic employment, the salary problem is a difficult one in recruiting for overseas personnel. The 1962 pay legislation mentioned in Chapter 14 provided salary increases for the foreign services of the State Department, USIA, and AID, along with those for the other federal employees. So there has been some improvement here, although there is room for more, particularly at the highest levels.

[49] *Ibid.*, p. 75.
[50] *Ibid.*, p. 78.

The international agencies have certain unique salary problems. Salaries paid by national governments vary greatly. Although the pay of United States public employees has lagged behind that in industry, it is much higher than that received by government workers in many other countries. Nor need the United States be used as the only example: such countries as Great Britain, Sweden, West Germany, and many others pay both public and private workers much more than in lesser-developed nations.

Since all member states are entitled to representation in the secretariats of the international agencies, on what basis should the salary scales be set? How high should the scales be set in relation to pay for comparable work in the public services of the member countries? Should the principle of equal pay for equal work be followed, regardless of the nationality of the employee? In answer to these questions, the United Nations follows the same policy as did the League of Nations. It is to pay salaries which compare favorably with those of the member governments which pay the highest salaries. The same salary is paid for comparable work, regardless of the nationality of the individual. This means that an employee who comes from a country with low wage levels earns much more than he could in his home environment: in fact, he may double or even treble his earnings, depending on how low the salaries are in his country. To establish salary scales below the pay rates of the countries paying the most would be neither realistic nor equitable, for the best available talent must be drawn from all the member states. Furthermore, the national from a poor country who does the same work as someone from a much more prosperous nation is entitled to be paid what others get for the same work.

A system of differential salary rates based on nationality would have a disastrous effect on staff morale. During part of its existence, the United Nations Relief and Rehabilitation Administration used such a system. Salaries were set sufficiently high to attract qualified staff, but they varied at the same work location. For the same kind of job, an American might get a thousand dollars a year more than a Frenchman, and the Frenchman a thousand more than someone from India. The only equality was that all received the same amount for cost-of-living allowance. The trouble with this kind of policy, as Tien-Cheng Young points out, is that despite its economies "it would destroy the very foundations of the international civil service and consequently reduce an international secretariat to a name only."[51] Actually, there is a clear justification for paying salaries even higher than those of the best-paying member governments. The official incurs additional expenses when he lives outside his home country. The extra costs of expatriation are usually very substantial, even not taking into account "the losses caused by lack of personal and professional contacts and from being remote from normal spheres of employment."[52] In actual practice, the international organizations take the expatriation factor into account in fixing the salary levels. They also give special grants in addition to salary, such as an installation allowance when the official takes up residence at his post and a termination indemnity when he is returned home.

International Loyalty v. National Loyalty

A final personnel problem meriting discussion is that of "international loyalty versus national loyalty." No one expects an international civil servant to cast off his sentiments of patriotism and affection for his home country. Once he joins the staff of an international agency, however, he must regard it as his *sole* employer. His country of origin may not like the policies he carries out as a staff member of the international agency, but he must not allow this to influence him in discharging his duties. As did the League of Nations, the United Nations requires the new employee to take an oath of office in which he pledges that he will not seek or accept instructions from any government or other authority external to the organization. Any international civil servant who accepted such instructions clearly would be disloyal to the organization. Such cases have occurred, but the problem goes deeper than this. The individual may accept no outside instructions, but still be greatly influenced by national biases in the opinions he expresses within the organization and in the contacts he has with other members of the secretariat. So long as he and other employees maintain such a narrow attitude, the work of the organization will not progress as it should. What is needed is what the International Civil Service Advisory Board dubs an "international

[51] Tien-Cheng Young, *op. cit.*, p. 131.
[52] *Ibid.*, p. 130.

outlook." The Board is very clear about the ingredients of such an outlook:

> It involves willingness to try to understand and be tolerant of different points of view, different cultural patterns, and different work habits. It also entails willingness to work without prejudice or bias with persons of all nationalities, religions, and cultures. It means a readiness to be continually conscious of how proposals, events, and statements of opinion may appear to a very wide range of nationalities. It involves conduct of the highest type and exercise of judgment and restraint in all expressions of view whether public or private; any expressions which could be construed as biased or intolerant, particularly in respect of national interests or political issues with which the organization is confronted, must be scrupulously avoided.[53]

This is no easy order. As Tien-Cheng Young observes, "there is nothing so difficult as transforming one's outlook, uprooting prejudices, replacing feelings and emotions, dictated by egoism, in favor of feelings which may lead to the love of one's neighbor and to living in harmony with peoples of other cultures, languages, and races."[54] Cliques based on nationality and similar cultural bonds easily form in international organizations. No matter how stern the statements in the Charter and the staff regulations about the obligation to maintain international loyalty, the individual staff member can easily rationalize that he is "right" in his opinions and not evidencing any national prejudices. Frequently, he is totally unaware of his biases. He expects others in the secretariat to behave like his fellow countrymen do in his home government. This to him is correct behavior; any other comportment is wrong. Such an official has failed to acquire the quality of *international-mindedness*. In the opinion of the International Civil Service Advisory Board, every "true international civil servant" must develop this quality, not only in his work contacts with the other members of the secretariat but also in his social relations with them.[55]

[53] International Civil Service Advisory Board, *Report on Standards of Conduct in the International Civil Service*, New York: United Nations, 1954, p. 4.

[54] Tien-Cheng Young, *op. cit.*, p. 22.

[55] *Report on Standards of Conduct in the International Civil Service*, *op. cit.*, pp. 5–6.

Political Activities of International Officials

What about the political activities of international officials? One of the United Nations' regulations states that "staff members may exercise the right to vote but shall not engage in any political activity which is inconsistent with or might reflect upon the independence and impartiality required by their status as international officials."[56] It is up to the Secretary-General to decide when a staff member has exceeded permissible bounds in his political activities. The United Nations has no elaborate set of regulations such as those developed by the United States Civil Service Commission under the Hatch Acts. In general, the guiding policy is as stated by the International Civil Service Advisory Board. The international official is not expected to be a political eunuch. In fact, the Board encourages him to "take a lively interest in the important public questions of the day." Such activities as the following are, however, considered improper: candidature for public office of a political character and the holding of such office; public support of a political party by speeches, statements to the press, or written articles; the holding of political party office; membership on any political campaign committee; acceptance or solicitation of any financial contributions for political purposes; and initiation or signature of petitions involving political candidates or political issues.

The Board did not think it was possible to lay down a fixed rule on membership in a political party. It did say that it was "inadmissible" for the staff member to belong to a party which was illegal in his country, however, and ruled out "membership in any group, whether political or not, which imposes on the staff member an obligation to action incompatible with his oath of office and responsibilities as an international civil servant."[57] The problem of membership in illegal parties is not a simple one. What if the party was legal when the staff member joined the international organization, but there is a change in regimes back home and the party is outlawed? Under such circumstances it is not fair to dismiss him, but it is correct to require

[56] Tien-Cheng Young, *op. cit.*, p. 35.

[57] *Report on Standards of Conduct in the International Civil Service, op. cit.*, p. 11.

him not to engage in political activities aimed at overthrowing the new regime. Furthermore, he should be expected not to show hostility to the new government's delegation to the United Nations. In practice, it is difficult for the United Nations and the other international agencies to check so closely upon the activities of staff members to be sure that they are not involved in clandestine efforts to dislodge the new regime. The United Nations has on occasion hired political exiles who have at least given moral support to movements to overthrow the governments which sent them into exile. So long as changes in governments through use of force occur with any regularity, this problem will remain delicate.

BIBLIOGRAPHY

Anderson, Nels, and Nijkerk, K. J., "International Seminars: An Analysis and an Evaluation," *Administrative Science Quarterly*, **III,** No. 2 (September, 1958).

Bailey, Sidney D., *The Secretariat of the United Nations*, New York: Carnegie Endowment, 1962.

Beckett, Paul L., "Ad Astra Per Aspera: Meditations on the Ecology of Technical Assistance Administration," *Western Political Quarterly*, **XI,** No. 3 (September, 1958).

Cleveland, Harlan, and Mangone, Gerard J. (eds.), *The Art of Overseasmanship*, Syracuse, N.Y.: Syracuse Univ. Press, 1957.

Cleveland, Harlan, Mangone, Gerard J., Adams, John Clarke, *The Overseas Americans*, New York: McGraw-Hill, 1960.

Fedder, Edwin H., "United States Loyalty Procedures and the Recruitment of International Personnel," *Western Political Quarterly*, **XXV,** No. 4 (December, 1962).

Keenleyside, H. L., "Administrative Problems of the United Nations Technical Assistance Administration," *Public Administration*, **XXXIII** (Autumn, 1955).

Loveday, A., *Reflections on International Administration*, Oxford, England: Clarendon Press, 1956.

Montgomery, John, "Crossing the Culture Bars: An Approach to the Training of American Technicians for Overseas Assignments," *World Politics*, **XIII,** No. 4 (July, 1961).

Personnel for the New Diplomacy, Report of the Committee on Foreign Affairs Personnel, New York: Carnegie Endowment, 1962.

Peter, Hollis W., and Henry, Edwin R., "Steps to Better Selection and Training for Overseas Jobs," *Personnel*, **XXXIX,** No. 1 (January–February, 1962).

Report on Recruitment Methods and Standards for the United Nations and the Specialized Agencies, New York: United Nations, 1950.

Rosen, S. McKee, *The Combined Boards of the Second World War: An Experiment in International Administration*, New York: Columbia, 1952.

Sharp, Walter, *Field Administration in the United Nations System*, New York: Frederick A. Praeger, 1961.

Singer, J. David, "The United Nations Advisory Committee on Administrative and Budgetary Questions," *Public Administration*, **XXXV,** (Winter, 1957).

Young, Tien-Cheng, *International Civil Service: Principles and Problems*, Brussels, Belgium: International Institute of Administrative Services, 1958.

INDEX